T0190425

# Lecture Notes in Information Systems and Organisation

## Volume 24

More information about this series at http://www.springer.com/series/11237

Rita Lamboglia · Andrea Cardoni
Renata Paola Dameri · Daniela Mancini
Editors

# Network, Smart and Open

Three Keywords for Information Systems
Innovation

 Springer

*Editors*
Rita Lamboglia
Parthenope University of Naples
Naples
Italy

Andrea Cardoni
University of Perugia
Perugia
Italy

Renata Paola Dameri
University of Genoa
Genoa
Italy

Daniela Mancini
Parthenope University of Naples
Naples
Italy

ISSN 2195-4968          ISSN 2195-4976   (electronic)
Lecture Notes in Information Systems and Organisation
ISBN 978-3-319-62635-2          ISBN 978-3-319-62636-9   (eBook)
https://doi.org/10.1007/978-3-319-62636-9

Library of Congress Control Number: 2017957832

Printed on acid-free paper

This Springer imprint is published by the registered company Springer International Publishing AG part of Springer Nature
The registered company address is: Gewerbestrasse 11, 6330 Cham, Switzerland

# Program Committee

# Reviewers

Arru, Brunella
Bruno, Elena
Caserio, Carlo
Chiucchi, Maria Serena
Corsi, Katia
Di Vaio, Assunta
Fiorentino, Raffaele
Fradeani, Andrea
Garelli, Roberto
Gesuele, Benedetta
Greco, Giulio
Iacoviello, Giuseppina
Lamboglia, Rita
Landriani, Loris
Lazzini, Arianna
Lepore, Luigi
Metushi, Eldi
Nespeca, Andrea
Paolone, Francesco
Pisano, Sabrina
Ramassa, Paola
Resta, Marina
Roncagliolo, Elisa
Soverchia, Michela
Trucco, Sara
Varriale, Luisa

# Contents

**Business Information Systems in a Networked, Smart and Open Environment** . . . . . . . . . . . . . . . . . . . . . . . . . . . . . . . . . . . 1
Rita Lamboglia, Andrea Cardoni, Renata Paola Dameri and
Daniela Mancini

**Information Systems Implementation and Structural Adaptation in Government-Business Inter-organization** . . . . . . . . . . . . . 21
Daniel N. Treku and Gamel O. Wiredu

**Management Control Systems in Inter-organizational Relationships for Environmental Sustainability and Energy Efficiency: Evidence from the Cruise Port Destinations** . . . . . . . . . . . . . . . . . . . . . . . 43
Assunta Di Vaio and Luisa Varriale

**The Role of Supply Chain Resilience on IT and cyber Disruptions** . . . . . . . . . . . . . . . . . . . . . . . . . . . . . . . . . . . . . . . 57
Giorgia Giusi Siciliano and Barbara Gaudenzi

**Virtual Entrepreneurship and e-Residency Adoption** . . . . . . . . . . . . . . . 71
Linda Uljala and Ada Scupola

**Stakeholder Accountability Through the World Wide Web: Insights from Nonprofits** . . . . . . . . . . . . . . . . . . . . . . . . . . . . . . . . . . 85
Gina Rossi, Sara Moggi, Paul Pierce and Chiara Leardini

**From Smart Work to Digital Do-It-Yourself: A Research Framework for Digital-Enabled Jobs** . . . . . . . . . . . . . . . . . . . . . . . . . . . . 97
Aurelio Ravarini and Gianmaria Strada

**Citizens Coproduction, Service Self-Provision and the State 2.0** . . . . . . . 109
Walter Castelnovo

**How Digital Transformation is Reshaping the Manufacturing
Industry Value Chain: The New Digital Manufacturing Ecosystem
Applied to a Case Study from the Food Industry** . . . . . . . . . . . . . . . . . 127
Marco Savastano, Carlo Amendola and Fabrizio D'Ascenzo

**Leverage Once, Earn Repeatedly—Capabilities for Creating and
Appropriating Value in Cloud Platform Ecosystems** . . . . . . . . . . . . . . 143
Christopher Hahn, Jan Huntgeburth and Ruediger Zarnekow

**Information Systems Architecture and Organization
in the Era of MicroServices** . . . . . . . . . . . . . . . . . . . . . . . . . . . . . . 165
Maurizio Cavallari and Francesco Tornieri

**Hosting Mission-Critical Applications on Cloud:
Technical Issues and Challenges** . . . . . . . . . . . . . . . . . . . . . . . . . . . . 179
Massimo Ficco, Alba Amato and Salvatore Venticinque

**The Impact of XBRL on Financial Statement Structural
Comparability** . . . . . . . . . . . . . . . . . . . . . . . . . . . . . . . . . . . . . . . 193
Steve Yang, Fang-Chun Liu and Xiaodi Zhu

**Digital Governmental Financial Reporting:
First Evidence from Italy** . . . . . . . . . . . . . . . . . . . . . . . . . . . . . . . . . 207
Andrea Fradeani, Michela Soverchia and Eldi Metushi

**The Propensity of Being "Openness" of Italian LGAs.
A Study of Possible Relationships with Financial Performance** . . . . . . . 223
Lepore Luigi and Paolone Francesco

**Exploring the Effects of Sustainability on Accounting
Information Systems: The Role of SBSC** . . . . . . . . . . . . . . . . . . . . . . 235
Katia Corsi and Brunella Arru

**The Moderating Effect of Proprietary Costs in the Relation
Between Ownership Structure and Human Capital Disclosure in
Sustainability Report** . . . . . . . . . . . . . . . . . . . . . . . . . . . . . . . . . . . 257
Sabrina Pisano, Luigi Lepore, Assunta Di Vaio and Loris Landriani

**Mapping Financial Performances in Italian ICT-Related
Firms via Self-organizing Maps** . . . . . . . . . . . . . . . . . . . . . . . . . . . . 271
Marina Resta, Roberto Garelli and Renata Paola Dameri

**The Impact of Business Intelligence Systems on Management
Accounting Systems: The Consultant's Perspective** . . . . . . . . . . . . . . . 283
Andrea Nespeca and Maria Serena Chiucchi

# Business Information Systems in a Networked, Smart and Open Environment

**Rita Lamboglia**ⓘ, **Andrea Cardoni**ⓘ, **Renata Paola Dameri**ⓘ
**and Daniela Mancini**ⓘ

**Abstract** Network, Smart, and Open are three keywords that nowadays guide information systems (ISs) research. We discuss the relevance that these three topics, concerning technological and organizational innovations (i.e. cloud, smart technologies and networking), play for the development of accounting and management information systems. The aim is to investigate how these innovations could influence ISs, with a particular focus on accounting and management information systems, enhancing their information potentialities and their ability to support decision making processes, and improving accounting methodologies; performance measurement systems; data management; information systems architecture, external and internal reporting.

**Keywords** Network · Smart · Open data · Innovation · Accounting information systems · Management information systems

## 1 Introduction

The research works published in this book are a selection of the best papers—original double blind contributions—submitted at the XIII Annual Conference of the Italian chapter of Association for Information Systems (ItAIS 2016), which was

R. Lamboglia · D. Mancini (✉)
Parthenope University of Naples, Naples, Italy
e-mail: mancini@uniparthenope.it

R. Lamboglia
e-mail: lamboglia@uniparthenope.it

A. Cardoni
University of Perugia, Perugia, Italy
e-mail: andrea.cardoni@unipg.it

R. P. Dameri
University of Genoa, Genoa, Italy
e-mail: dameri@economia.unige.it

held in Verona in October, untitled "ICT and innovation: a step forward to a global society". The volume also include three invited paper presented at the European Conference of Information Systems 2016 (ECIS 2016).

This book presents a collection of original research papers that mainly concern the relationships between Information Systems and three currently relevant keywords, as network, smart and open.

The remainder of this contribute is structured as follows. The next section, written by Andrea Cardoni, discuss the relationship between innovation in information technologies (IT) and management information systems in business networks. The second section, written by Renata Paola Dameri, discuss the role of Web 2.0 and smart technologies in managing information and affecting relationships among firms, public administration, customers, citizens. The last section, written by Rita Lamboglia and Daniela Mancini, analyses innovation of accounting and management information systems in an open context.

## 2  Exploring the Impact of Innovation and the Role of Management Information Systems in Network Settings

Nowadays digital technologies and innovation are broadly recognized as disruptive driving factors of change, impacting on almost every aspects of daily human and organizational behavior [1]. One of the most visible and pervasive effect on the current socio-economic environment is the influence of technology on network reconfiguration of society, both at individual [2] and organizational level [3].

Indeed, even if the emergence of the knowledge economy [4] inaugurated the new era of "network society" [2] since few decades, the diffusion of web-based technology, platforms and devices [5] has radically accelerated the process of networking reconfiguration affecting people and firms [6].

In a broader perspective, this phenomenon led to a massive increase of interconnections. Digital networking technologies have allowed social and organizational networks to expand and reconfigure way beyond the complexity of traditional network forms [2]. The change brought about the networked information environment is defined deep and pervasive, leading to structural change in the nature of economic and social organization [7].

From a business perspective, the digital economy is radically influencing markets and business models. In the post-fordist reorganizing strategies that first emerged in 70s and 80s anticipating the diffusion of networking technologies, the new digital communications platforms are expanding the capabilities for fostering the networked organizing logic [8]. This is stimulating the firms operating at every dimensional level and competing in every industry to follow in a reactive or proactive manner the "network imperative" [9].

Performing a study of digital network business models through a multi-year, in-depth study based on wide range of qualitative and quantitative analyses, recent literature [9] proposes a classification of business in four different models: "asset builders" that deliver value through the use of physical goods making, marketing, distributing, selling, and leasing physical things; "service providers" that deliver value through skilled people hiring and developing workers who provide services to customers for which they charge; "technology creators" that deliver value through ideas developing and selling intellectual property, such as software, analytics, pharmaceuticals, and biotechnology; "network orchestrators" that deliver value through connectivity creating a platform that participants use to interact or transact with the many other members of the network. Each model is based on a specific form of capital asset, respectively represented by physical capital, human capital, intellectual capital and social capital. Adopting this framework for a quantitative study involving the S&P 1500 (a combination of the S&P large, mid, and small cap indices), network orchestrators obtained on average faster revenue growth and higher profit margins than companies utilizing the other three business models. This led to identify a relevant difference between the "firm-centric" and the "network centric" business models, highlighting the importance to change radically some founding management principles on technology (from physical to digital), asset investment (from tangible to intangible), strategy (from operator to allocator), information and measurement (from accounting to big data). The latter claims for a shift from basic accounting data, focused on the physical assets and with significant time delays, to big data analytics, that still measure all these dimensions but also track their external, intangible assets and use this data to improve the speed and quality of decision-making [10].

It is then considered a key for innovative networked organizations to move beyond traditional forms of information and measurement, which have not kept up with the technologies and priorities of the market. With the rise of new assets (digital, intangible assets) new processes of information and measurement are needed [11, 12] as traditional systems focus almost entirely on the physical, they are internally focused do not support a timely decision-making process.

Consequently, in today environment the link between technology, business models, networked structures and information systems needs to be carefully investigated. In the attempt to frame all these changes in the theoretical view, the key principles of cybernetics [13, 14] help to understand the relationship between the digital age and the network society, evaluating the impact of digital innovation on organizational design [15] and information systems.

While technology disrupts, it can also be used to help cope with complexity. Networked IT enables forms of collaborative networked organisation that offer the sort of agility and flexibility hierarchically integrated businesses struggle to achieve [2]. It can also be used to capture and analyse intelligence about the environment (markets, customers, competitors) to support better decision-making about strategy and tactics. For cyberneticists such as Ashby [16], complexity can be understood in terms of the 'variety' exhibited by a system. Variety here refers to the number of distinguishable states a system (such as an organisation or organism) can assume.

Where a system can match the disturbances to its environment's states, it is said to have 'requisite variety'; that is, it can change its own internal states to respond to the world beyond [16].

The notion that 'only variety absorbs variety' is at the heart of work by Beer in his development of the Viable System Model (VSM) [13, 14]. The VSM identifies the functional requirements of an organization if it is to have the capacity for self-regulation, based on five component subsystems: System 1—*operations* that produce the organization's key outputs (such as products or services); System 2—*coordination*, which enables operational units to work together without clashes and oscillations; System 3 *delivery management* (including 3*, monitoring), which distributes resources between operations and support overall cohesion; System 4—*development management* (such as marketing, training and R&D), which prepares the organization for the future; and System 5—*policy and governance*—which sets overall direction and ensures there is a balance between operations and development.

In the process of erosion of the organizational and industrial boundaries occurred by the digitalization, a paradox encompassed by the opposed logics of stability and flexibility emerge [15]. Digital infrastructures need to be stable enough to allow the enrolment of new artefacts, processes and actors, but also assuring the flexibility to allow unbounded growth [17]. The critical issue involves the concept of 'control point' [8], that is how to define and control a set of connections in a socio-technical system that help determine behaviours and constraints for other elements in the system. Rooting the analysis of that paradox on the Viable System Model [13, 14] and Ashby's Law of requisite variety [16], networks are interpreted like complex structures in search for self-organization mechanism that helps to regulate the behaviour of the system and maintain its integrity within particular limit [13].

This is the context in which it is increasingly important to discuss the theoretical and empirical implications for accounting and management information systems (MIS) in the inter-organizational settings and networks [15]. The role of MIS has always been recognized as an important source of competitive advantage [18] but new challenges are emerging, as the MIS conceptualization, design and implementation, have to effectively integrate human and organizational structures, acting as 'control point' [8] and supporting the viable system coordination and monitoring mechanisms [13, 19].

Since the last decades of the past millennium, the management and accounting literature has deeply discussed the relationship between networks and MIS. One of the most relevant contribution [20] focuses on the strategic benefits of implementing an inter-organizational information system (IOS). The fundamentals of the IOS concept were developed in the 80s [20, 21] and the IOS term was first used by Barret and Konsynski [22] referring to systems that involve information "resources", like hardware, software, transmission facilities, rules and procedures, data/databases, and expertise, "shared between two or more organizations". Cash and Konsynski [23] finally adopted the term IOS defined as "automated information systems shared by two o more companies". Strong efforts have been undertaken in literature to explore the IOS subject in different perspectives [24] but a lack of a generally accepted framework of analysis led to the proliferation of IOS typologies. Many researchers in the Information Systems (IS) field referred to institutional economics' concepts, while a literature review performed by Kern and Willcocks [25] reported that the IS research on inter-organizational relationships adopted four main conceptual models: the life cycle dynamics, the exchange theory, the resource dependence theory, the transaction cost theory and organizational learning. More recent models have been trying to extend managerial theories such as the resource based view model [26] and the dynamic capabilities theory by taking into consideration the contribution of IT to company performance.

From an accounting perspective, new approach to re-think the lateral process on accounting information [27, 28] emerged in accounting literature since the mid-1990s, when many important scholars [29] emphasized the importance of extending the domain of accounting across the traditional boundaries and called for a need to encourage the research accounting in inter-organisational settings [30]. In this evolutionary perspective, Italian literature has traditionally accorded much importance to the study of accounting issues for networks. Consistent with a solid tradition, this subject is considered to be central for the understanding of the new organizational structures and needs to be investigated in close connection with the management issues. Even more the gap between the evolution of managerial and organizational structures and the definition of adequate information systems can influence the development of more effective forms of networking, as the support of managerial and organizational processes is not considered a crucial role of information [31]. By broadening the analysis perspective, Mancini focuses on the issues of "relational control" [32, 33] and illustrates an integrated scheme "information-governance-control-performance" where the differentiating factor of information sharing—together with the information system which it originates from —are the main components on which a company can implement an effective governance and control of its alliances [33].

Even in the light of this scientific maturity, it is widely recognized the technological innovation are bringing new criticalities and opportunities to be investigated [34, 35]. The challenges posed by the open and smart society are twofold, as the MIS design, implementation and use have to continuously fit the technological evolution and the network configuration [36]. This will assure the needed support to innovation dynamics and relational dimension allowing individuals and firms to achieve the complex set of strategic and operational objectives of collaborative processes.

In the need to thoroughly explore these issues, the first four papers included in this book provide some relevant scientific advancements, investigating the relationship between innovation, technology and MIS on different network settings (business and government, organizational and individual). The implicit question arising from the contributions is to whether inter-organizational relationships are following the technological innovations and the information systems (IS) are adequately designed and implemented to achieve the complex set of networking performance.

Particularly, the work of Treku and Wiredu focuses on Government to business inter-organizational relationship (G2B), analyzing a case of IT innovation platform (GIFMIS) involving the Government of Ghana and a private firm committed in the project to help with specifications, acquisition and deployment of IBM systems for the inter-organizational information system (IOS). Adopting the theoretical lens of structuration theory and transaction costs theory, the paper investigates how the technology induce organizational changes and, more specifically, which kind of influence the information systems (IS) implementation lead on structural adaptation of IOS. The qualitative data collection performed through open-ended interviews, document studies and non-participatory observations demonstrate that the structural adaptation derives from tensions between economic, technological and governance mechanisms, aiming at balancing IT infrastructure with inter-organizational governance to maintain low transaction costs. The work also illustrates the dynamics of inter-organizational transactions and the role of human agency in structural adaptation, highlighting the influence of strategic level agency by executive decisions.

In a similar networking arrangement, the manuscript of Di Vaio and Varriale deals with inter-organizational relationship involving public authorities and private operators assuming the management control systems (MCS) and inter-organizational information system (IOS) as main research objectives. The specific context is referred to the seaport activities and the focus is devoted to the administrative interconnections linking port authorities, shipping agents and cruise as companies to assure the regular operational and information flow related to arrival, mooring and departure of ships in the port destinations. Rooting the discussion on the MCS and environmental literature of seaport activity, the paper investigates the role of IOS on preventing and reducing the environmental effects and supporting the environmental strategic decision. The qualitative approach adopted interviewing two users in the Italian port of Naples investigate different relationship systems between shipping agency, cruise company and between port authorities (PA). The exploratory study found relevant differences in terms of information systems adopted for adequately managing the process and a lack of specific IS for supporting port users. Quality and quantity of information for environmental effect reduction are really scarce and the functions analyzed in the two inter-organizational systems do not allow the integration of operational and informational flow for effective relationship management and reduction of environmental effects.

The next two papers complete the analysis of technology evolution and accounting and MIS in the relational view, enabling a broader understanding of networking relationship in the open and smart society at organizational and individuals level. The work presented by Siciliano and Gaudenzi relates to industrial firms and consider the disruptive effects for modern supply chains (SC) deriving from information technology (IT) and cyber risks. The central issue discussed is the evaluation of the level of knowledge acquired and the risk management approach adopted by SC and IT managers. Framing the theoretical analysis on IS security literature and referring to the emerging research stream of cyber supply chain risk management, the paper collects data from fifteen selected industrial supply chains headquartered in Europe, composed by medium/large companies operating in different private industries. Providing a questionnaire based on security and risk management standards the research highlights a lack of knowledge sharing between IT manager and SC manager, poor communication processes and overconfidence in technical investments. In the absence of integration between the different functions the paper proposes an holistic IT and Cyber risk management framework based on resilience and discusses empirical implications.

In the last work written by Uljala and Scupola the analysis context moves from organizational to personal level, and the relational view is referred to the networking effects lead by technology innovation in developing the virtual entrepreneurship of individuals. The paper adopts the Rogers' diffusion of innovation (DOI) theory and take into consideration the case of E-Residency project implemented in Estonia. This is a transnational digital identity in the form of an eID card allowing individuals to electronically identify and authenticate encrypt and digitally sign documents, accessing electric services, aiming at contributing to the development of the Country's economic and cultural development. Selecting seven individuals adopting E-Residency technology for entrepreneurial purpose and submitting them a web-questionnaire accompanied by interviews, the case highlights the difficulties emerging on innovation diffusion and e-services. Despite the rather simple procedure designed, the scheme implemented encountered some obstructions due to the lack of integration between legal, administrative and policy capacities. The harmonization of these different dimensions of innovation from the users point of view is considered as a fundamental attribute in launching new e-service, especially at government level.

Summarizing, the overall contribution provided by the papers define a relevant view involving technology, organization and MIS that is fundamentally concerned with the reticular interaction between the innovation, organization and information processes (Fig. 1).

Framing the findings in this logic, the first paper demonstrate the existence of three forms of inter-organizational structural adaptation (legitimation, domination and signification) related to the need to balance efficiency and effectiveness between

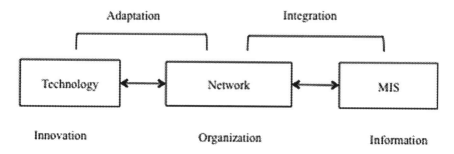

Fig. 1 Technology and MIS in network settings

governance, IT sources and capability, and simultaneously achieving cost efficiency of shared goals.

Viceversa, the remaining papers mostly focus on the issue of integration between networking and MIS and highlight the crucial role of the latter on supporting the relational systems to achieve the various kind of strategic objectives at organizational and individual level. Here the findings show the difficulties and obstacles encountered in different network settings to adequately integrate the information processes with the reticular organization in order to achieve some relevant strategic objectives in the open and smart society like environmental performance, risk management for IT and cybers risks and virtual entrepreneurship development.

Above all, it emerges the importance of a holistic approach and the integration of MIS with transversal organizational structures, which in turn are increasingly shaped by technology. In this context a comprehensive design and implementation of MIS has to be able to consider the interaction between innovation, organizational and information processes, moving from an "integration" to a "sharing" logic. Only this will allow to exchange not only information but also feed-back, ideas, suggestions, opinions between people, inside and outside companies, in order to create value by interaction [36].

These issues are raising the most significant challenges at operational and theoretical perspective that future research will have to investigate to develop the full potential of networking in an open and smart society. The Italian literature has traditionally accorded much importance to the study of the connections between management and information processes, even focusing on networked structures [31] and accounting in inter-organizational settings. For future researches and challenges there is the opportunity to discover the value of this holistic approach to study the continuous interaction between technology, networking settings and MIS, integrating this vision with theoretical concepts provided by the cybernetics.

The cybernetic view has always been consistent with the Italian holistic approach and provide a comprehensive framework that can allow to integrate the different level of analysis involving the impact of innovation and digital technology on networked structures and their related MIS. The adoption of cybernetic tools, already occurred to interpret the firm system of transformation [37] and recently discussed with reference to Management Control Systems [19] should then be extended to investigate networks and MIS in open and smart society, to discover the self-regulating mechanism ad support individual and firms to achieve performance in network settings.

# 3 The Transformation Role of Smart Management Information Systems

Since ten years environ, Web 2.0 has been transforming the way ICT is affecting both the economic environment and the daily life of people and business. Born from the financial bubble and the failure of several old-fashion ICT companies, the label Web 2.0 is nowadays a buzzword used here and there sometimes without a clear awareness about its real meaning [38]. The Internet is no more an instrument, but it becomes a platform without boundaries or dimensions, transforming the way people and firms interact each other in the digital milieu [39]. It emerges the potential driven by the Web to harness collective intelligence and to enforce participation [40].

At the origin, Web 2.0 was conceived in the ICT technology production context as a disruptive technology, as Web 2.0 is much more than just pasting a new user interface onto an old application. It is indeed a way of thinking, a new perspective on the entire technological environment. In the further, Web 2.0 has becoming a new vision of the whole business and finally also of the way people live, work, relate each other [41].

These transformations driven by the Web (r)evolution have cross impact on all the economic sectors and social contexts, therefore interesting a very large set of different aspects. Transformations especially modify the role of actors and stake-holders in the social, political, economic systems [42].

Traditionally, the value chain was conceived like a linear relation regarding one player and linked with other value chains of suppliers and customers [43]. Using ICT and especially the Internet, value chains become bi-directional or multi-directional, deeply changing the way firms interact each others [44–46]. From competition, the new organizational frameworks shift towards cooperation and finally coopetition, conceived like new way to add value in the production chain thanks to information and activities sharing [47]. The ICT pervasiveness produces cooperative exchange relationships on the Internet, involving both firms and customers [48]. New paradigms emerge, such as economies of aggregation, where the Internet deploys its ability to modify the value proposition of a company [49].

The most interesting effect of the deep use of the Internet 2.0 is that it increases the involvement of people in all the daily activities, not only economic ones, but also social and political ones. It produces intra-organizational networks that consist of both collaborative and competitive ties among organizational units [50]. Several cases are nowadays well known: for example, value chains where customer coop-erate in creating the final product, such as in MyPhotoBook, where the customer creates his own photo booklet building the frames and then the book is printed and sent by mail; or business networks where suppliers become partners involved in the co-design of the final products of their customer firms; or citizens cooperating with the local or central government in governing their city or country [51].

Also the relationship between the public administration and citizens is deeply changed, thanks to a set of technologies and applications forming the so-called e-government: government's use of technology, particularly web-based Internet applications to enhance the access to and delivery of government information and services to citizens, business partners, employees, other agencies, and government entities [52]. E-government is not only a way to speed or make more efficient the delivery of information and services: it is indeed an instrument to create new relationships between the government and the citizens and to increase trust and dialogue [53]. The use of Web 2.0 platforms and behaviors is especially a driver towards e-democracy, that is, the Internet potential to reshape democratic life and the use of digital network technologies to shape public policy [54].

Examining the Web 2.0 wave in its cross impact, some keywords strongly emerge, bringing together all the different fields of digitalization: they are participation, communication, smartness, co-creation, and network. These keywords depict a scenario where the traditional relationships tying different actors in a context are modified in a new way not known before.

This transformation clearly emerges from four papers included in the present book, regarding different implementation of Web 2.0; all the works highlight the capability of new technology to transform processes and relations, instead of simply improve old ways-to-do.

Rossi, Moggi, Pierce, and Leardini, in their paper face the topic of using a digital platform not only to communicate, but to exchange information and to involve stakeholders in understanding the goals and the activities in the not-for-profit sector. Corporate social responsibility is an emerging topic in the 21st century [55], and it is especially important for not-for-profit organizations. Technologies have improved interactivity between firms and their stakeholders, and the use of 2.0 technologies to have a better dialogue should be central in Nonprofits, even if they have not moved since now from web 1.0 [56]. The authors focus their research on Italian bank foundations, exploring the use of the Web as a tool for discharging accounts to stakeholders and involving them in dialogue. The data show that most of the foundations do not use websites to communicate interactively with their stakeholders, and communication is limited to one-way disclosure of information. The results suggest more steps can be taken to ensure increased responsiveness to community needs.

Ravarini and Strada, and Castelnovo too, both explore the Digital Do It Yourself (DDIY) behavior, in two different fields of investigation; the workplace and the government. DDIY is defined on the EU website as "a new socio-technological phenomenon which stems from the widespread availability of digital devices that support the convergence of physical ("atoms") and informational ("bits") components (ABC), as well as the growing accessibility of related knowledge and data through open online communities" (http://www.didiy.eu/home?page=1). DDIY is reshaping organization and work, education and research, impacting on social and legal systems, changing creative design and ethics.

Ravarini and Strada's paper explores the use of digital platforms in the workplace. Even if information and communication technology (ICT) has been used in production and business processes from longtime, its effects are unexpected when using new disruptive technologies. To better understand this heterogeneous panorama, the authors define a four-folded taxonomy that highlights the differences between traditional automation, self service and virtualization applications of digital technology and Digital Do-It-Yourself (DDIY). Their findings outlines as DDIY means rethinking the work in a more intelligent way, challenging the traditional constraints related to location and working hours, leaving to workers more autonomy in defining the modalities of work, be it intellectual or manual, compared with greater responsibility for results.

Castelnovo in his paper faces the topic of e-government using new technologies, defining a specific DDIY behavior in the public sector. Recent forms of citizens' participation to the public debate, such as emerging Do-It-Yourself (DIY) and Do-It-With-Others (DIWO) movements (with the key contribution of ICT) have further challenged our traditional vision by showing a variety of different forms of engagement with technology and participation in its design and use [57]. The author of this paper, assuming the concept of co-production as the lens through which to look at citizen's participation in civic life, shows how, when supported by a real redistribution of power between government and citizens, citizens' participation can determine a transformational impact on the same nature of government, thanks to disruptive technologies. Finally, the paper shows how the weakening of the distinction between service producers and service users, analogous to the weakening of the distinction between content producers and content users typical of the Web 2.0 paradigm, can lead to a radical redrawing of the relationship between government and citizens.

Finally, Savastano, Amendola, and D'Ascenzo in their work address the transformation of the manufacturing processes, using digital technologies. Based on the emerging Industry 4.0 paradigm, the authors explore this emerging trend through a case study carried out with an Italian company world leader in the food industry, aiming to shed light on opportunities and threats connected to digital transition. Business process digitalization is reconfiguring every aspect of organizational and operating activities along the entire value chain, defining a networked digital ecosystem allowing firms to achieve important gains in terms of value creation [58]. Even if this papers seems not too similar to the previous ones, it remarks that also in manufacturing the emerging paradigm regards a self-organizing digital infrastructure, aimed at creating a digital environment for networked organizations, to support the cooperation, the knowledge sharing and the interaction between different actors.

In conclusion, these four papers, although addressing very different field of research—accountability in not-for-profit organizations, digital enabled jobs, citizens coproduction in public services, and industry 4.0—contribute to outline the ongoing transformation driven by the Web 2.0 and the new digital platforms. This transformation is deep and effective if it is linked with a behavior transformation, involving people in their different roles of citizens, workers, entrepreneurs, political leaders, technicians, and so on. The joint efforts between technology, institutions and people could conduct ICT towards a new networked ecosystem.

## 4   The relationship between Open Data and Management Information Systems

Open data is a recent phenomenon that has received a considerable attention in recent years [59], because of a wide variety of open data policies developed for instance in the United States [60, 61], Europe [62, 63] and individual countries. But, despite their similarities, open data policies highlights different scopes. While the European Commission emphasizes the direct and the indirect economic gains coming from the use of open government data, the Obama regulation focuses on developing transparency, participation and collaboration, in order to improve services for American people.

In general, literature shows the relevance of open data policies, as their scopes is to achieve the long term transparency of government information and to contribute to citizens' rights to public access to government information. Furthermore, "open data policies have the potential to increase the participation, interaction, self-empowerment and social inclusion of open data users and providers alike, stimulating economic growth and realizing many others advantages" [59: 17]. Besides, previous studies in the area of open data supposes that open data positively influence the development of social, environmental and economic value [64].

Starting from Open data government initiatives, even private companies have begun to develop open data initiatives. In the private sector, open data seem to include business news, marketing information and competitor data that are available from an assortment of web sites. It is argued that open data can stimulate innovation, deliver new opportunities to companies and influence also the company reputation [65].

Literature review on open data reveals two aspects.

The first is that most of the research on open data have been carried out on public administrations. In general, these studies analyse the contingency factors that determine the development of open data policies in public government or they develop frameworks to compare open data procedures in different governments. These frameworks include factors as environmental and context, policy content, performance indicators, and public values. The findings of the works show that current policies are rather inward looking, while open data policy could be improved by collaborating with other organizations, focusing on the impact of the policy, stimulating the use of open data and looking at the need to create a culture in which publicizing data is incorporated in daily working processes [59].

The second aspect concerns the theoretical perspectives used to study open data. Literature review shows that several and different perspectives are used to study open data: legislative, political, social, economical, institutional, operational and technical [64]. The legislative perspective underlines how open data regulation, including open data directive and open data policies, are essential. The political perspective emphasizes the relevance of political developments and political changes between the countries. The social perspective focuses on cultural differences among countries and differences in programmes related to the social benefits of opening data, such as transparency and accountability. The economical perspective considers the financial benefits and gains that can be created by open data. The institutional perspective analyses the way in which institutions permit the publication and the use of open data. The operational perspective focuses on the use of the open data and the requirements to be able to use open data. Standards are considered very important for open data operations. The technical perspective reveals the importance of open data technologies, open data platforms and open data infrastructures.

In general, open data research seems to be still in its infancy, and as a result, the extent literature uses limited application and development of theory toward understanding the open data phenomenon. Furthermore, very little research has been also performed on how open data can exactly result in innovation [64].

Literature which explore the relationship between open data and innovation, defines innovation as an act or set of acts aiming to do something better, to meet a new need or respond to new circumstances [64]. In this context, innovation can be articulated in several typologies, including the development of a new product or a modification in an existing product; a process innovation that is new in the industry, opening a new market, development of new sources of supply for raw materials or other inputs, or any change in an business organization.

Open data seem to be potentially relevant for increase each innovation type, though stimulating innovation through open data practices is not easy. The complexity of this relationship derives from several factors, including: the large number of actors involved in the process, the variety of social and technical context, uncertainty surrounding how open data will be used, and the difficulty to assess intangible impacts generated through open data innovation [64].

First, several stakeholder are involved in the open data practices. Citizens, researchers, journalists, developers, entrepreneurs, archivist, and so on, are focused on their own activities and have different interests in open data process. The complexity systems from the fact that these interests could be in conflict.

Second, the open data process can be develop in a variety of context. Each context has specific characteristics (legal, cultural, technical) which influence how open data are collected, elaborated and disseminated.

Third, it is difficult to hypothesize how users will use open data, when they will use it and how it will be used in the future. Therefore, it is complex to define the characteristics that open data processes must possess.

Fourth, it is problematic to assess the value created from open data innovation and, in particular, how public value is generated. Several studies focuses on the analysis of the public value. They show that public value can have many levels of observation and that it is generally derived from the direct usefulness, fairness and equitability of benefits to a variety of stakeholders. Realising public and private open data formats creates significant benefits for researchers, citizens, companies and other stakeholder, such as business creation or having the ability to understand public or private problems in new ways through advanced data analytics.

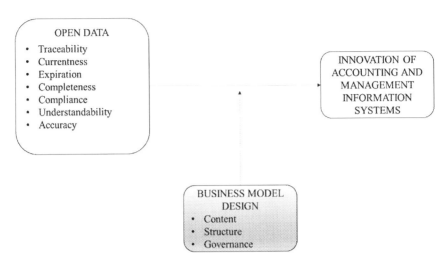

**Fig. 2** The relationship between open data and accounting/management information systems

Analyzing the literature regarding open data and innovation, emerges as another research gap is almost the lack of studies that examine the impact of the open data on the innovation of accounting and management information systems.

Starting from this consideration, we analyse the relationship between open data and the innovation of the accounting and management information systems, in order to answer to the following research question: how is the influence of the open data practices on the innovation of the management and accounting information systems?

To answer to this research question we build a theoretical model. Figure 2 depicts our basic research model.

Our conceptual model shows that open data practices impact on the innovation of the accounting and management information systems. We also propose a contingency approach to analyse this relationship, hypothesizing that the design of a specific business model influence and differentiate the effects of open data processes on the innovation of the accounting and management information systems.

Business model is understood as manifestation of how organizational variables are configured, how the company structures its relations with external stakeholders and the consequences of this configurations on company performance. Thus, according to the literature, we describe the business model as the content, structure and governance transactions within the company and between the company and its external partners that support the company in the creation, delivery and capture of value [66]. Following this definition, a business model need to specify [67]:

1. The content: the set of essential activities.
2. The structure: the organizational units performing those activities and the ways in which these units are linked.

3. The governance: the mechanisms for controlling the organizational units and the linkages between the units.

Based on the different possible configurations of these elements, companies can design different business model to achieve their scopes.

Another important element in our model is represented by the features of open data. We suppose that disclosing open data is not sufficient, but we need also to consider data quality in order to avoid an inefficient reuse of open data.

We suggest that a set of metrics are necessary tools to achieve data quality improvement, as it has been recently advocated by the literature [68]. Open data quality concerns the following characteristics: traceability, currentness, expiration, completeness, compliance, understandability, accuracy. Traceability (track of creation and track of updates) indicates the presence of data associated with the process of creation of a dataset, and with the updates done to a dataset. Currentness indicates the number of days passed between the moment in which the information is available and the moment in which the dataset is ready. Expiration reveals the ratio between the delay in the publication of a dataset after the expiration of its previous version and the period of time referred by the dataset. Completeness reveals that the dataset is complete and includes all the date. Compliance indicates the degree to which dataset follows specific standards. Understandability indicates the percentage of columns in a dataset that is represented in a format that can be easily understood by users. Accuracy indicates the percentage of data in a dataset that have a correct value.

The last ten research works included in this book are related, to some extension, to the implication of ICT in building on open context.

The first three papers concern cloud platforms, that are one of the IT infrastructure able to support an open view of information management systems. They debate on the implications of cloud platforms on information systems from different points of view.

The next two papers regard XBRL, which is an electronic language for financial reporting in private companies and public administration and it enable business data to be used interactively and reusable. The two research works highlights the impacts of XBRL on comparability and its role within governmental financial reporting.

The following three papers debate on the meaning of openness considering the relationship between companies and their stakeholders through financial, non financial and social communication.

The last two papers discuss the implication of new technologies on decision making tools, management accounting technics and accountants' role.

The contribution of Hahn et al. discusses about the capability to create and appropriate value in an interfirm collaboration in IT industry when the collaboration is based on a cloud platform ecosystem that push the firms to search new business models. The research work, based on empirical data from four case studies of cloud platform ecosystems, confirm the validity of the framework of Ray and Tang and add interesting contribution to the field of business model of Cloud platform ecosystems extending value appropriation mechanisms and improving the knowledge on IT capabilities. In terms of value appropriation mechanisms the authors add two new mechanisms as downstream capabilities and platform resourcing.

The research of Cavallari et al. discusses about MicroServices as a new Information Systems Architecture based on micro-components with specific functionalities, independent life-cycles yet interconnected and correlated. Based on a literature analysis, the authors highlight the implication of this new approach in terms of advantages and disadvantages. They also propose an interesting framework, the "Onion Model", to represent the ability to enhance eService security within a MicroService environment.

The contribution of Ficco et al. concerns the migration of mission-critical applications on an inter-Cloud ecosystem made by a federation of distributed Clouds of multiple heterogeneous organizations. In such environment some challenges have to be addressed: IT resource planning; scalability and elasticity metrics, forecasting models to predict behaviours of service level agreements violation; monitoring security issues. The authors suggest to integrate Cloud services with a Web dashboard which includes tools able to monitor and predict SLA violation, security issues, and the application resources.

The contribution of Yang et al. investigates wether the comparability of financial reporting has improved after the mandatory introduction of XBRL. The authors adopt an interesting methodology in order to measure not only the use of accounting taxonomy but also to evaluate the relative structure of semantic structures. They applied the local outlier detection method combined with the distance matrix from the graph similarity measure. Considering the three main financial statements taken from the XBRL annual report submitted to the SEC, the authors highlights that accounting semantic quality has improved and there is a significant convergence of statement structure that suggest a the improvement of comparability over time.

The paper of Fradeani et al. investigates the role that XBRL could play within governmental financial reporting. Through the case study of two Italian projects of the Court of Auditors and the State General Accounting Department, the authors affirm that the mandatory adoption of XBRL in public sector is possible and that the real challenge is the full use of XBRL both for private and public sector. On the base of the Italian experience, the paper also demonstrate that XBRL adoption cannot be considered an additional burocratic tool, but a different tool able to improve the reliability, timeliness and efficiency of information processing.

The contribution of Lepore et al. regards the relationship between openness and performance in Italian Local Government Authorities. In particular the authors propose an OLS regression based on the openness score and the financial distress indexes. Results show that the propensity of being more open (in terms of presence of open data, social media and Youtube Channel) is positive related to the financial distress score, and positive performance allows to be more open.

The paper of Corsi et al. discusses the openness of firms in terms of tools used to formulate, control and communicate the sustainability strategy, in the light of the triple bottom line model. Based on a case study, the research investigate the relationship between different level of accounting information systems for sustainability and three different approaches to Sustainability Balanced Scorecard. The authors propose an interesting framework which put in relation sustainability communication tools and accounting information systems.

The paper Pisano et al. examines the disclosure of human capital in sustainability reports considering the role of cost of capital and ownership structure. The authors propose a disclosure index that includes both the stock of knowledge and capabilities of employee and the human resources management practices.

The contribution of Resta et al. explores the potential of machine learning models to the analysis of firms' performance. They propose a Self-Organizing Map to exploit the complexity of financial data and apply it to a sample of ICT companies. They identify five clusters characterized by different dominant financial dimensions and offer a handy way to visualize the analysis of firms' performance.

The paper of Nespeca et al. investigates the impact of ICT tools on management accounting and on management accountants' role. Considering Business Intelligence (BI) tools, the authors developed an exploratory field study based on semi-structured interviews to consultants that manage BI implementation projects. The results highlights that advanced ICT tools like BI makes accounting processes more structured, more rational and faster, fostering the implementation of advanced management accounting tools like Balanced Scorecard. BI also affects management accountants' competencies, in particular it stimulate the development of business-oriented and business analytics competencies.

# References

1. Brynjolfsson, E. & McAfee, A. (2014). *The Second Machine Age. Work, progress, and prosperity in a time of brilliant technologies*. New York, USA: W.W. Norton.
2. Castells, M. (2010). *The rise of network society* (2nd ed.). Chichester, UK: Wiley-Blackwell.
3. Yoo, Y., Boland, K., Lyytinen, K., & Majchraz, A. (2012). Organizing for Innovation in the digitized world. *Organization Science, 23,* 1398–1408.
4. Mokyr, J. (2002). *The gifts of athena: historical origin of the knowledge economy*. Princeton: Princeton University Press.
5. Yoo, Y. (2010). Computing on everyday life. A call for research on experimental computing. *MIS Quarterly, 34,* 213–231.
6. Tiacci, L., & Cardoni, A. (2011). How to move from traditional to innovative models of networked organizations: A methodology and a case study in the metal-mechanic industry. In: L. M. Camarinha-Matos, A. Pereira-Klen, H. Afsarmanesh (Eds.), *PRO-VE 2011. IFIP AICT* (vol. 362, pp. 413–420). Heidelberg: Springer.
7. Benkler, Y. (2006). *The wealth of networks. How social production transforms markets and freedom*. New Haven, USA: Yale University Press.
8. Sambamaurthy, V., Bharadwaj, A., & Grover, V. (2003). Shaping agility through digital options. Reconceptualizing the role of information technology in contemporary firms. *MIS Quarterly, 27,* 237–263.
9. Libert, B., Beck, M., & Wind, J. (2016). *The network imperative, how to survive and grow in the age of digital business models*. Brighton: Harvard Business Review Press.

10. McAfee, A., & Brynjolfsson, E. (2012, October) *Big data: The management revolution.* Brighton: Harvard Business Review.
11. Vasarhely, M. A., Kogan, A., & Tuttle, B. M. (2015, June). Big data in accounting: An overview. *Accounting Horizons, 29*(2), 381–396.
12. Marchi, L. (2011). L'evoluzione del controllo di gestione nella prospettiva informativa e gestionale esterna. *Management Control, 3,* 5–16.
13. Beer, S. (1985). *Diagnosing the system for organizations.* Chichester, UK: Wiley.
14. Espejo, R., & Reyes, A. (2011). *Organizational systems, managing complexity with the viable system model.* Heidelberg, UK: Springer.
15. Jackson, P. (2015). *Networks in a Digital Age: A cybernetics perspective.* In European Conference of Information Systems (ECIS), Completed Research Papers, Paper 85.
16. Ashby, W. R. (1960). *An introduction to cybernetics.* London, UK: Chapman & Hall.
17. Tilson, D., Lyyttinen, K., & Sorensen, C. (2010). Digital Infrastructures: The missing IS research agenda. *Information Systems Research, 4,* 748–759.
18. Powell, T. C., & Dent-Miccallef, A. (1997). Information Technology as competitive advantage: The role of human, business and technology resources. *Strategic Management Journal, 5,* 375–405.
19. O'Gradie, W., Morlidge, S., & Rouse, P. (2016). Evaluating the completeness and effectiveness of management control systems with cybernetic tools. *Management Accounting Research, 33,* 1–15.
20. Johnston, H. R., & Vitale, M. R. (1988, June). Creating competitive advantage with inter-organizational information systems. *MIS Quarterly,* 153–165.
21. Venkatraman, N. (1994). IT-enabled business transformation: From automation to business scope redefinition. *Sloan Management Review, 35,* 73–85.
22. Barret, S., & Konsynski, B. R. (1982). Inter-organization information sharing systems. *MIS Quarterly, 6,* 93–105.
23. Cash, J. I., & Konsynski, B. R. (1985). Is redraws competitive boundaries. *Harvard Business Review, 2,* 134–142.
24. Haugland, S. A. (1999). Factors influencing the duration of international buyer-seller relationships. *Journal of Business Research, 3,* 273–280.
25. Kern, T., & Willcocks, L. (2000). Exploring information technology outsourcing relationships: Theory and practice. *Strategic Information Systems, 4,* 321–350.
26. Bharadwaj, A. S. (2000). A resource-based perspective on information technology capability and firm performance: An empirical investigation. *MIS Quarterly, 1,* 169–196.
27. Caglio, A., & Ditillo, A. (2008). A review and discussion of management control in inter-firm relationships: Achievements and future directions. *Accounting, Organizations and Society, 33,* 868–989.
28. Tomkins, C. (2001). Interdependencies, trust and information in relationship, alliances and networks. *Accounting, Organizations and Society, 26,* 161–191.
29. Hopwood, A. (1996). Looking across rather than un and down: On the need to explore the lateral processing of information. *Accounting, Organizations and Society, 29,* 51–72.
30. Hakansson, H., Krauss, K., & Lind, J. (2010). *Accounting in networks.* London: Routledge.
31. Lai, A. (1991). *Le aggregazioni di imprese. Caratteri istituzionali e strumenti per l'analisi economico-aziendale.* Milano: Franco Angeli.
32. Mancini, D. (2010). *Il sistema informativo e di controllo relazionale per il governo della rete di relazioni collaborative d'azienda.* Giuffré: Milano.
33. Mancini, D. (2011). L'azienda-rete e le decisioni di partnership: Il ruolo del sistema informativo relazionale. *Management Control, 1,* 65–97.
34. Mancini, D., Vaseen, E. H. J., & Dameri, R. P. (2014). Trends in Accounting Information Systems. In D. Mancini, E. H. J. Vaseen, & R. P. Dameri (Eds.), *Accounting information systems for decision making, LNISO.* Heidelberg: Springer.
35. Mancini, D., Lamboglia, R., Castellano, G., Corsi, K. (2017). Trends of digital innovation applied to accounting information and management control systems. In K. Corsi, N.

Castellano, R. Lamboglia, & D. Mancini (Eds.), *Reshaping accounting and management control systems. Lecture notes in information systems and organisation, 20*. Cham: Springer.

36. Mancini, D. (2016). Acounting information systems in an open society. *Emerging Trends and Issues. Management Control, 1*, 5–16.

37. DeMartini, C. (2014). *Performance management systems. Design, disgnosis and use*. Berlin: Springer.

38. O'Reilly, T. (2012). What is web 2.0. In H. M. Donelan et al. (Eds.), *Online communication and collaboration: A reader*. Abingdon: Routledge.

39. O'Reilly, T. (2009). *What is Web 2.0*. Sebastopol: O'Reilly Media Inc.

40. Bricklin, D. (2001). *The cornucopia of the commons. Peer-to-peer: Harnessing the power of disruptive technologies* (pp. 59–63).

41. Musser, J., & O'Reilly, T. (2006). *Web 2.0. Principles and Best Practices* [Excerpt]. Sebastopol: O'Reilly Media.

42. Thomas, J. C., & Streib, G. (2005). E-democracy, E-commerce, and E-research: Examining the electronic ties between citizens and governments. *Administration & Society, 37*(3), 259–280.

43. Porter, M. E., & Millar, V. E. (1985). *How information gives you competitive advantage* (Vol. 63, Issue NO. 4). Brighton: Harvard Business Review.

44. Porter, M. E. (2001). *Strategy and the internet*. Brighton: Harvard Business Review.

45. Narasimhan, R., & Kim, S. W. (2001). Information system utilization strategy for supply chain integration. *Journal of Business Logistics, 22*(2), 51–75.

46. Barnes, S. J. (2002). The mobile commerce value chain: Analysis and future developments. *International Journal of Information Management, 22*(2), 91–108.

47. Dagnino, G. B., & Padula, G. (2002, May). Coopetition strategy: a new kind of interfirm dynamics for value creation. In *Second Annual conference, Innovative Research in Management, European Academy of Management (EURAM)* (Vol. 9). Stockholm.

48. Hemetsberger, A. (2002). Fostering cooperation on the internet: Social exchange processes in innovative virtual consumer communities. *NA-Advances in Consumer Research, 29*, 354–356.

49. Bakos, Y., & Brynjolfsson, E. (2000). Bundling and competition on the internet. *Marketing Science, 19*(1), 63–82.

50. Tsai, W. (2002). Social structure of "coopetition" within a multiunit organization: Coordination, competition, and intraorganizational knowledge sharing. *Organization Science, 13*(2), 179–190.

51. Kahler, M. (Ed.). (2015). *Networked politics: Agency, power, and governance*. Ithaca: Cornell University Press.

52. McClure, D. L. (2000). Statement of David L. McClure, U.S. General Accounting Office, before the Subcommittee on Government Management Information and Technology, Committee on Government Reform, House of Representatives. Available: http://www.gao.gov.

53. Dameri, R. P., Ricciardi, F., & D'Auria, B. (2014). Knowledge and intellectual capital in smart city. *Proceedings of the European Conference on Knowledge Management, ECKM, 1*, 250–257.

54. Chadwick, A. (2008). Web 2.0: New challenges for the study of e-democracy in an era of informational exuberance. *I/S: A Journal of Law and Policy for the Information Society, 5*(1), 9–41.

55. Snider, J., Hill, R. P., & Martin, D. (2003). Corporate social responsibility in the 21st century: A view from the world's most successful firms. *Journal of Business Ethics, 48*(2), 175–187.

56. Waters, R. D., & Feneley, K. L. (2013). Virtual stewardship in the age of new media: Have nonprofit organizations' moved beyond Web 1.0 strategies? *International Journal of Nonprofit and Voluntary Sector Marketing, 18*(3), 216–230.

57. Buechley, L., Paulos, E., Rosner, D., & Williams, A. (2009). DiY for CHI: Methods, communities, and values of reuse and customization. In *Proceedings of Conference on Human Factors in Computing Systems (CHI)*. New York: ACM Press.

58. Chang, E., & West, M. (2006, December). Digital ecosystems a next generation of the collaborative environment. In *International Conference on Information Integration and Web-based Applications & Services (iiWAS)* (pp. 3–24).

59. Zuiiderwijk, A., & Janssen, M. (2014). Open data policies, their implementation and impact: A framework for comparison. *Government Information Quarterly, 31,* 17–29.

60. Obama, B. (2012). Open government directive. Retrieved September 15, 2012 from http://www.whitehouse.gov/sites/default/files/omb/assets/memoranda_2010/m10-06.pdf.

61. Obama, B. (2012). Digital government. Building a 21st century platform to better serve the American people. Retrieved September 15, 2012 from http://www.whitehouse.gov/sites/default/files/omb/egov/digital-governement/digital-government.html.

62. European Commission. (2003). Directive 2003/98/EC of the European parliament of the council of 17 November 2003 on the re-use of public sector information. Retrieved December 12, 2012 from http://ec.europa.eu/information_society/policy/psi/rules/eu/index_en.htm.

63. Commission, European. (2011). *Communication from the commission to the European parliament, the council, the European economic and social committee and the committee of the regions. Open data. An engine for innovation, growth and transparent governance.* Brussels: European commission.

64. Zuiderwijk, A., Helbig, N., Gil-García, R., & Janssen, M. (2014). Special issue on innovation through open data—A review of the state of the art and emerging research agenda: Guest editors' introduction. *Journal of Theoretical and Applied Electronic Commerce Research, 9* (2), I–XIII.

65. Stepashkin, M. V., & Khusnoiarov, F. F. (2015). Risk analysis for reputation based on assessments and ranking of information events and specific data from open sources of information. *Problems of Economic Transitions, 57*(12), 8–16.

66. Winter, S. G., & Szulanski, G. (2001). Replication as strategy. *Organization Science, 12*(6), 730–743.

67. Saebi, T., & Foss, N. J. (2015). Business models for open innovation: Matching heterogenous open innovation strategies with business model dimensions. *European Management Journal, 33,* 201–213.

68. Vetrò, A., Canova, L., Torchiano, M., & Minotas, C. O. (2016). Open data quality measurement framework: definition and application to open government data. *Government Information Quarterly, 33,* 325–337.

# Information Systems Implementation and Structural Adaptation in Government-Business Inter-organization

**Daniel N. Treku**[ID] **and Gamel O. Wiredu**[ID]

**Abstract** The adaptation of inter-organizational structure occasioned by organizational and information technology agency in government-to-business (G2B) relations has been quite under-researched. Drawing upon structuration and transactions costs theories, this paper analyzes how and why IS implementation causes structural adaption. Based on analysis of a case of an inter-organizational implementation of a financial management information system, the paper argues that: legitimation structural adaptation is occasioned by the need to balance efficiency and effectiveness between governance and IT sourcing; domination structural adaptation is occasioned by the need to balance efficiency and effectiveness between governance and business IT capability; and signification structural adaptation is occasioned by the need to achieve cost efficiency of shared goals and by availability of IT to preserve what is achieved over the long term. It is argued that this implementation perspective on structural adaptation deepens our understanding of socio-technical shaping of structure. It also offers far-reaching benefits to structure conception and its organizational application than the previous ones.

**Keywords** Implementation · Structural adaptation · Inter-organizational
Information systems · Government · Business

## 1  Introduction

The structure of inter-organizational relations plays an important role in successful implementation of inter-organizational information systems (IOS). Yet, how inter-organizational structures are produced and reproduced as they adapt to IOS

D. N. Treku (✉) · G. O. Wiredu
Ghana Institute of Management and Public Administration, Greenhill Close, Achimota,
Accra, Ghana
e-mail: dtreku@gimpa.edu.gh

G. O. Wiredu
e-mail: gwiredu@gimpa.edu.gh

© Springer International Publishing AG, part of Springer Nature 2018
R. Lamboglia et al. (eds.), *Network, Smart and Open*, Lecture Notes in Information
Systems and Organisation 24, https://doi.org/10.1007/978-3-319-62636-9_2

implementation circumstances remains quite under-researched. Organizational structures adapt to circumstances such as technology and human agency [1, 2]. In information systems (IS) research, structural adaptation has been explained from the IT perspective as witnessed in headlines such as "technology as an occasion for structuring" [3], "adaptive structuration" [4], "structurational model of technology" [5], "using technology and constituting structures" [6] "information technology and the structuring of organizations" [7], and "structuration theory and information systems research" [8].

These explanations are important contributions to IS, but broader explanations can be proffered because of two reasons. Firstly, the aspect of IT that dominates these explanations is use. However, IT use is just one among many aspects such as IT implementation, design, adoption, management and maintenance. Similarly, the organizational level of analysis dominates these explanations while other levels such as inter-organizational, national and global have been overlooked, probably, on assumption that they carry similar context underpinnings to organizational analysis. Therefore, it can be said that existing explanations that are focused on IT use and the organizational level of analysis are quite narrow.

Secondly, researchers' pursuit of technological explanations has advertently or inadvertently led them to project technology which leaves other non-technological factors in the background. Thus, even though technology may relate with economics, control, and strategy of organization to produce structural adaptations, these factors are treated as contexts in the various investigations that have been done. Consequently, existing explanations are rich with the technology perspective on structural adaptation but bereft of socio-technical systemic perspectives that show how technology and other organizational factors produce and reproduce structures. Because a socio-technical perspective is richer and more encompassing in its representation of IS reality, it can also be said that existing explanations which focused on technology alone are also narrow.

Barley [3] gives a hint of the second problem in his suggestion that technology influences organizational structure by taking account of historical and cultural circumstances. Hence, studies of the structuring process require "a methodology and a conception of the technical change" open to the construction of grounded, population specific theories" (p. 107). Informed by this suggestion, this study seeks to explain how adaptation of inter-organizational structures is induced by IS implementation. Thus, the study is based on three interrelated premises: first, IOS, which is constituted by IT, governance and economics, is the socio-technical systemic perspective taken to proffer a richer explanation; second, inter-organization is the level of analysis; and, third, implementation is the aspect of IS that is the focus.

The IOS perspective is important because inter-organization constitutes a more complex system than organization [9]. For instance, where economic transactions are at the core of human agency to implement IS, the understanding of structural adaptation cannot avoid embodiments and instantiated practices that may be economically binding on actions producing and reproducing structures. An IOS with specific instance of government-to-business (G2B) inter-organizational relationships "that define structure include trading, communicative, economic, corporate, power, cultural and geographical relationships" [10, p. 7]. In this, government's dominant institutional frame makes G2B relationships different from business-to-business ones. Government also has unique public welfare goals. It has strong affinity for centralization of structure, power and authority to deal with actors' clandestine activities [3]. However, in G2B relationships, it is more difficult to centralize because the relationship enables negotiability of structure and power [3, 11]. These underpinnings and instantiated practices are such that they cannot be adequately accounted for by existing explanations.

The implementation focus is also important because so far, the dynamics of IS implementation have not been explored in existing research on structural adaptation. IS implementation; refers to the process of integrating IT into a social setting with the aim of achieving stakeholder-acceptance. Unlike the IS use stage which signifies high levels of user acceptance and greater stability, the implementation stage is characterized by high levels of user resistance and fluidity due to power, politics, technology functionality, and organizational structure [12]. Because IS implementation entails greater dynamics than use; it has more diverse study elements that can be used in this study to provide a more robust explanation of structural adaptation.

This study is an attempt to extend technological explanations of structural adaptation by accounting for the antecedent and consequent IOS implementation requirements. The empirical case used in exploring these issues is the implementation of Ghana Integrated Financial Management Information System (GIFMIS) that was studied in its second phase after a successful first phase implementation. GIFMIS is a public financial management (PFM) tool aimed at bringing sanity, efficiency, transparency, accountability and effectiveness into the country's financial administration. The study analyzes why and how IS implementation by government and business partners induces structural adaptation using structuration and transaction cost theories. The analysis shows that government adapts structure to G2B IOS implementation by balancing high cost of change in governance mechanism with low cost of IT infrastructure use and with low cost of business IT capability. It also adapts structure to implementation by embodying low-cost clan relationship with business into IT to preserve it over the long-term. The paper argues that these findings extend explanations of how IT occasions structural adaptation, provide novel insights for analyzing how IS implementation shapes structural adaptation, and contributes more refined explanations of the relationship between human agency and structural adaptation.

The next section presents reviews of the literature on IOS implementation and the theories used. It is followed by presentation of the methodology, results, analysis and discussion of contributions.

## 2   IOS Implementation

Tan and colleagues [13] argue for a dyadic framework for IOS implementation based on the various typologies that have been used to classify IOS implementation. Their argument is that an implementation based on a dyadic framework helps to reveal superior insights between cooperating organizations that serve as a leverage for competitive advantage and business value whereas Johnstone and Vitale [14] had earlier authored the creation of competitive advantage with a complex and multi-lateral view of IOS; a pre-conception of contemporary value chain phenomena. These divergent yet complementary arguments for addressing IOS research design and implementation point to one theme: inter-organizational dynamics are driving the interactions, decisions, and structural changes during and after IOS implementation.

As noted in the IOS literature, complex dynamics exist in IOS implementation. They are normally characterized by process-oriented works flows and variances in the information resources available and the processing needs of the information for fashioning out standardization agreed upon by the organizations engaged in the implementation [15]. Indeed, Tan and colleagues [13] alludes to the positive effect of such interesting and complex perspectives of Bensaou and Venkatraman's [15] IOS implementation conceptions. However, they argue that the degrees in fit across multiple relationships hides the interplay between facilitators and inhibitors of value across the flow of events between implementing organizations. This interplay could be revealed by careful understanding of the human agency and the socio-technical 'affordances' [16] generated during implementation. The focus of this research is to understand how underlying structural constructs adapt to the implementation processes and the reasons for this perspective are categorized into two in the following arguments.

Firstly, numerous arguments in IOS implementation have focused on implementation as the dependent variable. With literature extant on the nature and operation of the IOS implementation variable, as espoused in the paragraphs above, there is the need for coherent application of IOS implementation process as an independent variable in revealing phenomena that shape the interplay amongst organizations, technology and socio-technical practices.

Indeed, Ginzberg and Schultz [17] argued that implementation could be viewed as managing future impacts of the system which implies future appropriation and practice instantiations. They came to this conclusion after careful studies of several implementation research works that revealed three underlying themes: (1) management practices to improve chances of successful implementation, (2) "the effects of changing technology on implementation practice" (p. 1) and (3) "changing views of the implementation process" (p. 1). The analysis of these thematic areas in the implementation literature informed their stance that implementation processes "have moved from an era of implementing large discrete projects to one of incremental changes in a broad, organizational computing environment" (p. 4). This is a coherent view that underscores the need to begin interrogating other IS phenomena such as structural adaptation with understanding of the level of analysis at play in light of IS implementation. The assumption here is, systems do not remain static, they provoke actions and these actions respond. There is thus the existence of complex organizational dynamics which an implementation process can help reveal.

Secondly, the production and reproduction of social structures have never been theorized from the perspectives of implementation, more so IOS implementation. When we focus on technology use as the extant literature has in theorizing structure and agency, arguments of emergence [6] and embodiment [4] of structures would continue to rob the field of what participants must do irrespective of the circumstances they face to make the interaction with the technology efficient and effective. Structural adaptation via Implementation lens embraces these two concepts (emergence and embodiment) in a way such that an organization could then make the choice to lean towards what would contribute to the attainment of their strategic goals. Perhaps this is what Bensaou et al. [15] forcefully advanced, as mentioned in the third paragraph of this section, but then again, for social structural considerations; we propose that implementation must be conceived as the independent variable to better the prevailing structural arguments. If IT use could be treated as an independent variable to theorize structure, then implementation must even more be the better phenomenon for theorizing structures and agency.

# 3   Theory

## 3.1   Structuration

The paper draws primarily on the work by Jones and Karsten [8] who explained how structuration theory may be incorporated in IS research. Their argument reflects the adoption of Giddens' [1] conceptualization of duality of structure which provides the boundary specifics (structural dimensions, antecedents and consequents) for IS researchers that may theorize structure. The boundary specifics provide the dimensions of structure for this study. Thus, it shows the extent to which different structures can be conceived (mentally represented to cause an action), how they are produced or reproduced by various forms of antecedent and consequent inter-actions being re-constituted by the same structure. The types of structures that are produced and reproduced are signification, domination and legitimation. These structures are primarily enacted by some interactive forms (communication, power and sanction). The interactive forms leverage or are leveraged by respective conceptual modal frames (i.e., modalities of interpretation, facility and norm) to enact the structures. Additionally, these structures can be produced from secondary bases when a particular structure produces other structures without leveraging the interactive forms.

Structures of signification are enacted by the meanings (interpretive schemes) that actors assign to entities or their coordinated actions. Although on daily basis, actors in the social system assign several meaning to occurrences, the consideration here refers to those meanings that influence a routinized way of doing things. The primary source of structures of signification are basic communications; for example, spoken language, sign language and mannerisms, and attitude towards work interdependencies. Apart from the signs, schemas and speech acts of communication, job functions about IT and how they are appropriated is necessary to determine signification structures. The import of this submission is that, production of signification structures must encompass a broader view of interaction between the participating organizations in an inter-organizational network. The task is to capture complex adaptive dynamics in a strategic implementation of G2B IOS. Thus, this view of interaction is adopted to broaden what constitute the interactions and how they routinize to develop signification structures.

Structures of domination are primarily developed from the exercise of power. To identify them, an understanding of power and politics in the organization must be resourced thoroughly to collect rich data. Pfeffer [18] defines power as the potential ability to influence behavior, to change the course of events, to overcome resistance and to get people to do what they would not otherwise do. Thus, domination structures are created through the modalities or media that actors leverage upon to exercise their power bases. Orlikowski and Robey [7] explain that all social systems and for that matter inter-organizational systems have in them asymmetric resources, that is, actors in the system have different pieces of information on these resources. As a result, one's actions or ways of interacting using his/her knowledge of the resource determines whether a dominative structure is created, reaffirmed or challenged. Thus, domination structures can be explained as the institutionalized structures of the routines that have characterized the exercise of power. They determine actions and the actions shape them.

An understanding of the modalities (norms) that mediate legitimated structure and its constitutive interactive base (sanction or rules and obligations) help to better appreciate what structures of legitimation are. Orlikowski and Robey [7] define norms as "organizational [systemic] rules or conventions governing legitimate or appropriate conduct". They explain that as individuals interact, they sanction certain codes amongst themselves. These codes legitimize their action, keep them in check and guide the manner in which future interactions may go. These norms or codes may be challenged, modified or entrenched by other rules (norms) or other resources (facilities). Primarily, the perspectives taken by this paper to theorize structuration harmonizes the dichotomous arguments in the field of structuration, presents a strong case that it is possible to have a theory that focuses on a working context and appreciates.

## 3.2   Transactions Costs

Transactions costs theory (TCT) usually "focuses on organizational transactions as its unit of analysis" [19]. Primarily, TCT is based on two assumptions, bounded rationality and opportunism. The basic criterion for organizing transactions is to economize on the sum of both production expenses and transactions costs [20]. In a G2B IOS implementation context, the decision to acquire, outsource or build technology in-house provides a setting for understanding transactions costs in that a transaction may be said to occur when a product is traded across a technologically-separable interface [20].

Transaction between any two parties are characterized by frequency of trans-actions, environmental uncertainty and asset specificity [21]. At all times, parties may look to reduce transaction costs or maximize transaction benefits by altering the characteristics of the transactions. Transactions cannot be overlooked in an organization's contractual relations. Williamson [20] asserts that "if TC are negli-gible, the organization of economic activity is irrelevant, since any advantages one mode of organization appears to hold over another will simply be eliminated by costless contracting". There are four possible relationships that are used to govern inter-organizational transactions to reduce costs—market (using prices), bureau-cracy (using rules), clan (using norms) and network (using mutual understanding). These relationships are framed by two conditions that increase transactions costs: performance ambiguity and goal incongruity [22].

Transaction benefits have been argued to be premised on how the intensity, segmentation, dispersion and scarcity of knowledge are fostered [23]. According to Boudreau and colleagues, an organizational need of maximizing transaction ben-efits while minimizing transaction costs "result in the mixing of governance structures, where two or more 'pure' governance structures [market, hierarchy and network] are combined". By this argument, we understand that neglecting the advantageous or disadvantageous positions of either government or business in their interaction only serves to hide certain causal elements that may influence structuring in the G2B context. TCT serves as a useful lens which "provides guidance on how a transaction might best be structured based on its internal and external coordination and control costs" [19].

## 4 Research Setting and Methodology

### 4.1 Setting

The government of Ghana (GoG) was considered as one giant organization or group of collectives and mostly, their implementable activities are piloted before an across-the-board application is done. The Government entered into an agreement with Net Solutions (a business entity) to implement GIFMIS technology that would among other things allow for all government transactions with businesses. GoG transacts business through Ministries, Departments and Agencies (MDAs) and Municipal, Metropolitan and District Assemblies (MMDAs) such as Ministry of Finance and Economic Planning (MoFEP), Controller and Accountant General's

Department (CAGD) and Accra Metropolitan Assembly. GoG projects are cate-gorized under various ministries through the departments or assemblies. MoFEP through CAGD set up GIFMIS Secretariat headed by a project director to specif-ically oversee the implementation process and onward management of the system with oversight responsibilities exercised by the Controller and Accountant General's Department. The GIFMIS Secretariat was a major site for data collection as the organogram championing the implementation process was domiciled there. All sub-units or departments operated from the Secretariat. Data centres had been set up at seven MMDAs and the CAGD to allow for piloting and preliminary use of the deployed artefacts and processes as at the time of data collection.

## 4.2  Design

This research was informed by critical realism which assumes an underlying causal reality that is objective and independent [24], and by interpretivism which assumes a subjective construction and interpretation of reality [25]. The idea is that expla-nation of structural adaptation in this research depends upon the technical reality of IT and the social reality of the implementation processes. Critical realism describes causality by detailing the means or processes by which events are generated by structures, actions, and contextual conditions involved in a particular setting [24]. Interpretivism allows for an appreciation of the diverse and inter-subjective meanings held by government and business organizations in the inter-organizational relationship under investigation. At the same time, critical realism enables the identification of whether the meanings could not have come about had it not been for underlying independent technical and social mechanisms in the IOS [26, 27]. The combination of these philosophies enabled a better explanation of structural adaptations during implementation than other existing ones.

This case was selected based on 'intensity sampling' logic espoused by Patton [28] where a single but broad implementation effort was being undertaken by GoG with the cooperation of other businesses. For a case to be selected based on intensity sampling, Patton [28] explains that there must abound critical issues but limited time for data collection and limited resources for the study; whereas more learning is required of the phenomenon of interest to make valid conclusions. More learning means gaining access to all relevant and loaded data within the limited time so that limited time does not negate the validity of claims. Thus, documents studies must be a characteristic feature and interviewees must be carefully chosen to reflect the case in its entirety. Additionally, the case must be unique, it must provide a very rich example of the phenomenon even if found elsewhere.

In this research, the information system implementation case studied was an Integrated Financial Management Information System which was the biggest IS implementation effort in terms of cost, time and scope by the government. The implementation was undertaken cooperatively by the government and businesses and the phenomenon could not be replicated in the same country. It is essentially a country-specific case which had overwhelming data, rich in nature, and at the disposal of the researcher. The case sufficiently showed the literature definition of a G2B IOS implementation. The case studied was not about producing, necessarily, statistical generalization of findings but to bring out rich insights that explain structural adaptation. Thus, the case was intrinsic [29] and causal [30] in nature. Intrinsic and causal case studies are not for generalization of findings but rather afford the use of the knowledge produced as an instrumental case to generate quantitative analysis in a different research on a similar phenomenon. Thus, from this study, another research undertaken could be championed in a different country where there is a similar implementation agenda. That research then would use, for instance, the knowledge in this paper to predict and explain the existence of certain mediating or impact factors. This is mainly done in a research program in building a conclusive theory on the original knowledge, so proffered in this paper.

## 4.3  Data Sources and Methods

Triangulation and multimethods were employed for data collection. They have various combinations either in data sources or theories or investigators and even methods in program based research [31]. Yin [30] explains that the triangulation of data sources may involve data collection via interviews, observation, physical artifacts and document studies. Wynn and Williams [32] cautioned that triangulation is not an issue of "repeated confirmations of event, structure, or context specifics, but the potential to abstract to a clearer understanding of causal factors and relationships" (p. 803). One key aspect of triangulation in critical realism is the use of multi-method. This is exemplified by the work of Zachariadis and colleagues [33] which integrates different studies on survey data, interview data, historical analysis among others to explain the cause-effect of economic benefits of innovation using the banking industry as context. The idea is that the triangulation within critical realism provided a richer data in understanding of the phenomena under investigation.

Open-ended interviews, rather than focused ones, were conducted over a period of two and half months. Eighteen sessions of formal interviews were held with twelve implementation members and businesses. Interviews spanned an average time of thirty-eight minutes per session. There were approximately eight informal interview sessions which averaged fifteen minutes per session. These were follow-ups, confirmatory as well as per chance interview sessions. On few occasions the researcher was granted permission to record the sessions. Recorded sessions were transcribed and coded. Interviewees were selected from various units or team leads and business representatives. The interviewees were selected for four reasons: Firstly, they represented all areas of the project that impacted on G2B relations and system functionalities. Secondly, they were most closely related to decision making processes that informed changes in technology features or systems.

Thirdly, they had a long standing relationship with the GIFMIS project and historical depth of government transactions. For instance, the deputy project director was a key interviewee because he had been around from conceptualization stages as far back as 2006 when earlier systems existed. This is significant considering the fact that political power had changed hands within over the course of implementation. Ministerial oversight from MoFEP had also changed considerably in terms of personalities. Fourthly, they have general understanding of government business and transactions.

Formal interviews begun with the Deputy Project Director after confidentiality issues had been discussed. The interview with the deputy project director continued in different sessions. There were phone conversations with him to clarify indistinct elements of texts during the document studies. Nevertheless, there were some trepidations regarding giving out some information about meeting briefs. Such issues were not a feature in subsequent sessions as familiarity grew with the interviewer. Other implementation officers were interviewed based on the section criteria already established.

For document studies, access was gained to policies, system audit reports on GIFMIS right from inception, procurement processes and technical reports as well as some internal memos within and without sub-units engaged in the entire implementation process. Document studies were used to confirm the interview data as well as to appreciate the history of interactions that had contributed to the implementation and structuring processes. Half way through data collection, the researcher was handed the project charter of GIFMIS implementation. Although this document was sought earlier, its absence initially meant that interviews were highly exploratory without biasness towards what the charter set itself to achieve. This helped in contesting or confirming interview texts. During this period, some memos were exchanged between CAGD and GIFMIS secretariat. Notices of sensitization meetings between government, and suppliers and contractors were cited and dates recorded. Follow ups on such notices and memos were done during interview sessions.

During the period of data collection, there were six high profile meetings that brought together stakeholders of the GIFMIS implementation. Most of these stakeholders were on the government end of the implementation. The implementation officer explained that negotiations for funding for phase two of GIFMIS implementation had begun. Secondly the preparation of the first phase review report was ongoing. These two main reasons, he explained, had necessitated these meetings. There were other meetings that took place once a month to review system implementation. The researcher was a non-participatory observer in the second session of one high profile meeting. Briefs from meetings were inquired from some stakeholders and compared with researcher's observations. Themes that reflected G2B interactions were sought from these experiences.

## 4.4 Data Analysis

Analysis of codes to ascertain construct condition and construct impact were conducted using principles of hermeneutics [34]. For a multimethod research employing interpretivism as well as critical realism, data collection and analysis were not too segmented. This is because processes of data reduction and display begin in the course of the collection process. Iteratively, data collected underwent rigorous dissections and integrations by the authors who were the primary instruments for data collection. Our understanding and theory were used to code and analyze texts with relevant themes.

The focus of data collection followed through G2B dynamics and interactions. That is to say not all data on interactions and functions of the GIFMIS and the implementation informed the analysis of the case. G2B data was also reduced by open coding texts and transcribed texts from interviews into a database system (a qualitative coding software). For instance, sentences that had 'business', 'suppliers', 'contractors', 'tax payers', transactions, meetings, Net Solutions and [other company names] were all coded as 'businesses'. The list is not exhaustive. It was assumed that since the implementation team was constituted and dominated by government, data without business connotations or deliberations were sifted. The process was done employing the adapted spiral hermeneutic to make sure more words were coded in order not to miss critical data that revealed causes of stated outcomes. The same was done for coded texts that show interactive linkages to other block codes. The researcher read and re-read contexts and materials together with interview sheets to ascertain the validity of grouping certain texts as connoting a particular code or name. Further reduction was done to reveal data with G2B transactions related with GIFMIS or IT implementation. Care was taken to ensure stated outcomes or effects did not have different interpretations assigned to their causal mechanisms.

## 5 Results

First phase of GIFMIS was launched in September, 2009 under the auspices of the Accountant General, among other things to provide the IT platform for these inefficiencies and consolidate gains of the Budget and Public Expenditure Management System (BPEMS) platform—a legacy system being done away with to pave way for GIFMIS. The full Implementation structure has the Minister of Finance and Economic Planning, as the project champion. The GIFMIS Secretariat made up of various units and headed by Project Director handles all the day to day implementation processes as well as the management of the system. The implementation process is in phases. The entire implementation plan of GIFMIS project for the phases contains areas that require an effective G2B IOS operationalization for the implementation goals to be met.

To avoid the hardware and software challenges of the BPEMS, Government contracted Oracle consultants from India, South Africa and USA. The Implementation Chairman remarked "[w]e brought top Oracle consultants to help with the project scoping. The existing modules that were running would be integrated with GIFMIS modules". In addition, "IBM computers and systems have been deployed countrywide to support the Oracle suite". After the initial work by these consultants, the implementation team contracted Net Solutions Ghana (NS), a private firm (business) to help with the specifications, acquisition and deployment of IBM systems. NS offered IT support services on GIFMIS and were paid as businesses like any supplier to engage the GIFMIS platform in transaction and also to handle the technical attributes with the implementation process.

It was understood from another officer's perspective that the GIFMIS system would run on E-business suit, an Oracle product, at a time when Oracle was partnering IBM Systems worldwide for large project implementations such as GIFMIS. By this knowledge, the implementation team identified IBM through NS as ideal system supplier, but more importantly the interphase of IBM and Oracle served as a good cost cutting measure for government hence its close association deepened with NS leading to a more bureaucratic relationship. Another interviewee was of the view that the main reason for the decision on implementing with NS was that Oracle, the parent company sells their products through consultants and local agents of which NS by their affiliation with IBM fits the bill.

Initially, the government per the verbal agreement was not obliged to stick with only NS for the IT systems they needed for the implementation. It could acquire the technology from anyone. This was evidenced by its decision at the initial stages of the implementation to bring in IT consultants in 2009 whose services could have been offered by NS. Thus, the government was not obliged under such network relationship with NS to look nowhere else for their IT needs. As one officer puts it, "they [Net Solutions Ghana] were [also] just brought in briefly because their systems [IBM] was going to be used so we needed their expertise". This means NS was not initially thought of as a partner for the entire implementation. However, an NS IT officer mentioned that, "GIFMIS [was] going to run on Oracle E-business suit and Oracle [was] partnering IBM Systems worldwide for large project implementations". By that knowledge, the implementation team identified IBM through Net Solutions as ideal IBM systems supplier who could offer some transactions advantage.

When asked how NS had managed to keep such an enviable relationship with government when others could not, one IT expert explained that their technical expertise was unparalleled. As earlier mentioned, an officer said, "they [Net Solutions Ghana] were just brought in briefly because their systems [IBM] was going to be used so we needed their expertise". He also maintained that their installed base as the dominant IBM experts who could configure Oracle suits on their hardware at prices better than what expatriates would offer made it difficult for government to poach their members in joining GIFMIS's technical Unit. Net Solutions by virtue of their expert knowledge and position as a local partners of IBM-Oracle-infused systems, were certified by Oracle and IBM Corporations.

For NS, it was living out its goal for operation: "our goal is to project IBM in all public Sectors in Ghana and West Africa". The contract with government was part of their strategic goal.

According to the Task Leader for World Bank (WB), the bank would support the second phase of GIFMIS project during the 7th WB implementation review. The following remarks were noted from the report on the meeting between World Bank and GIFMIS dated 12th December 2014. "Based on my assessment, I think the Public Financial Reforms have been successful for the past four years and we appreciate it"; "…It is important that the achievement chalked is not allowed to go waste, hence the support of the World Bank for the next phase of the project". The project champion was quoted by the same report. It read "the purpose of the review was to take stock of the GIFMIS phase one, in order to prepare for phase two". The mid-term review on GIFMIS covered the period May 20–23, 2013 and was carried out jointly by the "fact finding mission" of the funding partners (World Bank, UK Department for International Development, the Danish Internal Development Assistance and the Delegation of European Union). Their report noted, "based on satisfactory progress achieved against milestones in the various components, overall project implementation has been rated as satisfactory". However, the following recommendation was made about the contractual relationship between GoG and NS.

"The mission recommends that Oracle experts be deployed to configure multi-year commitment recording and tracking functionality in the GIFMIS by October 1, 2013 to allow tracking of contracts. The Oracle P2P system has capability by way of a sub-module, to generate a contract database so that ongoing commitments against multi-year contracts can be tracked, and obligations or arrears clearly identified". The mission recommends PD (post-dated): (a) issue appointment letter to the 2 techno-functional individual Oracle technical/functional consultants being currently hired to provide Oracle support, by July 1, 2013; (b) finalize the support agreement with *Net Solutions* for extended support by May 31, 2013; (c) finalize the SLA with NITA by June 30, 2013…".

Thus, GoG's initial plan to sign a short term (one-off) agreement with Net Solutions as the consultants for the implementation but ended up with the signing of a 3-year minimum term contract.

# 6 IOS Implementation and Structural Adaptation

## 6.1 Adaptation of Legitimation Structure

The change of the contractual relationship between GoG and NS from a verbal understanding to a formal agreement signifies a reproduction of a structure of legitimation. The initial structure of legitimation (L1), reflecting the verbal agreement, was enacted when funding for the project had not been received from the

World Bank by the government. This structure was enacted because the IT equipment was already in the domain of government. NS had supplied the equipment for a different project (not for GIFMIS project) but that project was yet to start. As funding issues prevailed in the initial stages of GIFMIS implementation, deploying this already-supplied technology under a verbal agreement was seen as sensible. The structure was also legitimized by the fact that government urgently needed NS to prepare a physical site for hardware deployment and installation. The equipment was to be installed at various transaction processing sites earmarked for piloting of the technology.

The government, per the verbal agreement, was not obliged to stick with only NS for the IT systems they needed to implement GIFMIS. It could acquire the technology from any other supplier, but it opted to use what was available. This action of the government, based on L1, demonstrates the freedom it had over determining whether or not to use the available technology that was not officially part of the project. There was no evidence from the empirical study that suggested any misgivings by NS to government's action. The action, plus the fact that this verbal agreement was in place from 2009 to 2013, imply the predominance of mutual understanding as the scheme of interpretation of such actions. Mutual understanding is the mechanism used to execute network governance, as it occurred between the government and NS. Network governance is preferable for inter-organizational relations which are characterized by low goal congruence and low performance ambiguity between the organizations [22, 35]. It was preferable in the empirical case because it guaranteed the lowest transactions cost of governing the relationship.

Upon the directive by the World Bank for a formal contract to be written to replace the verbal one, the government was required to follow the provisions of the Public Procurement Act of Ghana (Act 663). Thus, the formal contract changed the governance mechanism from network to bureaucracy because the new rules replaced the mutual understanding between the parties. The assumption undergirding the replacement of mutual understanding with rules is the presence of low goal congruence and high ambiguity between parties [22]. But rules are more expensive than mutual understanding to administer, and so the governance mechanism of bureaucracy is more expensive to administer than network. Therefore, the World Bank's directive and subsequent acceptance by the government suggest that effectiveness in inter-organizational governance was prioritized over efficiency. The government's action was informed by the quest for low cost of search for IT infrastructure. However, the Act (Act 663) has a three-fold proviso for sole sourcing that can be urged by a public organization to procure urgent products: justify urgent services due to unforeseeable circumstances; to explain capability and qualification of proposed firm; and to state conditions of contract and financial proposal. The government urged this proviso to procure the existing equipment supplied by NS.

This action however suggests the quest for efficient (less costly) IT sourcing for IOS implementation because alternative means of IT procurement would imply more expensive sourcing using the costlier (multi-sourcing) public procurement process. The quest for efficient IT sourcing is appropriate to maintain low transactions costs especially in the face of increased cost of bureaucratic governance—that is, the change from a network to bureaucratic governance mechanism. Balancing effective bureaucratic governance with efficient IT sourcing in IOS implementation is the underlying reason for legitimation structural adaptation. Because balancing is connected to the change from one legitimation structure to another, it is the means of adapting legitimation structure to IOS implementation. Therefore, we conclude that legitimation structural adaptation occurs because of the need to balance effective inter-organizational governance with efficient IT sourcing.

Before the structural adaptation (before production of the new structure; during the days of the verbal contract in the empirical case), the reverse was the case. There was efficient governance because network relations cost less than bureaucracy [35]; and there was effective sourcing of IT from business by government through the mutual understanding. In that scenario, balancing efficient network governance with effective IT sourcing was the underlying reason for structural adaptation. Therefore, we conclude that legitimation structural adaptation also occurs because of the need to balance efficient inter-organizational governance with effective IT sourcing.

Both scenarios and conclusions confirm that low transaction cost is the locus of structural adaptation to IOS implementation. But beyond confirmation, they suggest that legitimation structural adaptation to IOS implementation is occasioned by the need to balance efficiency and effectiveness between inter-organizational governance and IT sourcing. Stated differently, when a government and business are implementing IOS, their *need to balance efficiency and effectiveness between governance and IT sourcing* occasions the production and reproduction of legitimation structures.

## 6.2  Adaptation of Domination Structure

As a result of the written contract, a shared domination structure between GoG (2D1) and NS (1D1) was created. The domination structure was shared because, on the one hand, NS had power by virtue of its technical capability as an IT solutions provider. GoG also had power to grant NS higher level of access to the GIFMIS implementation team for troubleshooting and maintenance services (P1b). NS was the sole local partner of IBM Corporation in Ghana. It was certified by IBM to sell its products. The certification, named "IBM Corporation—Partner World Certification" was the highest form of certification given by IBM to all its trusted and qualified partners. Thus, the certification was also a facility that enabled NS to exercise power over critical technical features of GIFMIS and gain unrestricted access to its database. On the other hand, the ultimate power to grant the access still rested with GoG which used this 'high level of access granted to Net Solutions' to exercise domination over its partner. By giving NS the right to grant access to GIFMIS artifact, the government required it to follow certain regulations stipulated in the written contract. For instance, the contract demanded that NS should be present at any implementation ad hoc meetings, respond to any electronic message for IT services and carry out routine maintenance services at designated times.

This shared domination structure was produced in the wake of L2, and it represents a network governance mechanism. This is because it was characterized by low ambiguity in the performance of NS, and by high congruence or low goal incongruence in the goals of the government and NS. Hence, there was mutual understanding between the two parties as it was under L1 the analysis of the legitimation structure. Given that network is the least costly mechanism for governing an inter-organizational relationship, the government preferred it to a more costly bureaucracy, market or clan mechanism [22]. The shared domination structure was also preferred by government because the dominance of NS, by virtue of its technical capability, was inevitable. In transactions costs terms, technical capability is a transaction-specific asset [36]. A transaction-specific asset is an investment that is so highly valuable to a transaction that it is not subject to redeployment. NS's technical capability was so valuable to GIFMIS implementation that its deployment elsewhere would make for a costly decision. Hence, the shared domination structure was reflecting the need to achieve a balance between low cost of governance and high cost of business IT capability during implementation.

Government's dependence on high cost of business IT capability may imply inefficiency, but it generates effective G2B IOS implementation especially in the light of efficient governance. High cost of business IT capability that gives the business partner dominance in the inter-organizational structure is a prerequisite for attaining a successful IOS implementation. This is because governments usually lack this capability, and so they form G2B relationships to leverage it.

Governments are usually unqualified to gain efficient IT capability, and so they aim to achieve low transactions costs by drawing effective IOS implementation from IT capability and by generating an efficient governance mechanism. Hence, governments must be dominated to some degree by business IT capability—they must prefer a shared domination structure that represents a network governance mechanism. The combination of business IT capability, government IT incompetence, and preference for shared domination structure is in harmony with the quest for low cost of transactions between government and business. Therefore, we conclude that domination structural adaptation occurs because of the need to balance efficient inter-organizational governance with effective business IT capability. Stated differently, when a government and a business are implementing IOS, their *need to balance efficiency and effectiveness between governance and business IT capability* occasions the production and reproduction of domination structures. Adaptation of Signification Structure.

Although it was not a characteristic feature at the time of data collection, the creation of an extranet as a medium of communication between GoG and NS which ensured proper evaluation and better coordination of tasks was as a result of the success of their informal meetings. Before the institution of that extranet, the IT officer mentioned the use of their personal phones, mainly, for informal communication between the two parties. The extranet formed a structural feature [4] which embodies the kind of spirit which is explained as a reflection of shared inter-organizational goals of GoG and NS. This is because the Saturday meetings were a normal procedure for the NS IT officers in how to carry out work—generally, not peculiar to only the GIFMIS project. Thus, the will to achieve inter-organizational goals represented an embodied spirit that was impacted into the GIFMIS implementation process.

The quest to coordinate activities and the prevailing well-defined work-flows reflected strategic organizational goals. These goals were motivated by the fact that the initial enterprise system by the government (BPEMS) had woefully failed and everything was being done to make GIFMIS a success. Although the meetings that necessitated (presumably) the setting up of the technology medium was not a characteristic feature at the time of data collection, they were important reasons for how and why the implementation process produced the prevailing structure of signification. In adaptive structuration terms, the spirit that is passed unto IT constitutes a structure [4].

Additionally, there continued to be quests for tighter coordination which reflected ideals of the shared inter-organizational goals of the implementation process. This was in spite of the fact that the meetings that necessitated the technology medium were not a characteristic feature anymore at the time of data collection. These show the consequences of an overarching structure of the 'spirit' characterizing the project in spite of the changing implementation circumstances enumerated above. Another constituent of the signification structure so permeating as a result of the tighter coordination is the *Collaborative Authority* that existed due to the context of ideas on how best decisions could be made to increase efficiency in the implementation process. This authority was fundamental to the dynamics in producing the domination structure already explained. Its importance stems from the fact that the meetings and better still the exchanges via the extranet always brought a finality to the next line of action so that whatever activity was performed on the technology by each party had the full backing of the other.

The transaction cost interpretation of the adaptation of this structure to implementation is that there was again, a network relationship between GoG and NS. Network relationships signify development of shared goals and socialization between organizations whereby each one's interests are accommodated [35]. Powell explains that "the reduction in uncertainty, fast access to information, reliability, and responsiveness" are mainstays that motivate network relationships. In the GIFMIS case, the Collaborative Authority, albeit informal authority and an antecedent of the embodying spirit (shared by the implementing teams) contributed to the production of the shared domination structures. This can be explained by the emergence of a low performance ambiguity characterizing the exchanges as they wore on. Thus, over time the activities or issues that required Collaborative Authority to be exercised to achieve effectiveness in the course of implementation became repetitive and well-known and hence preemptive.

Therefore, expected outcomes were no longer ambiguous just as much as goal incongruence remained low but shared goals shifted or dissolve due to the emergence of different interpretive schemes or evolution of existing ones. This was costly because the shift or dissolution could increase goal incongruence or performance ambiguity or both. Therefore, the embodiment of signification structure in IT as its spirit implies a transaction cost reduction by government and business in IOS implementation. The embodiment of signification structure in IT in the GIFMIS case signifies its reification that preserved it in the face of the adaptations of domination and legitimation structures to G2B IOS implementation. To wit, signification structural adaptation is occasioned by the need to achieve cost efficiency and by the availability of IT to preserve what is achieved over the long term. Stated differently, when a government and business are implementing IOS, their *need to achieve cost efficiency of shared goals and availability of IT to preserve what is achieved over the long term* occasions the production and reproduction of signification structures.

## 7  Discussion

In order to overcome the limitations in prior research on technology-induced adaptive structuration, this paper has explained how and why G2B IOS implementation engenders an adaptive structuration process. Through this contextualized explanation of structuration, firstly, the paper contributes new reasons for how and why G2B IOS implementation causes structural adaptation. It ascribes structural adaptation to tensions between economic, technological and governance mechanisms. As the analysis showed, maintaining low transactions costs is a motive held by government to balance inter-organizational governance mechanisms with IT infrastructure use and business capability. This ascription transcends previous explanations of structural adaptation which focused primarily on IT as the variable that occasioned structuring [e.g., 3–6 and 37]. This paper's explanation expands the variables that occasion structuring to include economics of IT and governance mechanisms. Therefore, it extends the conceptualization of how IT occasions structural adaptation.

Secondly, the paper provides new insights at the inter-organizational level for analyzing how IS implementation shapes structural adaptation. Previous theories have been developed at the organizational level, and they do not incorporate the dynamics of inter-organizational transactions that this paper espouses. For instance, the balancing acts between inter-organizational governance mechanism and IT infrastructure use or IT capability of business as means of structural adaptation are missing in previous literature. DeSanctis and Poole [4] work seemed to be an exception because they asserted that their adaptive structuration framework could be applied to broader units of analysis (broader level). However, they only mentioned its application based on the fact that at the broader level "the goal is to identify persistent changes in behavior following introduction of the technology, such as shifts in how problems are described, decisions are made, or choices legitimated" [4, p. 138]. In this paper, a better explanation of the need for broader level (inter-organizational) of analysis of structural adaptation has been provided.

The third contribution is an IT implementation perspective to the understanding of human agency in structural adaptation. Previous explanations are informed by workers' use of IT to develop use perspectives to the understanding of agency. Use perspectives ascribe structural adaptation to operational level agency by worker actions; and they constitute micro-level explanations. Consequently, strategic level agency by managerial or strategic level agency has been quite lacking in the literature. By focusing on IT implementation in the inter-organizational transactions, this paper has explained structural adaption with strategic level agency by executive decisions. This explanation is in harmony with accounts of how technology is deployed by powerful actors in society for political and economic gains [e.g., 3–6 and 37]; and with accounts of the relationship between technology and centralization of authority, control and formalization of rules [38]. This is because their accounts also ascribe the effects of technology deployment to strategic level agency. However, this paper's explanation is different because IT and inter-organization are ontologically different contexts that generate different understandings of human agency and hence a different conception of structure. Moreover, the particularity of these contexts has led to the development of a more refined explanation of the relationship between human agency and structural adaptation.

One research implication of these contributions is that it opens research opportunities for explanation of structural adaptation with different aspects of human agency. This paper has shown that executive decisions on IT implementation provide new explanations that are different from those derived from workers' actions on IT use. Therefore, future research endeavors can focus on other types of human agency around issues such as IT development, adoption, maintenance, and management. Other factors in addition to IT economics and governance mechanisms can also be explored to extend explanations of the relationship between complex IT consideration and structural adaption.

Practically, these contributions suggest that governments can use them to manage structural adaptation even in the face of changing implementation circumstances that are beyond their control. Moreover, ideas from ideas such as human agency and IT implementation provide guidelines for appropriate decision making that will adapt G2B inter-organizational structures to implementation. Similarly, ideas from tensions between economics, technological and governance mechanisms provide guidelines for harmonizing G2B inter-organizational relations and attaining needed competitive advantage.

To conclude, the paper sought to explain how G2B IOS implementation shapes structural adaptations by drawing upon the theories of structuration and transactions costs. The theories were used to analyze data from an empirical study of the implementation of a financial management information system by the government of Ghana. The paper's explanation is positioned as a complementary perspective on technology-induced adaptive structuration. This socio-technical perspective is argued to be distinctive because of the IT implementation approach, the context of G2B, and the inter-organizational level of analysis.

# References

1. Giddens, A. (1984). *The constitution of society: Outline of the theory of structure*. Berkeley, CA: University of California Press.
2. Leonardi, P. M. (2011). When flexible routines meet flexible technologies: Affordance, constraint, and the imbrication of human and material agencies. *MIS Quarterly, 35*(1), 147–167.
3. Barley, S. R. (1986). Technology as an occasion for structuring: Evidence from observation of CT scanners and the social order of radiology departments. *Administrative Science Quarterly, 31*(1), 78–108.
4. DeSanctis, G., & Poole, M. S. (1994). Capturing the complexity in advanced technology use: Adaptive structuration theory. *Organisation Science., 5*(2), 121–147.
5. Orlikowski, W. J. (1992). The duality of technology: Rethinking the concept of technology in organizations. *Organization Science, 3*(3), 398–427.
6. Orlikowski, W. J. (2000). Using technology and constituting structures: A practice lens for studying technology in organisations. *Organization Science, 11*(4), 404–428.
7. Orlikowski, W. J., & Robey, D. (1991). Information technology and the structuring of organizations. *Information Systems Research, 2*(2), 143–169.
8. Jones, M. R., & Karsten, H. (2008). Giddens' structurational theory and information systems research. *MIS Quarterly, 32*(1), 127–157.
9. Sutanto, J., Kankanhalli, A., Tay, J., Raman, K. S., & Tan, B. C. Y. (2009). Change management in interorganizational systems for the public. *Journal of Management Information Systems, 25*(3), 133–176.
10. Gregor, S., & Johnston, R. B. (2000) Developing an understanding of interorganizational systems: Arguments for multi-level analysis and structuration theory. In *ECIS 2000*. Vienna, Austria.
11. Cordella, A., & Willcocks, L. (2009). Outsourcing, bureaucracy and public value: Reappraising the notion of the "Contract State". *Government Information Quarterly, 27*(1), 82–88.
12. Kim, H.-W., & Kankanhalli, A. (2009). Investigating user resistance to information systems implementation: A status Quo Bias perspective. *MIS Quarterly, 33*(3), 567–582.
13. Tan, M. T. K., Raman, K. S., & Wei, K. K. (2003). Implementing Inter-Organizational Systems (IOS) for strategic advantage : A value-flow framework. In *11th European Conference on Information Systems*. Naples, Italy.
14. Johnstone, H. R., & Vitale, M. R. (1988). Creating competitive advantage with inter-organizational system. *MIS Quarterly, 12*(2), 153–165.
15. Bensaou, M., Venkatraman, N., Bensaou, M., & Venkatraman, N. (1995). Configurations of interorganizational relationships: A comparison between U.S and Japanese Automakers. *Management Science, 41*(9), 1471–1492.
16. Robey, D., Anderson, C., & Raymond, B. (2013). Information technology, materiality, and organizational change: A professional Odyssey. *Journal of the Association for Information Systems, 14*(7), 379–398.
17. Ginzberg, M. J., & Schultz, T. W. (1991). Information systems implementation: Testing a structural model. *Interfaces, 21*(5), 88–89.
18. Pfeffer, J. (1992). Understanding power in organizations. *California Management Review, 1992*, 29–50.
19. Gregory, T. (2011). Transaction cost economics and directions for relational governance research. In *Southern Association for Information Systems Conference*. Atlanta, GA.
20. Williamson, O. E. (1979). Transaction-cost economies: The governance of contractual relations. *Journal of Law and Economics, 22*(2), 233–261.
21. Anding, M., & Hess, T. (2002) Online content syndication—A critical analysis from the perspective of transaction cost theory. In *European Conference on Information Systems*. Gdansk, Poland.

22. Ouchi, W. G. (1980). Markets, Bureaucracies and Clans. *Administrative Science Quarterly, 25*(1), 129–141.
23. Boudreau, M.-C. (2007) The benefits of transaction cost economics: The beginning of a new direction. In *ECIS 2007 Proceedings*. University of St. Gallen. In *European Conference on Information Systems*. St. Gallen, Sweden.
24. Bhaskar, R. (1978). *A realist theory of science*. Hemel Hempstead: Harvester.
25. Walsham, G. (2006). Doing interpretive research. *European Journal of Information Systems, 15*(3), 320–330.
26. Avgerou, C. (2013). Social mechanisms for causal explanation in social theory based IS Research. *Journal of the Association for Information Systems, 14*(8), 399–419.
27. Bhaskar, R. (1979). *The possibility of naturalism*. Brighton: Harvester.
28. Patton, M. (1990). Designing qualitative studies. In M. Patton (Ed.), *Sage*. CA: Beverly Hills.
29. Stake, R. E., & Trumbull, D. J. (1982). Naturalistic generalizations. *Review Journal of Philosophy and Social Science, 7*, 3–12.
30. Yin, R. K. (2003). *Case study research—Design and methods*. London: Sage.
31. Denzin, N. K. (1978). *The research act: A theoretical introduction to sociological methods*. New York: Praeger.
32. Wynn, D., Jr., & Williams, C. K. (2012). Principles for conducting critical realist case study research in information systems. *MIS Quarterly, 36*(3), 787–810.
33. Zachariadis, M., Scott, S., & Barret, M. (2010). Designing mixed-method research inspired by critical realism philosophy: A tale from the field of IS Innovation. In *International Conference on Information Systems*. St. Louis, MO.
34. Klein, H. K., & Myers, M. D. (1999). A set of principles for conducting and evaluating interpretive field studies in information systems. *MIS Quarterly, 23*(1), 67–93.
35. Powell, W. W. (1990). Neither market nor hierarchy: Network forms of organization. *Research in Organizational Behavior, 12*, 295–336.
36. Wareham, J. D. (2003). Information assets in interorganizational governance: Exploring the property rights perspective. *IEEE Transactions on Engineering Management, 50*(3), 337–351.
37. Barley, S. R. (1990). The alignment of technology and structure through roles and networks. *Administrative Science Quarterly, 35*, 61–103.
38. Kallinikos, J. (2009). The regulative regime of technology. In F. Contini & G. F. Lanzara (Eds.), *Palgrave Macmillan*. UK: Basingstoke.

# Management Control Systems in Inter-organizational Relationships for Environmental Sustainability and Energy Efficiency: Evidence from the Cruise Port Destinations

**Assunta Di Vaio**(iD) **and Luisa Varriale**(iD)

**Abstract** This paper aims to analyse the role of Management Control Systems (MCS) for supporting the decision making process of Port Authorities (PAs), shipping agents and cruise companies, in preventing and reducing negative environmental effects from the seaports. The paper focuses on information management (data collecting, processing and reporting) in the relationships system established among the players involved in the arrival, mooring, and departure of ships in the port destinations. This work investigates the content of control function by PAs, in the landlord port model, evidencing if it pays attention only to verify the compliance of the declarations according to MARPOL convention and port regulations. Starting from a deep review of the literature on environmental issues in the seaports and MCS and information systems for environmental sustainability and energy efficiency applied in port sector, and specifically in the cruise industry, we conducted two semi-structured interviews to port users as shipping agents and service providers in one Italian seaport. The first results of the research outline the need to get more detailed information and reporting on environmental sustainability and energy efficiency, above all when the ships are morning on the quays, and, also, it has been evidenced how MCS, supported by information system, could help to improve the information basis for PAs, shipping agents and cruise companies in the future developmental decisions of seaports. Theoretical and managerial implications are discussed.

**Keywords** Management control systems · Environmental sustainability
Cruise ports

---

A. Di Vaio (✉) · L. Varriale
Parthenope University of Naples, Naples, Italy
e-mail: susy.divaio@uniparthenope.it

L. Varriale
e-mail: luisa.varriale@uniparthenope.it

© Springer International Publishing AG, part of Springer Nature 2018          43
R. Lamboglia et al. (eds.), *Network, Smart and Open*, Lecture Notes in Information
Systems and Organisation 24, https://doi.org/10.1007/978-3-319-62636-9_3

# 1   Introduction

In the last decades, researchers, institutions and operators are paying an increasing attention to the environmental impact of port operations and development. The port industry have to follow rigid scrutiny and rules systems in terms of environmental regulatory compliance, because of the high price related to climate change and global warming deriving from their activities and operations.

Hence, on one side, ports must acquire and demonstrate higher levels of environmental performance for ensuring community support [1–3]. On the other side, ports have to comply with ever higher regulatory and societal requirements for environmental protection with significant impact on their space/room for the growing [2]. Thus, the increasing relevance of environmental issues in the port industry is very challenging because it concerns different aspects, such as the need to minimize any emissions from existing and future port activities and the necessity to modify their logistics area.

Focusing the attention on the ports, which tend to assume environmentally sustainable and energetically efficient behaviour, thanks to a review of the literature, some authors frame the concept of "green ports" developing one of the first frameworks for sustainable and aware port strategies, where "a green port will lead to positive outcomes on port's customer retention and economic performance" [4: 424, 5]. Thus, green ports can be conceptualized as all ports with proactive orientations which develop, implement and monitor practices addressed to prevent and reduce the environmental impacts of ports at local, national and international level over regulatory compliance [3].

Briefly, green ports combine three different dimensions, that is the social, economic and environmental goals adopting a microeconomic standpoint [6, 7], overcoming regulations because the environmental and sustainable practices are encouraged voluntary [3].

As such, strategies and policies in port management have to consider environmental issues moving to the development of green ports. The literature on these topics is still scarce and needed to identify and analyze the concrete port industry requirements. After all, in order to support the "green port decision making processes" of PAs, the environmental regulations would provide also information and details about the instruments able both to measure the effects of the "green choices" and to control the effectiveness and efficiency of decision making processes, i.e., all the decision making processes concerning the waste pollution of ships and other port users operating in the seaport areas. In the perspective of normative requirements, the adoption of the rules does not concern their only respect through reporting activities, that is certifications and permissions, but it requires the consideration of a specific "green behavioural orientation", in fact, measurement and control instruments need to be implemented allowing PAs and all the port users to make investment choices for reducing the negative environmental impact and to manage the processes effectively and efficiently. In this scenario, the role of management control systems and, also new technologies is crucial because for supporting the decision making process and operating activities of port users in the perspective of sustainable and green port industry. For achieving high competitiveness in seaports, also responding to the environmental needs, PAs, policy makers, and local communities must invest growing financial and economic resources.

This paper aims to analyse the role of MCS, and its main instruments, to support the decision making process of PAs, shipping agents and cruise companies, in preventing and reducing negative environmental effects from the seaports. The paper focuses on the management of information (data collecting, processing and reporting) in the relationships system established among the players involved in the activities related to arrival, mooring, and departure of ships in the port destinations. Hence, our manuscript aims to verify if the control function of PAs, in the landlord port model,[1] regards only the duty to verify the compliance of the declarations according to MARPOL convention and port regulations,[2] or the public authority with cruise companies are involved in the overall information and data management process to support also the general environmental strategic decisions in the seaport.

This is an explorative study conducted through a qualitative approach using a case study methodology. This research is composed by two phases. First, we deeply review the literature on MCS and information systems in inter-organizational relationships for environmental sustainability and energy efficiency applied in port sector, and in particular in the cruise industry. Second, in order to understand the role of MCS within port industry for preventing and reducing the environmental impact of the main port operations, specifically in the inter-organizational relationships among PAs, shipping agents and cruise companies, we conducted two semi-structured interviews to port users as shipping agents (1 interview) and services providers about ships classification with details on environmental certifications and others documents related to the quality of the processes (1 interview) in Italy. In order to acquire more knowledge about the control function of PAs, we started to analyze the "informative base" that is the information that are supplied to the Authorities by the shipping agents/cruise companies, and service providers about the certification of the processes quality. The paper is organised as follows. In the second section, a deep review of the main contributions in the literature on the environmental impact of port operations and development gives a clear scenario about the phenomenon highlighting the existing gap in the research. In the third section, the focus is on MCS and its instruments for collecting, managing and reporting information and data about the environmental impact of port users. Then,

---

[1]The landlord port model occurs when the PA provides the infrastructure, while investments in superstructure (equipment, port facilities, and so forth) and port operations are contracted out to private operators, mostly the shipping or cruise companies [8].

[2]The International Convention for the Prevention of Pollution from Ships, introduced in 1973 and modified by the Protocol of 1978 and 1997, is shortly named MARPOL. It is one of the most important international marine environmental conventions developed by the International Maritime Organization for minimizing pollution of the oceans and seas, including dumping, oil and air pollution [9].

the forth section provides details about the methodology adopted with the case study and the semi-structured interviews conducted. Finally, the last section presents final considerations and suggestions for future research.

## 2   Environmental Sustainability and Energy Efficiency for Ports in the Literature

In the last decades the climate change, especially the global warming, is increasingly gaining a relevant importance in all economic sectors gradually restructuring them, mainly some sectors whose activities and functioning have high environmental impact, such as the port industry. Around the world port operators are beginning to understand the main implications for environment and, mostly, climate change, resulting in increasing adaption efforts and variations in port destinations, e.g., the great impact of larger, faster and most luxurious vessels or the growing of cruise passengers flow, mainly in the cruise industry [10–14]. Consequently, we observe an increasing share of national and global budgets, hence, most economic operators, in tourism and aviation travel, as well as in the port industry, tend to attract the attention of environmental groups and politics [2, 13–18]. The port industry, including the cruise sector, is trying to respond to this challenge with calls adaptation and by setting inspirational emission targets [19–26]. Ports are concerned with environmental and social impacts because they produce substantial external effects [3, 27].

Through a deep review of past literature several studies can be identified which have addressed various aspects of environmental impacts generated by seaport industry [28]. In the past literature on the topic, most scholars usually tend to distinguish the study of environmental risks related to the seaport industry into two main categories [28]: the impact assessments and optimal solutions [29, 30] and environmental risk perception [31, 32]. Despite the increasing attention paid by researchers on the topic, still only few environmental risk-based studies are focused on the impacts generated by shipping and maritime activities following mostly a managerial and economic perspective [28], especially this scarcity suggests to better clarify the phenomenon and systematize the contributions already existent in the literature.

Thus, this review allows outlining that scholars tend to adopt different reading lens, that is the main studies on the environmental issues in seaport industry can be categorized into three perspectives: technical, managerial and economic, and legal viewpoint.

Indeed, some studies adopt a technical viewpoint focusing their attention on seeking and developing instruments aimed at reducing, for instance, the gas emissions or emissions for particulate matter and carbon monoxide [33, 34]. Other researchers pay their attention on managerial and economic perspective related to energy efficiency and environmental sustainability, for example, they look for developing and introducing specific effective policies in measuring and controlling the future cost scenarios for reduction of ship $CO_2$ emissions [35]. Finally, most studies pay their attention on the main implications deriving from the regulatory system, mostly from the rules and norms at global and national level which have introduced relevant limitations and behavioural obligations for port operators. More specifically, firstly with reference to the technical perspective, several studies mostly investigate the $CO_2$ emissions or other dangerous gas emissions derived from international shipping [13, 15, 18, 24, 34, 36, 37], also e.g., carbon emissions per passenger-kilometre (p-km) specifically for cruise ships [38]. The burning of oil (heavy fuel oil, mainly, and as marine diesel oil) from international vessels concerns mostly $CO_2$, $SO_2$, $NO_x$ and hydro carbon into the atmosphere [38, 39].

Considering both technical and economic perspectives, the most significant and common approach consisted into the 'resource' approach, or the so-called 'damage cost' approach, addressed to estimate the opportunity costs related to damages occurred to natural resources or social welfares [18, 40, 41]. Another approach named the 'prevention' approach, differently from the previous techniques focused on estimating the damage costs, addressed to estimate the costs related to escape the potential environmental impacts, especially climate changes [40, 41].

In an effort to provide and develop approaches and methodologies able to monitor, control, quantify and measure the environmental impacts of shipping activities in economic and monetary terms, Etkin [42] proposed a logical methodology to evaluate oil spill impacts of shipping activities. In this methodology both natural environmental and socio-economic losses were identified and quantified, also for determining the damage and costs related to different spill types and for assessing all the necessary prevention and reduction measures [42].

Unfortunately, in spite of the relevance of methodology provided by Etkin [42], because it considered many "spill-specific factors" able to influence oil spill impact costs, such as spill amount, oil type, location specific socio-economic value, freshwater vulnerability, habitat/wildlife sensitivity and location type, this approach did not have empirical evidence in maritime industries outside US, of course due to the specific American situation, including geographical, environmental and socio-economic conditions [18].

Lately, other authors proposed a set of economic evaluation models for assessing the environmental impacts due to accidental oil spills [43]. This model defined two main steps, one related to the measure of lost services for an injured natural resource, and the other one consisting in integrating the lost services with a unit value of the injured natural resource, where other economic valuation methods were used to measure them. In this model the main innovation was the 'service recovery function' concept with a wider definition of 'environmental impact cost', including 'natural environmental', 'social-economic', 'responding', and 'research' costs [43]. Both natural damages and economic losses summarized all the opportunity costs within the market.

Further scholars introduced similar models but with focus mostly on 'economic losses' and 'response costs' due to accidental (rather than routine) maritime pollutions adopting historically observed data analysis [44]. In summary, numerous studies introduced models and mechanisms aimed to estimate and assess the environmental impact within the maritime sector, paying more attention to the impacts of routine shipping operations [40, 42, 45], but mostly they had similar deficiencies related to their geographic restrictions and their focus on large scale accidental pollutions [43, 44, 46, 47].

Other studies tried to overcome these deficiencies using different models to assess small and large scale accidental oil spills but always missing other maritime pollution sources, or any detailed evaluations of environmental impacts along coastal areas [48–50]. In these circumstances ethical concerns, regarding the risks and negative effects for maritime accidents, need to be managed, evaluating and implementing various assisting actions and policies, such as clean-ups, impact assessments, the enactments of various international, national and local, like the US Oil Pollution Act 1990 (OPA-90) [18, 51, 52]. Finally, most studies, defining environmental impacts of maritime and shipping industry, focused only on natural damages completely ignoring economic losses for the coastline, and also the details about environmental impacts by maritime industry suggested by MARPOL 73/78/97.

## 3 Management Control Systems and Information System in Inter-organizational Systems

Some scholars have recognized a software as the main factor in managing and supporting knowledge and information sharing, because of the crucial role played by the control as a key driver for effectively functioning of the management process [53, 54].

Thanks to an integrated information system, the management and exchange of information allow the coordination and control of activities among firms [55].

Also, in order to stimulate the partners in assuming "performance oriented" behaviours and coordinating the input-output information process within the relationship, the control into Inter-Organizational Relationships plays a crucial role [56]. In the port industry innovative IT tools have been adopted to collect and manage information traffic flows, also for managing some specific decision making processes in particular areas, like environmental issues related to the port operations. The management accounting and control systems can facilitate and support all the organizational processes, especially the decision making process, in the port community collecting and analyzing information and data. Differently, during the last two decades, IT role in seaport systems has already been recognized by most scholars [57–59]; indeed, IT constitutes a crucial part in improving the operational systems in cargo handling with reference to the transfer and processing of broad volumes of data within seaport organizations [57]. Likewise, the port management information system is relevant, above all because of the involvement of private operators in the ownership structure of the concessionaires due to the complexity of data and information to manage [59].

In the past, port users usually used paper-based methods, such as sending fax or handing in documents directly for the delivery of cargo. Besides, port users tend to send the documents via e-mail thanks to the internet channel. But information and data needed to be typed again every time in the port's information systems requiring more time and increasing the risks of mistakes [60].

In this context, interesting and relevant advantages in the port community have been provided by the technology adopted by port users especially considering the integrated information technologies useful for the Management Control Systems (MCS). Some scholars argue that MCS plays a crucial role in supporting the business strategy in order to achieve the competitive advantage and high standards of performance [61, 62]. In this direction, information and data management and sharing, regarding the processes within the inter-organizational relationships established between PAs, shipping agents and cruise companies with focus on the environmental impact of their operations, require more attention in order to be effectively provided. Thus, these port users have to manage and share a lot of information, both internal and external, making more complex the decision making processes.

These port players can be significantly supported by IT in rapidly sharing and managing information and data in the real time and also the accounting activities and controlling functions can be supported in preventing and reducing the negative effects on the environment of their activities.

Most literature, theoretical and empirical studies, have outlined the positive effects of IT on the organizations performance, also showing its key role to support management accounting activities and facilitating exchange of information among public and private organizations [58, 63–65].

According to this perspective, considering MCS we might create positive conditions for the improvement of the relationships between PAs, shipping agents and cruise companies in the port community, also making more effective and efficient the different port organizational models, that is service port, tool port, landlord port, and private port models [8].

## 4 Methodology

This paper adopts a case study methodology investigating one port experience in Italy, the Port of Naples. We have chosen Naples seaport responding to specific criteria, that is: the relevance of cruise traffic, indeed Naples is the second transit port in the Mediterranean region and, regarding both transit and home ports, it is classified at third position [66: 7, 10]; the frequency and continuity of events planned and managed using the cruise terminal spaces; the entity of the revenue events on the total of the revenues obtained by cruise terminal concessionaire (as shown below); the presence of the cruise companies in the ownership structure of the concessionaire.

This is an explorative study conducted through semi-structured interviews to key actors in the investigated sector through face-to-face and phone meetings. During the month of May 2016 we conducted two semi-structured interviews to port users, that is one shipping agent (1 face-to-face interview) and one services provider about ships classification (1 phone interview). In details, we gathered information and data during our interviews to these key actors, that is shipping agent and port environment certification agent in the port of Naples. Each interview lasted from about one hour (phone interview) to three hours (face-to-face interview). The interviews followed a detailed semi-structured questionnaire with focus on crucial aspects regarding the actions required during the arrival, mooring and departure of ships for waste management and duties for preventing and reducing environmental impact of port operations.

## 4.1  Case Study Description

In our case study we investigate two main inter-organizational relationship systems: the first one between shipping agency and cruise company, and the second one between the shipping agent and PA of Naples.

Thanks to early results of our interviews, in the first relationship, we evidence that the shipping agency (Marinter S.r.l.) is mainly involved in managing all the practices about the waste management process derived from the ships in the port of Naples. This function is named "Garbage Declaration" and consists of collecting, processing and reporting all information and data about the waste management process for the ships. More specifcally, the shipping agency manages all the process adopting an information system. In this relationship we can observe three distinguished phases: before, during and at the end of mooring on the quay. Each step requires specific documents for the waste management process, in fact, the Master ship has to fill specific schedules about the amount and nature of waste produced on the ship, specifying the intention to use the waste services in the port. These schedules filled for the port in Naples represent the "Garbage Declaration" that is necessary for the shipping agency to require the following intervention of PA and the specialized organization for certification about the environmental impact of shipping operations. In the collecting and sharing process for information and data, the shipping agency adopts a specific digital platform, called PMIS (PORT MANAGEMENT INFORMATION SYSTEM), that allows to be in attach with external organizations for environmental management control and monitoring processes.

In the second relationship, the company interviewed, that is RINA Services S.p. A. in Genoa (Italy), is involved in the environmental certification for waste management from ships. Its geographic competence concerns different Italian ports like Naples. In particular, this private organization makes inspections for monitoring and evaluating the application of MARPOL convention about the waste and pollution derived from all the ships, also cargo and passenger. In this case, the company without using any software or digital platforms, checks all the documents (e.g., "Garbage Declaration") related to waste and pollution from the ships managed at the port. Hence, this company only certificates the respect of environmental regulations by the port.

In the two inter-organizational relationships investigated, we can observe really great differences in terms of information systems adopted for managing the specific processes. In fact, in the first case, a digital platform, conceived as an application of MCS, is adopted, while in the second case there aren't specific software or information systems that support the overall functions regarding the waste and pollution management process.

## 5  Final Remarks and Future Perspectives

This paper can contribute to the existing literature by investigating the inter-relationships systems established between port users for collecting, processing and reporting information and data about the environmental effects derived from ships in the port industry. We observe still the lack of specific information systems for supporting the port users in their activities and, also, they don't share information, data and practices about that, with high risk to miss relevant data, information and specific steps during the overall processes. Thus, the quality and quantity of information about the environmental services are really poor. Also, the functions analyzed in both the inter-relationships systems merely concern descriptions and documentation related to waste and pollution emissions.

Hence, our working progress study has evidenced some relevant criticisms in the relationship between the port users analyzed. In fact, the findings have outlined that the management control, information system and reporting are still missing regarding the crucial aspects related to the environmental issues and the consequent activities in the port.

This paper presents several limitations, related mainly to its exploratory nature with focus only on some criticisms, but it can be considered as an interesting research starting point in order to find new and more intriguing aspects to investigate, which can explain the different role and use of the management control, information system and reporting tools in the seaport system.

**Acknowledgements** The authors are grateful for the contributions of the operators interviewed. A special thanks to Dr. Luisa Mastellone, shipping agent and board member at Marinter S.r.l. in Naples (Italy), and Dr. Paolo Teramo, Environmental Engineering at RINA Services S.p.A. in Genoa (Italy). Any errors are entirely attributed to the authors. The research has been published thanks to the financial support received by the Parthenope University, Naples, entitled "Bando di sostegno alla ricerca individuale per il triennio 2015–2017. Annualità 2017".

# References

1. European Sea Ports Organisation (ESPO). (2012). *Towards excellence in port environmental management and sustainability*. ESPO Green Guide, Brussels (2012).
2. Lam, J. S. L., & Notteboom, T. (2014). The greening of ports: A comparison of port management tools used by leading ports in Asia and Europe. *Transport Reviews, 34*(2), 169–189.
3. Acciaro, M. (2015). Corporate responsibility and value creation in the port sector. *International Journal of Logistics Research and Applications, 18*(3), 291–311.
4. Lam, J. S. L., & Van de Voorde, E. (2012). Green port strategy for sustainable growth and development. In *Transport Logistics for Sustainable Growth at a New Level, International Forum on Shipping, Ports and Airports (IFSPA)* (pp. 27–30).
5. Pavlic, B., Cepak, F., Sucic, B., Peckaj, M., & Kandus, B. (2014). Sustainable port infrastructure, practical implementation of the green port concept. *Thermal Science, 18*(3), 935–948.
6. Majeure Alternative Management—HEC Paris. (2009–2010).
7. Henriques, A., & Richardson, J. (2004). *The triple bottom line: Does it add up*. London: Earthscan.
8. World Bank. (2007). World Bank port reform toolkit. www.worldbank.org/transport/ports/toolkit.
9. MARPOL 73/78/97. (1997). International Convention for the Prevention of Pollution from Ships (MARPOL): 1973 Convention, 1978 Protocol, 1997 Protocol—Annex VI; Entry into force: 2 October 1983 (Annexes I and II).
10. Murugesan, S. (2008). Harnessing green IT: Principles and practices. *IT professional, 10*(1), 24–33.
11. Walker, G., & King, D. (2008). *The hot topic: What we can do about global warming*. Boston: Houghton Mifflin Harcourt.
12. Nordhaus, W. D. (2008). *A question of balance: Economic modeling of global warming*.
13. Hwang, J., & Hyun, S. S. (2016). Perceived firm innovativeness in cruise travelers' experience and perceived luxury value: The moderating effect of advertising effectiveness. *Asia Pacific Journal of Tourism Research, 21*(supp1), 101–128.
14. Gibbs, D., Rigot-Muller, P., Mangan, J., & Lalwani, C. (2014). The role of sea ports in end-to-end maritime transport chain emissions. *Energy Policy, 64*, 337–348.
15. Lin, J., Lin, C. C., Cleland-Huang, J., Settimi, R., Amaya, J., Bedford, G., Zou, X. (2006). Poirot: A distributed tool supporting enterprise-wide automated traceability. In *Requirements Engineering, 14th IEEE International Conference* (pp. 363–364). IEEE.
16. Bows, A., Anderson, K., & Peeters, P. (2009). Air transport, climate change and tourism. *Tourism and Hospitality Planning & Development, 6*(1), 7–20.
17. Grech, A., Bos, M., Brodie, J., Coles, R., Dale, A., Gilbert, R., Rasheed, M. A. (2013). Guiding principles for the improved governance of port and shipping impacts in the Great Barrier Reef. *Marine Pollution Bulletin, 75*(1), 8–20.
18. Lu, C. S., Liu, W. H., & Wooldridge, C. (2014). Maritime environmental governance and green shipping. *Maritime Policy & Management, 41*(2), 131–133.
19. Johnson, D. (2002). Environmentally sustainable cruise tourism: A reality check. *Marine Policy, 26*(4), 261–270.
20. Butt, N. (2007). The impact of cruise ship generated waste on home ports and ports of call: A study of Southampton. *Marine Policy, 31*(5), 591–598.
21. Eijgelaar, E., Thaper, C., & Peeters, P. (2010). Antarctic cruise tourism: The paradoxes of ambassadorship, "last chance tourism" and greenhouse gas emissions. *Journal of Sustainable Tourism, 18*(3), 337–354.
22. Brida, J. G., & Zapata, S. (2010). Economic impacts of cruise tourism: The case of Costa Rica. *Anatolia, 21*(2), 322–338.

23. Howitt, O. J., Revol, V. G., Smith, I. J., & Rodger, C. J. (2010). Carbon emissions from international cruise ship passengers' travel to and from New Zealand. *Energy Policy, 38*(5), 2552–2560.
24. Poplawski, K., Setton, E., McEwen, B., Hrebenyk, D., Graham, M., & Keller, P. (2011). Impact of cruise ship emissions in Victoria, BC, Canada. *Atmospheric Environment, 45*(4), 824–833.
25. Strazza, C., Del Borghi, A., Gallo, M., Manariti, R., & Missanelli, E. (2015). Investigation of green practices for paper use reduction onboard a cruise ship—A life cycle approach. *The International Journal of Life Cycle Assessment, 20*(7), 982–993.
26. de Grosbois, D. (2016). Corporate social responsibility reporting in the cruise tourism industry: A performance evaluation using a new institutional theory based model. *Journal of Sustainable Tourism, 24*(2), 245–269.
27. Dinwoodie, J., Tuck, S., Knowles, H., Benhin, J., & Sansom, M. (2012). Sustainable development of maritime operations in ports. *Business Strategy and the Environment, 21*(2), 111–126.
28. Ng, A. K., & Song, S. (2010). The environmental impacts of pollutants generated by routine shipping operations on ports. *Ocean and Coastal Management, 53*(5), 301–311.
29. Anderson, J. W., & Lee, R. F. (2006). Use of biomarkers in oil spill risk assessment in the marine environment. *Human and Ecological Risk Assessment: An International Journal, 12*, 1192–1222.
30. Nasiri, F., Manuilova, A., & Huang, G. H. (2009). Environmental policy analysis in freight transportation planning: An optimality assessment approach. *International Journal of Sustainable Transportation, 3*(2), 88–109.
31. Bohm, G., & Pfister, H. R. (2005). Consequences, morality, and time in environmental risk evaluation. *Journal of Risk Research, 8*(6), 461–479.
32. El-Zein, A., Nasrallah, R., Nuwayhid, I., Kai, L., & Makhoul, J. (2006). Why do neighbors have different environmental priorities? Analysis of environmental risk perception in a Beirut neighborhood. *Risk Analysis, 26*(2), 423–435.
33. Jalkanen, J. P., Johansson, L., Kukkonen, J., Brink, A., Kalli, J., & Stipa, T. (2012). Extension of an assessment model of ship traffic exhaust emissions for particulate matter and carbon monoxide. *Atmospheric Chemistry and Physics, 12*(5), 2641–2659.
34. Villalba, G., & Gemechu, E. D. (2011). Estimating GHG emissions of marine ports—The case of Barcelona. *Energy Policy, 39*(3), 1363–1368.
35. Eide, M. S., Longva, T., Hoffmann, P., Endresen, Ø., & Dalsøren, S. B. (2011). Future cost scenarios for reduction of ship $CO_2$ emissions. *Maritime Policy & Management, 38*(1), 11–37.
36. Buhaug, O., Corbett, J. J., Endresen, O., Eyring, V., Faber, J., Hanayama, S., et al. (2009). *Second IMO GHG Study*. London, UK: International Maritime Organization (IMO).
37. Contini, D., Gambaro, A., Belosi, F., De Pieri, S., Cairns, W. R. L., Donateo, A., et al. (2011). The direct influence of ship traffic on atmospheric PM 2.5, PM 10 and PAH in Venice. *Journal of Environmental Management, 92*(9), 2119–2129.
38. Howitt, O. J. A., Revol, V. G. N., Smith, I. J., & Rodger, C. J. (2010). Carbon emissions from international cruise ships passengers' travel to and form New Zealand. *Energy Policy, 28*, 2552–2560.
39. Buhaug, Ø., Corbett, J. J., Endresen, Ø., Eyring, V., Faber, J., Hanayama, S., Lee, D. S., Lee, D., Lindstad, H., Mjelde, A., Pålsson, C., Wanquing, W., Winebrake, J. J., & Yoshida, K. (2008). Updated study on greenhouse gas emissions from ships: Phase I Report. International Maritime Organization (IMO) (included as Annex in document MEPC58/INF.6).
40. INFRAS/IWW. (2000). *External costs of transport: Accidents, environmental and congestion costs of transport in Western Europe*. Paris: INFRAS/IWW, International Union of Railways.
41. Daniels, R. H. O. N. D. A., & Adamowicz, V. (2000). *Environmental valuation. Handbook of Transport Modelling*. Pergamon, Amsterdam.
42. Etkin, D. S. (2003). Modeling oil spill response and damage costs. In *Proceedings of the 2003 International Oil Spill Conference*. Washington DC: American Petroleum Institute.

43. Liu, X., & Wirtz, K. W. (2006). Total oil spill costs and compensations. *Maritime Policy & Management, 33*(1), 49–60.
44. Garza-Gil, M. D., Prada-Blanco, A., & Vazquez-Rodriguez, M. X. (2006). Estimating the short term economic damages from the Prestige oil spill in the Galician fisheries and tourism. *Ecological Economics, 58*(4), 842–849.
45. IFAW. (2007). *Chronic oil pollution in Europe*. Brussels, Belgium: IFAW.
46. Sirkar, J., Ameer, P., Brown, A., Goss, P., Michel, K., Nicastro, F., et al. (1997). A framework for assessing the environmental performance of tankers in accidental groundings and collisions. SNAME T and R ad hoc panel.
47. Rawson, C., Crake, K., & Brown, A. (1998). Assessing the environmental performance of tankers in accidental grounding and collision. *SNAME Transactions, 106*, 41–58.
48. GESAMP. (2001). A sea of troubles. IMO/FAO/UNESCO/WMO/WHO/IAEA/UN/UNEP Joint Group of Experts on the Scientific Aspects of Marine Pollution (GESAMP) and Advisory Committee on Protection of the Sea. Reports and studies no. 70, IMO, London.
49. Bigano, A., & Sheehan, P. (2006). Assessing the risk of oil spills in the Mediterranean: The case of the route from the Black Sea to Italy. Working paper. Milan: Fondazione Eni Enrico Mattei, 32.
50. Adler, E., & Inbar, M. (2007). Shoreline sensitivity to oil spills, the Mediterranean coast of Israel: Assessment and analysis. *Ocean and Coastal Management, 50*(1, 2), 4–34.
51. Bohm, G., & Pfister, H. R. (2005). Consequences, morality, and time in environmental risk evaluation. *Journal of Risk Research, 8*(6), 461–479.
52. El-Zein, A., Nasrallah, R., Nuwayhid, I., Kai, L., & Makhoul, J. (2006). Why do neighbors have different environmental priorities? Analysis of environmental risk perception in a Beirut neighborhood. *Risk Analysis, 26*(2), 423–435.
53. Marchi, L. (1993). *I sistemi informativi aziendali*. Giuffré: Milano.
54. Mancini, D. (2010). *Il sistema informativo e di controllo relazionale per il governo della rete di relazioni collaborative d'azienda*. Giuffrè: Milano.
55. Choe, J. M. (2008). Inter-organizational relationships and the flow of information through value chains. *Information & Management, 45*, 444–450.
56. Dekker, H. C. (2004). Control of inter-organizational relationships: Evidence on appropriation concerns and coordination requirements. *Accounting, Organizations and Society, 29*(1), 27–49.
57. Kia, M., Shayan, E., & Ghotb, F. (2000). The importance of information technology in port terminal operations. *International Journal of Physical Distribution & Logistics Management, 30*(3/4), 331–344.
58. Lee-Partridge, J. E., Teo, T. S., & Lim, V. K. (2000). Information technology management: The case of the Port of Singapore Authority. *The Journal of Strategic Information Systems, 9* (1), 85–99.
59. Park Nam Kyu, K., Choi, H. R, Lee, C. S., Kang, M. H., & Yang, J. W. (2005). Port management information system towards privatization. In *Proceedings of IAME 2005 Annual Conference, International Association of Maritime Economists*. Limassol, Cyprus.
60. Keceli, Y., Choi, H. R., Cha, Y. S., & Aydogdu, Y. V. (2008). A study on adoption of port community systems according to organization size. In *Convergence and Hybrid Information Technology, 2008. ICCIT'08*. Third International Conference on Seaport Industry and Port Community System, 1, 493–501, IEEE.
61. Kaplan, R. S., Norton, D. P. (1996). Using the balanced scorecard as a strategic management system.
62. Langfield-Smith, K. (1997). The management control systems and strategy: A critical review. *Accounting, Organizations and Society, 22*(2), 207–232.
63. Teo, T. S. H., & King, W. R. (1996). Assessing the impact of integrating business planning and IS planning. *Information & Management, 30*, 309–321.

64. Kia, M., Shayan, E., & Ghotb, F. (2000). The importance of information technology in port terminal operations. *International Journal of Physical Distribution & Logistics Management, 30*(3/4), 331–344.
65. Marlow, P. B., & Casaca, A. C. P. (2003). Measuring lean ports performance. *International Journal of Transport Management, 1*(4), 189–202.
66. CLIA Europe. (2015). Cruise industry. Contribute Contribution of cruise tourism to the economies of Europe 2015 Edition. http://www.cliaeurope.eu/.

# The Role of Supply Chain Resilience on IT and cyber Disruptions

Giorgia Giusi Siciliano🆔 and Barbara Gaudenzi🆔

**Abstract** This study considers two major disruptions for modern supply chains: IT and cyber risks. As they may significantly impact the business continuity, the service quality, the investor confidence and the reputation of companies, more effective solutions are needed. We conducted an empirical study having as unit of analysis the supply chains of fifteen European companies, leaders in their industry. The findings show a misalignment of awareness between IT and SC managers toward these sources of disruption and the need of enhancing the traditional Supply Chain Risk Management process. We propose a framework that may improve the management of these unpredictable, high-consequence risks for the supply chain through a key element: the resilience.

**Keywords** IT and cyber risks · Risk management · Supply chain resilience

## 1 Introduction

The "IT threat evolution report" of 2016 by Kaspersky highlights the first three months of 2016 have seen the same amount of IT and cybersecurity events that just a few years ago would have seemed normal for a whole year.

Thus, if on one hand Information Technology (IT) and cyber-based technologies have been considered by both academics and practitioners as a resource that may enhance information flow about products, inventory, manufacturing, and logistics [1–4], they may generate two of the main source of business disruption within networks [5–9]: IT and cyber risks. Supply chains are called to develop the ability to cope with them, but both practitioners and academicians state there is still poor awareness and knowledge [10, 11].

G. G. Siciliano (✉) · B. Gaudenzi
University of Verona, Verona, Italy
e-mail: giorgiagiusi.siciliano@univr.it

B. Gaudenzi
e-mail: barbara.gaudenzi@univr.it

© Springer International Publishing AG, part of Springer Nature 2018
R. Lamboglia et al. (eds.), *Network, Smart and Open*, Lecture Notes in Information
Systems and Organisation 24, https://doi.org/10.1007/978-3-319-62636-9_4

The purpose of this study is to answer the following research questions:

– "What is the level of knowledge about IT and cyber risks among IT and SC managers?"
– "Which are the directions to build an effective and holistic IT and cyber Risk Management in the supply chain?"

Thus, we developed a qualitative research based on an interpretative and grounded theory approach [4, 12, 13]. We involved Supply Chain managers and IT executives of fifteen European leaders, operating in different industries. The unit of analysis has been the whole supply chain. The study is organized as follows. First, we provide an up-to-date literature review about how these threats are defined, focusing mainly on their role as business disruptors. Secondly, the cyber Supply Chain Risk Management (SCRM) literature is analyzed. The fifth section provides a model based on the Zsidisin and Wagner [14] study. Finally, in the last section conclusions and directions for practioners and future research for academicians are provided.

## 2   Knowing IT and cyber Operational Risks

The Information Systems (IS) security literature highlights the importance of awareness about IT and cyber operational risks to facilitate the correct detection of malicious events [15, 16], to effectively allocate the investments in specific security-enhancing assets [11] and to train employees [17, 18]. At the intersection of operations and supply chain management literature there is a growing body of research studying how sharing a deeper knowledge and communication [1, 4, 19–21] may lead to an effective assessment of the operational supply risks [22] and a better alignment throughout the value chain, lowing the exposure and vulnerability toward SC risks [23–26].

With respect to IT and cyber operational risks, there is a call for investigation about the alignment of knowledge and subsequent actions between IT and Supply Chain Personnel [6, 7, 27–30].

Thus, we aim to fill this gap providing a review about how IT and cyber risks have been described by the literature of the last five years. The scope is to test whether (or not) IT and Supply Chain executives share the same awareness and knowledge and if they align the SCR measures and procedures accordingly [28].

The Basel II Committee defines an "operational risk" as "the risk of loss resulting from inadequate or failed internal processes, people and systems or from external events" [24, 31–33].

This definition describes also IT and cyber risks, which the operations management literature encounters among the operational risks [12, 34]. The literature highlights some commonalities between the two risks. In particular, their nature may be both malicious and accidental [12, 34]. Moreover, both these threats negatively impact the confidentiality, integrity, and availability of the system and may be classified as unforeseeable events, characterized by unpredictability, low-probability and high-gravity. On the other hand, some differences seem to arise. In fact, the same authors seem suggesting that cyber operational risks stem more from malicious intent while IT operational risks appear to be more accidental by nature. The IS security literature seems to confirm the aforementioned categorization of the nature of IT and cyber operational risks.

In fact, with respect to cyber threats, Shackelford [9, p. 351] encounters fraud, identity theft among them, calling the actors "cyber criminals" and Mukhopadhyay et al. [35, p. 11] states, "cyber-risk is defined as the risk involved with a malicious electronic event that causes disruption of business and monetary loss". Öğüt et al. [36] talk about "attackers", Khan and Estay [37] about "talented criminals" and Hiller and Russell [38], say that cyber-attacks are made from criminals, which aim to gain some profit from cyber breaches. Moreover, the cyberspace has often been considered a fertile place for offences against confidentiality, integrity, and availability [39] and for terrorism [39–41].

With respect to IT operational risks, instead the accidental component seems significant. In fact, Benaroch et al. [42] underline accidental factors have been identified by IT executives as two of the top three threats to IS and Von Solms and Van Niekerk [26] speak about human errors.

Therefore, IT and cyber risks show differences and commonalities that both IT and SC managers should be aware of, in order to align their actions. Thus, the first contribution of this study is answering the following research question:

RQ1: "what is the level of knowledge about IT and cyber risks among IT and SC managers?

## 3 The IT and cyber SCRM

cyber-attacks and IT breakdowns may be considered like "black swans", for their unpredictability, low-probability but high-gravity. The growing interest toward these threats has led to a new stream of research, at the intersection of cybersecurity, supply chain management, and enterprise risk management [6, 7]: the cyber supply chain risk management. The discipline is still in its infancy, so while it has the great merit to shed light on these new SC risks, suffers from some gaps as well.

First of all, it has highlighted how IT and cyber risks may be a significant threat [43, 44], both for the upstream [13, 45] and downstream supply chain, in terms of loss of investors' confidence [11, 33, 36, 38, 46] or loss of reputation among customers [36, 47, 48]. However, at the best of our knowledge, there is lack of studies about the simultaneous impact of IT and cyber risks upstream and downstream.

Another lack lies in the focus of the stream, which is mainly on cyber threats, while the IT failures are not explicitly considered [28].

Furthermore, studies have solely focused on insurance [34, 49, 50], mitigation measures [27, 30, 49] and assessment procedures [7, 22, 27, 37, 49, 51–53]. Thus, at the best of our knowledge, there is a lack of studies providing an holistic supply chain risk management (SCRM) framework, which covers the SC from upstream to downstream, considers both IT and cyber operational risks and implements all the risk management process, from prevention to mitigation.

As a consequence, our second research question is:

RQ2: "Which are the directions to build an effective and holistic IT and cyber Risk Management in the supply chain?".

# 4   Methodology and Data

In conducting our qualitative research, we initially identified the questionnaire items mainly according to the security and risk management standards [54–57], as the literature of the last five years seems to have poorly investigated the actual alignment among IT and SC executives of aware-ness, knowledge and measures toward IT and cyber risks and the role of supply chain resilience on effective SCRM. We also included some questions to confirm, integrate or contradict the academic definitions about the nature of these risks.

The resulting open-ended questionnaire is composed by 26 items, which were designed to cover the dimensions as follows: 8 for the definitions about the nature of IT and cyber risks, 5 for the IT and cyber risk assessment, 4 for the IT and cyber risk prevention, 2 for the IT and cyber risk mitigation, 3 for the IT and cyber risk compliance and 4 for the IT and cyber risk governance.

The unit of analysis has been the whole supply chains' IT and cyber risk practices of assessment, mitigation, compliance and governance. Companies in the sample (Table 1) have been chosen according to the following criteria.

First, they had to have the IT function and an SC manager, as it was important to capture a representative sample of participants with work experience in managing IT, cyber and SC risks [58]. Second, they had to operate in different industries, to answer the calling for further investigation of different industrial sectors. In fact, a heterogeneous sample should increase the understanding of the occurrence, detection, and reaction to cyber-attacks and IT failures, validating theory and conceptual frameworks [16, 28] and providing the general trend [59]. Third, companies' headquarter had to be in Europe, as the extant literature lacks of studies about the level of awareness in the European private sector [38, 60–62]. Forth, the sample is composed by medium/large companies, as the literature found they may have more negative effects from an IT or cyber breach [12].

When possible, the interviewees were more than one within the same company (SC manager and IT manager). They have been identified in accordance with our aim to investigate the real alignment of knowledge and actions of different roles [63] towards these two risks. This process allowed us to reach the point of

**Table 1** Sample characteristics

| Firms | Sector | Size |
|---|---|---|
| | | **Small**: revenues under €1 million and between 10 and 100 employees<br>**Medium**: revenues between €1 million and €500 million under 50 thousand employees<br>**Large**: revenues exceeding €10 billion and more than 50 thousand of employees |
| C1 | Apparels | Large |
| C2 | Metalcasting | Medium |
| C3 | Services | Medium |
| C4 | Services | Large |
| C5 | Oil and Gas | Large |
| C6 | Finance | Large |
| C7 | Software | Medium |
| C8 | Healthcare | Medium |
| C9 | Apparels | Medium |
| C10 | Healthcare | Medium |
| C11 | Finance | Medium |
| C12 | Tobacco | Medium |
| C13 | High Technology | Medium |
| C14 | Heating | Medium |
| C15 | Food Products | Large |

theoretical saturation with fifteen organizations. Some evidences from our research are summarized in Table 2.

As a second step, the textual data of the questionnaire have been transcribed and coded using the grounded theory approach [64–66].

# 5 Results

IT managers confirm the classification provided by the current literature: operational cyber risks appear to be mainly malicious by nature, while IT operational risks are more accidental. Also the common threats of unpredictability, low-probability and high-gravity are confirmed. Instead, with respect to SC managers, they do not see any significant difference.

The IT and cyber SCRM suffers from a general misalignment between knowledge and actions. In fact, the IT security managers suggest the assessment and prevention measures suffer from an overconfidence in technical solutions (e.g., firewalls, anti-virus, digital signature and encryption), unable to identify breaches on critical

**Table 2** Some evidences from the interviews

| The nature of IT and cyber operational risks | C10. IT security manager: IT risk is more a risk of software and procedures. cyber risks are related to external attacks from hackers. These penetrate the systems through the web, emails and smartphones<br>C10. SC manager: I think IT and cyber risks are the same thing<br>C6. IT security manager: If it is online, it is cyber, if it is offline, it is IT<br>C6. SC manager: I do not think the difference is important to manage IT and cyber risks |
|---|---|
| IT and cyber Supply Chain Risk Assessment | C2. IT security manager: I think the SC risk assessment of IT and cyber risks in the organization is fundamental, but I do not have the chance to suggest the appropriate measures, as I am not in direct contact with the SC function<br>C2. SC manager: At the moment the organization's staff does not receive systematic training in Information System Continuity Management, but we are working on it<br>C9. IT security manager: I manage an IT budget, but there is not an ad hoc percentage for security<br>C9. SC manager: We run the risk assessment every year, but it is not specifically on IT and cyber risks. At the moment there is neither a dedicated budget to IT Security Management, it is all in the Risk Management budget |
| IT and cyber Supply Chain Risk Prevention | C3. IT security manager: There should be more effort in risk prevention, working towards both evident risks and the most hidden ones<br>C3. SC manager: The prevention is based for the 50% on good hardware and software. It would be a great improvement to integrate them throughout the supply chain<br>C8. IT security manager: Decisions concerning the prevention within the SC are taken by who has poor knowledge about IT and cyber risks<br>C8. SC manager: The IT personnel is not able to transmit effectively the IT and cyber risks concept |
| IT and cyber Supply Chain Risk Mitigation | C5. IT security manager: The mitigation relies only on technical solutions, but they cannot solve issues related to breaches towards the consumers' reputation or the suppliers' trust<br>C5. SC manager: We are working on securing physical and virtual area. We are planning to adopt systems based on password sharing and dual certification<br>C7. IT security manager: There is a general SC Risk Mitigation plan, but I am not involved in it<br>C7. SC manager: The mitigation is not structured, but I would say the level of coverage is good. We work on supply contracts with response time of 2–4 h, partnership vendors and usage of replicated systems |

(continued)

**Table 2** (continued)

| IT and cyber Supply Chain Risk Compliance | C14. IT security manager: Conforming to the Information Security Standards may improve the general culture and awareness. Moreover, they may support IT managers to convince SC managers to do some changes<br>C14. SC manager: We conform to the general Risk Management Official Standards, not the Information Security Standards |
|---|---|
| IT and cyber Supply Chain Risk Governance | C15. IT security manager: I think there is a communication problem. For example, the company hired a consultant that reports to me, but I am not in the management board, so there is a gap in the information flow<br>C15. SC manager: I think all the companies within the value chain are totally risk adverse<br>C1. IT security manager: My area produces data for the SC risk management but there is not a real interaction<br>C1. SC manager: If we had more supply chain integration, we would have a better defense. We should work in this direction |

dimensions such as investors' reputation and suppliers' trust. The solution may be enhancing the cross-functional culture and communication. However, SC supply managers admit the promotion of an IT and cyber culture and specific training courses are not a priority, yet.

SC managers prefer to rely on risk mitigation strategies (e.g., physical entry controls, secure areas, equipment security level, and insurance). However, IT managers suggest a better integration of IT mitigation measures among companies (e.g., contractual agreements with key-suppliers). In sum, SC and IT managers acknowledge the relevance to enhance their traditional SCRM, but the novelty of these risks renders difficult planning concrete and effective ways to cope with them.

# 6   Model

The contribution of our study is an holistic risk management framework, which embraces the supply chain from upstream to downstream, considering both IT and cyber operational risks.

In particular, we suggest developing a superior level of resilience to compensate the greatest weakness of traditional SCRM: its inability to adequately characterize low-probability, high-consequence events [67–69] such as IT and cyber risks.

The SCRM literature has increasingly recognized the advantages related to resilience, namely recovery, flexibility, crisis preparedness [2, 21, 70, 71], and business continuity system [15, 68, 71]. Recently, among the advantages has been encountered also the enhancing of the traditional SCRM [71]. These advantages have attracted the interest of academicians: in 2015, for the first time Khan and Estay (p. 10) have talked about supply chain cyber resilience as "the capability of a supply chain to maintain its operational performance when faced with cyber-risk". However, the two authors also highlight a lack of frameworks that link SCRM, resilience and the phenomenon of cyber-risk or IT risk explicitly, while the literature has focused more on the positive impacts of IT and cyber capabilities on supply chain resilience [45, 72].

We try to fill this gap, suggesting resilience as an element to enhance the traditional SCRM when dealing with IT and cyber operational risks. Specifically, we adapt the model proposed by Zsidisin and Wagner [14] that suggests how supply chain resiliency practices may support a risk mitigation strategy and particularly risk prevention. However, while these authors investigate how "supply resiliency practices" impact on disruption occurrence, we aim at analyzing the role of resiliency practices in coping with two specific,—IT and cyber risks— throughout the whole supply chain risk management process. The literature considers the resilience as characterized by four abilities, namely the ability to plan/ prepare (or readiness), to absorb (or respond), to recover and to adapt to known and unknown threats [20, 28, 35, 73]. We also consider the fourth dimension identified by Hohenstein et al. [67, p. 96], the "growth", which "exceeds recovery by not only returning to a normal state after a risk event but achieving a new and improved position".

In particular, the plan/prepare ability implies the systematic identification and prevention of risks; absorbing allows the business continuity while dealing with a disruption; the recovering skill involves the successful coming back of all the functions to the status quo, while the adaptation requires adjusting plans and procedures to the specific business needs. The model shown in Fig. 1 considers the integration of the aforementioned four abilities in a systematic IT and cyber SCRM process.

Firstly, the improvement of the traditional SCRM lies in the ability to plan and prepare an early assessment and prevention of risks, in order to identify priorities and allocate resources. This phase should be based on a strong cultural revolution upstream and downstream (e.g., common training courses, shared budget to potentiate detection) and a better integration and collaboration between IT and SC functions (e.g., through team working, systemic updating and training courses). If the process of identification and evaluation of IT and cyber risks is applied thoroughly, the decision-making should be well supported and timely (e.g., if the identification and evaluation procedure turns out to be "secure" or "successful", no action should be planned).

The subsequent IT and cyber risks mitigation should present the ability to absorb and to recover from any type of IT and cyber risk, synchronizing the timing response to the different degree of urgency different types to IT failures and cyber breach they may present [74]. In addition, this phase requires boosting the traditional SCRM upstream and downstream, collaborating to share crucial information and valuable data with suppliers and customers, organize meetings across IT and SC managers of companies within the whole supply chain, using safety stocks to reduce stock outs and lost sales, predefine communication systems to reduce errors upwards and to prevent reputation damages downwards.

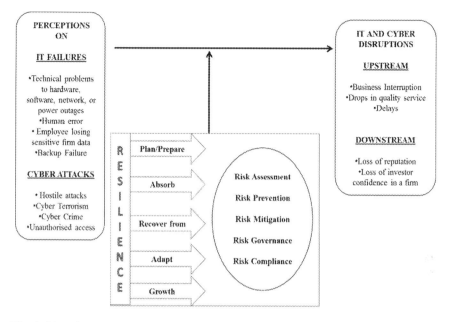

**Fig. 1** Managing IT and cyber risk in supply chains: The role of resilience

With respect to the IT and cyber risk management governance, this should involve IT managers to acquire all the critical information. This would allow monitoring the continuous alignment of the real risk appetite with the actual risks companies may face. Moreover, conforming to the Information Security Standards would give the advantage to enhance the overall culture and communication, supporting IT managers' suggestions through competent guidelines to the specific business needs and the specific IT and cyber threats the company may face.

# 7 Discussion and Conclusion

Nowadays, supply chains have to deal with fast-changing, unpredictable and high-consequence threats, such as IT and cyber risks. In front of these emerging threats, traditional supply chain seem to be less effective, while resilient supply chain can be better prompt to react.

Through a qualitative research, we investigated organizations' perceptions and risk management approaches about these emergent risks. In particular, with regard to the first research question, "what is the level of knowledge about IT and cyber risks among IT and SC managers?", the results indicate IT managers have a deeper knowledge and awareness towards IT and cyber risks, but they rarely have the chance to share information with SC managers. As a consequence, companies suffer from poor communication, overconfidence in technical investments and a lack of integration and alignment of measures and procedures throughout the whole SC. The findings related to this first research question confirm the extant literature in more than one sense.

First of all, we validate previous studies stating that companies still do not recognize IT and cyber risks as relevant threats [50], invest less than the optimal level [11, 30], weakening all the supply chain [16, 30, 34, 38]. In particular, companies invest in specific security-enhancing assets (e.g., fire-walls, anti-virus) [49] that may leave them vulnerable over a longer period, as IT and cyber change suddenly and drastically [11, 17, 34, 40]. Thus, our findings confirm it would be more appropriate to complement the aforementioned measures with long-term tools such as a deeper cross-functional communication [16, 30, 49].

With respect to the second research question, "Which are the directions to build an effective and holistic IT and cyber Risk Management in the supply chain?", we suggest an holistic risk management framework, that may enhance the traditional risk management process from downstream to up-stream, thanks to the contribution of a key element: the resilience.

# References

1. Chewning, L. V., Lai, C. H., & Doerfel, M. L. (2013). Organizational resilience and using information and communication technologies to rebuild communication structures. *Management Communication Quarterly, 27*(2), 237–263.
2. Mensah, P., & Merkuryev, Y. (2014). Developing a resilient supply chain. *Procedia-Social and Behavioral Sciences, 110,* 309–319.
3. Mensah, P., Merkuryev, Y., & Longo, F. (2015). Using ICT in developing a resilient supply chain strategy. *Procedia Computer Science, 43,* 101–108.
4. PWC Report. (2015). Information security breaches survey 2015. https://www.pwc.co.uk/assets/pdf/2015-isbs-technical-report-blue-03.pdf. Last accessed September 12, 2016.
5. Aon Risk Solutions, Global Risk Management Survey. (2015). www.aon.com/2015GlobalRisk/. Last accessed March 12, 2016.
6. Bartol, N. (2014). Cyber supply chain security practices DNA–Filling in the puzzle using a diverse set of disciplines. *Technovation, 34*(7), 354–361.
7. Boyson, S. (2014). Cyber supply chain risk management: Revolutionizing the strategic control of critical IT systems. *Technovation, 34*(7), 342–353.
8. Krebs, B. (2014). Target hackers broke in via HVAC company. Krebs on Security. http://krebsonsecurity.com/2014/02/target-hackers-broke-in-via-hvac-company/. Last accessed April 25, 2016.
9. Shackelford, S. J. (2012). Should your firm invest in cyber risk insurance? *Business Horizons, 55*(4), 349–356.
10. Jüttner, U. (2005). Supply chain risk management: Understanding the business requirements from a practitioner perspective. *The International Journal of Logistics Management, 16*(1), 120–141.
11. Sokolov, A., Mesropyan, V., & Chulok, A. (2014). Supply chain cyber security: A Russian outlook. *Technovation, 34*(7), 389–391.
12. Goldstein, J., Chernobai, A., & Benaroch, M. (2011). An event study analysis of the economic impact of IT operational risk and its subcategories. *Journal of the Association for Information Systems, 12*(9), 606.

13. PWC Report. (2015). 2015 Addressing security risks in an interconnected world. Key findings from The Global State of Information Security® Survey 2015. https://www.pwc.ru/ru/industrial-manufacturing/assets/pwc-global-state-of-information-security-survey-industrial-products.pdf. Last accessed September 12, 2016.
14. Zsidisin, G. A., & Wagner, S. M. (2010). Do perceptions become reality? The moderating role of supply chain resiliency on disruption occurrence. *Journal of Business Logistics, 31*(2), 1–20.
15. Ben-Asher, N., & Gonzalez, C. (2015). Effects of cyber security knowledge on attack detection. *Computers in Human Behavior, 48,* 51–61.
16. Ghadge, A., Dani, S., & Kalawsky, R. (2012). Supply chain risk management: Present and future scope. *The International Journal of Logistics Management, 23*(3), 313–339.
17. Ifinedo, P. (2014). Information systems security policy compliance: An empirical study of the effects of socialisation, influence, and cognition. *Information & Management, 51*(1), 69–79.
18. Ponomarov, S. Y., & Holcomb, M. C. (2009). Understanding the concept of supply chain resilience. *The International Journal of Logistics Management, 20*(1), 124–143.
19. Leat, P., & Revoredo-Giha, C. (2013). Risk and resilience in agri-food supply chains: The case of the ASDA PorkLink supply chain in Scotland. *Supply Chain Management: An International Journal, 18*(2), 219–231.
20. Lim, J. H., Stratopoulos, T. C., & Wirjanto, T. S. (2011). Path dependence of dynamic information technology capability: An empirical investigation. *Journal of Management Information Systems, 28*(3), 45–84.
21. Ward, J. M. (2012). Information systems strategy: Quo vadis? *The Journal of Strategic Information Systems, 21*(2), 165–171.
22. Sturm, P. (2013). Operational and reputational risk in the European banking industry: The market reaction to operational risk events. *Journal of Economic Behavior & Organization, 85,* 191–206.
23. Brewer, N. T., Weinstein, N. D., Cuite, C. L., & Herrington, J. E., Jr. (2004). Risk perceptions and their relation to risk behavior. *Annals of Behavioral Medicine, 27*(2), 125–130.
24. Heckmann, I., Comes, T., & Nickel, S. (2015). A critical review on supply chain risk–Definition, measure and modeling. *Omega, 52,* 119–132.
25. Jensen, L. (2015). Challenges in maritime cyber-resilience. *Technology Innovation Management Re-view, 5*(4), 35.
26. Von Solms, R., & Van Niekerk, J. (2013). From information security to cyber security. *Computers & security, 38,* 97–102.
27. Ellison, R. J., & Woody, C. (2010). Supply-chain risk management: Incorporating security into software development. In *43rd IEEE Hawaii International Conference on System Sciences, (HICSS)*, (pp. 1–10). Honolulu: IEEE Press.
28. Kasperky. (2016). Report 2016 IT Threat Evolution In Q1 2016 https://securelist.com/files/2016/05/Q1_2016_MW_report_FINAL_eng.pdf. Last accessed April 25, 2016.
29. Linkov, I., Eisenberg, D. A., Plourde, K., Seager, T. P., Allen, J., & Kott, A. (2013). Resilience metrics for cyber systems. *Environment Systems and Decisions, 33*(4), 471–476.
30. National Academy of Sciences. (2016). Disaster resilience: A national imperative. Washington DC, United States. http://www.nap.edu/catalog.php?record_id=13457. Last accessed June 01, 2016.
31. Gatzert, N., & Kolb, A. (2014). Risk measurement and management of operational risk in insurance companies from an enterprise perspective. *Journal of Risk and Insurance, 81*(3), 683–708.
32. Hora, M., & Klassen, R. D. (2013). Learning from others' misfortune: Factors influencing knowledge acquisi-tion to reduce operational risk. *Journal of Operations Management, 31*(1), 52–61.
33. Strauss, A., & Corbin, J. (1998). *Basics of qualitative research: Procedures and techniques for developing grounded theory*. Thousand Oaks, CA: Sage.
34. Biener, C., Eling, M., & Wirfs, J. H. (2015). Insurability of cyber risk: An empirical analysis. *The Geneva Papers on Risk and Insurance Issues and Practice, 40*(1), 131–158.

35. Mukhopadhyay, A., Chatterjee, S., Saha, D., Mahanti, A., & Sadhukhan, S. K. (2013). Cyber-risk decision models: To insure IT or not? *Decision Support Systems, 56*, 11–26.
36. Öğüt, H., Raghunathan, S., & Menon, N. (2011). Cyber security risk management: Public policy implications of correlated risk, imperfect ability to prove loss, and observability of self protection. *Risk Analysis, 31*(3), 497–512.
37. Khan, O., & Estay, D. A. S. (2015). Supply chain cyber-resilience: Creating an agenda for future re-search. *Technology Innovation Management Review, 5*(4).
38. Hiller, J. S., & Russell, R. S. (2013). The challenge and imperative of private sector cybersecurity: An international comparison. *Computer Law & Security Review, 29*(3), 236–245.
39. Tehrani, P. M., & Manap, N. A. (2013). A rational jurisdiction for cyber terrorism. *Computer Law & Security Review, 29*(6), 689–701.
40. Hua, J., & Bapna, S. (2013). The economic impact of cyber terrorism. *The Journal of Strategic Information Systems, 22*(2), 175–186.
41. Tazelaar, F., & Snijders, C. (2013). Operational risk assessments by supply chain professionals: Process and performance. *Journal of Operations Management, 31*(1), 37–51.
42. Benaroch, M., Chernobai, A., & Goldstein, J. (2012). An internal control perspective on the market value consequences of IT operational risk events. *International Journal of Accounting Information Systems, 13*(4), 357–381.
43. Boyes, H. (2015). cybersecurity and cyber-resilient supply chains. *Technology Innovation Management Review, 5*(4), 28.
44. Konchitchki, Y., & O'Leary, D. E. (2011). Event study methodologies in information systems re-search. *International Journal of Accounting Information Systems, 12*(2), 99–115.
45. Davis, A. (2015). Building cyber-resilience into supply chains. *Technology Innovation Management Review, 5*(4), 19.
46. Knowles, W., Prince, D., Hutchison, D., Disso, J. F. P., & Jones, K. (2015). A survey of cyber security management in industrial control systems. *International Journal of Critical Infrastructure Protection, 9*, 52–80.
47. Gaudenzi, B., Confente, I., & Christopher, M. (2015). Managing reputational risk: Insights from an European Survey. *Corporate Reputation Review, 18*(4), 248–260.
48. Scholten, K., Sharkey Scott, P., & Fynes, B. (2014). Mitigation processes–antecedents for building supply chain resilience. *Supply Chain Management: An International Journal, 19*(2), 211–228.
49. Moore, T. (2010). The economics of cybersecurity: Principles and policy options. *International Journal of Critical Infrastructure Protection, 3*(3), 103–117.
50. Sen, R., & Borle, S. (2015). Estimating the contextual risk of data breach: An empirical approach. *Journal of Management Information Systems, 32*(2), 314–341.
51. Deane, J. K., Rees, C. L., & Baker, W. H. (2010). Assessing the information technology security risk in medical supply chains. *International Journal of Electronic Marketing and Retailing, 3*(2), 145–155.
52. Feng, N., Wang, H. J., & Li, M. (2014). A security risk analysis model for information systems: Causal relationships of risk factors and vulnerability propagation analysis. *Information Sciences, 256*, 57–73.
53. Kim, W., Jeong, O. R., Kim, C., & So, J. (2011). The dark side of the Internet: Attacks, costs and respons-es. *Information systems, 36*(3), 675–705.
54. ISO 31000—Risk management. http://www.iso.org/iso/home/standards/iso31000.htm. Last accessed February 14, 2016.
55. ISO/IEC 27001:2013 Information technology—Security techniques—Information security management systems—Requirements http://www.iso.org/iso/iso27001. Last accessed February 14, 2016.
56. ISO/IEC 27036-1:2014 Information technology—Security techniques—Information security for supplier relationships. http://iso.org/standard/59648.html. Last accessed February 14, 2016.

57. ISO/IEC 27032:2012 Information technology—Security techniques—Guidelines for cyber-security http://iso.org/standard/44375.html. Last accessed February 14, 2016.
58. Hofmann, D. A., & Stetzer, A. (1998). The role of safety climate and communication in accident interpretation: Implications for learning from negative events. *Academy of Management Journal, 41*(6), 644–657.
59. Linton, J. D., Boyson, S., & Aje, J. (2014). The challenge of cyber supply chain security to research and practice–An introduction. *Technovation, 34*(7), 339–341.
60. Irion, K. (2013). The governance of network and information security in the European Union: The European Public-Private Partnership for Resilience (EP3R). In *The Secure Information Society,* (pp. 83–116). London: Springer.
61. Mensah, P., Merkuryev, Y., & Manak, S. (2015). Developing a resilient supply chain strategy by exploiting ICT. *Procedia Computer Science, 77,* 65–71.
62. Waters, D. (2011). *Supply chain risk management: Vulnerability and resilience in logistics.* London: Kogan Page Publishers.
63. Gibbert, M., & Ruigrok, W. (2010). The "what" and "how" of case study rigor: Three strategies based on published work. *Organizational Research Methods, 13*(4), 710–737.
64. Glaser, B. G., & Strauss, A. L. (2009). The discovery of grounded theory: Strategies for qualitative research. Transaction publishers.
65. Srinidhi, B., Yan, J., & Tayi, G. K. (2015). Allocation of resources to cyber-security: The effect of misalignment of interest between managers and investors. *Decision Support Systems, 75,* 49–62.
66. Strauss, A. L. (1987). *Qualitative analysis for social scientists.* Cambridge: Cambridge University Press.
67. Hohenstein, N. O., Feisel, E., Hartmann, E., & Giunipero, L. (2015). Research on the phenomenon of supply chain resilience: A systematic review and paths for further investigation. *International Journal of Physical Distribution & Logistics Management, 45* (1/2), 90–117.
68. Pearson, N. (2014). A larger problem: Financial and reputational risks. *Computer Fraud & Security, 2014*(4), 11–13.
69. Ranganathan, C., Teo, T. S., & Dhaliwal, J. (2011). Web-enabled supply chain management: Key antecedents and performance impacts. *International Journal of Information Management, 31*(6), 533–545.
70. Christopher, M., & Peck, H. (2004). Building the resilient supply chain. *The international journal of logistics management, 15*(2), 1–14.
71. Pettit, T. J., Fiksel, J., & Croxton, K. L. (2010). Ensuring supply chain resilience: Development of a conceptual framework. *Journal of Business Logistics, 31*(1), 1–21.
72. Tehrani, P. M., Manap, N. A., & Taji, H. (2013). cyber terrorism challenges: The need for a global response to a multi-jurisdictional crime. *Computer Law & Security Review, 29*(3), 207–215.
73. Hollnagel, E., Paries, J., Woods, D., & Wreathall, J. (2011). *Resilience engineering in practice: A guidebook.* United Kingdom: Ashgate.
74. Wachinger, G., & Renn, O. (2010). Risk perception and natural hazards, CapHaz-Net WP3 Report, DIALOGIK Non-Profit Institute for Communication and Cooperative Research, Stuttgart. caphaz-net.org/outcomes-results/CapHaz-Net WP3 Risk-Perception.Pdf. Last accessed May 14, 2016.
75. Martin, J. A., & Eisenhardt, K. M. (2010). Rewiring: Cross-business-unit collaborations in multibusiness organizations. *Academy of Management Journal, 53*(2), 265–301.
76. Posey, C., Roberts, T., Lowry, P. B., Bennett, B., & Courtney, J. (2013). Insiders' protection of organizational information assets: Development of a systematics-based taxonomy and theory of diversity for protection-motivated behaviors. *MIS Quarterly, 37*(4), 1189–1210.
77. Urciuoli, L. (2015). cyber-resilience: A strategic approach for supply chain management. *Technology Innovation Management Review, 5*(4), 13.

# Virtual Entrepreneurship and e-Residency Adoption

## Linda Uljala and Ada Scupola

**Abstract** The purpose of this article is to investigate the technological attributes of Estonian e-Residency that facilitates or hinder its adoption for international virtual entrepreneurship. To conduct the study, the theory of Diffusion of Innovations is applied and a qualitative study of adopters of e-Residency for entrepreneurial purposes is conducted. The findings show a variety of attributes of e-Residency that to varying degrees influence the adoption process including felt needs, perceived risk and uncertainty. The article corroborates and adds to previous research on the adoption of technology and e-services by investigating a particular type of e-service, namely e-Residency.

**Keywords** E-services · e-Residency · Innovation · Adoption · Entrepreneurship

## 1 Introduction

In recent years, entrepreneurship has been undergoing a fundamental transformation due to synergies between Information and Communication Technology (ICT) development and changing paradigms of economic transactions. This has reflected rapid and radical changes that are influencing the global marketplaces, and new forms of entrepreneurship as well as practices of conducting business have begun to emerge [1]. Although some of the long-established entrepreneurial concepts might still be applicable, much of the context in which activities related to entrepreneurship are manifested has changed significantly in a relatively short period of time. Thus, the full economic impact of the technological development on entrepreneurship has not been thoroughly recognized [1].

L. Uljala · A. Scupola (✉)
Department of Social Sciences and Business, Roskilde University, 4000 Roskilde, Denmark
e-mail: ada@ruc.dk

L. Uljala
e-mail: lindauljala@gmail.com

© Springer International Publishing AG, part of Springer Nature 2018
R. Lamboglia et al. (eds.), *Network, Smart and Open*, Lecture Notes in Information Systems and Organisation 24, https://doi.org/10.1007/978-3-319-62636-9_5

One of the recent technological innovations influencing entrepreneurial practices in the global sphere is the Estonian e-Residency, launched in 2014. E-Residency is a transnational digital identity in the form of an eID card [2] defined here as a set of information about an individual, constructing "a unique identifier for an individual which can be stored in an electronic form" [3]. E-Residency allows individuals to electronically identify and authenticate oneself, encrypt and digitally sign documents, and access electronic services in Estonia, regardless of where one is physically residing [2, 4].

Estonia's objective with the launch of e-Residency is to contribute to the development of the country's economy, science, culture and education [5]. E-Residency is promoted in the official homepage in the following way: "e-Residency offers to every world citizen a government-issued digital identity and the opportunity to run a trusted company online, unleashing the world's entrepreneurial potential" [6]. Particularly, e-Residency is seen as having potential in making the difference for individuals who are from countries where electronic services for businesses might be lacking, or setting up a business can be time consuming and challenging due to national level bureaucracy. In such cases, e-Residency can be seen as a solution [2].

As the e-Residency project was initiated in 2014, very little research has been conducted on the subject. Furthermore, the adoption of electronic identities in general has not received wide academic attention either especially from a virtual entrepreneurship perspective [3]. To address this gap, this research addresses the following research question: Which are the attributes of e-Residency that virtual entrepreneurs have perceived important during the e-Residency adoption process? To explore the attributes of e-Residency adoption, this paper applies Rogers' [7] Diffusion of Innovations theory (DOI) and conducts a qualitative study of entrepreneurs that have started an online company in Estonia through the e-Residency eID card.

The article is structured as follows. The introduction has presented the background of the article. The second section briefly presents the theoretical background including concepts of virtual entrepreneurship and technology adoption. The third section illustrates the research method and data collection. The fourth question illustrates the results. Finally, the last section presents some concluding remarks.

## 2   Theoretical Background

### 2.1   Virtual Entrepreneurship

Generally entrepreneurship has been distinguished as a major force in the economy on a global scale [8], and it has been recognized in terms of creation of new business enterprises, innovation, introduction of new products or services, and/or entering new markets [8, 9]. Often the term entrepreneurship is also used syn-onymously with start-ups [9].

The Internet can be seen as a new and pioneering area for entrepreneurship [9] as it offers opportunities for "developing new markets where virtual prod-ucts/services are offered in a virtual small business by entrepreneurs" [9]. As a subcategory of entrepreneurship, virtual entrepreneurship can be characterized as "an innovative business practice that enables business opportunities to be detected and seized", which is primarily based on technological innovations [10]. These entrepreneurs are oriented at digitalization of some or all areas of business operations and activities [10]. The activities include seeking for opportunities to implement innovations, such as new internet technologies, to change traditional business practices into e-business models as well as improve and accelerate information exchange [10].

## 2.2   Adoption of Innovation

Rogers' [7] defines an innovation as "an idea, practice, or object that is perceived as new by an individual". Rogers [7] further explains, that the perceived newness of the idea for the individual defines whether something is an innovation or not, rather than the idea being "objectively new as measured by the lapse of time since its first use or discovery". An innovation offers a new alternative as well as completely new means of solving problems for an individual or an organization. As majority of new ideas, which diffusion has been scrutinized, are technological innovations, Rogers often used the word "innovation" and "technology" synonymously [7]. For Rogers, technology consists of two aspects: (1) hardware and (2) software. (1) Hardware is defined as "the tool that embodies the technology in the form of a material or physical object" and (2) software is outlined as "the information base for the tool" [7].

Diffusion is characterized by Rogers' [7] as "the process by which an innovation is communicated through certain channels over time between the members of a social society". In this process, four main elements have been identified, which can be highlighted and analyzed in every innovation diffusion research: (1) the inno-vation, (2) communication channels, (3) time, and (4) the social system [8]. Along with these elements highlighted by Rogers, Xiaojun et al. [11] emphasized the characteristics of the units of adoption as determinant for the diffusion of an IT innovation in particular.

## 2.3   Attributes of Innovation

Attributes of innovation influence the adoption of innovation as they consist of user-perceived qualities or characteristics of new idea [11, 12]. Rogers' [7] outlines five attributes that are relative advantage, compatibility, complexity, observability, and trialability [7, 13]. These five different attributes determine the success of the adoption of the innovation [8], as they have an influence on whether an individual adopts or rejects a particular innovation [13].

**Relative Advantage**. Relative advantage is "the degree to which an innovation is perceived as being better than the idea it supersedes" [7]. Relative advantage is the extent to which a new idea can bring benefits to an individual [13], and is the strongest predictor of the rate of adoption of a new idea [14]. Black et al. [15] describe relative advantage as being essentially domain specific. However, some dimensions of relative advantage have been found to have some degree of generality, such as reduced costs and greater convenience [15].

**Compatibility**. Compatibility is "the degree to which an innovation is perceived as consistent with the existing values, past experiences, and needs of potential adopters" [7]. Rohani and Hussin [13] state that this attribute is referring to the degree to which a new idea is being consistent with existing business practices, processes and value systems. Black et al. [15] as well as Sahin [14] emphasize that the level of compatibility directly influences the rate of adoption.

**Complexity**. Complexity is "the degree to which an innovation is perceived as relatively difficult to understand and use" by an individual [7]. This attribute is negatively related to the adoption of an innovation [15], and thus high level of complexity negatively correlates with the rate of adoption [14].

**Observability**. For Rogers [7] the attribute of observability is "the degree to which the results of an innovation are visible to others". The characteristic of observability is the extent to which a new idea is visible to others in a social system [15]. Furthermore, Black et al. [15] state the following: "the more visible an innovation (and its benefits), the greater the likelihood of adoption, simply because the gains from adoption will be more easily recognized". Therefore, peer observation or role modeling is one of the key motivational elements in the diffusion and adaptation of technology. Hence, observability is positively correlated with the rate of adoption [14].

**Trialability**. Trialability is "the degree to which an innovation may be experienced with on a limited basis" [7]. Black et al. [15] explain trialability as referring to the extent to which a new idea is perceived by an individual as being trialable on a limited ground before any decision to adopt has been done. The opportunity to trial an innovation is an effective mechanism for reducing uncertainty and the perceived risk of adoption. Therefore, similar to relative advantage, compatibility and observability, trialability is positively correlated with the rate of adoption of a new idea [14].

**Perceived Risk**. According to Miltgen [3], the attributes of innovation of Rogers' DOI theory are focusing on key factors of innovation adoption which are mainly measuring perceived advantages of a new technology, except for the attribute of complexity. However, because of novelty, innovation adoption inherently involves a risk [3], and thus an individual has to cope with degrees of uncertainty [7]. For Rogers [7] "uncertainty implies a lack of predictability, of structure, of information". The attribute of perceived risk is applied in the study to complement Rogers' DOI model.

# 3   Research Methods

Rogers' DOI theory can be acknowledged as a middle-range theory [16] as it "organizes a body of findings from replicated studies into a structured system of principles" [16]. In this paper Rogers' DOI serves as a guideline for defining the method. This will be used to (a) adjust the scope for data collection, (b) provide a fundamental chronology for primary data collection, as well as (c) organize the presentation of the findings and the analysis.

The qualitative research method was chosen in accordance to the nature of the object of study [17] to investigate the adoption process of e-Residency. Primary data was collected via interviews complemented with online observation of e-Residency and secondary data.

## 3.1   Data Collection Process and Analysis

The purpose of this section is to report the primary data collection process and analysis, which consists of three steps: (1) finding informants, (2) collecting data, and (3) data analysis.

**Finding Informants**. The first step of data collection began with identifying potential informants according to the following criteria: (a) had obtained e-Residency, and (b) were utilizing, or had intentions to utilize e-Residency for entrepreneurial purposes in Estonia. Potential informants were contacted through a Facebook group called 'Estonian e-Residents' by posting an invitation to the group's wall to take part in the research. The inquiry for informants in the Facebook group shortly explained the topic of the research as well as the criteria for participation described above.

**Collecting Data**. The primary data consisted of data collected via interviews as well as a web-based questionnaire. Before each interview session, the informants were requested to fill in a web-questionnaire which consisted of questions regarding their background. The background questions were decided to be separated from the interviews as to save more time for discussing the main object of study.

A total of seven interviews were conducted between December 2015 and February 2016 via Skype as the informants were geographically dispersed. Due to that reason the option such as personal interviewing was not considered any further. The informants represented different backgrounds and relations to the innovation, which allowed to understand the possible circumstances in the adoption process of e-Residency for entrepreneurial purposes in order to be able to identify and select the most relevant and critical factors for the study. Due to this and the in-depth nature of the interviews consisting of different themes around the topic of e-Residency, the amount of material collected from the seven informants was found adequate for the study.

**Data Analysis**. Each of the seven interviews lasted for approximately one hour and were recorded with a voice recorder. After their completion, the content of the recorded material was transcribed verbatim. The transcription of the interview material took place in parallel to data collection. The analysis of data was conducted according to Elo and Kyngäs' [18] three stages: (1) preparation, (2) organizing, and (3) reporting. At the preparation phase, the transcripts were read through several times to make sense of it as a whole [18]. The purpose with the analysis was not to conduct a line-by-line microanalysis of the data [17]. Strauss and Corbin [17] referred to such a coding method as open coding, in which the transcripts are perused and broad questions are raised, such as "what is going on here?" and "what makes this document the same as, or different from, the previous ones that I coded?" Therefore, at the organizing phase, sentences and paragraphs which were found essential for the study were selected for further inspection [18]. These selected parts of the data were analyzed and included to the presentation of the findings.

# 4   Analysis and Results: Perceived Attributes of e-Residency

## 4.1   Relative Advantage

In the initial stages of the adoption process the informants began to form a perception of the advantages in terms of the value that the adoption of e-Residency could potentially bring to them. The perceived relative advantages of e-Residency for the informants concerned mostly business related benefits such as an opportunity and means of managing an existing business in Estonia, to establish a new company, or to relocate an existing business to Estonia from outside Europe. Especially the informants located outside Europe saw e-Residency as a portal for establishing a business in Europe. These mentioned factors are consistent with the messages generally conveyed about the advantages of e-Residency [6, 19].

**Start-up and Maintenance Costs**. The topic of costs in relation to establishing a company in Estonia arose during the interview sessions among the informants regardless of which stage they were in the adoption process. The narratives on start-up and maintenance costs for a company consisted mainly of costs of virtual office providers. These perceptions varied among the informants, although the majority of the informants found the costs of services of virtual office providers reasonable and even cheaper compared to other countries in Europe. This was seen as beneficial for adopting e-Residency for entrepreneurial purposes as illustrated for instance by the statement of informant G:

> Compared to other locations … I think that the start-ups costs in Estonia are a lot lower than start-up costs in other countries (informant G).

Furthermore, the data suggests that the variations in perspectives concerning the costs among the informants can be seen influenced by the background of the unit of adoption. For instance, the perspectives could be explained by prior knowledge of the international scenery for start-ups, or the sociocultural context of the informant. It is acknowledgeable that an evaluation of a cost-benefit ratio and the perceived value is relational and should be considered critically as these perspectives may vary among the adopters due to their characteristics and prior conditions. For instance, the perspectives may vary among the units of adoption due to the standards and costs of living in the country they are residing. However, the data collected for the study does not allow to draw further arguments and generalizations on the matter. Such heterogeneity among the unit of adoption can lead to an uneven diffusion of e-Residency across countries with different economic, social and political environments, as argued by Zhu and Kraemer [20] in their study on diffusion of e-business. Therefore, it is suggested that the variations in perspectives could be possibly explained by sociocultural factors and prior conditions of the units of adoption. However, it would require more specific inspection on the units of analysis in a larger sample in order to be able to more solidly explain the variations among the perceptions based on the prior conditions and the characteristics of the adopters.

**Estonian Tax System**. The informants, who were at the latter phases of the adoption process, brought up the issue of taxation for business within the Estonian legal framework. These informants found the tax system beneficial for the type of businesses they were practicing, or were about to establish. The types of businesses mentioned were e-commerce, consulting and IT services. Without entering a detailed description of the Estonian tax system, the informants found favorable and support-ing that there is no tax on corporate income, as stated by informant G for in-stance:

> I like the fact that in Estonia they tax only the distributed profits ... I found it very good for my business (Informant G).

Taxation can be perceived as external driving force for the adoption of e-Residency, as it concerns the operational environment for businesses in Estonia, and thus it is not directly involved with the innovation itself.

**Time Efficiency and Flexibility**. Besides the perceptions on costs and legal framework, the fact that most of the adoption process as well as the post-adoption phases could be performed remotely online was perceived as time efficient and flexible. For example, informant A, with no previous entrepreneurial background, explains that simultaneously as becoming an entrepreneur by utilizing e-Residency to establish a company in Estonia, he is able to focus on other activities where he is physically residing. Informant A also exemplified how he approached the adoption of e-Residency as a learning process on how to establish and administer a company. The aspect of learning was also mentioned by Frølunde et al. [8] as a driver of getting involved in activities related to international entrepreneurship. Time efficiency and flexibility together with the perceptions of rather low start-up costs indicatively supported the motivation to learn and/or to approach the adoption of e-Residency as an opportunity to learn.

**Credential Status**. E-Residency was approached as a governmentally issued digital identity document, for what certain personal information and biometrics are required to be disclosed as a part of the application procedure. Furthermore, Estonian government was approached as a "trustable ID provider" (informant C). Disclosing the information as a part of the application process was found reasonable and also beneficial. Especially the background check procedure based on the disclosed information was seen as establishing a status of reliability and authenticity in digital identification as well as a credential of a noncriminal background. Such a credential status was further viewed as favorable when practicing international business. Therefore, credential status building can be seen as a motivational factor for obtaining e-Residency [8].

## 4.2   Compatibility

**Felt Needs**. According to the data, e-Residency was found to be consistent with existing entrepreneurial practices as well as to correspond with the felt needs of the adopters. The felt needs among the informants were commonly business related. This meant that they already had a business in Estonia, or they were already considering of establishing a business before learning about e-Residency and were looking for options of conducting business in and outside the country of residence. The considerations of starting a business outside their country of residence included seeking for methods and options among different countries. This can be further seen as suggesting some degree of familiarity with notions in relation to international entrepreneurship and location-independency, which are also embedded to the concept of e-Residency, as the activity of looking for new opportunities business-wise was not limited to any national borders specifically [21].

E-Residency can be seen as an opportunity that responds to the needs of the in-formants. In Rogers' [7] terms—a need preceded awareness-knowledge of the innovation. As such, the probability of satisfying one's own needs with the innovation can be seen as a motivation for applying for e-Residency, and thus getting involved with the activities related to it [8]. The following quote demonstrate the felt needs of informant B, which are thus explaining motivations for the adoption decision:

> I already have two start-ups in India… target market is in Europe … that pushed me to apply for the e-Residency card (informant B).

On the contrary, some of the informants seemed to attach some notions of physicality to the concept of e-Residency, such as intentions or thoughts of having a physical office in Estonia and/or physically residing in the country. This does not proclaim that these informants had not understood the nature of the innovation as not entailing for physical residency or right of entry to the country [22]. Rather, the idea of e-Residency was found to inspire ideas about the innovation as a medium or an enhancement which could lead to a situation where the unit of adoption had the possibility to entail rights to entry or reside in the country. For instance, this can be illustrated with a statement of informant B, who asserts the following reasoning for the notion of physicality attached to adopting e-Residency for entrepreneurial purposes:

> A physical presence is a must for any business (informant B).

**Experience with ICT**. Although this research did not particularly measure the familiarity and experience of the units of adoption with e-Residency, the data suggested a degree of compatibility with ICT among the informants. This became apparent in the narratives as some of the informants described that they had professional backgrounds in IT, which indicates for competency in ICT in general. The competence with ICT can enhance the initiation of usage of the innovation. Furthermore, as e-Residency is approached as a technological innovation, understanding the nature of the innovation and its features as well as using it can be seen as influenced by this dimension of the attribute, and thus drive the adoption process. Informant E, for instance, stated the following, which illustrates the compatibility of the unit of adoption in relation to ICT:

> I'm well enough versed in computed technology to know that a chip and pin card going through an x-road where you got independent safety and security and all of the different silos, I can get into the police system in Estonia, I can get into the medical records (informant E).

## 4.3   Trialability

The unit of adoption cannot concretely try e-Residency prior to obtaining it, i.e. log in with the eID card to the Estonian e-Government systems. Instead, in order to internalize its meaning and value prior to adoption, trialability of e-Residency is highly dependent on the available information about it from the channels of communication: the official sources, media, social media as well as interpersonal channels. Through the content of these communication channels, e-Residency can be experienced on a limited basis, which contains some degree of demonstration of how it can be utilized and what procedures are required in order to meet with the anticipated consequences. This was evident from the narratives that the informants did search for information about it in order to be able to conceptualize the concept of e-Residency the best they could and how it could be used before making the decision to apply for it. Some of the informants found that there was a limited amount of information on e-Residency at the early phases of the adoption process. Depending on the time of learning about e-Residency, some of the informants acknowledged that the available information regarding e-Residency has been certainly improved since their initial stages of the adoption process. The official website of e-Residency (www.e-estonia.com/e-residents) evidently has a crucial role as an official source of information as it was often referred to by the informants. The official website was found to be if not the first then one of the first sources to seek information from, although, the narratives are suggesting that the information from this channel was not adequate enough. Therefore, the adopters had the need to search information from other, unofficial sources in order to create a complete understanding of the innovation, especially in regards to the implementation, as exemplified by informant C by stating:

> First checked the e-Residency site … well nothing much there, just marketing I suppose. I joined the Facebook group, and there were somewhat clear points what do you have to do in real life when founding a company (informant C).

This indicates that one source was insufficient to experience and understand the idea of e-Residency. Therefore, media posts, social media and blogposts were found to play a role as well, indicating the importance of the evaluations of near-peers— individuals who have already adopted the innovation [7, 23]. The combinations of different sources of information were also sought to assure that the concept of e-Residency was correctly understood. The issues related to quality of the information as well as the reliability of the source regarding e-Residency was also raised in the data. Informant D suggests that although near-peers can be perceived as an important source of information, this information from the near-peers through social media should be treated with some particular concern regarding its accuracy. Due to the perceived newness and the level of complexity involved in comprehending the concept of e-Residency, the reliability of the channels of communication is in important role to avoid and correct misunderstandings.

## 4.4 Complexity

According to the informants, the concept of e-Residency and relative features can be perceived as entailing different levels of complexity. As exemplified in the quote below, informant F describes how he somewhat understood what e-Residency is about based on the initial channel of communication, although more comprehensive picture of the innovation came later on:

> The first time I really didn't understand what it was and what was the impact of it, but after a while I saw it was much more than something I can use to make some income (informant F).

The data illustrated that e-Residency can be rather difficult to comprehend and further effort in seeking and interpreting information is required. Therefore, the comprehension and internalization of the idea can be time-consuming. This is in line with Laukkanen et al. [24], as they argued that especially the adoption of technological innovations requires considerable learning effort, which thus involves willingness and ability to learn and acquire knowledge. The level of complexity perceived by the units of adoption can be seen to be connected with the prior conditions of the adopter and the perceived compatibility with the innovation, such as the level of compatibility with ICT. This can be especially the case when all the features of the innovation are not already familiar to the unit of adoption, such as electronic signatures for instance. Understanding the features of e-Residency equals internalizing the value of the innovation, which thus can be the final key to drive the prospective adopter to apply for e-Residency. The challenge to understand the value of e-Residency can thus have influence on the rate of adoption—prolonging the innovation-decision process. The issue with complexity can be also related to the attribute of trialability and the matters related to information about e-Residency. The combination of the two attributes can be identified as a barrier in the adoption process, although it is left questionable, whether it is an issue with the way of transmitting and/or the content of a message, or the prior condition of the unit of adoption.

## 4.5 Perceived Risk

The attribute of perceived risk refers to perceived uncertainty attached to the adoption of the innovation [25]. In our study, the perceived risk mainly implies a lack of predictability with the implementation of e-Residency for entrepreneurial purposes. In other words, the act of obtaining e-Residency does not guarantee that the unit of adoption will complete the adoption process as the barriers involved particularly in the implementation of the innovation may hinder or even cause a discontinuance to the process. Therefore, the unit of adoption encounters a risk consisting of potential undesirable results when adopting e-Residency.

**Information Regulating Levels of Uncertainty**. According to the narratives, some degrees of uncertainty correlates with the available information regarding e-Residency. The informants who were found to be more thorough and involved in seeking and interpreting information about e-Residency prior the application expressed that they had an adequate amount of information regarding the innovation which reduced the perceived uncertainties. On the contrary, similar to the attribute of complexity, the narratives also suggested that there can be identified a lack of information regarding the implementation of the innovation for entrepreneurial purposes. This lack of information creates uncertainty, and thus increases the perceived risks when applying for e-Residency while not completely comprehending the concept, the ways of utilizing the innovation and thus gaining value. Regardless of the experienced lack of information, the informants had applied for e-Residency. The informants with entrepreneurial needs, curiosity and willingness to accept new and even uncertain ideas had the driving characteristics to encounter the risks related to the adoption of e-Residency.

**Attitudes Towards a Risk of Personal Data Violation**. The informants were also inquired whether they had any concerns in relation to a risk of privacy or security violations in regard to disclosing their personal information as a part of the application for e-Residency. The informants found it reasonable to disclose personal information and biometrics as a part of the application procedure, which is an indication of a lower level of risk perception [3]. The informants expressed of not having particular high risk perceptions of their personal information getting into wrong hands. This suggests a confidence in security and trust towards the innovation. However, risks attached to the establishment of a digital identity in the form of a threat of prospective misusage were acknowledged, for instance, by informant F in the following statement:

> Because I have it, I have one more way to be hacked, I have one more piece of identity so I have one more way to be stolen that… Sure it's a risk, I did think about it a bit I mean there is much more benefits that there is risk (informant F).

**Lack of Know-how**. Another dimension influencing the degree of uncertainty found in the data was the perceived lack of know-how of the units of adoption in relation to implementing the innovation. The backgrounds of the informants regarding their experience and knowledge of starting and managing a business influenced the perceived uncertainty regarding the adoption of e-Residency. The informants with no previous entrepreneurial background expressed of having uncertainties in regards to the implementation phase.

## 5   Conclusions

By applying Rogers' Diffusion of Innovation theory, this paper has contributed to the existing literature on innovation diffusion and e-services by providing insights on the e-Residency attributes that facilitate or hinder its adoption process for business related purposes. The findings show that the application procedure for e-Residency can be characterized as a rather simple and straightforward procedure, and that most of the complications occur during the implementation of the innovation. This is an illustration of what was argued by Rogers [7]: it is a different thing to decide to adopt an innovation, and actually use it. This research confirms what was found by Kerikmäe and Särav [5] that since the introduction of e-Residency, the scheme has been encountering obstructions due to lack of thorough judgement and "harmonization between the legal, administrative and policy capacities". Moreover, the findings can be seen as a further refinement of Kerikmäe and Särav's [5] findings by providing insight about how these attributes are perceived from the users' point of view, and how they influence the adoption process of e-Residency. Therefore, the main lesson that can be learned from the study is the importance of harmonization of the legal, administrative and information policy capacities in launching new e-services, especially at e-government level.

However, this study presents a number of limitations. The qualitative nature and relatively little number of interviews make it difficult to generalize the results. In addition, this study partially corroborates previous studies' results such as using e-Residency to create a virtual team of consultants geographically dispersed, but with a common virtual residency as suggested by Matlay and Westhead [1]. Future research could therefore replicate the same study with a bigger number of interviews, conduct a survey among e-Residency adopters or focus on replicating other studies such as Matlay and Westhead [1].

# References

1. Matlay, H., & Westhead, P. (2005). Virtual teams and the rise of e-Entrepreneurship in Europe. *International Small Business Journal, 23*(3), 279–302. https://doi.org/10.1177/0266242605052074.
2. Kotka, T., Castillo, C., & Korjus, K. (2015). *Estonian e-Residency: Redefining the nation-state in the digital era*. In: Working Paper Series, no. 3. Oxford: Oxford University.
3. Miltgen C (2010, May) Adoption of new identity-based services: Proposition of a conceptual model based on TAM, DOI and perceived risks. *Congrès International de l'AIM*, La Rochelle, 1.
4. Sullivan, C. (2014). *Digital identity's new frontier: The political, economic, and legal ramifications of Estonian e-Residency*. In: Georgetown Journal of International Fairs. The Edmund A. Walsh School of Foreign Service. Georgetown University. http://journal.georgetown.edu/digital-identitys-new-frontier-the-political-economic-and-legal-ramifications-of-estonian-e-residency/.
5. Kerikmäe, T., & Särav, S. (2015). Legal Impediments in the EU to New technologies in the Example of E-Residency. *Baltic Journal of Law & Politics, 8*(2), 71–90. https://doi.org/10.1515/bjlp-2015-0019.
6. Estonian e-Residency: About. e-Estonia. https://e-estonia.com/e-residents/about/.
7. Rogers, E. M. (2003). *Diffusion of innovations* (5th ed., pp. 6, 15, 16, 37, 229, 259). New York: Free Press.
8. Frølunde, L., Teigland, R., & Flåten, B.-T. (2011). *Final scientific/expert report on virtual world entrepreneurship: A look at entrepreneurs in the Nordic Region exploring the use of virtual worlds for entrepreneurial activity*. Nordic VW Network 09045, Nordic Innovation, Oslo.
9. Frølunde, L., & Flåten, B.-T. (2011). *Selection of best entrepreneurship practices in relation to the emerging 3D Internet, Nordic VW Network Project 09045* (p. 9). Oslo: Nordic Innovation.
10. Jelonek, L. (2015). The role of open innovations in the development of e-entrepreneurship. *Procedia Computer Science, 65*, 1014.
11. Xiaojun, Z., Ping, Y., Jun, Y., & Spil, A. M. (2015). Using diffusion of innovation theory to understand the factors impacting patient acceptance and use of consumer e-health innovations: A case study in a primary care clinic. *BMC Health Services Research, 15*(1), 1–15. https://doi.org/10.1186/s12913-015-0726-2.
12. Dearing, J. W. (2009). Applying diffusion of innovation theory to intervention development. *Research on Social Work Practice, 19*(5), 503–518. https://doi.org/10.1177/1049731509335569.
13. Rohani, M. B., & Hussin, A. R. C. (2015). An integrated theoretical framework for cloud computing adoption by universities Technology Transfer Offices (TTOs). *Journal of Theoretical and Applied Information Technology, 79*(3), 415–430.
14. Sahin, I. (2006). Detailed Review of Rogers' diffusion of innovations theory and educational technology-related studies based on Rogers' theory. *TOJET: The Turkish Online Journal of Educational Technology, 5*(2).
15. Black, N. J., Lockett, A., Winklhofer, H., & Ennew, C. (2001). The adoption of internet financial services: A qualitative study. *International Journal of Retail & Distribution Management, 29*(8), 390–392.

16. Roman, R. (2003). Diffusion of innovations as a theoretical framework for telecenters. *Information Technologies & International Development, 1*(2), 55.
17. Strauss, A., & Corbin, J. (1998). *Basics of qualitative research: Techniques and procedures for developing grounded theory* (2nd ed., p. 120). Thousand Oaks, California: Sage Publications, Inc.
18. Elo, S., & Kyngäs, H. (2008). The qualitative content analysis process. *Journal of Advanced Nursing, 62*(1), 107–115. https://doi.org/10.1111/j.1365-2648.2007.04569.x.
19. Estonian e-Residency. e-Estonia. https://e-estonia.com/e-residents/welcome/.
20. Zhu, K., & Kraemer, K. L. (2005). Post-adoption variations in usage and value of e-business by organizations: Cross-country evidence from the retail industry. *Information Systems Research, 16*(1), 61–84.
21. McDougall, P. P., & Oviatt, B. M. (2000). International entrepreneurship: The intersection of two research paths. *The Academy of Management Journal, 43*(5), 902–906. http://www.jstor.org/stable/1556418.
22. eGovernment in Estonia. (2015). Edition 17.0, European Commission, ISA Editorial Team, Kurt Salmon S.A.
23. Murray, C. E. (2009). Diffusion of innovation theory: A bridge for the research-practice gap in counseling. *Journal of Counseling & Development, 87*, 108–116. https://doi.org/10.1002/j.1556-6678.2009.tb00556.x.
24. Laukkanen, T., Sinkkonen, S., Laukkanen, P. (2007). Information as a barrier to innovation adoption. In: *Proceedings of the Australian and New Zealand Marketing Academy Conference, Dunedin*, New Zealand, December 3–5, 2007. http://www.anzmac.org/conference_archive/2007/papers/T%20Laukkanen_1a.pdf.
25. Al-Jabri, I., & Sohail, M. S. (2012). Mobile banking adoption: Application of diffusion of innovation theory. *Journal of Electronic Commerce Research, 13*(4), 379–391.

# Stakeholder Accountability Through the World Wide Web: Insights from Nonprofits

**Gina Rossi⬭, Sara Moggi⬭, Paul Pierce⬭ and Chiara Leardini⬭**

**Abstract** Accountability to stakeholders has always been pivotal in supporting nonprofit organizations in legitimizing their existence within local communities and building public trust. The development of Web-based accountability tools has offered growing possibilities to communicate and engage in dialogue with stakeholders. However, nonprofit organizations are not yet fully exploiting the potential of the Web. By focusing on Italian bank foundations, this study explores the use of the Web as a tool for discharging accounts to stakeholders and involving them in dialogue. The data show that most of the foundations do not use websites to communicate interactively with their stakeholders, and communication is limited to one-way disclosure of information. The results suggest more steps can be taken to ensure increased responsiveness to community needs.

**Keywords** Accountability · Web disclosure · Stakeholder engagement
Foundations

## 1 Introduction

There is general agreement within the literature that accountability practices based on a continuing dialogue and exchange of views with stakeholders are essential for legitimizing nonprofit organizations (NPOs) [1]. As NPOs must account for how

G. Rossi (✉)
University of Udine, Udine, Italy
e-mail: gina.rossi@uniud.it

S. Moggi · C. Leardini
University of Verona, Verona, Italy
e-mail: sara.moggi@univr.it

C. Leardini
e-mail: chiara.leardini@univr.it

P. Pierce
Lund University, Lund, Sweden
e-mail: paul.pierce@ics.lu.se

© Springer International Publishing AG, part of Springer Nature 2018
R. Lamboglia et al. (eds.), *Network, Smart and Open*, Lecture Notes in Information
Systems and Organisation 24, https://doi.org/10.1007/978-3-319-62636-9_6

they provide public benefits and meet stakeholders' needs, they need to renew their accountability practices on an ongoing basis to make sure they are appropriate and effective [2]. New information technologies can help NPOs pursue this goal.

The diffusion of the Internet has deeply changed how NPOs relate to and communicate with a wide range of stakeholders at limited cost [3, 4]. Several studies have examined the potential of the Web in providing accounts to multiple stakeholders and engaging them in dialogue for building public trust [3–6]. What has emerged is that the Web has become both the public face of NPOs and a tool for managing inclusive and intense public relations [6].

Despite the large amount of literature on these issues, little remains known about how European NPOs use the 'dialogic potential of the Internet' [4]. Aiming to fill this gap, our study focuses on Italian bank foundations (IBFs) and explores how they use the Web to communicate and interact with their communities. IBFs are a particular type of community-based NPO born from the privatization of community-owned public savings banks. Their mission is to provide grants or realize their own projects that foster the welfare of the community in which they are rooted [7]. Therefore, the local community is one of the most salient recipients of IBFs' accountability.

Recently, IBFs have been affected by a significant change. At the beginning of 2015, an agreement signed by the Ministry for Economic and Financial Affairs (MEF) and the Association of Italian Foundations and Savings Banks (ACRI) clearly defined the Web-disclosure principles that IBFs have to follow in engaging stakeholders. This agreement (hereafter referred to as the 'ACRI-MEF agreement') encouraged foundations to use their websites to inform the local community about their philanthropic activities. Moving from the need to strengthen public confidence and trust through greater transparency in decision-making processes, the ACRI-MEF recommendations depicted the IBFs' websites as mirrors of these organizations that community members can easily access at any time.

Through descriptive statistics, this study analyses which kinds of information IBFs provide through their websites, distinguishing between general information on the foundations' life and activities, reporting to stakeholders and links to social media. The results contribute to a better understanding of IBFs' Web-based accountability practices, providing insights into stakeholders' involvement in dialogic activities and how this can differ depending on foundation size.

The remainder of this study is structured as follows. In the next section, an overview of the nonprofit literature on the use of the Web for accountability purposes is provided. The methodology section underlines the main features of the data collection and data analysis carried out, and the results section describes the main Web-based accountability practices recently employed by IBFs. Finally, a discussion of the results and conclusions are presented to underline the role of Web-based accountability in enhancing legitimacy and trust.

## 2 Accountability for Stakeholders Through the Web

The nonprofit literature strongly highlights the importance of NPOs legitimizing their existence and increasing public trust and confidence by effectively demonstrating how they provide public benefit to their communities [2, 8, 9]. Accountability is 'a duty—sometimes empirical (typically legal), sometimes moral—and it arises from the responsibility that individuals and organisations have to provide "accounts" of their activities. The accountable entity is typically subject to two responsibilities: the responsibility to act; and the responsibility to provide an account of those actions (these may be synonymous)' [10]. In this sense, NPOs' accountability to constituents is considered essential for demonstrating that strategic-level decisions accord with stakeholders' needs [11, 12] and for providing signals of good housekeeping [13].

As NPOs are democratic organizations serving a community [14], there has been a growing call for dialogue-based accountability [15] with greater inclusion of community representatives in organizational activities. However, accountability to the community is usually limited to one-way communication mechanisms, in which information about financial and social performance flows from the organization to the stakeholders without feedback [16]. Further, it is important to remember that non-accountability is in itself a mirror of what organizations decide to (or not to) communicate [17].

The rapid diffusion of Internet-based technologies among NPOs has revealed considerable potential for more diffused and involving accountability practices, but this potential has not been completely exploited [18]. Several studies have examined the role of the Web in supporting nonprofit accountability. According to Kent and Taylor [19], a website responsive to stakeholders' information needs should be easy to interface with, provide useful information and be attractive to generate return visits. Additionally, it should allow feedback from the audience by creating a 'dialogic loop' [19] that offers organizations the opportunity to respond to the public's questions, concerns and problems.

Empirical research has highlighted that NPOs use the Web to discharge accountability by informing stakeholders about who they are and what they do. This use depends on the availability of financial resources, the attitude to Web disclosure and the compatibility of this disclosure with current organizational practices [9]. However, NPOs are still behind in using the Web to engage stakeholders in dialogue through interactive and relational communications.

In a study on how large United States (US) NPOs use the Web to accomplish organizational goals, Kang and Norton [3] found that websites usually presented traditional public relations materials, such as information about organizational history, mission, performance and services delivered to beneficiaries. Only a few websites provided interactivity functions for requesting information and providing feedback, such as discussion forums, chat rooms, online polls and surveys. As so few NPOs websites provide such opportunities, this represents a failure on NPOs' role to create a dialogic loop with the public [3].

Similar results characterize Ingenhoff and Koelling's study [4] on the potential of websites to be used as online-communication tools for Swiss charities. Although most of these organizations acknowledged the importance of engaging stakeholders in dialogue, they did not use the Internet efficiently for two-way communication purposes. Information for the public was provided through annual reports, mission statements, organizational history and other information concerning organizational activities, while interaction with stakeholders was usually limited to general contact information or forms.

Recent studies have revealed that even the use of social media by NPOs did not significantly enhance interaction with stakeholders. For example, Lovejoy et al. [20] highlighted that NPOs primarily use Twitter to relay information using it as a one-way communication method.

In an effort to conceptualize and operationalize Web-based accountability practices in NPOs, Saxton and Guo [5] proposed a theoretical framework based on two core dimensions of online accountability: disclosure and dialogue. The first dimension concerns the transparent provision of financial and performance information to stakeholders, while the second relates to the solicitation of input from stakeholders and their interactive engagement. By testing the framework on US community foundations, the authors found websites were used mostly for providing disclosures on organizational performance, while they lacked mechanisms for engaging in dialogue with stakeholders, thus confirming that NPOs are failing to maximize the opportunities offered by the Web to engage with stakeholders.

One reason for this failure is the limited technological capacity of NPOs to develop and implement these kinds of tools [3]. According to Lee and Bhattacherjee [21], this failure is often linked to organizational size and the availability of financial resources. They observed that a digital divide separates large NPOs with more assets from small and micro NPOs, producing inequalities between organizations that can use the Web to advance their mission and those that cannot. This assumption was confirmed by Ingenhoff and Koelling [4], who found that the capacity to develop interactive communication with stakeholders is greater for large NPOs. Similarly, Saxton and Guo [5] found that the asset size is one of the most significant factors in the adoption of both disclosure and dialogue Web-based accountability practices, thus confirming that resources matter.

The Web's potential as a tool for responding to stakeholders' information needs is also affected by the extent to which organizations depend on the public to accomplish their mission. According to Kent et al. [22], membership-based NPOs employ more dialogic principles in constructing their websites, because they need to solicit, consider and adjust to stakeholder feedback for achieving their goals.

Moreover, since websites are not optimally designed for all potential users, the amount of information provided and the level of interaction they allow depend on the salience of the stakeholders targeted by the organizations as the main recipients of their communication efforts [18]. The more managerial attention given to specific stakeholder groups, the greater and more interactive the content addressed to them [6].

# 3   Methodology

With the aim to investigate how NPOs use the Web for supporting accountability practices, this research focuses on IBFs, a particular kind of Italian NPO recently called on to better exploit the Web's potential for communicating to and engaging with local stakeholders.

Content analysis [23] of the websites of the 87 IBFs operating in Italy in March 2016 was undertaken to better understand what kind of information is provided online, distinguishing between general information on the foundations' life and activities, reporting to stakeholders and links to social media.

A team of three researchers defined the list of codes following the categories (and sub-categories) of Web-based accountability tools proposed by the ACRI-MEF agreement, as integrated by the literature on online accountability. Table 1 presents the coding rules followed for each category and sub-category.

**Table 1**   Coding rules

| Category | Coding rule |
| --- | --- |
| *General information* | Pool of information provided on the foundation's life and activities |
| Mission | The foundation's long-term aims |
| History | Description of the foundation's history |
| Investment policies | Policies on asset investments |
| Grant-making policies | Policies related to the disbursement of grants in order to respond to community needs |
| Guidelines | General rules to follow in disbursing grants |
| Announcements | Announcements on funding disbursements and instructions on how to submit applications |
| *Reporting to stakeholders* | Documents available to report the foundation's activities |
| Strategic planning | Programmatic document explaining the foundation's long-term goals and polices to achieve them |
| Financial statement | Formal accounts for the results achieved during the past year through asset management and grant-making activities |
| Mission report | Stand-alone report accounting for the achievement of the foundation's aims |
| Social report | Social accounting tools providing social, environmental and economic information to stakeholders |
| Integrated report | Document integrating financial information with the social and environmental impacts of the foundation's performance |
| Code of ethics | Code describing the correct behaviour the foundation has to follow |
| *Social media* | Web based/online tools that allow foundations to share information and ideas |
| Facebook Twitter YouTube Google+ Pinterest Instagram | Different types of social media detected |

**Table 2** Number of IBFs by size

| Size | Large | Medium-large | Medium | Medium-small | Small | Total |
|------|-------|--------------|--------|--------------|-------|-------|
| N. of IBFs | 18 | 17 | 17 | 17 | 18 | 87 |

Clear definition of the coding rules enhances the content analysis reliability. The analysis was carried out by two researchers, and, in case of disagreement, a third researcher was called on to resolve the discrepancy in data collection.

Since the availability of financial resources is one of the most significant factors affecting Web-based accountability practices in NPOs [5], a more in-depth analysis of the results considered IBFs by their size (see Table 2). The classification has been realized by considering the amount of net assets. According to the ACRI [24], five groups of IBFs of similar size have been identified using the criterion of statistical quintiles.

# 4 Results

To describe the Web-based accountability practices of the 87 IBFs better, the results consider separately information provision on the foundations' life and activities, the presence of reports describing foundations' social and financial performance and the existence of links to social media.

## 4.1 Information on NPOs' Life and Activities

IBFs use websites to provide stakeholders with general information on their history, mission, investment and grant-making policies; for describing the guidelines they follow in disbursing grants; and for publishing announcements to beneficiaries calling for project submissions.

As shown in Fig. 1, information on grant-making policies is the most diffused on websites (76 out of 87 IBFs), followed by a usually detailed history of the organization that retraces its origins and evolution over time and shows how much the foundation is rooted in the local community (59). Information on announcements to beneficiaries aimed at soliciting proposals also appears quite frequently (41). Information about organizational mission (32), guidelines (12) and investment policies (6) is diffused less.

Considering IBFs by asset size (see Table 3), the results show that the Web is used in quite similar ways by foundations to provide general information. Although small foundations usually appear less active than larger ones, there are few remarkable differences; those that do exist mostly concern guideline disclosures and announcements. Information on investment policies does not appear on the

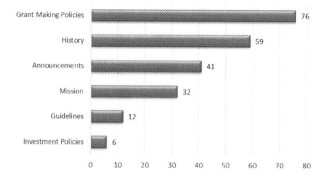

**Fig. 1** General information provided on the websites

**Table 3** Number and percentage of IBFs providing general information by asset size

| IBF Size | Mission | | History | | Investment policies | | Grant-Making policies | | Guidelines | | Announcements | |
|---|---|---|---|---|---|---|---|---|---|---|---|---|
| | N | % | N | % | N | % | N | % | N | % | N | % |
| Large | 6 | 33.33 | 11 | 61.11 | 3 | 16.67 | 15 | 83.33 | 4 | 22.22 | 11 | 61.11 |
| Medium-large | 10 | 58.82 | 12 | 70.59 | 2 | 11.76 | 14 | 82.35 | 3 | 17.65 | 8 | 47.06 |
| Medium | 4 | 23.53 | 12 | 70.59 | 1 | 5.88 | 16 | 94.12 | 3 | 17.65 | 9 | 52.94 |
| Medium-small | 6 | 35.29 | 13 | 76.47 | 0 | 0 | 16 | 94.12 | 1 | 5.88 | 9 | 42.94 |
| Small | 6 | 33.33 | 11 | 61.11 | 0 | 0 | 15 | 83.33 | 1 | 5.55 | 4 | 22.22 |
| Total | 32 | | 59 | | 6 | | 76 | | 12 | | 41 | |

websites of small IBFs. Conversely, the attention paid to informing stakeholders about the foundation's history, mission and grant-making-activity policies is very similar between foundations of all sizes.

## 4.2 Reporting to Stakeholders

IBFs usually communicate with their stakeholders by providing reports illustrating how they carry out their organizational activities. Some of these documents are required by law, while others are optional though recommended by the ACRI.

As highlighted in Fig. 2, the report most diffused on IBFs' websites is the financial statement (85 out of 87 IBFs). This report accounts for the results achieved through the organization's asset management and grant-making activities during the past year. Since the preparation and presentation of this report is mandatory by law, this document is readily accessible online.

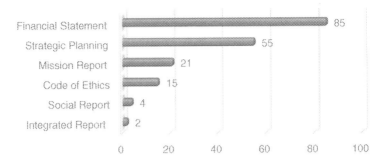

**Fig. 2** Reports provided on IBFs' websites

Strategic-planning documents providing accounts of how IBFs formalize their strategies through action plans are widely disclosed on voluntary bases (55). These documents identify long-term goals and polices to achieve them, areas of intervention, and funds expected to be employed in asset management and grant-making activities.

Less diffused is the stand-alone mission report. IBFs usually provide information on their mission and its achievement within a dedicated section of their financial statement. However, 21 out of 87 foundations have voluntarily prepared a separate document reporting on their grant-making activities and the use of financial resources.

Codes of ethics are presented on a few websites (15), while social reports (4) and integrated reports (2), as voluntary social accounting tools, are sporadic.

The analysis of Web-based reporting practices by IBF size (see Table 4) shows that medium-large foundations are the more active users of the Web. Compared with foundations of other sizes, they more frequently disclose information on strategic plans, mission, and social and integrated reports. Although social accountability is generally weak irrespective of organizational size, it is interesting to observe that small and medium-small foundations do not use the Web at all for presenting social and integrated reports. The attention paid to providing codes of ethics online is extremely differentiated among IBFs and not apparently linked to IBF size.

**Table 4** Number and percentage of IBFs providing reports by asset size

| IBF Size | Strategic planning | | Financial statement | | Mission report | | Social report | | Integrated report | | Code of ethics | |
|---|---|---|---|---|---|---|---|---|---|---|---|---|
| | N | % | N | % | N | % | N | % | N | % | N | % |
| Large | 12 | 66.67 | 18 | 100.00 | 6 | 33.33 | 1 | 5.55 | 0 | 0 | 6 | 33.33 |
| Medium-large | 13 | 76.47 | 17 | 100.00 | 6 | 35.29 | 2 | 11.76 | 1 | 5.88 | 3 | 17.65 |
| Medium | 12 | 70.59 | 16 | 94.12 | 5 | 29.41 | 1 | 5.88 | 1 | 5.88 | 2 | 11.76 |
| Medium-small | 8 | 47.06 | 16 | 94.12 | 2 | 11.76 | 0 | 0 | 0 | 0 | 0 | 0 |
| Small | 10 | 55.55 | 18 | 100.00 | 2 | 11.11 | 0 | 0 | 0 | 0 | 4 | 22.22 |
| Total | 55 | | 85 | | 21 | | 4 | | 2 | | 15 | |

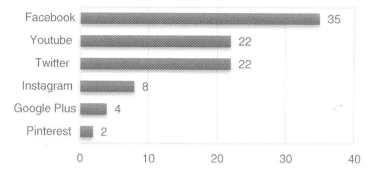

**Fig. 3** Links to social media on IBF websites

## 4.3 Social Media

IBF websites can also present links to social media for interacting more actively with their communities and providing them with the opportunity to raise questions and provide feedback. As shown in Fig. 3, the most common social media linked to on the foundations' websites are Facebook, Twitter and YouTube, with links to other social media quite sporadic.

Since more than 50% of IBFs do not link to any social media on their websites (see Table 5), social networking seems scarcely diffused in this NPO context. However, the data show that most of the foundations employing social media use more than one to engage in dialogue with stakeholders.

As highlighted in Table 6, large IBFs' websites provide links to a more remarkable variety of social media than those of the foundations of other size. Additionally, when the analysis focuses on the most diffused social media

**Table 5** Number of social media used by IBFs

| N. of Social media | 0 | 1 | 2 | 3 | 4 | 5 | Total |
|---|---|---|---|---|---|---|---|
| N. of IBFs | 47 | 12 | 9 | 15 | 3 | 1 | 87 |

**Table 6** Social media employment per IBFs' size

| IBF Size | Facebook | | Twitter | | YouTube | | Google+ | | Pinterest | | Instagram | |
|---|---|---|---|---|---|---|---|---|---|---|---|---|
| | N | % | N | % | N | % | N | % | N | % | N | % |
| Large | 8 | 44.44 | 8 | 44.44 | 6 | 33.33 | 1 | 5.55 | 2 | 11.11 | 3 | 16.67 |
| Medium-large | 10 | 58.82 | 4 | 23.53 | 7 | 41.17 | 0 | 0 | 0 | 0 | 4 | 23.53 |
| Medium | 7 | 41.17 | 3 | 17.65 | 6 | 35.29 | 2 | 11.76 | 0 | 0 | 0 | 0 |
| Medium-small | 5 | 29.41 | 3 | 17.65 | 0 | 0 | 0 | 0 | 0 | 0 | 1 | 5.88 |
| Small | 5 | 27.78 | 4 | 22.22 | 3 | 16.67 | 1 | 5.55 | 0 | 0 | 0 | 0 |
| Total | 35 | | 22 | | 22 | | 4 | | 2 | | 8 | |

(Facebook, Twitter and YouTube), it emerges that large and medium-large foundations are particularly attentive to using the Web for communicating their availability to interact with stakeholders through social media.

## 5   Discussion and Conclusions

This study explores the role of the Web in supporting nonprofit accountability by investigating how IBFs use their websites for communicating and engaging in dialogue with local stakeholders and the public. According to the previous literature, the case of IBFs confirms that the Web supports accountability mostly through one-way communication [16], by providing disclosures on traditional information to demonstrate what they aim to do and how they perform [3–5]. Information on financial performance, grant-making policies and organizational history is what foundations pay the most attention to and what most diffuse on their websites.

Surprisingly, the mission—that is, the *raison d'être* of an NPO [13]—is infrequently disclosed online. This lack, added to the limited presence of mission reports, reduces the capacity to account for progress towards achieving organizational goals. Since NPOs legitimize their existence by demonstrating they provide public benefit to their communities, this lack could weaken their ability to increase public trust and confidence [2, 8, 9].

With regard to online disclosure on their policies, almost all IBFs communicate about grant-making policies, explaining how they meet the needs of local communities. Conversely, only a few organizations disclose online their investment policies on how they manage their assets. This hampers NPOs' accountability and deprives the community of knowing how incomes used to finance grant-making activities have been generated.

According to prior studies [3–5, 18], the potential of the Web has not yet been completely exploited by IBFs. The majority of them do not use websites to communicate interactively with their stakeholders or engage them in dialogue by asking for comments and feedback. Links to social media are limited and does not seem to enhance interaction with stakeholders significantly [20]. However, this lack highlights interesting possibilities to implement more involving Web-based accountability practices that will improve IBFs' responsiveness to community needs.

The case of IBFs confirms the general assumption that organizational size can affect Web use [4, 5, 21]. Larger organizations seem to disclose a greater number and variety of documents and information through websites, thus demonstrating greater attention to accounting for foundation activities and their impact on the local community. Moreover, larger foundations make more use of the Web by providing links to social media, therefore communicating their availability to interact with their stakeholders in a more active way.

Since broader disclosure to—and more involving dialogue with—stakeholders require technological capacities and financial resources, the case of IBFs confirms that organizational size matters [9]. However, despite larger IBFs seeming to perform better in the use of Web-based technologies, they still appear weakly engaged in a 'dialogic loop' [19] with their local stakeholders. Therefore, the overall picture emerging from this study suggests more steps can be taken to ensure they are more responsive to community needs.

To improve the reliability of the study, further research could employ degrees-of-freedom analysis [25] by subjecting the data collected to an a priori set of predictions grounded in the extant literature. In this way, it would be possible to better understand if the research findings support theories on Web use by NPOs.

Additionally, since Web-based accountability practices continuously evolve over time, it would be interesting for future research to investigate how IBFs take on the new challenge set out by the ACRI-MEF agreement to be more accessible to and interactive with their local communities.

# References

1. Hoque, Z., & Parker, L. (eds.). (2015). *Performance management in nonprofit organizations: Global perspectives*. New York, London: Routledge.
2. Connolly, C., & Hyndman, N. (2013). Towards charity accountability: Narrowing the gap between provision and needs? *Public Management Review, 15*(7), 945–968. https://doi.org/10.1080/14719037.2012.757349.
3. Kang, S., & Norton, H. E. (2004). Nonprofit organizations' use of the World Wide Web: Are they sufficiently fulfilling organizational goals? *Public Relations Review, 30,* 279–284. https://doi.org/10.1016/j.pubrev.2004.04.002.
4. Ingenhoff, D., & Koelling, A. M. (2009). The potential of Web sites as a relationship building tool for charitable fundraising NPOs. *Public Relations Review, 35,* 66–73. https://doi.org/10.1016/j.pubrev.2008.09.023.
5. Saxton, G. D., & Guo, C. (2011). Accountability online: Understanding the web-based accountability practices of nonprofit organizations. *Nonprofit and Voluntary Sector Quarterly, 40*(2), 270–295. https://doi.org/10.1177/0899764009341086.
6. Saxton, G. D., & Guo, C. (2012). Conceptualizing web-based stakeholder communication: The organizational website as a stakeholder relations tool. *Communication & Science Journal, 18*.
7. Leardini, C., Rossi, G., & Moggi, S. (2014). *Board governance in bank foundations*. Berlin: Springer.
8. Ebrahim, A. (2010). *The Many faces of nonprofit accountability*. Harward Business School Working paper 10-069.
9. Lee, R. L., & Blouin, M. C. (2014). *Towards a model of web disclosure adoption by nonprofit organizations*. Twentieth Americas Conference on Information Systems http://aisel.aisnet.org/cgi/viewcontent.cgi?article=1268&context=amcis2014.
10. Gray, R. (2008). Social and environmental accounting and reporting: From ridicule to revolution? From hope to hubris?—A personal review of the field. *Issues in Social & Environmental Accounting, 2*(1), 3–18. https://doi.org/10.22164/isea.v2i1.22.
11. Murtaza, N. (2012). Putting the lasts first: The case for community-focused and peer-managed NGO accountability mechanisms. *Voluntas, 23,* 109–125. https://doi.org/10.1007/s11266-011-9181-9.
12. Conway, S. L., O'Keefe, P. A., & Hrasky, S. L. (2015). Legitimacy, accountability and impression management in NGOs: the Indian Ocean tsunami. *Accounting, Auditing & Accountability Journal, 28*(7), 1075–1098. https://doi.org/10.1108/AAAJ-04-2012-01007.

13. Ebrahim, A. (2009). Placing the normative logics of accountability in "Thick" perspective. *American Behavioral Scientist, 52*(6), 885–904. https://doi.org/10.1177/0002764208327664.
14. Taylor, M., & Warburton, D. (2003). Legitimacy and the role of UK third sector organizations in the policy process. *Voluntas, 14*(3), 321–338. https://doi.org/10.1023/A:1025618720650.
15. Roberts, N. C. (2002). Keeping public officials accountable through dialogue: Resolving the accountability paradox. *Public Administration Review, 62*(2), 658–669. https://doi.org/10.1111/1540-6210.00248.
16. Moggi, S., Leardini, C., & Rossi, G. (2015). Mandatory or not mandatory reporting? Insights from Italian bank foundations. *International Journal of Public Administration, 38*(10), 734–742. https://doi.org/10.1080/01900692.2014.969842.
17. Broadbent, J., Laughlin, R., & Willig-Atherton, H. (1994). Financial controls and schools: Accounting in 'public' and 'private' spheres. *The British Accounting Review, 26*(3), 255–279. https://doi.org/10.1006/bare.1994.1017.
18. Taylor, M., Kent, M. L., & White, W. J. (2001). How activist organizations are using the Internet to build relationships. *Public Relations Review, 27,* 263–284. https://doi.org/10.1016/S0363-8111(01)00086-8.
19. Kent, M. L., & Taylor, M. (1998). Building dialogic relationships through the World Wide Web. *Public Relations Review, 24*(3), 321–334. https://doi.org/10.1016/S0363-8111(99)80143-X.
20. Lovejoy, K., Waters, R. D., & Saxton, G. D. (2012). Engaging stakeholders through Twitter: How nonprofit organizations are getting more out of 140 characters or less. *Public Relations Review, 38*(2), 313–318. https://doi.org/10.1016/j.pubrev.2012.01.005.
21. Lee, R. L., & Bhattacherjee, A. (2011). A theoretical framework for strategic use of the web among nonprofit organizations. In: *Proceedings of the Southern Association for Information Systems Conference* (pp. 103–108). Atlanta: Association of Information Systems.
22. Kent, M. L., Taylor, M., & White, W. J. (2003). The relationship between Web site design and organizational responsiveness to stakeholders. *Public Relations Review, 29,* 63–77. https://doi.org/10.1016/S0363-8111(02)00194-7.
23. Krippendorff, K. (2013). *Content analysis: An introduction to its methodology.* Thousand Oaks: Sage.
24. ACRI. (2015). Ventesimo rapporto sulle Fondazioni di origine bancaria - Anno 2014. Rome: ACRI.
25. Woodside, A. G. (2010). *Case study research: Theory, methods.* Practice: Emerald Group Publishing.

# From Smart Work to Digital Do-It-Yourself: A Research Framework for Digital-Enabled Jobs

**Aurelio Ravarini**[ORCID] **and Gianmaria Strada**

**Abstract** This position paper proposes a framework to study the effects of emerging digital technologies on work. We frame such effects in a four-folded taxonomy that highlights the differences between traditional automation, self service and virtualization applications of digital technology and a new genre of applications, that we name Digital Do-It-Yourself (DiDIY), funded on the concepts of knowledge worker and knowledge sharing. By leveraging on DiDIY, we propose to challenge the dramatic scenarios of job destruction portrayed by recent economical reports, and, on the other hand, we discuss the actual novelty of smart working, as it is carried out now.

**Keywords** Smart work · Digital transformation · Jobs · Skills

## 1 Introduction

The fundamentals of management and organizational science have been developed and consolidated in an era structurally different from today [1]. Economy was mainly based on goods (atoms) and not on services (bits), economic transactions mainly occurred at the local and not international level (when globalization was not yet a mature phenomenon), and the so-called first world experienced a constant economic growth. In that era technology used to provide tools supporting materials

This article has been developed under the DiDIY project funded from the European Union's Horizon 2020 research and innovation programme under grant agreement No. 644344.

A. Ravarini (✉) · G. Strada
Università Carlo Cattaneo—LIUC, Castellanza, Italy
e-mail: aravarini@liuc.it

G. Strada
e-mail: gstrada@liuc.it

© Springer International Publishing AG, part of Springer Nature 2018
R. Lamboglia et al. (eds.), *Network, Smart and Open*, Lecture Notes in Information Systems and Organisation 24, https://doi.org/10.1007/978-3-319-62636-9_7

handling (atoms) and not information management (bits). The managerial models developed in that era, when the concept of physical goods were set against the concept of intangible services, leveraged on an analytical approach synthetized in the Taylor's model of work.

Nowadays, business services are central to competition, business models are changing fast and the impact of technology on the entire society is pervasive. The rapid growth of digital technology and a change in paradigms affects the everyday life and organizational contexts, and–in particular–job occupations: "thanks to digital technology … business is evolving into an office-less enterprise that's more mobile and fluid than the "desk jobs" of decades past—which presents a challenge to the companies that supply businesses with the nuts-and-bolts of their physical infrastructure" [2].

The so called "4th industrial revolution", which includes developments in pre-viously disjointed fields such as artificial intelligence and machine-learning, robotics, nanotechnology, 3D printing, and genetics and biotechnology, is claimed to cause over the next five years a widespread disruption in business models but also to labour markets, with enormous change predicted in the skill sets needed to thrive in the new landscape [3].

This new environment is quickly reshaping–besides business models–also skills and abilities. According to the Strategic Policy Forum on Digital entrepreneurship [4] "reskilling the workforce in different EU industrial sectors is a major priority and challenge". People will need to learn new skills, otherwise they will risk to fall into obsolescence: the rising of technology is radically transforming several industries and is making many manual jobs obsolete, while the demand of new types of skills, not only technical but also relational, are even more useful [5].

Technological disruptions create substitute specific tasks. New technical skills will need to be supplemented with strong social and collaboration skills. Digital technologies can create and expand virtual work spaces, enable and support new ways of working, facilitate communication, collaboration and the creation of net-works of professional relationships across the boundaries of organizations. The development of such "professional clans" is possible thanks to the diffusion of digital mobile tools that turn to zero the issue of space and time distance [3].

However, while the new so-called "gig economy" may be one of the most visible and current manifestations of disruptions to the labour market, many more changes—both positive and negative—are expected in most industries, leading to new man-agement and regulatory challenges. In this paper we present a conceptual framework showing the bright side of digital technologies as their impact on jobs is concerned. While machines get smarter, many jobs will keep on maintaining critical components that are social, emotional, where the presence of individuals' skills is essential. We provide support to the thesis that technologies can help organizations evolve beyond the mere substitution of men power if workers will be able to empower themselves becoming knowledge workers.

## 2  Theoretical Background

### 2.1  The Impact of Digital Technology on Organizations Besides Automation

The findings of a recent report by the World Economic Forum [3] pointed out that the fourth industrial revolution is consolidating new ways of working and new organizational models. The report presents a framework to classify digital dependent phenomena and their effect on work, among which a loss of 5.1 million jobs, due to the advent of this "revolution" and the related automation of increasingly complex tasks.

However, the report provides several other relevant insights beside this worrying forecast.

The changing nature of work, and skills instability–the rapid change in the skills requirements of all existing jobs–are nowadays among the most important drivers of change. These phenomena are further compounded by the rise of mobile internet and cloud technology, enabling the rapid spread of internet–based service models, where the relevance of the physical components of organizations, including employees, appear to fade [3].

The impact of concurrent disruptions in technological, demographic and socio-economic level will transform the employment landscape and skills requirements, resulting in substantial challenges for recruiting, training and managing talent, new emerging job categories and functions are expected to become critically important by the year 2020 [3, 4].

For example, developments in technologies related to coding have facilitated the rapid growth of new roles and lowered the barriers to entry. Or, in another business domain: Google Analytics, marketing automation software tools, and the accessibility of growing volumes of data have raised employers' expectations that a broader set of employees—not just statisticians or business analysts—will drive analytic insights. Roles such as Digital Marketer, Data Analyst and Mobile Application Developer are often times accessible to job seekers with technical training short of a computer science degree.

This drastic change of profiles is not perceived or implemented by all the firms in many different industries undergoing digital transformation, due to several factors: resistance to change by entire established firms and their executive managers, traditional mind sets and old procedures, scarce urgency pushed from the market (so far) towards change.

### 2.2  From Teleworking to Smart-Working

In opposition to this scenario, where technology is seen as inevitable and problematic, since the early 90's another stream of research has been highlighting that digital tools can open up many options in terms of the location and timeframes of work.

Digital is said to bring value to work within those organizations able to exploit technology to create a variety of workplace settings, and tools that support different types of work: individual or collaborative, focused individual procedural work or work based on social interactions and improvisation, and even the opportunity to work in a variety of different locations throughout the day. At the same time, such a flexible work configuration allows to fulfil improvements in term of work-life balance [6–8]. Employers who can accommodate this new way of working are finding it easier to attract and to retain digital-savvy employees [6, 9].

During the 90's, the popular (although broad) term used to describe such arrangements was *telework* [10]. According to Sparrow (2000), teleworkers represent "privileged core employees, enjoying high trust relationships, and given autonomy over work location and time, i.e. the re-emergence of industrial guilds serviced by a small technical and commercial elite". Telework initially aimed at cutting organizational costs associated with maintaining and leasing property, and more recently has been implemented to reduce work pressures and facilitate work-life balance [5, 8]. Kossek and Friede [11] suggest four types of work-life policies: flexibility of working time, flexibility of working place, support with care responsibilities and informational and social support. Flexibility of working time includes reduced hours or part-time; flexitime; compressed work-week; job-sharing; compensatory time (extra time gets recouped) and leaves of absence. According to [7], flexibility of working place refers to "teleworking, that is working from another location other than the office".

More recently, following the diffusion of the adjective *smart* to generally address business components supported by digital technology, the term *smart work* has been largely adopted to refer to employers providing employees with flexibility in their working hours, following practices of part-time working or flexi-hours, that–however–do appear essentially similar to those described already two decades ago under the term telework. A recent survey on 100 large Italian companies [12] identified four categories of smart working organizations: inconsistent, analogical, digital and complete. If we exclude the last category, the large majority of companies claiming to have adopted smart work have actually carried out initiatives limited to the adoption of digital devices and policies of work time flexibility. Some of them are even mere employer branding initiatives, as it has been confirmed in a more recent report [13].

In other words, one may question whether the main innovation between the current initiatives labelled "smart working" and the telework of two decades ago, consists in the technological innovations available (high-speed Internet, cloud computing and mobile devices) that let companies displace workers at their own houses.

## 2.3 A taxonomy of the effects of Digital Technology on Work

If this is the case, the promised, positive disruptive potential of the scenario depicted by the World Economic Forum [3] appears to be very limitedly exploited, leaving the stage to the darkest forecasts on job occupation.

We believe that the roots of the lack of full exploitation can be found in the pervasivity of the impact of digital technology on work, which leads to overlap different effects that technology can enable:

1. Automation, i.e. independence on humans or "Do Without People". It consists in substituting individuals with machines to perform certain tasks. Emerging digital technologies such as the Internet of Things and Big Data appear to enable computers to perform highly sophisticated tasks, typically qualifying the so-called white-collars, while the application of artificial intelligence to robotics let machines to cover complex operative tasks, until now requiring the work of the "blue-collars" [3, 14].
2. "Self-service": i.e. operational autonomy, or "Do Without Asking". It consists in allowing individuals becoming independent on certain organizational entities for carrying out operative tasks. It is the typical effect enabled by the adoption of intranets to support employees in many administrative and communication tasks.
3. Virtualization: i.e. independence on physical proximity or "Do Without Touching". It enables the employees to overcome space constraints by carrying out tasks involving distant organizational resources (e.g. people, plants, archives) as if she was in presence of such resources.

One might observe that the current "smart working" practices exploit self-service and virtualization. These technology-enabled effects–although relevant–don't add value to the workforce: they provide workers with new, efficient (hardware and software) means, without significantly changing the way they work. It seems unlikely that, by these means, companies can compensate the occupation losses inevitably consequent to automation.

Conversely, as reported by Quinones [15] in its qualitative study: "the challenge is not just to design innovative ICTs with tailorable system design principles, but to consider the appropriation work that occurs at the user level—supporting good understandings of technology and cultivating practices around it. Such work is akin to establishing what MacLean et al. (1990) called the culture of tailoring".

To evaluate the impact on occupation we should change paradigm and move from a paradigm based on space, time and efficiency (the bases of the three effects mentioned above) to a new paradigm, focused on the effect of technology on the value of the competence at work.

Within a EU funded project under the H2020 framework, we have named this fourth effect Digital Do-It-Yourself: by exploiting the availability and ease of use of digital technologies, organizational roles typically dependent on experts (internal or external to the organization) can carry out–autonomously–innovative practices.

For example: workmen in the production plants can set up a pilot project to monitor the production flow (using Arduino boards and sensors) without or limitedly asking support to the IT department; R&D employees can create (with 3D printers) prototypes of new products, without requiring consultancy from R&D consulting firms; marketing employees can set up a marketing campaign by creating a mobile app, without or limitedly asking support to the IT department.

By enabling disintermediation of experts, the DiDIY effect shakes organizational roles, something that can be recognized in the Makers communities [16], and has been described with the term "democratization of manufacturing" [17, 18].

In synthesis, we can add a fourth item to the list introduced above:

4. Digital Do-It-Yourself, i.e. the integration of activities, amplification of roles and empowerment of workers, autonomy of decision making, knowledge sharing. Contrary to the previous effects, it is not qualified by independence, but rather by inter-dependence between individuals (sometimes described as a "Do-It-Together" practice) and between an individual and technology.

By assuming the very existence of this effect, we can introduce the role of the "digital Do-It-Yourself worker" (or "DiDIYer"), a type of proactive, digitally-enabled knowledge worker [19–21] that exploits digital technology both to exert her creativity and to share knowledge to achieve higher goals. At the organizational level the effect of DiDIY is effectiveness and not increased efficiency [14, 22]. In other words, a DiDIYer is the really "smart" variant of the current actual "smart worker".

## 3   Research Design

The novelty of the paradigm introduced in this paper requires, besides a solid theoretical background, the identification of potential organizational domains in which empirical research should explore the applicability of the paradigm. So far we have identified six domains, that are introduced in the following section. Each domain can represent a research topic, a specific area of investigation under the general umbrella of a general research framework.

### 3.1   Potential Empirical Domains

**Manufacturing Workers** Manufacturing workers can exploit digital technologies to develop new methods and technologies for production (e.g. digital desktop fabrication): knowledge work, craft, and design are recombined in novel ways (Ratto and Ree 2010). The diffusion of 3D printing, laser cutting, and garage-scale

CNC mills have created contexts of democratized technological practices. It has given hackers and hobbyists modes of production previously only available to large organizations [17]. Rapid prototyping technologies are impacting business processes because they enable sharing knowledge about product design and fabrication (Oxman 2007).

**Makers** The rise of the maker culture [16] is closely associated with the rise of a totally new entrepreneurial ecosystem made of hacker spaces, fab labs makers spaces, tech-shops, co-working spaces, crowdfunding platforms, related and supporting industries (such as laser cutters and 3D printer makers and consultants; dedicated vocational training and education; academic and corporate research), local and international associations, clubs and institutions. Makers tend to concentrate mainly around large and medium cities, forming local communities. Often physical proximity and geographical clustering play a critical role in the rise and success of such communities and in the exploitation of their capacity to act as incubators for knowledge creation and sharing and eventually for innovation, leading to entrepreneurial initiatives.

**CIOs and Other Executives** The role of the CIO is undergoing major changes in relation with the DiDIY affecting other managerial roles. CIOs work is progressively overlapping with the work of designers, Operations managers and particularly Chief Marketing Officers (Ariker 2014, Deloitte 2015). In this new scenario a new executive position is getting increasing credit: the CDO (Chief Digital Officer), typically emerging from the marketing department, where abilities related to e-Commerce and web-based communication are increasingly available.

**Networkers** This is a new type of professional, gaining market space at the expenses of sales agent. In certain B2C industries, e.g. cosmetics, companies are transforming the sales department by welcoming initiatives of network marketing spontaneously growing from single individuals. Networkers are able to exploit their knowledge of the business (the product and the market), to launch sales initiatives based on the effective use of digital tools and enabling the creation of a social network of dealers and final customers.

**Administrative Employees** Administrative employees can create software tools to improve their job, giving life at what is also defined a "private information system", that responds to highly specific purpose, and by default is highly customized because developed by the end–user possibly with the support of an intra-organizational community of other administrative employees.

**Shoppers** Shoppers of retail chain are progressively capable to run certain step of the buying process on their own, by collecting information on the web and/or by creating on-line communities where they share the expertise on producers of goods. The changes in the shopper buying behaviour process have a fall-out on the retailer structures, marketing strategies and organization. In this case the subject is not a worker, but the DiDIY behavior of shoppers possibly would have a relevant impact on work in the retailer industry (Fig. 1).

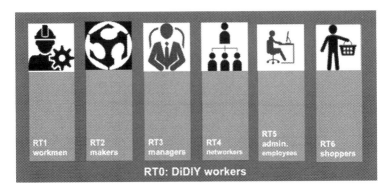

**Fig. 1** General research framework and vertical research topics

## *3.2 Towards a General Research Framework*

The domains of application of the DiDIY phenomenon presented above belong to a widely heterogeneous set of environments (different industries, different business processes, different organizational roles). However, it is possible to recognize a common ground, that can be synthesized in terms of a general framework enabling defining constraints (although blurred to some extent) for the identification of any domain of application of the DiDIY effect.

We can state that DiDIY is present whenever:

a. a DiDIYer, i.e. a certain organizational role,
b. carries out on their own certain activities, activities previously carried out by experts or specialized companies (this aspect deals with the traditional notion of Do-It-Yourself),
c. by exploiting certain digital technologies,
d. possibly exploiting the knowledge sharing within a certain community of individuals, or of organizational entities (this aspect deals with the innovative notion of Do-It-Together, where "together" refers to a community the DiDIYer belongs to).

## 4  Implications of the DiDIY Paradigm

In recent years the interest in the Digital Do-It-Yourself organizations have grown significantly, as per all the latest research related to smart working. Digital Do-It-Yourself means rethinking the work in a more intelligent way, challenging the traditional constraints related to location and working hours, leaving to workers more autonomy in defining the modalities of work, be it intellectual or manual, compared with greater responsibility for results.

Not simply autonomy, but also flexibility, accountability and trust are the key principles of this new approach to work. The DiDIYer seen as a knowledge worker elaborates and programs his activities without the need of specialists in the field, but not alone: together–i.e. sharing knowledge with–other DiDIYers operating in the same application domain. This helps her to identify the objective, focusing on the problems that she likely will have to face to achieve it.

At the organizational level, the presence of DiDIYers has several implications.

Firstly, it requires monitoring skills of the context in which she operates, not only the mere execution of her tasks.

Secondly, the value of an individual is not related to her position in the hierarchy but to the contribution that he is able to provide to the community in which she is recognized.

Thirdly, if the DiDIY paradigm is based on value, it does not matter how much a DiDIY worker takes to perform an activity: "time is money" is not meaningful anymore. What matters is not how much time she needs to perform a task but the added value generated. This conclusion is openly in conflict with the traditional approach to the evaluation of work, based on the effort measured in time units. It is worth noting that in some contexts such an approach is already in place. For example, sales agents are measured in sales orders and not in hours of work. Thus the point is how to measure the value added by other jobs were time is the traditional measure.

In general, the HR function, more than the IT department, appears to be affected by the emergence of the DiDIY worker. HR professionals should develop new skills (or at least be aware of some techniques) in order to fully grasp the rapid current developments in the digital landscape. Furthermore, the human resources should also optimize internal communication making an appropriate use of all the available channels such platforms of social intranet or business social networks, besides the traditional communication channels.

In this sense the digital transformation process can be seen as a socio-technological transformation process that requires the development of new skills in the HR function and, more generally, a change in the organizational culture. To this aim, HR people should work together to the marketing and communication functions.

## 5   Conclusions and Future Work

In this position paper we study the effects of emerging digital technologies on work. We frame such effects in a four-folded taxonomy that highlights the differences between traditional automation, self service and virtualization applications of digital and a fourth, new genre of application, that we name Digital Do-It-Yourself, funded on the concepts of knowledge worker and knowledge sharing.

By leveraging on DiDIY, we propose to challenge the dramatic scenarios of job destruction portrayed by recent economical reports, and, on the other hand, we discuss the actual novelty of smart work practices, as they are carried out now.

We have developed and propose a research framework that can be used—descriptively—to identify organizational contexts where the DiDIY effect occurs, or —prescriptively—to design DIDIY based initiatives. Six domains of applications have been identified: they represent possible streams of research that we expect to explore in further studies.

**Acknowledgements** We acknowledge doct. Marina Leandri for her work on this research during the internship at the CETIC Research Center, Università C. Cattaneo—LIUC.

# References

1. Dobbs, R., Manyika, J., & Woetzel, J. (2015). *The four global forces breaking all the trends.* Book excerpt from No Ordinary Disruption, Ed. Public Affairs 2015. Retrieved March 30, 2015. http://www.mckinsey.com/insights/strategy/The_four_global_forces_breaking_all_the_trends.
2. Kane, G. C. (2015, June 09). The workplace of the future. *MIT Sloan Management Review.*
3. World Economic Forum. (2016). *The future of jobs: Employment, skills and workforce strategy for the fourth industrial revolution.* Geneva, Switzerland: World Economic Forum.
4. Strategic Policy Forum on Digital Entrepreneurship. (2016, March). *Accelerating the digital transformation of European industry and enterprises.*
5. Wang, J., & Verma, A. (2012). Explaining organizational responsiveness to work-life balance issues: The role of business strategy and high-performance work systems. *Human Resource Management, 51*(3), 407–432.
6. Morganson, V. J., Major, D. A., Oborn, K. L., Verive, J. M., & Heelan, M. P. (2010). Comparing telework locations and traditional work arrangements: Differences in work-life balance support, job satisfaction, and inclusion. *Journal of Managerial Psychology, 25*(6), 578–595.
7. Krishnakumar, S., & Choudhury, J. (2014). Understanding the nuances of work-life balance. *Review of HRM, 3,* 81.
8. Irfan, A. (2015). Antecedents and outcomes of work-life balance. *The International Journal of Business & Management, 3*(1), 1.
9. Attia, E. A., Duquenne, P., & Le-Lann, J. M. (2014). Considering skills evolutions in multi-skilled workforce allocation with flexible working hours. *International Journal of Production Research, 52*(15), 4548–4573.
10. Niles, J. M. (1998). *Teleworking: Strategies for managing the virtual workforce.* New York, NY: Wiley.
11. Kossek, E., & Distelberg, B. (2009). Work and family employment policy for a transformed work force: Trends and themes. In N. Crouter & A. Booth (Eds.), *Work-life policies* (pp. 1–51). Washington, DC: Urban Institute Press.
12. Gastaldi, L., et al. (2014). Smart working: Rethinking work practices to leverage employees' innovation potential. In *15th International CINet Conference, Operating Innovation–Innovating Operations.* Budapest, Hungary.
13. Osservatorio Smart Working. (2016, April). *Nuovi modi di lavorare: una panoramica sullo smart working* (in Italian: *New ways of working: Overview on smart working*). Research Report. Politecnico di Milano.

14. Lacity Mary, C., & Willcocks, L. (2015, June). What knowledge workers stand to gain from automation. *Harvard Business Review*.
15. Quinones, P. A. (2014). Cultivating practice & shepherding technology use: Supporting appropriation among unanticipated users. In *Proceedings of the 17th ACM Conference on Computer Supported Cooperative Work & Social Computing*.
16. Anderson, C. (2012). Makers: The new industrial revolution. Crown Publishing Group.
17. Tanenbaum, J., Williams, A. M., Dejardins, A., & Tanenbaum, K. (2013). Democratizing technology: Pleasure, utility and expressiveness in DIY and Maker Practice. In *Conference CHI 2013: Changing Perspectives* (pp. 2603–2612). Paris, France.
18. Williams, A., & Nadeau, B. (2014). Manufacturing for makers: From prototype to product. *Interactions, 21*(6), 64–67.
19. Mikulecký, P. (2008). Towards smart working environments. *IADIS Conference*.
20. Moon, M. (2009). Knowledge worker productivity. *Journal of Digital Asset Management, 5* (4), 178–180.
21. Cannella, A. A., & Ann McFadyen, M. (2013). Changing the exchange the dynamics of knowledge worker ego networks. *Journal of Management*. doi:0149206313511114.
22. Kinnie, N., & Swart, J. (2012). Committed to whom? Professional knowledge worker commitment in cross-boundary organisations. *Human Resource Management Journal, 22*(1), 21–38.
23. Assenza, P. (2015). If you build it will they come? The influence of spatial configuration on social and cognitive functioning and knowledge spillover in entrepreneurial co-working and hacker spaces. *Journal of Management Policy and Practice, 16*(3), 35.
24. General Assembly + Burning Glass Technologies. (2015). *Blurring lines: How business and technology skills are merging to create high opportunity hybrid jobs*. http://burning-glass.com/research/hybrid-jobs/.
25. Lake, A. (2013). Smart flexibility: Moving smart and flexible working from theory to practice. *Leadership & Organization Development Journal, 34*(6), 588–589.
26. Lee, J. (2013). Cross-disciplinary knowledge: Desperate call from business enterprises in coming smart working era. *Technological and Economic Development of Economy, 19*(sup1), S285–S303.
27. Meier, J., & Crocker, M. (2010). Generation Y in the workforce: Managerial challenges. *The Journal of Human Resource and Adult Learning, 6*(1), 68.
28. Noel, A. (1989). Strategic cores and magnificent obsessions: Discovering strategy formation through daily activities of CEOs. *Strategic Management Journal, 10*(S1), 33–49.
29. Petrick, I. J., & Simpson, T. W. (2013). 3D printing disrupts manufacturing: How economies of one create new rules of competition. *Research-Technology Management, 56*(6), 12–16.
30. Schneckenberg, D. (2009). Web 2.0 and the empowerment of the knowledge worker. *Journal of knowledge management, 13*(6), 509–520.
31. Wu, F., & Zhang, X. (2014). Employees' positions in virtual working community and their job performances: A social network analysis. *Human Resource Development International, 17*(2), 231–242.
32. Xiao-dong, J. I., & Cong-Zhen, A. N. (2010). *Working smart, working hard or social network. The determinants of salespersons' performance in direct selling firm*. School of IBA, Shanghai University Press.

# Citizens Coproduction, Service Self-Provision and the State 2.0

Walter Castelnovo

**Abstract** Citizens' engagement and citizens' participation are rapidly becoming catch-all concepts, buzzwords continuously recurring in public policy discourses, also due to the widespread diffusion and use of social media that are claimed to have the potential to increase citizens' participation in public sector processes, including policy development and policy implementation. By assuming the concept of co-production as the lens through which to look at citizen's participation in civic life, the paper shows how, when supported by a real redistribution of power between government and citizens, citizens' participation can determine a transformational impact on the same nature of government, up to the so called 'Do It Yourself government' and 'user-generated state'. Based on a conceptual research approach and with reference to the relevant literature, the paper discusses what such transformation could amount to and what role ICTs (social media) can play in the government transformation processes.

**Keywords** Co-production · Participation · User-generated public services
Public value · Social media · Do it yourself government

## 1 Introduction

Governments have been using information processing technologies for a long time even before people started to talk of Information and Communication Technologies (ICTs) and e-Government. The main reason for governments to resort to those technologies was to improve the governments' operations, which mainly means 'doing the same things differently', i.e. possibly better. This implies transforming governments' operations, although this transformation involves only changes to operational and management practices, what O'Neill [1] calls instrumental transformation and Scholl [2] calls first-order transformation. While these transforma-

W. Castelnovo (✉)
Department of Theoretical and Applied Sciences, University of Insubria, Varese, Italy
e-mail: walter.castelnovo@uninsubria.it

© Springer International Publishing AG, part of Springer Nature 2018                    109
R. Lamboglia et al. (eds.), *Network, Smart and Open*, Lecture Notes in Information
Systems and Organisation 24, https://doi.org/10.1007/978-3-319-62636-9_8

tions can deliver benefits of increased speed, greater consistency and quality of service and lower transaction costs, 'the order of socio-political relationships and the referent framework of public governance remain unchanged' [1, p. 753].

Starting from the late 1980's, with the advent of e-Government a new perspective has emerged that focuses on the possibility of transforming government and governance in a deeper sense, thanks to the transformational impact that ICTs can have on them. For many years, scholars, professionals and policy makers have been working on the, explicit or implicit, assumption that governments would achieve systemic or 'second-order' transformations by relying on ICTs. The expectation was that ICTs could be used not only for doing the same things differently but also, and more importantly, for 'doing different things'. This implies that the relationships, and thereby the behaviors, of politicians, the public and public officials will be radically altered and new forms of public management and new models of governance will emerge [1, p. 754].

However, notwithstanding this widely-shared expectation, after 30 years of e-Government whether it has succeeded or not in enabling and supporting any systemic transformation of government and governance is still an open question more and more debated by scholars, practitioners and policy makers [2–6]. Based on this critical discussion, a more realistic view has recently emerged concerning the real capability of ICTs of inducing systemic transformations in government and governance. As observed by Scholl [2, p. 4], citing Orlikowski and Barley's works, 'human agents, organizational systems, and ICT are linked in a circular fashion, such that information technologies are produced by the very social structures that they promise to transform'. From this point of view, to achieve substantial transformations both the technical and social aspects should be considered, whereas when researchers talk about change usually one aspect is privileged over another [7]. This seems particularly true for many e-Government strategies implemented worldwide during the past years that have been strongly influenced by the technological determinism, or at least by the myth of technical rationality [8], that resides in the minds of many policy makers and e-Government practitioners [9].

As a consequence, the need of transforming human agents and organizational systems, i.e. the 'soft elements' of the e-Government systems [10, 11], has received less attention than needed. As Fountain observed in [12], 'whenever possible, decision-makers have used technology in ways, however innovative, that leave deeper structures and processes—such as authority relations, political relations and oversight processes—undisturbed' (p. 19). With the advent of web technologies, 'technology, which was previously used primarily in back office operations came between service providers and users and thus opened up an entirely new space and models of government operations and government organization' [5, p. 112]. However, this new space of opportunity has not always been covered with new models of operations and new models of relations between service providers and service users. In many cases, the main difference between the model of online services typical of the e-Government systems and the traditional public services delivery models only concerns the channel used. User centricity, which is claimed to be a foundation principle for e-Government, did not change in any fundamental way the supply-driven and government push approach to public services design and delivery [13–16]. This is completely in line with the unidirectional relation between content providers and content consumers typical of the so-called Web 1.0 [17].

The advent of the social media and Web 2.0 raised a new expectation concerning the capability of ICTs of enabling systemic transformation in government and governance. As Linders [18, p. 446] points out 'much hope is placed on the advent of social media, ubiquitous mobile connectivity, and web 2.0 interactivity, which for the first time provide channels not just for mass dissemination but also for mass production and collaboration'. What makes the governments' use of social media particularly interesting is their 'ability to transform governance by increasing a government's transparency and its interaction with citizens' and to 'create new ways of democratic participation, pressures for new institutional structures, and processes and frameworks for open and transparent government on an unprecedented scale' [19, p. 1]. All this can lead to rethinking the structure and nature of government in ways that 'dramatically alter how the public and government interact, develop solutions, and deliver services' [19, p. 5].

The impact of social media on government can be much deeper than the impact the traditional web technologies had on governments during the past 20 years, mainly due to the intrinsic interactive nature of social media that enables new forms of relationship both between citizens and government and between different government organizations. As Linders [18, p. 451] points out, social media 'appear to enhance and expand the viability of and capacity for citizen coproduction, not only in traditional citizen-to-government arrangements ("citizen sourcing"), but also in arrangements whereby the government informs, assists, and enables private actions ("government as a platform") or whereby citizens assist one another, with IT replacing government as vehicle for collective action ("Do-It-Yourself government")'.

In this paper, starting from Linders' statement above, and focusing particularly on the concept of Do-It-Yourself government (and the related concepts of user-generated state and State 2.0), I will use the concept of co-production as the lens through which to look at the new forms of citizens' engagement and participation that are emerging from the spreading of the participatory and collaborative culture typical of the Web 2.0 paradigm. To this end, I will consider under what conditions citizens can participate as co-producers in public value generating initiatives and what implications can derive from this in terms of a second-order transformation in government.

More specifically, by considering co-production as an enhanced form of participation, the paper tries to answer two related research questions:

- Q1: Under what conditions can co-production represent a truly new relationship between governments and citizens?
- Q2: Under what conditions can the Do-It-Yourself government be considered as a second-order transformation of government resulting from a joint effort between citizens and governments?

To answer these questions, in the paper I assume a conceptual research approach [20] and discuss at some length the literature on public services co-production and citizens' participation in public initiatives. The aim of this discussion is to provide an explication/clarification of the concepts involved in the answers to the two research questions above, i.e.: co-production, participation, user-generated services and Do It Yourself state.

Based on the discussion of those concepts, I will conclude that the answer to both the research questions above lays on the rebalancing of the power relationships between government and citizens, which does not depend on ICTs but strictly pertains to the realm of policy and political representativeness. This will lead to the conclusion that the widespread diffusion and use of ICTs (and social media) by itself can neither deterministically determine nor directly enable a second-order transformation in government. As a conclusion of the paper, I will argue that, by impacting heavily on society, culture, life-styles, interpersonal relationships and economic relationships as well, the use of social media can change the context dramatically, making traditional forms of government more and more dysfunctional, what [21] calls policy entropy. The Do-It-Yourself government (and the State 2.0) can thus be considered as a possible ending of a second order policy innovation/transformation process aiming at maintaining/restoring the fit between government and society in the era of Web 2.0.

## 2   Citizens as Public Services Co-producers

Co-production of public services as a theoretical concept has been around for more than thirty years but it has assumed an increasing significance in the agenda of public sector reform during the past years. The recent renewed interest toward co-production appears to have been stimulated mainly by two phenomena: the global financial crisis that forced governments worldwide to reduce public spending thus putting a squeeze on public services; and the widespread diffusion and use of social media that strongly support a culture of self-organization and participation.

On the one hand, the need to reduce the public spending has triggered a renewed interest in co-production as a way of reducing the costs of services or even rescuing services, which might otherwise be entirely cut [22–24]. However, as reported by Linders [18, p. 447], looking at co-production simply from the point of view of public cost savings opens the way to many criticisms of coproduction as a 'cynical attempt to dignify [the government's] cuts agenda, by dressing up the withdrawal of support with the language of reinvigorating civic society.'

On the other hand, the widespread diffusion and use of social media, related to the advent of the so-called Web 2.0, enables the creation of new connections between government and citizens that are essential for the co-production model to work [25]. Besides this, and even more importantly, the interactive and collaborative nature of Web 2.0 weakens the distinction between content producers and content consumers, which matches well with ideas about co-production as they have been developed in the administrative sciences.

The literature (both scientific and grey) on the collaborative production of public services is continuously growing, as it is the range of the government-citizens' relationships that have been analyzed through the lens of the co-production concept [22–29]. As defined by Bovaird [22, p. 847], co-production amounts to 'the provision of services through regular, long-term relationships between professionalized service providers (in any sector) and service users or other members of the community, where all parties make substantial resource contributions'. Alford [23] observes that there is a considerable disagreement over the definition of co-production within the relevant literature, especially concerning what constitutes the results or 'products' of co-production, and what kinds of activities should be considered as part of the process of co-production.

Co-production is much more than user/consumer involvement. It is a value-creating activity that challenges the traditional conception of the value creation process and the role that the users/consumers can play in it. Prahalad and Ramaswamy [30] observe that, in the more common variations of consumer involvement, the firm is still in charge of the overall orchestration of the experience, with consumers treated as passive. Managers partition some of the work usually done by the firm and pass it on to their consumers. The firm decides what products and services to produce and, by implication, it decides what counts as value and what is of value to the customers. Some scholars consider this kind of user/consumer's involvement as a form of co-production, although in this case users/consumers have little or no role in the value creation process. By strategically managing this kind of client co-production, the firm only aims at improving operational efficiency, developing more optimal solutions, and generating a sustainable competitive advantage [31].

Different from this kind of consumer involvement, co-production gives the users an active role in the (co)creation of value; for this reason, co-production entails the redefinition of both the meaning of value and the process of value creation, which takes well beyond considering user/consumer's involvement as a way to improve the organization's operational efficiency. Looking at the involvement of the users/consumers only, or mainly, from an efficiency-based point of view obscures the transformational impact of the co-production model, which is crucial when considering citizen's involvement in government activities as co-producers. In fact, the adoption of the co-production model in government entails transforming the organizational structures, staff attitudes and the processes of the government agencies, up to the possible transformation of the same nature of government toward the so-called 'user generated state', or the state 2.0 [32, 33].

As observed above, the transformational potential of the co-production model is magnified by the use of social media to increase citizen's engagement in government activities [18, 32, 34–37]. However, the simple adoption of new technological tools by government organizations in no way can deterministically force transformational effects on government, and this holds also with respect to the relation between the use of social media and the advent of the user-generated state [37]. The embracing of the culture of self-organization and participation emerging from the Web 2.0 paradigm can nevertheless stimulate the adoption of new ways of creating public goods by encouraging them to emerge from within society and by collaboratively involving users in public service co-production [32].

Linders [18] describes different degrees and typologies of co-production in the age of social media. To do this end, Linders defines a 'structured classification scheme for ICT-facilitated citizen coproduction initiatives' (p. 447), based on two dimensions: stages of service delivery (design, execution, monitoring) and distribution of power and responsibility between providers and beneficiaries (citizens sourcing, government as platform, do it yourself government). Linders' schema allows classifying a large number of citizen co-production initiatives in the age of social media and helps clarifying what the implications are for governments, in terms of both possible benefits and criticalities. Quoting [19], Linders observes that 'while the potential impact of social media technologies on the functioning of government is "profound," they come with challenges in the areas of policy development, governance, process design, and conceptions of democratic engagement' (p. 452). In particular, Linders identifies two major criticalities in the involvement of citizens in ICT-based co-production: new roles and responsibilities that governments will need to perform to enable and support citizens' co-production (taking it beyond government cost-savings); and the redistribution of power and responsibilities between governments and the newly empowered citizen. Both these elements impact on the cases of co-production considered by Linders. However, although in his paper Linders discusses government's new role and responsibilities at some length, he only mentions the redistribution of power and responsibilities between governments and citizens that, on the other hand, is fundamental for better understanding what the 'Do It Yourself government', the 'user-generated state' [32] and the 'state 2.0' [33] could mean. In the following, I will focus specifically on this topic that I will discuss with the aim of finding an answer to the research questions Q1 and Q2 above.

## 3 Bringing the Power of People into Public Services

Participation is a central concept in the contemporary public policy discourse to the point that it has become one of the mantras of the digital age. However, as Cornwall [38] points out, this widespread adoption of the language of participation raises questions about what exactly this much-used buzzword has come to mean, since 'participation' can be used to evoke almost anything that involves people.

Participation is most often related to the citizens' involvement in the decision-making processes though consultation exercises. The literature provides plenty of examples of initiatives involving citizens through a variety of tools and methods for consultation from face-to-face events and surveys to the use of Web 2.0 interactive technologies that allow the possibility to reach out to a much wider audience and provide channels for mass consultation, production and collaboration

[18]. This is the basis for a new trend in the citizen-government relationship based on 'citizen sourcing' as a way to foster citizens' participation by engaging citizens in government related activities [35]. However, as Linders [18] points out, even when citizens are engaged in government related activities through citizen sourcing, government still holds the primary responsibility for them. How government exercises this responsibility determines the effectiveness of citizen sourcing as a public participation model. In fact, if government agencies are not willing to actually consider and put into practice the results of a citizen sourcing exercise, it will seem like nothing more than rhetoric to citizen participants, which could undermine government-citizens' relationships and may be counterproductive if citizens discover that their efforts and feedbacks have no impact or remain unaccounted [35].

Irrespective of what the participation mechanisms implemented are and how innovative the tools that can be used are, in many cases participation is little more than a formality. As Timney [39] points out, 'while citizens are given the opportunity to provide input, their suggestions rarely change the outcomes of the process because the most critical decisions have been usually made already' (p. 87).

The relation between citizens contribution and public policy and action is crucial for every participation exercise [40]. This brings to the foreground the problem of how power and authority are distributed in citizens' participation exercises. In fact, participation is the process 'by which members of a society (those not holding office or administrative positions in government) share power with public officials in making substantive decisions related to the community' [41, p. 5]. Kweit and Kweit [42] consider power redistribution as one of the outcomes of successful participation that, among other things, depends on the characteristics of the organization implementing the participation exercise, the nature of the administrative processes [43], the form of government and the political culture [44]. Not surprisingly, [45] found empirical evidence confirming that red tape and hierarchical authority, which entail a centralization of power and authority, are negatively associated with good participation outcomes.

The relation between participation and power is the core of one of the most influential works on citizens' participation, i.e. the paper in which Sherry Arnstein first introduced her well-known ladder of citizen participation [46]. Arnstein considers participation as valuable only to the extent that it involves a redistribution of power without which participation is 'an empty and frustrating process for the powerless. It allows the powerholders to claim that all sides were considered, but makes it possible for only some of those sides to benefit' [46, p. 216]. Although Arnstein's approach may appear obsolete and it has been criticized as defective in some ways [38, 40, 47], the idea that sharing power and authority between the power-holders (public officials) and the have-nots (citizens) is a fundamental condition for participation is still widely shared within the literature.

Most of the frameworks that examine the influence of participants on the final outcomes of participation exercises describe a spectrum of power relationships between citizens and public officials (considering as such both decision makers and public servants). These go from arrangements in which public officials maintain all the power, to arrangements that are more balanced or even to arrangements in which citizens obtain the majority of decision-making seats, or full managerial power [46]. When the power relationship is balanced, participation can be considered as a form of cooperation between citizens and public officials. Arnstein defines as partnership this form of participation, whereas in the often-cited IAP2 framework it is defined as collaboration [48]. By discussing citizens' participation in complex governance, Fung [40, p. 69] observes that some participation mechanisms allow citizens to exercise direct power jointly with public officials; she defines this balanced power arrangement as 'co-governing partnership'. Similarly, Timney [39] considers the collaboration between citizens and public officials based on balanced power relationships as an example of the collaborative network paradigm. He characterizes this form of participation as 'government with the people', as opposed to 'government for the people', i.e. participation exercises in which citizens are allowed to advise and express preferences, but the public officials retain for themselves the right (power) to decide.

What is at stake here actually are different power arrangements, not different participation mechanisms [49]. Even when the most collaborative tools are used, as it happens with crowdsourcing exercises, citizens are not allowed to influence the design and the implementation of public programs if public officials are not willing to give back to citizens some power [35, p. 18]. In their study of idea generation and selection through crowdsourcing as implemented by the city of Ghent (Belgium) as a first step in its smart city-strategy, Schuurman et al. [36] observe that citizen-sourcing exercises are quite likely to result in choices conflicting with the goals and policies of the city governments, which indicates a gap between the city and its citizens. This is a problem for city governments, but it could also be an opportunity if a genuine citizen-centric approach is assumed that allows public officials to use crowdsourcing exercises to stay in touch with citizens [36]. This, of course, holds at the condition that public officials are willing to share power with citizens.

There is a very strong overlap between approaches to encourage co-production as an element of participative democracy and approaches to encourage citizens' participation and involvement more generally [50]. One important aspect on which co-production and participation overlap significantly concerns power distribution between public officials and citizens. In fact, the achievement of the benefits deriving from co-production depends on 'the ways in which the power of people can be brought into public services' [50, p. 3]. As observed by [51] 'co-production is a potentially transformative way of thinking about power, resources, partnerships, risks and outcomes, not an off-the-shelf model of service provision or a single magic solution' (p. 1). It follows that co-production 'is not the same as consultation or the types of tokenistic participation of people who use services and their carers which do not result in meaningful power-sharing or change' (p. 3). Hence, co-production can be related to participation but only at the higher rungs of Arnstein's ladder, i.e. partnership, delegated power and citizen control [46].

By considering different levels of power sharing between public officials and citizens, Needham and Carr define three levels of co-production: (i) simple co-production, in which people experience co-production simply as a description of how all services rely on some productive input from users; (ii) intermediate co-production, in which through shared decision-making the service deliverers are made more aware of the circumstances, needs, preferences and potential contributions of service users; (iii) transformational co-production, in which new user-led mechanisms of planning, delivery, management and governance are developed, requiring and creating a relocation of power and control.

Bovaird [22, p. 856] observes that 'as coproduction almost always means a redistribution of power among stakeholders, the very process of moving to greater coproduction is necessarily highly political and calls into question the balance of representative democracy, participative democracy, and professional expertise'. This strategic and highly transformative impact of co-production is particularly apparent when the power relationships between public officials and citizens are rebalanced in favor of citizens.

In his paper, Bovaird describes the different forms the value creation process can take when citizens are involved as co-producers by considering how the responsibility for service planning and service delivery can be distributed between public officials and citizens/communities. By considering the responsibility for an activity to be allocated (i) uniquely to the public officials, (ii) uniquely to the citizens/communities or (iii) shared between the two, nine possible configurations of the relationship between public officials and citizens/communities are possible, as summarized in Fig. 1.

Out of the nine configurations considered in the figure, two cannot be considered as forms of co-production, namely: public officials as the sole service planners and deliverers, which is the traditional service provision model (configuration 1); public officials as the sole deliverer of services designed by citizens/communities (configuration 3). The path from configuration one through configuration five (full co-production) to configuration nine corresponds to a complete redefinition of the

| | | Responsibility for designing public services | | |
|---|---|---|---|---|
| | | Public officials | Public officials and citizens | Citizens |
| Responsibility for implementing public services | Public officials | 1 Traditional development of a public initiative | 2 Mixed co-production (on the design side) | 3 Public officials as the sole implementers |
| | Public officials and citizens | 4 Mixed co-production (on the implementation side) | 5 Full co-production | 6 Mixed co-production (on the implementation side) |
| | Citizens | 7 Citizens as the implementers of an initiative designed by public officials | 8 Mixed co-production (on the design side) | 9 Self-organized citizens' development (design and implementation) of an initiative |

**Fig. 1** Roles in coproduction (adapted from [22])

power relationships between public officials and citizens. In configuration one, public officials have complete power with no active role for citizens that are simply considered as passive users of the services delivered to them. In configuration nine, citizens have all the power instead, which means that the role of public officials (and hence the role of the 'public') in service design and delivery should be completely redefined. When public officials have no direct involvement in services, their role is to support universal self-organized service provision by individuals and communities through advice, training, reassurance, quality assurance, and, only as a last resort, intervention at key moments [22, p. 850]. Following the path from configuration one to configuration nine entails giving government the role of convener and enabler rather than the first mover of civic action [34], which is one fundamental aspect of both the Digital Era Governance [52] and the Transformational Government paradigms [18].

The considerations above give the basis for answering to the research question Q1 (Under what conditions can co-production represent a truly new relationship between governments and citizens?). After discussing the relation between co-production, citizen participation and power, it is now clear that to be considered as a truly new relationship between governments and citizens' co-production should be based on the rebalancing of the power relationships between public officials and citizens. Without this transformation in the power relationships coproduction, as other forms of citizens' participation, is no more than a rhetorical or, even worse, a manipulation exercise. As Needham [53, p. 13] points out, 'co-production should not be a rationale for pushing the costs and risks of service provision onto the user —the emphasis is on collaboration not substitution. Nor should it be a form of DIY (do-it-yourself) welfare, analogous to the co-productive activities of the consumer of flatpack furniture'.

## 4    Do It Yourself Government: Where Is the Public Value?

Linders [18] observes that the advent of social media and Web 2.0 interactivity enable completely new forms of the relation between citizens and government, up to arrangements 'whereby (…) citizens assist one another, with IT replacing government as vehicle for collective action' (p. 451). Linders defines as Do It Yourself (DIY) government such arrangements enabled by mass coordination via social media that 'provides a vehicle for citizens to self-perform functions of government that the state has refused or is unable to provide on its own' (p. 450). Following Linders' observation, it should be concluded that the DIY government is related to a failure of government to deliver services to the citizens satisfying their needs and their quality requirements. From this point of view, it could seem that the DIY government is similar to the self-provision of public services that represents a possible solution citizens can resort to as a reaction to dissatisfaction towards the services delivered to them [54].

Service self-provision mechanisms are informal methods and strategies used by individuals and groups to satisfy their immediate interests and need for services when they are dissatisfied with the quantity or quality of services provided by either the state, the market or the third sector. In contexts in which more service providers are available in different sectors (public, private and third sector), when citizens are dissatisfied with a service provider, they can adopt one of two typical strategies: (i) demand the provider to improve the service (voice strategy) or (ii) turn to a provider in another sector (exit strategy). Self-provision of services is a further alternative citizens can resort to when they feel that both the exit and voice options have been exhausted [54].

Self-provision is a proactive and entrepreneurial response strategy citizens can assume by initiating, producing, and delivering alternative services, mainly for their own use. As such, self-provision entails questioning the status quo, 'it undermines the status of government as a body solely responsible for service management. Moreover, entrepreneurial exit often reflects policy non-compliance, i.e., a behavior that is inconsistent with current policy or contradicts it [55].

Service self-provision, and the DIY government as well, can be seen from two different perspectives. On the one hand, they can be considered mainly as exit strategies determined by high dissatisfaction and low trust in government (which lead to consider as ineffective the voice strategy). When considered as an exit strategy, the 'widespread self-provision of services may create the impression that major parts of society are interested in reducing the role of government in providing these services' [54, p. 290]. Moreover, the focus of self-provision is on an immediate improvement in the services citizens receive rather than long-term or fundamental changes in the system, which makes difficult (or even impossible) for self-provision to generate a public value that is a value for the wider population and for future generations of citizens as well [56].

On the other hand, self-provision can be considered as an active participation exercise that can be supported and encouraged by government, despite the initial conditions that lead to the development of self-provision mechanisms. This will 'help maximize the advantages of such initiatives while keeping them within the legal and democratic framework of society' [54, p. 290]. The new services, which were entrepreneurially initiated by dissatisfied citizens, can receive official legitimization from the government, or the government may change its policy to acknowledge citizens' new ideas as reflected in the new form of the services [55]. In both cases, the services initiated by the citizens through self-provision mechanisms evolve from sporadic instances to social acceptance, and then to official legitimizations and even to their integration within the portfolio of the services offered by government. By responding to the citizens' needs, the self-provided services deliver a value to them that, through social acceptance and legitimization can be considered a public value, to the point that the self-provided services can be included within the public sphere [57]. As such, they can be considered as citizen-generated public services, or public services 2.0 if the focus is on the enabling technologies [32, 58].

Considered as a participation exercise, service self-provision represents a form of co-production (under the arrangement 9 in the Fig. 1) that can help restore and reinvigorate the citizens' trust toward government, based on a rebalancing of the power relationships in favor of citizens. Different from the 'exit strategy view', the 'co-production view' of the DIY government and self-provision envisages a positive role for government and public officials, although quite different from the roles they usually play in the bureaucratic state. Linders [18] describes these new roles and responsibilities as framer, sponsor, mobilizer, monitor and provider of last resort. O'Relly [34] talks of convener and enabler of civic action. Margetts and Dunleavy [52] give government the fundamental role of enabler of co-production and isocratic administration. Alford [23] argues that public servants' jobs are not simply about producing services, but also influencing citizens to co-produce. Leadbeater and Cottam [32] view the role of government as helping people to exercise choice in a collectively responsible way and so participate in creating public goods, whereas for Morrison [33] what is required to government is re-working the nature of what is public and put citizens in control.

All these new roles and responsibilities entail a transformation of government that affects not only how government and public officials perform their activities (doing things differently) but also, and more importantly, what activities they have to perform (doing different things). Thus, seen through the lens of co-production, the DIY government entails a second order transformation of government and governance. By integrating citizens (and communities) generated services within the public sphere, such second order transformation entails 'a shift in the center of gravity of governance from state and market towards civil society; from regulation by exit and voice towards regulation by loyalty; and from coordination by hierarchies and markets towards coordination through networks' [57, p. 35]. Benington defines this new mode of governance based on a redrawing and rebalancing of the relationships between the state, the citizens and civil society as Networked Community Governance. The networked community governance entails some loss of control by government, policy-makers and public managers in favor of civil society, which, by the way, is one of the reasons that according to Bovaird [22] explain the public officials' reluctance to support co-production exercises. This loss of control determines the 'need for governments to discover new ways of indirect influence on the thinking and activity of other organizations and actors, in addition to direct use of "state assets" and "state authority" to achieve its end' [57, p. 36]. From this point of view, seen through the lens of co-production, the DIY government does not reduce the role of government. Rather, it requires a redefinition of government so that it will not be seen 'simply as to act as a referee between competing interest groups, but also to work proactively to try to develop some kind of shared vision or common purpose out of the diversity of perspectives, and to negotiate and mobilize coalitions of interest to achieve communal aims' (p. 36).

On the basis of the considerations above, it is now possible to answer to the research question Q2 (Under what conditions can the Do-It-Yourself government be considered as a second-order transformation of government resulting from a joint effort between citizens and governments?). The DIY government, as well as the user-generated state and the state 2.0, can determine a second order transformation of government under the following conditions:

1. the user generated services are developed under a co-production strategy and not simply as an exit strategy
2. the user-generated services are able to deliver a public value and not only to satisfy the immediate interests and need for services of the citizens developing them
3. the user-generated services achieve social acceptance and legitimization
4. the user-generated services are developed within a networked community governance framework
5. public value delivery is at the center of the activities of all the actors in the civil society, irrespective of their roles.

## 5   Conclusions

It is generally acknowledged that the widespread diffusion and use of social media facilitates citizens' participation and citizens' involvement as co-producers in traditionally government related activities. By considering the relevant literature, in this paper it has been shown how the weakening of the distinction between service producers and service users, analogous to the weakening of the distinction between content producers and content users typical of the Web 2.0 paradigm, can lead to a radical redrawing of the relationship between government and citizens. This would transform government radically, in line with developments in information and communication technology associated with the Web 2.0 phenomenon [33]. From this point of view, it seems possible to conclude that ICTs (social media in particular) can play a central role in the transformation of government; however, does this mean that Web 2.0 technologies can determine a transformative impact on government? In other words, can the possible impact of social media on government be seen as evidence supporting the ICT reform hypothesis?

The ICT reform hypothesis, that more or less explicitly has underlined much of the e-Government research, is based on the thesis according to which ICTs have the potential for dramatically changing organizations. When this does not happen, it is because top managers fail to distribute the technology efficiently, empower lower level staff and re-engineer the organization's processes [3].

Kraemer and King [3] examine in depth this thesis by surveying almost 30 years of US literature. The conclusion they reach is that, despite the policy rhetoric of transformation associated with e-Government, the findings support the so-called 'reinforcement' hypothesis instead: 'IT has been used most often to reinforce existing organizational arrangements and power distributions [3, p. 3]. At most, e-Government has been capable to determine 'incremental changes in the public sector as a result of introducing and using ICTs, leaving the deep structure of existing institutional arrangements and external relationships intact' [59, p. 744].

Mergel et al. [60] reconsider the Kraemer and King's analysis in the light of the changes determined by the advent of the Web 2.0 technologies that greatly facilitate interactive collaboration between organizations or between individuals and that can easily be deployed, often by people with very low technological abilities (p. 32). Despite the high expectations towards the use of social media by government, Mergel, Schweik and Fountain observe that the transformational potential of Web 2.0 technologies creates a paradox in the public sector, due to the conflict between the participatory and collaborative culture typical of the Web 2.0 paradigm and the highly regulated and constrained culture that characterizes government organizations. This leads to doubt that social media can have a direct transformational impact on government. Although ICTs (social media) can enable enhanced forms of participation (co-production) and the empowerment of citizens, up to allow them to self-provide services in an efficient and effective way, as the discussion in this paper shows, these emergent social phenomena positively impact on government only if government itself activates internal transformational processes that, first of all, concern policy and political representativeness.

How then this relates to ICTs and social media? The widespread diffusion and use of social media as well as of the culture of interactivity, participation and cooperation typical of the Web 2.0 paradigm, is progressively shaping the society in the digital era, affecting heavily life-styles, interpersonal relationships and economic relationships as well. This is changing dramatically the context, making traditional forms of government more and more dysfunctional, what Potts [21] calls policy entropy. The ongoing deep ICT enabled transformations in society and economy put pressure on government organizations to innovate and transform themselves to maintain/restore the fit between government and society in the era of Web 2.0. A better way to think about the transformational impact of social media is that it provides a 'window of opportunity' that government could exploit to comprehensively reexamine how it does things, which entails redefining the nature of government, representativeness, legitimacy and, in the end, redefining what is public.

# References

1. O'Neill, R. (2009). The transformative impact of e-government on public governance in New Zealand. *Public Management Review, 11*(6), 751–770.
2. Scholl, H. (2005). Organisational transformation through e-government: Myth or reality?. In M. A. Wimmer et al. (Eds.), EGOV 2005, LNCS *3591*, 1–11.
3. Kraemer, K., & King, J. L. (2006). Information technology and administrative reform: Will e-government be different? *International Journal of Electronic Government Research, 2*(1), 1–20.
4. Foley, P., & Alfonso, X. (2009). eGovernment and the transformation agenda. *Public Administration, 87*(2), 371–396.
5. Nograšek, J., & Vintar, M. (2014). E-government and organisational transformation of government: Black box revisited? *Government Information Quarterly, 31*(1), 108–118.

6. Meijer, A., Boersma, K., & Wagenaar, P. (Eds.). (2013). *ICTs, citizens and governance: After the hype!*. Amsterdam: IOS Press.
7. Gil-Garcia, J. R., Vivanco, L. F, Luna-Reyes, & L. F. (2014). Revisiting the problem of technological and social determinism: reflections for digital government scholars In M. Janssen, F. Bannister, O. Glassey, H. J. Scholl, E. Tambouris, M. Wimmer, A. Macintosh (Eds.), *Electronic government and electronic participation* (pp. 254–263). Amsterdam: IOS Press.
8. Bannister, F., & Connolly, R. (2012). Forward to the past: Lessons for the future of e-government from the story so far. *Information Polity: The International Journal of Government & Democracy in the Information Age, 17*(3), 211–226.
9. Taylor, J. A., & Lips, A. M. B. (2008). The citizen in the information polity: Exposing the limits of the e-government paradigm. *Information Polity, 13,* 139–152.
10. Johnston, E. W., & Hansen, D. L. (2011). Design lessons for smart governance infrastructures. *American Governance, 3,* 1–30.
11. Scholl, H. J., & Scholl, M. C. (2014). Smart governance: A roadmap for research and practice. In iConference 2014 Proceedings (pp. 163–176).
12. Fountain, J. (2001). *Building the virtual state: Information technology and institutional change*. Washington, DC: Brookings Institution Press.
13. Reddick, C. G. (2005). Citizen interaction with e-government: From the streets to servers? *Government Information Quaterly, 22,* 38–57.
14. Kunstelj, M., & Vintar, M. (2004). Evaluating the progress of e-government development: A critical analysis. *Information Polity, 9,* 131–148.
15. Verdegem, P., & Verleye, G. (2009). User-centered E-Government in practice: A comprehensive model for measuring user satisfaction. *Government Information Quarterly, 26,* 487–497.
16. Gauld, R., Goldfinch, S., & Horsburgh, S. (2010). Do they want it? Do they use it? The 'Demand-Side' of e-Government in Australia and New Zealand. *Government Information Quarterly, 27,* 177–186.
17. Cormode, G., & Krishnamurthy, B. (2008, June 2 ). Key differences between web 1.0 and web 2.0. *First Monday, 13*(6).
18. Linders, D. (2012). From e-government to we-government: Defining a typology for citizen coproduction in the age of social media. *Government Information Quarterly, 29,* 446–454.
19. Bertot, J., Jaeger, P., Munson, S., & Glaisyer, T. (2010). Engaging the public in open government: Social media technology and policy for government transparency. *Computer, 43* (11), 53–59.
20. Meredith, J. (1993). Theory building through conceptual methods. *International Journal of Operations & Production Management, 13*(5), 3–11.
21. Potts, J. (2009). The innovation deficit in public services: The curious problem of too much efficiency and not enough waste and failure. Innovation: Management. *Policy & Practice, 11,* 34–43.
22. Bovaird, T. (2007). Beyond engagement and participation—User and community coproduction of public services. *Public Administration Review, 67*(5), 846–860.
23. Alford, J. (2009). *Engaging public sector clients: From service-delivery to coproduction*. Basingstoke: Palgrave Macmillan.
24. Bovaird, T., & Loeffler, E. (2012). From engagement to coproduction: The contribution of users and communities to outcomes and public value. *VOLUNTAS: International Journal of Voluntary and Nonprofit Organizations, 23*(4), 1119–1138.
25. Meijer, A. (2012). Coproduction in an information age: Individual and community engagement supported by new media. *VOLUNTAS: International Journal of Voluntary and Nonprofit Organizations, 23*(4), 1156–1172.
26. Joshi, A., & Moore, M. (2004). Institutionalized co-production: Unorthodox public service delivery in challenging environments. *The Journal of Development Studies, 40,* 31–49.
27. NESTA. (2012). *People powered health co-production catalogue*. London: Nesta.

28. Voorberg, W. H., Bekkers, V. J. J. M., & Tummers, L. G. (2015). A systematic review of co-creation and co-production: Embarking on the social innovation journey. *Public Management Review, 17,* 1333–1357.

29. Fledderus, J., Brandsen, T., & Honingh, M. E. (2015). User coproduction of public service delivery: An uncertainty approach. *Public Policy and Administration.* 1–20.

30. Prahalad, C. K., & Ramaswamy, V. (2004). Co-creation experiences: The next practice in value creation. *Journal of Interactive Marketing, 18,* 5–14.

31. Bettencourt, L. A., Ostrom, A. L., Brown, S. W., & Roundtree, R. I. (2002). Client co-production in knowledge-intensive business services. *California Management Review, 44* (4), 100–128.

32. Leadbeater, C., & Cottam, H. (2007). The user-generated state: public services 2.0. In P. Diamond (Ed.), *Public matters: The renewal of the public realm.* Methuen, London.

33. Morison, J. (2010). Gov 2.0: Towards a user generated state? *The Modern Law Review, 73*(4), 551–577.

34. O'Reilly, T. (2010). Government as a Platform. In D. Lathrop & L. Ruma (Eds.), *Open government: Collaboration, transparency, and participation in practice.* USA: O'Reilly Media.

35. Nam, T. (2012). Suggesting frameworks of citizen-sourcing via Government 2.0. *Government Information Quarterly, 29,* 12–20.

36. Schuurman, D., Baccarne, B., De Marez, L., & Mechant, P. (2012). Smart ideas for smart cities: Investigating crowdsourcing for generating and selecting ideas for ICT innovation in a city context. *Journal of Theoretical and Applied Electronic Commerce Research, 7,* 49–62.

37. Meijer, A., & Thaens, M. (2013). Social media strategies: Understanding the differences between North American police departments. *Government Information Quarterly, 30*(4), 343–350.

38. Cornwall, A. (2008). Unpacking 'participation': Models, meanings, and practices. *Community Development Journal, 43,* 269–283.

39. Timney, M. (2011). Models of citizen participation: Measuring engagement and collaboration. in King, C.S., Sharpe, M.E. (eds.), Government is us 2.0 (86–100). Armonk, NY.

40. Fung, A. (2006). Varieties of participation in complex governance. *Public Administration Review, 66*(s1), 66–75.

41. Roberts, N. C. (2008). *The age of direct citizen participation.* Armonk, NY: M.E. Sharpe.

42. Kweit, M. G., & Kweit, R. W. (1981). *Implementing citizen participation in a bureaucratic society: A contingency approach.* New York: Praeger.

43. King, C. S., Feltey, K. M., & O'Neill Susel, B. (1998). The question of participation: Toward authentic public participation in public administration. *Public Administration Review, 58*(4), 317–326.

44. Ebdon, C., & Franklin, A. L. (2006). Citizen participation in budgeting theory. *Public Administration Review, 66*(3), 437–447.

45. Yang, K., & Pandey, K. S. (2011). Further dissecting the black box of citizen participation: When does citizen involvement lead to good outcomes? *Public Administration Review, 71*(6), 880–892.

46. Arnstein, S. (1969). The ladder of citizen participation. *Journal of the American Institute of Planner, 35,* 216–224.

47. Tritter, J. Q., & McCallum, A. (2006). The snakes and ladders of user involvement: Moving beyond Arnstein. *Health Policy, 76,* 156–168.

48. International Association for Public Participation (IAP2). (2007). *IAP2 Spectrum of Public Participation.* Tornton, CO: International Association for Public Participation. http://iap2. affiniscape.com/associations/4748/files/IAP2%20Spectrum_vertical.pdf.

49. Rowe, G., & Frewer, L. J. (2005). A typology of public engagement mechanisms. *Science, Technology and Human Values, 30*(2), 251–290.

50. Bovaird T., & Loeffler, E. (2014). *Bringing the power of the citizen into local public services —An evidence review* (Research Report 110/2014). Cardiff: Welsh Government.

51. Needham, C., & Carr, S. (2009). *Co-production: An emerging evidence base for adult social care transformation*. London: Social Care Institute for Excellence.
52. Margetts, H., & Dunleavy, P. (2013). The second wave of digital-era governance: A quasi-paradigm for government on the Web. *Philosophical Transactions of The Royal Society A 371*.
53. Needham, C. (2008). Citizens, consumers and co-producers. *Kurswechsel, 2,* 7–16.
54. Mizrahi, S. (2011). Self-provision of public services: its evolution and impact. *Public Administration Review, 72*(2), 285–291.
55. Gofen, A. (2012). Entrepreneurial exit response to dissatisfaction with public services. *Public Administration, 90*(4), 1088–1106.
56. Hartley, J. (2011). Public value through innovation and improvement. In J. Benington & M. Moore (Eds.), *Public value: Theory and practice* (pp. 171–184). Basingstoke: Palgrave Macmillan.
57. Benington, J. (2011). From private choice to public value? In J. Benington & M. Moore (Eds.), *Public value—Theory and practice* (pp. 31–51). Basingstoke: Palgrave.
58. Punie, Y., Misuraca, G., Osimo, D., Huijboom, N., Broek, T. A., van den Frissen, V., & Kool, L. (2010). *Public services 2.0: The impact of social computing on public services.* Brussels, Be: European Commission.
59. Lips, A. B. M., & Schuppan, T. (2011). Transforming e-government knowledge through public management research. *Public Management Review, 11*(6), 739–749.
60. Mergel, I., Schweik, C., & Fountain, J. (2009). The transformational effect of web 2.0 technologies on government. Accessed 1 June 2009. Available on SSRN, http://papers.ssrn.com/sol3/papers.cfm?abstract_id=1412796.

# How Digital Transformation is Reshaping the Manufacturing Industry Value Chain: The New Digital Manufacturing Ecosystem Applied to a Case Study from the Food Industry

**Marco Savastano⊙, Carlo Amendola⊙ and Fabrizio D'Ascenzo⊙**

**Abstract** The rapid development and adoption of Internet and digital technologies dramatically changed business processes, leading to a disruptive digital transformation of the whole industry value chain. The so-called Industry 4.0 refers to a complex evolution of the entire industrial sector that includes technological advances in production equipment (i.e. Additive Manufacturing), smart finished products (IoT), data tools and analytics, involving activities and stakeholders at all levels. Therefore, companies need to completely redesign their business processes and models in order to achieve the important benefits disclosed by these new settings. Even though actual and potential advantages are remarkable, only a limited number of companies has already made rapid advances by developing high digital capabilities necessary to obtain a competitive advantage. The purpose of this paper is to explore this emerging trend through a case study carried out with an Italian company world leader in the food industry, aiming to shed light on opportunities and threats connected to digital transition.

**Keywords** Industry 4.0 · Digital transformation · Business process digitalization Industrial internet · Manufacturing industry value chain · Additive manufacturing Direct digital manufacturing · Innovation · Internet of things · New product development · Value Co-creation · SMEs

M. Savastano (✉) · C. Amendola · F. D'Ascenzo
Management Department, Sapienza University, Rome, Italy
e-mail: marco.savastano@uniroma1.it

C. Amendola
e-mail: carlo.amendola@uniroma1.it

F. D'Ascenzo
e-mail: fabrizio.dascenzo@uniroma1.it

© Springer International Publishing AG, part of Springer Nature 2018
R. Lamboglia et al. (eds.), *Network, Smart and Open*, Lecture Notes in Information Systems and Organisation 24, https://doi.org/10.1007/978-3-319-62636-9_9

# 1   Introduction

Over the last decades, the rapid developments of the Internet and the information technologies have profoundly impacted every aspect of organizational and social activities through a disruptive digital transformation. A large number of companies, including small and medium-sized enterprises (SMEs), have accelerated the digitization of their business processes in order to gain market and operational efficiency while meeting the increasing customer expectations [1, 2].

In today's highly competitive environment, digital innovation is critical for addressing manufacturers' key business drivers and creating value. Indeed, digital tools and technologies allow manufacturing companies to reduce costs, increase productivity, improve product development, achieve faster time-to-market and enhance customer focus across various elements of the value chain [2]. On the other hand, also some threats exist: business models have to be redesigned and aligned with the innovative tools in order to effectively exploit their potentials and take full advantage of the high investment needed.

Different digital tools and innovations can be employed by manufacturers for enhancing each of the following stages of their value chain [3]:

- Product Design and Innovation.
- Manufacturing.
- Supply Chain Management.
- Marketing, Sales and Services.

This fourth wave of technological advancement, sometimes referred to as "*Industry 4.0*" (especially in Europe; "*Industrial Internet*" in USA), reflects in particular the rise of a basket of new digitally-enabled industrial technologies and seems to result in a new fundamental paradigm shift of the industrial production, supposed to realize the manufacturing of individual products in a batch size of one while maintaining the economic conditions of mass production. This transformation includes advances in production equipment (i.e. additive manufacturing, autonomous robots, adaptive CNC mills, etc.), smart finished products and objects (e.g. connected cars, ubiquitous computing and the Internet of Things—IoT), data tools and analytics. In addition to the aforementioned innovations, collaboration platforms, social networks, augmented reality, virtualization, cloud computing and crowdsourcing impact manufacturing companies to varying degrees. These technologies are changing the way things are designed, produced and serviced around the globe. In combination, they can create value by connecting different players and machines in a new "digital thread" across the value chain, relying on the availability of an unprecedented huge amount of data in order to address manufacturer's key business drivers. They are potential enablers of a disruptive change, comparable to the rise of consumer e-commerce [4, 5].

Although these wide potentialities, manufacturing companies from different industries have traditionally been slow to react to the advent of digital innovations and their impact across the manufacturing value chain and operating model. As resulted from a recent survey conducted by McKinsey [2], while there are some manufacturing companies that have made rapid advances by deriving significant benefits from digital transformation, their number is still small. In fact, 80% of the respondents consider digital manufacturing and design to be a critical driver of competitiveness, but only 13% rate their organizations' digital capabilities as high. And even among those pioneers, many believe that their firms and related industries they operate in currently lack necessary standards, data-sharing, and capabilities. At the same time, executives at several manufacturers in different industries identify a need for dramatic improvements in certain software applications in areas such as computer-aided design (CAD), enterprise resource planning (ERP), and manufacturing execution systems (MES), finding them difficult to learn, slow to evolve and adapt, closed and sometimes too expensive for being adopted by small businesses. On the contrary, for taking advantage of the transformative potential disclosed by digital manufacturing it is crucial for information systems to be open, interoperable, and user-friendly [5].

Starting from the definition of the Industry 4.0 and business process digitalization (BDP) concepts, our exploratory research focuses on the extensive use and development of Additive Manufacturing for industrial applications, aiming to analyze and understand the possible impacts of the rising digital manufacturing ecosystem on the current industry value chain. To this purpose, our research question emerged as follows:

- *RQ: How digital technologies are impacting the manufacturing value chain, enabling benefits for businesses in different industries?*

To achieve this goal, after taking into account the existing literature and several market evidences, we carried out a case study with an Italian company world leader in the food industry for better exploring possible scenarios and assessing practical implications.

## 2 Theoretical Background

### 2.1 Industry 4.0

In Europe the manufacturing industry represents an important axis of identity, which retains its strategic importance despite the violence of the crisis. For instance in Germany, according to the Eurostat data, it contributes to over 25% of the GDP and provides over 7 million jobs. Moreover, the share of GDP attributable to manufacturing industry in Italy was 15.5% in 2014, with more than 4.5 million people employed in the sector and manufactured products that represent more than 78% of total exports of goods and services [6, 7].

The three so called "industrial revolutions" of the past were paradigm shifts of the production process, all triggered by technical innovations: the advent of mechanization, the intensive use of electrical energy and the widespread automation of production and use of electronics. According to the existing literature on this topic and the experts from the industry, the advanced digitalization within factories in combination with Internet technologies and innovations in the field of *smart objects*—machines and products—enabled by the ubiquitous computing are the foundations of the upcoming fourth industrial revolution, characterized by smart factories and digital enterprises working together with customers and suppliers in industrial digital ecosystems. Alongside to technological innovation, the organization structure has undergone several major shifts to face fast changing markets [4, 8].

More in detail, the term Industry 4.0 (coined in Germany during the Deutsche Messe 2011) refers to a wide range of current concepts related to a disruptive transformation in the organization and management of the entire value chain process involved in manufacturing industry, driven by digital innovation [9]. It focuses on the end-to-end digitalization of all physical assets and the integration into digital ecosystems with value chain partners. Moreover, physical and virtual workflows will merge into cyber-physical systems (CPS), that will enable the communication between humans, machines and products within smart factories. At the base of the gains achievable by this new configuration, that networks a wide range of new technologies to create value, lies the seamless generation, gathering, analysis and communication of data [10]. In fact, smart factories have to deal with the need of rapid product development, flexible distributed production and complex environments [11].

Some specific settings drive the configuration of Industry 4.0 framework as follows [10]:

(1) **Digitisation and integration of vertical and horizontal value chains:**

*(i) vertical integration* of processes spans across the entire organisation, from procurement and product development, through manufacturing, logistics and services. All data about operations processes, process efficiency and quality management, as well as operations planning are available in real-time, supported by smart sensors and augmented reality and optimised in an integrated system; *(ii) horizontal integration* stretches beyond the internal operations, from suppliers to customers, including all key network partners. The organization in collaborative networks multiplies the available capacities without the need of further investments. Collaborative Manufacturing and Development Environments are important particularly for SMEs with limited resources; in fact, within these networks risks can be balanced and combined resources can increase the range of perceivable market opportunities [8, 12, 13].

(2) **Digitisation and customization of products and services:**

Digitisation of products refers to the expansion of existing products, for instance by adding smart sensors or communication devices to be used with data analytics tools (i.e. smart products), as well as to the development of brand new digitized products through entirely digitalized processes. By integrating new methods of data collection and analysis with flexible processes enabled by Modularization, Rapid

Manufacturing techniques and Reconfigurable Manufacturing Systems, companies are able to generate data on product use and quickly refine products requirements to meet the increasing needs of end-customers in a cost-efficient way.

(3) **Digital business models and customer access:**

Leading industrial companies can also expand their offering by providing disruptive digital solutions such as complete, data-driven services and integrated platform solutions. Innovative digital business models are often focused on generating additional revenues and optimising customer interaction and access. Digital products and services allow enterprises to serve customers with complete solutions in a distinct digital ecosystem.

Recent studies described also a set of *key technology trends* as the building blocks of Industry 4.0, which enable manufacturers to reach technical and economic benefits through faster, more flexible, and more efficient processes for the production of higher-quality goods at reduced costs. Many of the following advances in technology (such as additive manufacturing, smart sensors, advanced human-machine interfaces, big data analytics, etc.) are already employed by manufacturers, but within this comprehensive framework they will transform the production process: isolated cells will work together as a fully integrated, automated, and optimized production flow, leading to greater efficiencies and changing traditional production relationships among suppliers, producers, and customers—as well as between human and machine [14]. Figure 1 on the next page provides a representation of these essential innovative tools.

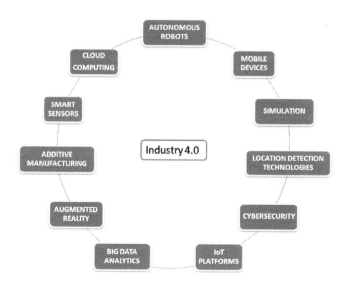

**Fig. 1** Industry 4.0 enabling key technologies. *Source* our elaboration

## 2.2 Business Process Digitalization

Closely linked to and somewhat forming part of the concept of industry 4.0, *business process digitalization (BPD)* can be defined as an enterprise-wide information system based on the technological foundation of the Internet. This means an extensive use of e-business tools and practices across the value chain, leading to a wide range of innovation opportunities [15, 16].

In particular, it refers to digital applications and internet technologies which affect several aspects of organizational activities and processes: B2S (business to suppliers), B2E (business to employees), B2C (business to customers) and B2O (business to others) IT applications that enhance various inter and intra-firm activities, such as customer and supplier services (i.e. computer-aided design and digital manufacturing; multi to omni-channel customer management enablers), employee services (i.e. education and training), industry scanning (technology sourcing), etc. [1].

As already mentioned, there are areas in the manufacturing value chain and operating model which can be radically transformed by digital innovation, representing a topic of great interest to many organizations. Digital capabilities help companies to rapidly exchange large amounts of data, store local data centrally, enrich processes with an increased knowledge base, generate valuable insights from this "big data" and facilitate communication and collaboration through digital channels within their value chain. These new capabilities transform the classic value chain model, represented by a linear flow of processes, into an integrated value circle (see Fig. 2 on the next page).

When properly exploited, digital technologies can help manufacturers to turn into highly innovative, fast-growing and agile companies. Product development experiences a significant increase of innovative power through open innovation and

**Fig. 2** Integrated value circle. *Source* Capgemini Consulting 2012

collaboration within integrated competence networks as well as by involving customers in the co-design and co-creation of products and services. In the manufacturing area, digital tools help companies to increase the productivity and agility of their factories and their responsiveness to rapid market changes. Digital supply chains can raise the efficiency of their logistics settings, covering even remote spots in their increasingly distributed configurations. Digital tools in marketing, sales and services can boost effectiveness, revenues and margins by multiplying the touchpoints to reach customers and addressing their expectations.

The impact of these advances on manufacturing companies activities varies depending on the sub-sector they operate in, defining which specific part of the value chain they need to focus on. Accordingly, on the one hand more business-to-business oriented sectors like Aerospace & Defense and industrial products have experienced the greatest impact on the operations area (i.e. product development, manufacturing, SCM); on the other one, apparel and part of the high-tech industry, with a stronger business-to-consumer orientation, are impacted the most in areas such as product innovation, marketing, sales, customer relationship management and service [3].

Results from a study conducted by Li et al. [1] with small and medium-sized manufacturers operating in different industries in USA, show a significant positive impact of the extensiveness of business process digitalization on SMEs' new product development (emphasizing a correlation between these two variables). These findings suggest that companies, and in particular SMEs, can achieve innovative competitive advantages by implementing and exploiting an enterprise-wide information system and digitalizing business processes. The extensiveness of BPD also allow firms to develop unique, hard-to-imitate IT capabilities and IT enabled knowledge base through synergy and learning effects. Moreover, a moderating effect of firm age on the relationship between BPD and new product development emerged. It is positive and significant and suggests an indirect impact of age on firm innovation, meaning that mature firms gain advantages in this regard because they are more stable than younger ones so that the enterprise-wide information system can be fully exploited and integrated with business and organization processes [1]. This datum results in contrast with some previous researches that relate firm age negatively with innovation, as one of the factors inhibiting it due to organizational inertia and path dependence in firm strategy [17–19].

Although a large amount of studies on the adoption of BPD provided good understanding by focusing on the different aspects at the organizational, industrial and institutional level, it is still unclear how it can enhance firm's market and operational performance along the value chain. In order to contribute to the literature on this topic, the present study explores this concept in this specific way focusing on the digitalization of new product development and manufacturing processes.

# 3   The Digital Manufacturing Ecosystem

Previously in this paper we described additive manufacturing (AM) as one of the key technology trends representing the basis of Industry 4.0.

There is a wide range of technologies covered under the umbrella of AM, with varying benefits, disadvantages and potential. The present analysis of the sector has its specific focus not on the different kinds of technologies used, but on the value the digitalization of manufacturing can create both for companies and consumers through an appreciation of the various benefits and challenges that AM methods present.

Unlike traditional manufacturing techniques, AM creates objects by adding different layers of material, rather than removing it in a subtractive manner. Paired with computer-aided design (CAD) software, this technique affords the creation of products with unique material and geometric properties [20]. From a technological point of view it is not a recent innovation (stereolithography was invented in 1983 by engineer Chuck Hull and used for rapid prototyping applications), but in recent years the opportunity to use this technology have expanded significantly due to the incremental ability to "print" larger objects of every kind of shape and material, and thus for every sector. Key drivers that made possible this evolution, pushing companies to invest in it as a production technique, are the following [21, 22]:

i. *the possibility to use a broader variety of materials*, including photosensitive resins, aluminium, super alloys, stainless steel, titanium, polymers, ceramics, cement, glass and new thermoplastic composites up to human tissues and edible substances for 3D food printing;

ii. *a significant production time reduction and substantial improvements in the quality of products*, in terms of higher resolution of industrial printers and increased strength and finish quality of goods;

iii. *3D printers rapid costs reduction,* thanks to their fast diffusion and the expiration of some critical patents that gave the possibility to Open Source hardware to lead to rapid innovation and improvements.

While scientific research is strongly polarized on technical characteristics of additive manufacturing [23], more efforts are needed concerning economic, strategic and organizational aspects of this domain, currently more important than in the past since digital manufacturing applications increasingly relate to the production of end products and components for final uses more than to prototyping purposes [24].

As already observed in our previous work [25], AM technologies offer several important advantages to manufacturer companies:

• To redesign products with fewer components, reducing material waste as well as obtaining lighter parts characterized by equal physical strength properties.
• To realize products on-demand closer to the customers (the so-called "distributed manufacturing"), simplifying the traditional supply chain and reducing delivery times together with warehousing, packaging and transportation costs.

- To produce any good—including customized ones—in small production batches (even batches of one) economically, with an enhanced flexibility in terms of locations and times.

In particular, compared to traditional production techniques, additive manufacturing exceeds any technical constraints related to the objects geometries. Complex shapes realized as one piece in a single run, with no assembly required, result not only in lower costs of labor per unit, but also in higher level of technical functionality [26]. At the same time, the production costs are nearly independent from the volumes. In fact, since each unit is built independently, it can easily be modified only by changing the digital design in order to accommodate improvements, demand variability or to suit unique requests. Combining these benefits with the enormous availability of data concerning customers needs, behavior and preferences, as well as the possibility to directly interact with them through several digital touchpoints, companies are able to achieve high degrees of product customization, with the possibility to delight customers by involving them in the co-design of goods [27].

On the other hand, since economies of scale are not feasible through this technology, it is not competitive in terms of costs for large scale production of standardized goods. This makes it suitable especially for small-scale and high-quality local productions characterized by a premium price.

Due to its features, additive manufacturing is an important success factor in industrial sectors and market niches where agility, speed and flexibility represent competitive advantages. For these reasons, the sectors most involved today are aerospace, automotive, biomedical, dental and packaging. In addition, AM is particularly widespread in jewelry and is currently recording a fast growth in fashion accessories and food industries [28].

# 4 Case Study

## 4.1 Research Design

In order to answer our research question and find out practical evidences for addressing the constructs emerging from the literature review, we conducted a case study research in a specific sector (agri-food) involving one of the most famous Italian and European food company, world leader in the production of pasta, sauces, ready meals and snacks: Barilla Group S.p.A.

Our purpose was to carry out an in-depth investigation to assess actual/possible benefits of process digitalization through the adoption of additive manufacturing, narrowing down a broad field of research into a more easily researchable topic [29]. To do so, in early June 2016 we visited the Barilla headquarter located in the city of Parma to perform in-depth interviews with two managers—Giacomo Canali and Fabrizio Cassotta—from the Group Research, Development and Quality division, in order to gain a deeper understanding of the company innovation strategy by obtaining a direct testimony from those who work daily in this environment. The face-to-face interviews (which lasted more than an hour) were based on a semi-structured track with open-ended questions in order to define the contents to be treated without, in any way, limiting the respondents to communicate freely their opinions and experiences. Indeed, respondents were solicited to describe objectives, insights and strategies of the innovative project under investigation in great detail and exhaustive explanations, with a specific focus on the benefits and potentials for the company and its customers. The interview guideline was structured on the following topics, which represent only a schematic summary of the specific questions realized:

(a) Type of digital/additive manufacturing technology adopted and implementation stage.
(b) Objectives, development time and investments.
(c) Expected benefits.
(d) Supply chain partners and competitors advances.
(e) Product categories involved.
(f) Make or buy decisions.
(g) Technical and organizational critical issues.
(h) Added value creation within the value chain.
(i) Sustainable competitive advantage.
(j) Expected future developments.

Furthermore, in order to guarantee greater validity to the investigation, a data triangulation has been implemented by combining evidences resulting from the interviews with ones gathered from secondary sources (e.g. websites, reports, research articles, etc.).

## 4.2 Food Industry: Trends and Perspectives

The food and drink industry is the EU's largest manufacturing sector in terms of turnover, value added and employment. It is also an important asset in trade with non-EU countries.[1] In 2013 it recorded a turnover of €1048 billion, generating a value added of €206 billion, and employed 4.2 million people. The industry remains stable, resilient and robust, even in times of economic downturn. Indeed, it is one of the very few manufacturing sectors to produce above its output level of 2008 (see Fig. 3, next page) [30].

It results in a diversified sector, characterised by a wide range of company sizes, with SMEs accounting for a large share of the activity (more than 50% of the industry turnover). It includes a variety of sectors: the top 5 sub-sectors (bakery and

---

[1]http://ec.europa.eu/index_en.htm.

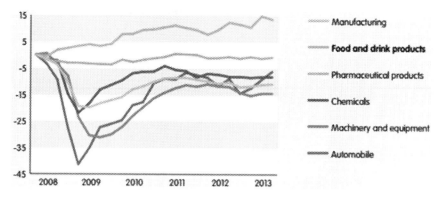

**Fig. 3** Production in the EU manufacturing industry, period 2008–2013 (% change since 2008). *Sources* Eurostat; FoodDrinkEurope 2014

farinaceous products, meat sector, dairy products, drinks and 'various food products' category) account for 75% of the total turnover and more than four fifths of the total number of employees and companies.

With reference to the Italian market, the manufacturing industry closed the year 2015 with an annual turnover growth rate of 2.5% (compared to 2014) spread to all sectors, with the only exception of metallurgy and chemical intermediates. The food and drink sector, leader in terms of turnover since 2009 and competitive at EU level, continues to contribute to the Italian manufacturing industry growth. Even among other key sectors of Made in Italy, the good results of this sector on international markets must be highlighted [31].

### 4.2.1 Additive Manufacturing for the Food Industry

Additive manufacturing of food is an emerging field characterized by great potential but limited application, in search of utility. The key motivators for the development of 3D printing of food are product customization, on-demand production, geometric complexity and direct-to-consumer relationships. For these reasons, recent applications of this technique focused mainly on intricate 3D shapes for artistic presentations and complex textures. As the custom cake market has shown, premium can be added to food products by customizing the shape on the base of consumers' requests [32]. Researchers have developed software applications to turn designs into 3D printed structures on food [33]. 3D printing systems have been used to create sugar sculptures by ink-jetting a binder, such as alcohol, onto layers of powdered sugar: for instance The Sugar Lab's core business is the production of custom shapes out of sugar. Moreover, ChocoEdge and PIQ Chocolates currently sell custom shaped chocolates to consumers while two of the world's largest 3D printing companies, Stratasys and 3D Systems, are developing 3D printers to produce chocolate treats.

Additive manufacturing allows food customization not only in terms of shapes, but also of content. According to this aspect, food can be designed and printed based on individuals' biometric data and personal taste preferences. Anyhow, AM technology in food industry is still in the early stages; companies need to continue investing in R&D and regularly develop new capabilities, so the examples cited here represent only the starting point of this field expansion [34].

## 4.3 Barilla "3D Pasta Printing"

Barilla company was founded in Parma in 1877 as a shop specialized in the production of bread and pasta. Today it is one of the top Italian food groups, world leader for pasta, leading producer for the ready-made sauces in continental Europe, the bakery products in Italy and the crispbread in Scandinavian countries. The Group owns 29 production sites (14 in Italy and 15 abroad) and exports to over 100 countries. Every year the Group's plants turn out more than 1,800,000 tons of food products, which are commercialized under several brands (Barilla, Mulino Bianco, Harrys, Pavesi, Wasa, Filiz, Yemina, Vesta, Misko, Voiello, Academia Barilla) and consumed all over the world.

Barilla recorded an excellent economic performance in 2015, even in a particularly complex economic situation. Italy still represents 47% of total sales (the datum is slightly decreasing), while the rest of Europe and the Americas are growing up (+4% in volumes), especially the United States, where Barilla is the leader with a market share of about 30% and opened three restaurants in New York. Concerning research and development activities, the Group invested 155 million Euro in equipment, research and development in 2014 (+6% compared to 2013), and 37 million specifically in research and development activities on processes and products in 2015 [35].

Barilla has recently developed in-house the first prototype of a 3D printer for pasta (within the "3D Pasta Printing" project) in collaboration with TNO, a Dutch Applied Research Centre located in Eindhoven. Through this collaboration it was possible to merge Barilla's know-how and experience about pasta with TNO's about 3D technologies. The various phases of project development have employed the work of several people from different functional areas of Barilla. In particular, agronomists, food technologists, chemists, microbiologists, engineers, as well as professionals from marketing and procurement areas. In addition, it was used the external contribution of consultants including *makers* and designers. The project was presented on several occasions and through different media platforms. At first in a TV-show on BBC in the Netherlands, then showcased during the Pasta World Championship 2015. The presentation at CIBUS International Food Exhibition 2016 was followed by a great media resonance with many interviews and articles, including on specialized websites and blogs (e.g. Wired, etc.). This was followed by the event at Fabbrica del Vapore for the XXI Triennale di Milano.

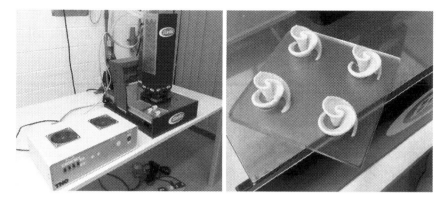

**Fig. 4** Barilla 3D Printer (**a**) and 3D-Printed Pasta (**b**)

Barilla 3D printer uses a Fused Deposition Modeling (FDM) manufacturing technology and pasta is made out of a mixture of durum wheat flour and water, basically the same ingredients used in the traditional process but with formulation and properties of the raw materials developed ad hoc (see Fig. 4a). The machine takes 2 min for the extrusion of pasta, which has the typical consistency of fresh pasta (the extrusion speed is about 2 g/min). Within 3 additional minutes it can be cooked and ready to be eaten. In this way it is possible to create a plate of pasta on-demand, from zero, in 5 min. Furthermore, it is also possible to customize the shape, colour and taste of pasta. Different shapes of pasta are designed throughout a specific CAD software, that allows to create a virtually endless library of geometries in addition to traditional formats (see Fig. 4b). In this regard Barilla launched an online contest based on a crowdsourcing platform for the co-creation of innovative shapes which could meet consumer tastes. Additive manufacturing's key strengths of geometric complexity, product customization and economy at low volume of production are therefore translated into benefits for the food industry.

Based on these evidences, we hypothesized some potential uses of Barilla 3D Pasta Printing, split up into the following industry levels and scenarios:

1. *Consumer produced pasta*: in this scenario Barilla would be considered the developer of the desktop 3D printer and the only supplier of the digital models for the domestic production of different types of pasta. "User interface would be as easy as possible, with plug and play cartridges and a dedicated mobile app to select the size/recipe and start the printing process". This would allow to achieve the food printing goal of producing shapes on-demand without the need for a multi-step process, enabling even less skilled users to produce any kind of fresh pasta in a short time. Furthermore it would be possible to adapt the ingredients to individual's health requirements and activity level, as well as tastes.

2. *Small scale food production*: would include mainly pasta shops, supermarkets and restaurants, both independent and directly managed by Barilla (i.e. the ones recently opened in New York). In any case, the technology and the whole

service (different pasta designs, sauces, etc.) would be provided by Barilla to ensure compliance with its quality standards. Pasta can then be printed according to specific customer requirements, for the direct consumption or the purchase. "This would ensure a unique gastronomic customer experience". Within this category is included also the idea of local "*printer farms*", spread over the whole country and ideally comparable to FabLabs.
3. *E-commerce*: online selling of 3D printed pasta, specifically created according to the individual consumer tastes and delivered at home.

We didn't include *Industrial scale food production(4)* in the previous list since Barilla will continue serving the mass consumer market (and the most traditional pasta formats) by using conventional manufacturing techniques, in order to avoid current technical limitations as well as to exploit economies of scale and higher efficiency in terms of production costs and times. It is also important to notice that the expected use of this technology, in any context, does not refer to rapid proto-typing, but to direct digital manufacturing (DDM). In order to find out the best business model for this innovation, Barilla is carrying out market researches with current and potential customers (prospects) by using different methodologies of investigation (e.g. design thinking, etc.). Early evidences show different results according to the market explored (Italy, Europe, USA). The project is still in the research stage; depending on the context chosen, then will be developed the specific technical prototype characterized by proper features: a compact, cheaper and user-friendly desktop printer for domestic use, a faster and bigger one for catering applications or an industrial-sized machine to be employed within a factory. Even if the technology is mature for each of the aforementioned applications, some time is still needed both for the technical development and business model design before the final market release. The group has strategically focused only on the pasta market for this innovation (as first mover), but in the future applications for bakery products could be possible. Currently no competitors exist for the 3D printing of pasta. Some independent makers have tried to develop similar solutions, but "there is no one with this level of resolution, able to produce these formats, and especially with this quality of the finished product".

## 5   Conclusions and Future Research

Innovative digitally-enabled technologies are leading to a new disruptive paradigm shift of the industrial production. Business process digitalization is reconfiguring every aspect of organizational and operating activities along the entire value chain. The integration and management of a wide range of advanced tools within a net-worked digital ecosystem, also known as Industry 4.0, allow firms to achieve important gains in terms of value creation for the different players involved at every level in the system. Manufacturing companies need to adopt a systematic approach, by drawing a digital roadmap, to address business opportunities across their value chain: (i) firstly they should clearly outline the strategic business objectives to be achieved. Objectives need to be explicitly defined and committed to by all functions before starting the project. (ii) secondly, manufacturers should identify and select potential innovation that can be applied and further developed, able to provide business value. To do so, they need to gain a good understanding of the latest digital applications across the manufacturing value chain through market analysis. (iii) finally, they have to prioritize the initiatives based on the perceived business benefits (e.g. financial, internal, for customers and innovation) and ease of implementation, according to the specific market.

As evidences from our case study demonstrate, innovation projects are often technology driven. While on the one hand technology is mature for almost any industrial application, on the other one business models need to be redesigned and aligned to it in order to achieve a real sustainable competitive advantage on the market.

Since the present work is an exploratory research, further studies are needed in order to analyze more in depth this rapidly growing phenomenon and test with quantitative evaluations the impact of digital transformation, in terms of real benefits for business and value added for consumers.

**Acknowledgements** We would like to thank Ing. Giacomo Canali (Group Research, Development and Quality Research manager), and Dott. Fabrizio Cassotta (Innovation Pasta, Ready Meals and Smart Food Manager, team leader for the 3D Pasta Printing project) from Barilla Group S.p.A., for their fundamental collaboration and professional support.

# References

1. Li, J., Merenda, M., & Venkatachalam, A. R. (2009). Business process digitalization and new product development: An empirical study of small and medium-sized manufacturers. *International Journal of E-Business Research, 5*(1), 49–64.
2. Markovitch, S., & Willmott, P. (2014). *Accelerating the digitization of business processes* (pp. 1–5). Newyork: McKinsey & Company.
3. Ebner, G., & Bechtold, J. (2012). Are manufacturing companies ready to go digital? *Capgemini Study.*
4. Lasi, H., Fettke, P., Kemper, H. G., Feld, T., & Hoffmann, M. (2014). Industry 4.0. *Business and Information Systems Engineering, 6*(4), 239–242.
5. Nanry, J., Narayanan, S., & Rassey, L. (2015). *Digitizing the value chain* (p. 4). McKinsey Quarterly.
6. Bricco, P. (2015). Così la manifattura resta decisiva per tornare a crescere. *Il Sole 24 Ore.*
7. ISTAT. (2014). *L'evoluzione Dell'economia Italiana: Aspetti Macroeconomici.*
8. Brettel, M., Friederichsen, N., Keller, M., & Rosenberg, M. (2014). How Virtualization, decentralization and network building change the manufacturing landscape: An Industry 4.0 perspective. *International Journal of Mechanical, Aerospace, Industrial and Mechatronics Engineering, 8*(1), 37–44.
9. Deloitte. (2015). *Industry 4.0. Challenges and solutions for the digital transformation and use of exponential technologies* (pp. 1–30). New york: Deloitte.
10. Geissbauer, R., Vedso, J., & Schrauf, S. (2016). *Industry 4.0 : Building the digital enterprise.*

11. Vyatkin, V., Salcic, Z., Roop, P. S., & Fitzgerald, J. (2007). Now that's smart! *IEEE Industrial Electronics Magazine, 1*(4), 17–29.
12. Lin, H. W., Nagalingam, S. V., Kuik, S. S., & Murata, T. (2012). Design of a Global Decision Support System for a manufacturing SME: Towards participating in Collaborative Manufacturing. *International Journal of Production Economics, 136*(1), 1–12.
13. Mendikoa, I., Sorli, M., Barbero, J. I., Carrillo, A., & Gorostiza, A. (2008). Collaborative product design and manufacturing with inventive approaches. *International Journal of Production Research, 46*(9), 2333–2344.
14. Rüßmann, M., Lorenz, M., Gerbert, P., Waldner, M., Justus, J., Engel, P., & Harnisch, M. (2015). *Industry 4.0. The Future of Productivity and Growth in Manufacturing* (pp. 1–5). Boston Consulting.
15. BarNir, A., Gallaugher, J. M., & Auger, P. (2003). Business process digitization, strategy, and the impact of firm age and size: The case of the magazine publishing industry. *Journal of Business Venturing, 18*(6), 789–814.
16. Johnston, D. A., Wade, M., & McClean, R. (2007). Does e-business matter to SMEs? A comparison of the financial impacts of Internet business solutions on European and North American SMEs. *Journal of Small Business Management, 45*(3), 354–361.
17. Hannan, M. T., & Freeman, J. (1984). Structural inertia and organizational change. *American Sociological Review, 49*(2), 149–164.
18. Hansen, J. A. (1992). Innovation, firm size, and firm age. *Small Business Economics, 4*(1), 37–44.
19. Henderson, A. D. (1999). Firm strategy and age dependence: A contingent view of the liabilities of newness, adolescence, and obsolescence. *Administrative Science Quarterly, 44*(2), 281–314.
20. Royal Academy of Engineering. (2013). *Additive manufacturing: Opportunities and constraints.*
21. Berman, B. (2012). 3-D printing: The new industrial revolution. *Business Horizons, 55*(2), 155–162.
22. Kietzmann, J., Pitt, L., & Berthon, P. (2015). Disruptions, decisions, and destinations: Enter the age of 3-D printing and additive manufacturing. *Business Horizons, 58*(2), 209–215.
23. Gibson, I., Rosen, D. W., & Stucker, B. (2010). *Additive manufacturing technologies—Rapid prototyping to direct digital manufacturing*, Springer (2010).
24. Confindustria. (2014). *Scenari Industriali.*
25. Savastano, M., Amendola, C., D'Ascenzo, F., & Massaroni, E. (2015). 3-D Printing in the Spare Parts Supply Chain: an Ex plorative Study in the Automotive Industry. In *Proceedings of the ItAIS Conference.*
26. D'aveni, R. (2015). The big idea. The 3-D printing revolution. *Harvard Business Review.*
27. Reeves, P., Tuck, C., & Hague, R. (2011). *Additive manufacturing for mass customization.* Fogliatto: Springer.
28. MaRs. (2013). Layer-by-Layer : opportunities in 3D printing technology trends, growth drivers and the emergence of innovative applications in 3D printing. p. 37.
29. Creswell, J. W. (2013). *Research design: Qualitative, quantitative, and mixed methods approaches.* Sage publications.
30. FoodDrinkEurope. (2014). *Data & Trends of the European Food and Drink Industry.*
31. Intesa San Paolo. (2016). *Rapporto Analisi dei Settori Industriali—Febbraio.*
32. Lipton, J. I., Cutler, M., Nigl, F., Cohen, D., & Lipson, H. (2015). Additive manufacturing for the food industry—A review. *Trends in Food Science & Technology, 43*(1), 114–123.
33. Wei, J., & Cheok, A. D. (2012). Foodie: Play with your food promote interaction and fun with edible interface. *IEEE Transactions on Consumer Electronics, 58*(2), 178–183.
34. Porter, K., Phipps, J., Adam, S., & Sam, A. (2015). *3D opportunity serves it up. Additive manufacturing and food.*
35. Barilla Group. (2015). *Good for you good for the planet.*

# Leverage Once, Earn Repeatedly— Capabilities for Creating and Appropriating Value in Cloud Platform Ecosystems

Christopher Hahn⬤, Jan Huntgeburth⬤ and Ruediger Zarnekow

**Abstract** Information technology (IT) advancements enabled new delivery models (i.e. Cloud Computing), thereby facilitating the emergence of new business models in the IT industry, such as Cloud platform ecosystems. With their growing acceptance and diffusion in practice, we need a deeper understanding of their IT capabilities in order to implement their business model, thereby creating and appropriating value. We draw on empirical data from four case studies of Cloud platform ecosystems utilizing a framework on IT-enabled business models for data analysis. We found four key motivations for interfirm collaboration that each generated business model requirements specified in the context of Cloud platform ecosystems. These drive the development of unique B2B IT capabilities enabling value creation and appropriation mechanisms. We propose three dyadic (relation-specific) IT customization and two network IT standardization (network-oriented) capabilities based on our cross case analysis. Furthermore, we describe prevalent value creation and appropriation mechanisms and suggest two additional mechanisms grounded in the data: downstream capabilities and platform resourcing. We provide a possible reasoning on the underlying logic of IT capabilities, value creation and appropriation of Cloud platform ecosystems.

**Keywords** Cloud platform ecosystems · Value creation · Value appropriation IT capabilities

C. Hahn (✉) · R. Zarnekow
Technical University Berlin, Berlin, Germany
e-mail: christopher.hahn@tu-berlin.de

R. Zarnekow
e-mail: ruediger.zarnekow@tu-berlin.de

J. Huntgeburth
University of Augsburg, Augsburg, Germany
e-mail: huntgeburth@is-augsburg.de

© Springer International Publishing AG, part of Springer Nature 2018
R. Lamboglia et al. (eds.), *Network, Smart and Open*, Lecture Notes in Information Systems and Organisation 24, https://doi.org/10.1007/978-3-319-62636-9_10

# 1  Introduction

> As digital deepens, it's clear that hardcoded business and operating models won't suffice
> […] What's changed is that there's a shift to platform thinking. […] Platform concepts need
> to penetrate all aspects of a business (Dave Aron, Vice President, Gartner [1]).

IT has enabled standardization and advancements resulting in changing delivery models of IT services (i.e. Cloud Computing) and the accompanying servitization in the IT industry [2, 3]. Traditional providers react by transforming their business models into service-centric approaches, resulting in e.g. market predictions of 22 Bln. US$ for Platform as a Service (PaaS) in 2019 [4]. Within this paper, our understanding of Cloud platforms is the offering of IaaS, PaaS or SaaS or combinations thereof complemented with management services. Prominent examples are Salesforce.com App Cloud, Amazon AWS or Google Cloud Platform. We conceptualize these as platform ecosystems drawing on Tiwana et al. [5] as a software-based platform that connects platform-specific module developers to end consumers (B2B) (or other developers) thereby acting as two-sided markets. Platform ecosystems combine the streams of product families (e.g. modularization and architecture) and market intermediaries (e.g. multi-sided markets) [6]. In practice, it is one of the most important concepts for progressing into digital business according to market researchers [1] and consulting companies alike [7]. Yoo et al. [8] emphasize that the emergence of software-based platforms is shifting competition and innovation toward platform ecosystems. These are able to create substantial competitive barriers for rival platforms and to foster value creation through generativity and heterogeneity [5, 8]. The combined offerings of Cloud platform ecosystems can exceed capacities and capabilities of what can be provided by any single company. Hence, the incentive for ecosystem participants lies in the generation of performance by leveraging complementary assets accessible through the platform [6, 9, 10]. This emphasizes the value creation potential of interfirm collaboration through platform-based business models. Best-practice firms for platform ecosystems (e.g. Apple, Google in mobile domain) excel in developing and leveraging IT capabilities to exchange content with partners, govern different types of interfirm relationships, and structure transactions in novel ways [11]. Empirical evidence suggests that value creation and appropriation are affected by firm's business model—which is operationalized by its (IT) capabilities [12]. Therefore, we argue that the underlying logic Cloud platform ecosystems' IT capabilities to operationalize the business model and eventually to create and appropriate value is an important—but understudied—phenomenon.

Within the information systems (IS) literature, Yoo et al. [8] highlight the necessity for more research on the phenomenon of platform-centric ecosystems. In line with a call of the IS community, we will approach (IT-enabled) business models within the IT industry (Cloud) and their respective mechanisms to create and appropriate value [13]. We argue that this is especially important in the case of Cloud platform ecosystems given the variety of participants engaged in resource generation and integration. There exists little research within our area of enquiry. Scholars have researched on value co-creation and value appropriation in platform ecosystems of ERP standard software [14–16]. Alike, value co-creation has also been explored within the cloud platform context within a single case study of an IaaS provider [17]. These studies are not discussing value creation and appropriation in relationship with the necessary IT capabilities required to implement the business model. Furthermore, preferences of PaaS consumers have been studied [18] as well as business models of PaaS platforms in terms of typology [19], dynamics, simulation and construction [20–22]. Again, these studies do not provide insights on the IT capabilities required to implement the business model. Thereby we will contribute to the research streams by offering another perspective on value creation and appropriation within the context of IT-enabled business models. Thus, we are addressing this research gap by examining the following research question: How do Cloud platforms create and appropriate value and which kinds of IT capabilities do they require?

The remainder of the paper is structured as follows. Section 2 introduces Rai and Tang's [12] framework on IT-enabled business models which we utilized as our theoretical lens. In Sect. 3, we describe the background of our case studies and methodology in terms of data collection and analysis in detail. Section 4 presents the results and interpretation of our empirical study. Eventually, Sect. 5 highlights this study's contributions to research and practice.

## 2 Theoretical Background

The business model (BM) is an important but understudied phenomenon, which affects value creation and appropriation besides accepted influence factors such as product-market-strategy and industry factors (e.g. speed of innovation) [12, 23]. Furthermore, it is becoming widely acknowledged that IT-enabled business models are a distinct source of value creation and appropriation [24, 25]. In this sense, the IT-enabled BM represents how interfirm exchanges and transactions with customers, suppliers or partners are structured and executed [12]. Despite the general recognition of the IT's critical role in enabling BMs [see e.g., 26], the relationship between IT enablement (through IT capabilities) and BMs has received limited attention [12]. Therefore, Rai and Tang [12] addressed this gap by proposing a framework for business value from IT-enabled business models (see Fig. 1). We utilized this framework as our theoretical lens as it provides a general understanding on the relationship between the strategic intent for interfirm collaboration, the respective business models requirements and the implementation through IT capabilities resulting in value creation and appropriation.

The first pillar of the framework is represented by the strategic intents of a company considering not only product market fit but also in terms of how to structure interfirm collaboration [27]. They operationalize this concept with five key strategic motivations for interfirm collaboration: (1) to achieve supply chain efficiencies, (2) to develop market responsiveness, (3) to design, develop, and/or commercialize innovative offerings, (4) to develop markets and customer

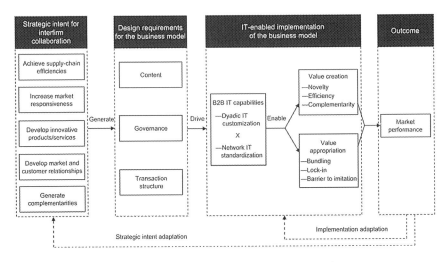

**Fig. 1** Framework: business value from IT-enabled business models [12]

relationships, and (5) to generate complementarities. The second pillar is driven by
the recognition that each strategic intent results in BM design requirements. These
comprise the following three constitutive elements [28]: (1) content: goods or
information exchanged with partners, (2) governance: control of goods/information
(incl. legal form of organization, participants incentives), and (3) transaction
structure: parties involved and the ways how they exchange. Accordingly, these
design requirements induce a focal firm to develop specific B2B IT capabilities
which are defined as the ability to manipulate the firm's digital network of information in order to create, control and execute interfirm transactions [29]. They
further argue that two IT capabilities need to be acquired functioning at distinct
levels: (1) IT customization at the dyadic interfirm level, and (2) IT standardization
at the network level. Dyadic IT customization considers idiosyncratic (i.e. relationship specific) requirements in a single relationship for the sharing of information, its governance and transaction structure. Examples include build-to-order
interfaces to exchange custom information and/or tailor business rules and processes to ensure proper collaboration [30, 31]. In contrast, the focal firm's ability to
leverage modularized IT resources and standards for facilitating information
exchange describes network IT standardization. Thereby common process for data
exchange or activity structuring can be leveraged in order to hamper the need for
relationship specific investments [32, 33]. Through these IT B2B capabilities, the
business model is implemented in conjunction with value creation and appropriation mechanisms. Value creation mechanisms describe the strategies in order to
create value for all stakeholders involved and specify the upper limit of value that
can be captured [34]. The three main mechanisms from Amit and Zott's [28] work
are used: (1) Novelty, (2) Efficiency, and (3) Complementarity. By drawing on
Teece [25] they suggest three value appropriation mechanisms: (1) Bundling,

(2) Lock-in and (3) Barrier to imitation. As a feedback loop, Rai and Tang [12] suggest that based on the market performance, either the implementation of the BM is adjusted (IT capabilities, value creation and/or appropriation) or the strategic intent needs to be adapted also resulting in an adjusted implementation.

## 3  Research Design

In this paper we employ an explorative multiple case study approach in the spirit of Eisenhardt and Graebner [35]. We opted for an interpretative case study approach since the phenomenon in practice is relatively new and practitioners as a source for information may be subject to different terminology still indicating the same meaning [36, 37]. Thus, we were able to better explore phenomena by accessing these meanings and thereby better capture ideas and actions in organizational contexts [36]. We believe that this understanding is essential in order to draw conclusions embedded into organizational contexts. As research on Cloud platforms is still in its infancy, our exploratory approach is particularly useful to discover not anticipated features or facets [36]. In that, we have chosen a diverse sampling strategy looking for cases that clearly adopted and represented one of the five key motivations for interfirm collaboration [38]. Thereby, we strive for case hetero- geneity only in this dimension while ensuring equality with respect to its business model (Cloud platform for B2B enterprise software). This results in higher repre- sentativeness of our cross case results [38]. We employed market research utilizing reports from market research institutes (e.g. Gartner, IDC, Forrester, Experton) on Cloud Platforms ('PaaS', 'aPaaS', 'iPaaS', 'Application Platform') in order to identify case candidates. We opted for market leading Cloud platforms to ensure that only cases with appropriate market performance are selected. Furthermore, it is important to understand that these platforms offer a combination of strategic intents to a different degree. We looked for the most prominent strategic intent in each of these cases by comparing the strength and frequency of the mentioned concepts. Matching of these cases to strategic intents was done based on a pre-study [39] utilizing secondary data (web pages, FAQs etc.) and will be further elaborated within the analysis section. Figure 2 shows the matching of strategic intents and our selected cases with a short context description. We have not yet identified a case that primarily aims at achieving supply-chain efficiencies.

By relying on a semi-structured interview guide with open-ended questions, we made sure to include all relevant aspects with a shared understanding while at the same time giving interviewees the freedom to enrich the discussion with aspect of his/her particular interest. The interview guideline was structured into the following four segments: (1) Introduction (role, experience, common agreement on terms), (2) Strategic intent, platform functionalities, transaction structure & governance, (3) Value creation and appropriation and (4) Key capabilities and resources. Based on the methodological guidelines of Sarker and Sarker [40] we chose suitable interviewees. In particular, we explicitly looked for product managers, sales

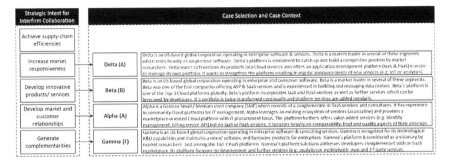

**Fig. 2** Case matching and case context

managers or partner managers of the identified platforms thereby ensuring appropriate experience and knowledge in the (architectural) design and value proposition. We opted for complementary roles of interviewees within a case to increase data triangulation and validity. A summary of the research project's objectives and interview guide have been sent upfront to ensure appropriate knowledge. We also considered other documents and information—either publicly available or received from the interviewee. In particular, we looked into company presentations, brochures, FAQs, videos and accessed the platform itself where possible. The interviews were scheduled between August and October 2015 of which three have been conducted face to face and five via phone. Interviews were held in German, which was the mother tongue of all participants. Each conversation was digitally recorded and subsequently transcribed by native speakers who were familiar with the subject matter and terminology. In total, 454 min were recorded and the transcribed material amounted to 43.042 words. Table 1 describes the interviewer details for each case.

**Table 1** Profiles of the interviewees and interview details

| Case # | Interviewer position | Size | Date | Duration/ transcription size |
|---|---|---|---|---|
| Alpha (A) | C-level (CMO) (A#1) | SME | 08/2015 | 55 min/6.102 words |
|  | C-level (CEO) (A#2) | SME | 09/2015 | 59 min/5.132 words |
| Beta (B) | Partner business development (B#1) | Corp. | 08/2015 | 48 min/4.335 words |
|  | Senior technical consultant (B#2) | Corp. | 09/2015 | 55 min/5.705 words |
| Gamma (Γ) | Platform product manager (Γ#1) | Corp. | 09/2015 | 55 min/5.376 words |
|  | Sales manager Europe (Γ#2) | Corp. | 10/2015 | 41 min/3.630 words |
| Delta (Δ) | Sales manager Europe (Δ#1) | Corp. | 09/2015 | 62 min/6.210 words |
|  | Senior technical consultant (Δ#2) | Corp. | 10/2015 | 79 min/6.552 words |

Overall, we followed the methodological guidelines summarized by Sarker and Sarker [40] to ensure rigorous data analysis and representation and applied conceptual coding as a tool in qualitative research to support data complexity reduction. Furthermore, we relied on a priori codes for our concepts based on the dimensions of IT-enabled business models framework [12]. We also applied conceptual coding in order to specify framework, utilizing its dimensions as category families. For example, the capability of standardizing a trading process was coded as 'Network IT Capability: Process Standardization'. Coding was performed with the help of qualitative research software tool ATLAS.ti 7. The constant comparative process involved data triangulation, i.e. whenever possible, we compared responses across interviewees, platform cases, and organizational roles of respondents [41].

# 4 Results and Interpretation

In the following section we will present the within-case analyses of the four cases, thereby empirically validating the framework of Rai and Tang [12] and extending it to the emerging context of cloud platform ecosystems. We will utilize empirical evidence from the interviews, documents and other sources to develop a contextual understanding of IT-enabled business models for Cloud platform ecosystems.

## 4.1 Within-Case Analysis

**Case Alpha (A)**. The dominant strategic intent of the first case organization is to develop market and customer relationships. This is apparent in the content aspect of the business model design requirements as they provide market intelligence, product entry, distribution strategies and personalized content. Market intelligence is provided in a wide choice of substitute SaaS services, which are presented in a standardized way with the same level of information as well as efficient processes for procurement and transaction execution. (*A#2.1*: *"We are organizing the whole procurement process which includes the catalogue portfolio and the platform [...] and the delivery processes as well [...]."*). Further, we found that Alpha tackles customer experience that calls for quality and trust assurance, customer ratings, recommendations, searching functionalities as well as complementary professional services (e.g. IT consulting). (*A#1.1*: *"[Our goal is] to offer the largest catalogue possible [...]. [...] we would like all solutions to present in the same standardized way [...] categorized by certain criteria, industry, domain, expertise, trust-level. [...] [We will integrate additional functionalities such as] identity management, central billing and invoicing [...] which are standardized processes. [...] differentiator is the offering of complimentary professional services (e.g. implementation)."*).

In terms of governance, the Cloud platform incorporates an electronic marketplace (EM) that presents the SaaS offerings in the previously described manner. The platform further automatizes the standard procurement and transaction processes (incl. delivery). (*A#1.2*: "*We as a sales channel take over a part of our partner's job.[We will integrate] recommendations and reviews [...]. We are trying to standardize all interfaces. Proprietary would be contrary to our approach of being an open platform [...].*"). With their approach, Alpha offers independent software vendors (ISVs) two novel distribution channels. The first channel represents online sales directly via their public cloud platform (see A#1.2). The second utilizes multipliers with an established end-customer base relying on the (customized) cloud platform. Thereby, the transaction structure is expanded with additional sellers previously not selling software. (*A#2.2*: "*We are not confident in end-customer access [...]. We approach multipliers offering our catalogue and platform which enables them to leverage existing end-customers with a fast time-to-market. [...].*").

Alpha has developed a set of IT capabilities in order to implement their business model. Dyadic IT customization capabilities can be found in the process of including a SaaS solution into the catalogue. This involves the technical integration to enable platform services (e.g., Single-Sign-On (SSO) or billing) and the quality check and trust rating given by the platform. At this stage, often business model development activities (pricing model or marketing) are supported by the platform as well (*A#1.3*: "*Since we all want to present them [SaaS solutions] equally, we do some business development for our partners. [...] The platform configurability allows us to adapt very flexibly [...] offering different integration levels [...].*"). In addition, the customization of the public platform into a sub-store for each multiplier in terms of individual requirements (i.e. design or specific catalogue) is a dyadic capability. Alpha has also developed a set of network IT standardization capabilities. In particular, they developed a standardized service description, price information and trust information to display each SaaS solution. The procurement process of end-customers and the resulting transaction (incl. delivery and payment) process have also been automated and standardized (*A#2.3*: "*You need to categorize the whole catalogue portfolio [...] which requires a lot of time and know-how [and] extensive process understanding.*"). Standardized interfaces have been implemented for integration of the value-added services (e.g. SSO). In the same vein, the architecture of the platform is prepared to allow for the creation of "sub-stores".

In terms of value creation, Alpha achieves novelty by providing novel distribution channels. Efficiency is created by automating and handling transaction processes for both parties as well as enabling efficient information search (cf. electronic marketplaces). Offering enhancing platform services (e.g. SSO, billing) for complementary modules results in the creation of complementarity. When it comes to value appropriation, Alpha bundles the aforementioned platform services into one offering with a price model consisting of a listing fee and success-based revenue share. Alpha also highlighted their independent access to a cloud ISV ecosystem as a barrier to imitation.

**Case Beta (B)**. The dominant strategic intent of Beta is to develop innovative services. The business model design requirements therefore consider the following aspects within the content dimension. Customer requirements of ISVs are followed in the form of processes, tools and architecture for SaaS application development and operations. Product ideas and breakthrough concepts are provided by several innovative platform modules (e.g. IoT, advanced analytics etc.) that can be used to develop new services. These modules capture knowledge and skills which can now be accessed by ISVs that had not had access before (*B#1.1*: *"The central value proposition is to help ISVs to focus on their core competencies enabling them to innovate by providing them with platform services. [...] such as machine learning and just use it like building blocks."*). Market intelligence is provided by partner business development roles that advise ISVs and developers on business model and monetization strategies (*B#1.2*: *"The central task of my role is to make partner solutions successful[...], we market them[...] and help go-to-market activities and build a sustainable business model."*). Within this strategic intent governance requires knowledge integration across the focal firm's boundaries and encapsulation of intellectual property (IP). Beta achieves the knowledge integration via a combination of platform functionalities and individual consulting for partners. The platform offers modularized services for application development and operations as well as other modules for specific areas (e.g. IoT or analytics). When new services are developed by ISVs these are encapsulated as a new solution that runs on the platform. IP rights remain with the ISV/developer (*B#1.3*: *"If these solutions meet the quality criteria they can be listed [in the marketplace] thus offering a new sales channel [...] IP rights remain with developers."*). The platform takes over tasks of developers or system houses thereby changing the 'traditional' transaction structure of enterprise application development and operations. Third party developers are incentivized by increased sales potential to offer their knowledge as platform services. The platform offers knowledge transfer through dedicated platform services, processes and documentation (incl. communities). These are complemented with a marketplace that helps to market and sell these newly developed SaaS services.

In the following, we will describe the IT capabilities Beta has developed to implement the design requirements. Dyadic IT customization capabilities can be found in the process of transforming existing solutions into a platform compatible architecture or by enabling hybrid architectures. Technical and business consulting is both dyadic in nature but helps to leverage the platform appropriately (*B#1.4*: *"One of our biggest advantages is the large portfolio [...] transformed into services as separate modules."*). Quality assurance of SaaS services that should be marketed via the marketplace is a dyadic capability as well. Beta has also developed a set of network IT standardization capabilities which can be manifested in the following aspects. In particular, the platform offers standardized tools and process for application development and operations (incl. the management of these services) (*B#1.5*: *"It is of utmost importance to be highly available and [...] fully automated infrastructure. [...] capabilities of managing data centers and services on a high security level, appropriate management processes."*). The platform offers flexible interface architecture to extend new services (modules) (*B#2.1*: *"Openness [...] means that I can not only use proprietary languages and technologies [...]. We offer SDKs [or] a developer can use the underlying RESTful API [...] which are documented."*). This includes the provision of self-learning and exchange mechanisms (tutorials, documentation and communities). In order to leverage marketing and sales knowhow as well as existing channels, a marketplace has been set up that offers value-added services such as central invoicing. The encapsulation of intellectual property has also been manifested in a set of agreed terms of services.

In the case of Beta, value is created in all three dimensions: novelty, efficiency and complementarity. Novelty is provided by the provision of additional sales channel (i.e. marketplace) that helps to market and sell these newly developed SaaS and add-ons. Efficiency is created by offering standardized development and operations environment that takes away effort from the developer (see #B2.1). Complementarity is achieved through the ability to build innovative services relying on other services and infrastructure and making some newly developed services reusable for other developers (**B#1.6**: "*There are numerous add-ins or plug-ins for other solutions which can be sold* via *the marketplace [...].*"). In terms of value appropriation, Beta bundles the aforementioned platform services into one offering and charges for the infrastructure that is used (**B#2.2**: "*The more this partner service is used, the more hardware resources are consumed.*"). Lock-in, though not intended, occurs inevitably via knowledge dependence on certain services and modules provided by Beta's platform. Another mechanism we noticed concerns the reusability of third party developed services. These third party modules (e.g. 'add-ins') thereby extend the core platform service and increase the total value of the platform, usually known as indirect network effects. In the context of cloud platform, this extended platform core leads to increased platform users and increased revenue for the platform provider.

**Case Gamma (Γ)**. The dominant strategic intent of Gamma is to generate complementarities. In the following, we will illustrate the business model design requirements for Gamma beginning with the content dimension. A catalogue of different developer services is provided which can be used to develop complementarities. These services range from development kits (SDKs) to infrastructure and operation services. Furthermore, more specific services which require deep expert knowledge are made available as well (**Γ#2.1**: "*It is one of our strategic intents to be the platform where cool and innovative ideas are implemented [...]. We have about 140 pre-configured developer services in our catalogue supporting in quite different areas, such as IoT, cognitive services, [...].*"). The interface specifications are publicly available to all interested parties. These complementarities can then be included in the catalogue of developer services as well, which means other developers can reuse these services in their own solution (**Γ#1.1**: "*These services are not only complementary solutions but also services in direct competition with our own from third party providers.[...] It is very easy to integrate these as building blocks in a similar way for developers.*"). Governance requires the support of industry standards (and the control of complements in terms of quality, intellectual property as well as availability and compatibility through the platform itself (**Γ#1.2**: "*We [product managers] control the catalogue of developer services [...] and decide according a list of quality measures[...] since we only want high quality services to be offered.*"). The transaction structure consists mainly of the interaction of services in horizontal (infrastructure, operations etc.) and vertical (analytics, special services) relationships. These complements are then encapsulated and IP rights remain with the developers. The platform then offers two ways of support in terms of marketing and sales: (1) integration into catalogue of developer services, (2) marketplace for stand-alone SaaS solutions.

Gamma has developed a set of IT capabilities derived from their business model requirements. Dyadic IT customization capabilities have evolved around the control of the complements, which includes quality assurance as well as IP considerations and legal agreements (*Γ#1.3*: *"Technical [integration] is not that difficult given the software is written modularized [...]. This is nothing compared to the effort required for quality assurance, discussing legal agreements* etc.*[...] IP rights remain with the developer."*). Business development and technical consulting are also offered (*Γ#1.4*: *"We offer on-site service where our top-programmers collaborate with clients [...] to support customers."*). The transformation of existing products into complements that are compatible with the platform architecture is also dyadic in nature. Gamma has developed a set of network IT standardization capabilities. In particular, the platform offers standardized tools and processes for application development and operations (incl. management of these services). The platform offers a flexible interface architecture to extend new services (modules) and supports standards that allow developers to just 'push' the code onto the platform. Additionally, the ability to offer, extend and transform an extensive catalogue of reusable developer services (incl. encapsulated complements) is of utmost importance. These services are partially very specific and extensively enrich the knowledge base of developers (e.g. cognitive services). Therefore, documentation on how to use and apply these is crucial. The capabilities to support in market and sales activities for these complements have also been highlighted.

Gamma creates value in all three dimensions: novelty, efficiency and complementarity. Novelty is provided by new distribution and monetization channels through the possibility to list new solutions in developer services catalogue or in the SaaS marketplace. Efficiency is created by offering standardized development and operations environment that takes away effort from the developer. Complementarity is achieved through the development of services that complement the developer service and platform portfolio, which then can be used as building blocks by other developers. Gamma appropriates value in several ways. Basic platform services are bundled and charged based on usage parameters (used storage, no. of transactions etc.) (*Γ#1.5*: *"We are charging based on the executed code on the platform (used main memory* etc.*) which is free within a certain threshold [...]. And you pay extra for used optional services as well [...]."*). A success-based revenue share has to be paid when third party services are consumed via the developer service catalogue or marketplace. Barrier to imitation are installed by patented services that also require enormous hardware capacities. In addition, Gamma offers downstream capabilities that are billed separately such as IT implementation services. We found a strong mechanism that extends the value of the platform. By incorporating complements into the service catalogue that can be recombined, the platform expands in its scope and offerings. Thus, other developers can develop even better solutions by reusing these building blocks. We found this mechanism to be stronger than in the case of Beta, since here exists a separate catalogue for developer services appearing as if it belongs to the platform (*Γ#1.6*: "*We asked an existing partner [...] to offer his existing SaaS solution for end-customers encapsulated with an API for developers.*").

**Case Delta (Δ).** The dominant strategic intent in Delta's Cloud platform business model is to increase market responsiveness so that capacity (infrastructure for operations and development) can be scaled efficiently. Content-wise Delta has considered the requirements by enabling a flexible switching between on premise and hybrid operations to react to performance peaks (*Δ#1.1*: "*This enables our customers to do load-balancing, migrate into hybrid scenarios, to buffer peak loads etc.[...] This is it: I want to be faster, seize market opportunities and not be slowed down by typical IT processes.*"). This further allows the transformation of development test environments into productive environments without much effort (*Δ#1.2*: "*All activities for test and development can be done within the cloud which is 60–70% in some companies.*"). In terms of governance, switching costs are reduced by only offering high quality ('best of breed') solutions from the portfolio of the platform owner, which are pre-integrated. Furthermore, while switching between on premise and hybrid operations the same software is provided (*Δ#2.1*: "*Therefore we are bridging by mirroring the possibilities of a public Cloud into the private Cloud [...] with exactly the same software and functionalities.*"). Hardly any 3rd party services are offered which reduce governance effort for these. The transaction structure calls for dyadic collaboration for relationship adaption which is enabled by the platform and the aforementioned mechanisms. These coordinate relationship specific signalling and enable specific adaption as well as unifying activities across the traditional value chain (e.g. application development and operations infrastructure).

Delta has acquired IT capabilities in both dimensions, dyadic IT customization and network IT standardization. The former can be manifested in a post-sales consulting organisation and adjacent IT consulting services (*Δ#1.3*: "*We have a customer success manager organisation that consults the customer after sales for free [...].*"). The integration of services and products into relationship specific services, such as the administration console is an individual task. Delta also has to transform and pre-integrate further products and services from their own and 3rd party portfolio into platform services and SaaS solutions (*Δ#1.4*: "*It is our goal that all these applications [Delta's SaaS] are available on the platform and can be integrated [...] via open standards.*"). Furthermore, existing solutions of customers also need to be transformed into a platform compatible architecture (*Δ#1.5*: "*We are collaborating with system integrators to support our platform by enabling them to join our platform[...].*"). Delta has developed a set of network IT standardization capabilities in order to leverage their business model. The administration console is able to work with the full stack of platform services. The platform itself also offers infrastructure, operation and development services as well as SaaS solutions. Delta has also developed standard requirements for operations on the platform, which enables scaling functionality. All functionalities of the platform and its services are documented and available for learning purposes.

In Delta's case, we find two value creation mechanisms to be present as well. By providing a new mechanism for hybrid solution architectures and operations enabling responsiveness, Delta achieves efficiency. Furthermore, efficiency can be found by offering standardized development and operations environment that takes away effort from the developer. In addition, the administration console for pre-integrated solutions also fosters efficiency. Through leveraging their existing applications portfolio and installed base as well as consulting services, Delta utilizes complementarity as a value creation mechanism. We found three mechanisms for value appropriation in place: bundling, lock-in and downstream capabilities. The bundle consists of basic platform services that are charged based on usage parameters (used storage, no. transactions etc.) with post-sales consulting services for free. Lock-in effects are established by offering a rather closed portfolio of these pre-integrated services (mostly provided by platform owner) (*Δ#1.6*: "*We want to increase our application business* via *platform and its integration and* vice versa. […]. *This is the strategy behind, lock-in is a strong driver* […]."). Furthermore, the consistent familiarity and ease of use of the platform tools (incl. administration console) will add to that. In addition, Delta offers downstream capabilities that are billed separately such as IT consulting and implementation services. In addition, based on their installed base cross selling and upselling opportunities are methods to capture further value.

## 4.2   Cross-Case Analysis and Discussion

This section provides a cross case analysis and discusses this in light of an underlying logic of IT capabilities, value creation and appropriation. First, we will introduce the results of our case comparison. Second, we address the validity of the framework in our context. Last, we will draw conclusions in the context of Cloud platform ecosystems that are enabled by the framework. Table 2 summarizes the findings of our within-case analysis.

In terms of novel findings—enabled by using the framework as theoretical lens—based on our sampling strategy it is apparent that all four cases differ in terms of their dominant strategic intent for interfirm collaboration. The resulting business model requirements instantiations vary widely. Nonetheless, we can generalize that dyadic IT customization capabilities revolve around three streams in the context of cloud platforms: (1) Transforming and integrating products/services into platform services (own portfolio or third party), (2) Onboarding (incl. quality assurance, connecting to interfaces for platform integration and added-value services) and integrating existing solutions of customers onto the platform, and (3) Individual familiarization, such as IT consulting. The transformation of products or services into platform services aims at increasing its functionality and scope. Onboarding describes the mechanism of bringing complements (e.g. add-ons or 3rd party platform services) on the platform. In light of existing theory, this relates to solving essential system or business problems acting as the core of a platform [42]. Within

**Table 2** Summary of the case results (IT capabilities, value creation and appropriation) (new concepts in italics)

| | | Alpha (A) | Beta (B) | Gamma (Γ) | Delta (Δ) |
|---|---|---|---|---|---|
| IT capabilities | Dyadic IT cust. | • Onboarding solutions (incl. integration, quality approval)<br>• Consulting and advisory for partners<br>• Platform customization for sales partners | • Transforming solutions into platform architectures<br>• Consulting and advisory for partners<br>• Onboarding solutions (incl. integration, quality approval) | • Onboarding solutions (incl. quality approval, IP, legal)<br>• Consulting and advisory for partners<br>• Transforming solutions into platform architectures | • Consulting and advisory for partners<br>• Integration of solutions into platform architecture<br>• Transforming solutions into platform architectures |
| | Network IT stand. | • Standardized processes and information for SaaS transactions<br>• Standardized interfaces for onboarding with architectural planning for customization | • Standardizing development, operations and transaction processes and governance<br>• Architectural flexibility through standardized APIs<br>• Learning resources (e.g. FAQs) | • Standardizing development, operations and transaction processes and governance<br>• Architectural flexibility through standardized APIs<br>• Catalogue service management for new services and complements<br>• Marketing and sales support<br>• Learning resources | • Standardizing application development, integration and operations processes<br>• Learning resources (e.g. FAQs) and platform services free for testing |
| Value creation | | • Novelty: new sales channels for SaaS and consulting services<br>• Efficiency: automating procurement and transaction processes | • Novelty: enabling new sales channels for SaaS and complements<br>• Efficiency: standardized development and operations processes | • Novelty: enabling new sales channels for SaaS and complements<br>• Efficiency: automating procurement and transaction processes | • Efficiency: automating enterprises business processes (pre-integration); Enabling hybrid architectures and responsiveness |

(continued)

**Table 2** (continued)

| | Alpha (A) | Beta (B) | Gamma (Γ) | Delta (Δ) |
|---|---|---|---|---|
| | • Offering enriching platform services (e.g. SSO, billing) | • Complementarity: enabling development of innovative services, add-ons or (re-) combinability of these | • Complementary: enabling development of innovative complementary platform services | • Complementary: leveraging existing portfolio and professional services to create complements (SaaS) |
| Value appropriation | • Bundling: platform services with revenue sharing<br>• Barrier to imitation through vendor ecosystem | • Bundling: platform services based on infrastructure usage<br>• Unintended lock-in through dependence on services<br>• *Platform resourcing:* extend scope through integration of 3rd party modules | • Bundling: platform services with revenue sharing<br>• Barrier to imitation: few IP protected services<br>• *Downstream capabilities* (billable consulting)<br>• *Platform resourcing:* extend scope through integration of 3rd party modules | • Bundling of platform services based on infrastructure usage<br>• Lock-in: through closed platform ecosystem<br>• *Downstream capabilities* (billable consulting) |

our study, all cases had IT products before which solved a range of these problems but needed to be transformed and integrated under the umbrella of the platform. Further, this also comprises the facilitation of external companies provision of complements and developing unique, compelling features in order to attract users representing a part of the 'coring' and 'tipping' strategy described by Gawer and Cusumano [42]. Individual familiarization (e.g. IT consulting) refers to the capabilities of the platform provider of getting used to the platform (e.g. technical standards) and receiving (individual) support. This has been found as a factor of perceived openness in mobile platform ecosystems [43] increasing complementors' satisfaction. Similarly, network IT standardization capabilities differ in detail but we can also draw some general tendencies: (1) Standardization of processes, information exchange formats as well as rules and regulations for participation within a platform, and (2) Modularization of the platform and its services with standardized interfaces in order to adapt to changing environments and requirements.

In terms of process standardization, we found that e.g. application development processes or application sourcing and transactions processes are standardized in order to increase efficiency. Nonetheless, these processes rather leave choices for individual ecosystem participants instead of commoditizing the process altogether [see e.g., 44]. Information exchange formats in this context relate to processing the information (e.g. product descriptions, invoicing information, programming code exchange etc.) which is discussed within the intermediary literature stream [see e.g., 45]. Specific to application development processes, standardization frameworks such as Cloud Foundry or OpenShift or container technologies (such as Docker) for transferring applications within different environments may play a crucial role. It further comprises requirements that must be fulfilled in order to participate within the ecosystem (quality norms, support, legal agreements) relating to further standardization and ensure quality of the platform [see e.g., 46]. When it comes to modularization of the platform, our cases highlighted the need for architectural planning and interface design. In all cases, we found that interfaces were designed according to open standards (REST API) and documentation was publicly available. The platform itself consisted of modularized platform services as well in order to give customers the choice on what to use. Recent literature highlighted the need of modularization in platform architectures [47] including its fit with platform governance [5]. Especially in terms of innovation platforms it is proposed that modularity is essentially changing the business architecture of different industries and markets alongside with interconnected data [48].

When it comes to value creation, almost all three mechanisms have been used by each case (except Delta) but they all differ in detail. Our empirical data suggests that in three cases, efficiency is provided by offering an application development and operations platform (IaaS & PaaS), standardizing enterprise processes by pre-integration or supporting the execution of procurement processes. Likewise, three cases offer additional sales channels in order to create novelty. Most notably, in the case of Alpha where the end customer access will be provided via sales multipliers. Complementarity is further created through the development of innovative services, which are supported by platform services. Gamma is strongly supporting the notion of innovative applications through assembling 'building blocks' (platform services). We propose that this can be interpreted as the recombination of malleable resources and resembles the generative innovation mechanism in digital infrastructures [49]. Further value creation through complementarity occurs in order to develop extensions or add-ons for existing applications or platform services [see e.g., 50].

The most prominent appropriation mechanism—employed by all cases—is the bundling of (basic) platform services. For example, the application development services (programming environment) including database services, infrastructure and additional support services are bundled. The pricing mechanism is then based on the infrastructure that is consumed. In the case of Delta, these services can be used for free until the application is deployed. Although, lock-in is not intended as an appropriation mechanism, it still occurs to a certain extent through technological (specific service APIs) and organizational (processes, governance) structures. By supporting industry standards (Docker, Cloud Foundry), our case organizations want to prevent technological lock-in and instead persuade complementors by offering superiors services. Barrier to imitation only plays a minor role in value appropriation since IP rights on software are hard to protect. Only few specific platform services with high knowledge are considered as IP protected property. Based on our data, we extended the value appropriation dimension with two additional mechanisms: (1) Platform resourcing, (2) Downstream capabilities. We propose the notion of 'platform resourcing' for platforms whose strategic intent is to develop innovations or to generate complementarities as a mechanism to capture the service developed via the platform to extend the platform core and its functionality base. We think that this relates to the increase of scope and reach by integrating partner solutions and resembles the generative scaling mechanism in digital infrastructures [49]. Downstream capabilities represent unique knowledge and can be translated into e.g. software consulting services [15, 51]. The three cases that employ these downstream capabilities have not built these capabilities specifically for the platform. We think that these complementary professional services help lower the entry barriers and fit into a value co-creation oriented strategy [see e.g., 15, 17]. Figure 3 summarizes our cross case findings.

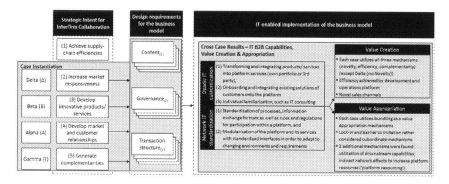

**Fig. 3** Cross case results and summary of contribution

Based on our empirical data, we are able to show that the framework is robust enough to capture the findings in our context. We could assign our empirical data to the (sub-)dimensions from strategic intent to business model design requirements into the IT-enabled implementation. From our perspective, this can be taken as an indicator for the suitability of the framework as theoretical lens.

The distribution of strategic intents and resulting BM requirements may underline the different needs in the enterprise Cloud application market and their respective priorities inferred by platform providers. We would also deduce from this finding that there exist different interpretations of product-market-fit targeting slightly different customer segments. At first sight, it may seem contradictory that platform-centric business models still require so many multifaceted dyadic IT capabilities. We think that the dyadic capabilities are necessary to advance the platform or to decrease entry barriers by providing familiarization services (e.g. consulting) or transforming solutions into platform compatible architecture. The network standardization capabilities are then required to multiply the possible value that is created on a much larger scale. Hence, once a solution is on the platform more value can be created by e.g. providing mechanisms to upscale infrastructure, to expand the solutions with further pre-integrated modules or providing additional sales channels. This is especially interesting because the cases differ in their strategic intent but still employ similar value creation strategies. In line with our previous argumentation, we would further conclude that there exists a variety of market needs of slightly different customer segments and every platform tries to create the largest value possible combining these strategies. We would further argue that once developers and services are on the platform, it is easier to provide additional services to increase value generation.

We infer that this also relates to the value appropriation strategies, especially bundling as the most prominent. The underlying mechanisms here are dynamic, i.e. grow with an increased usage of the platform infrastructure and services. Furthermore, we think there is a reinforcing effect that takes advantage of indirect network effects to capture more value by extending the resource base of the platform [e.g. Gamma (generate complementarities) and Beta (develop innovative services)]. Additionally, the companies that offer consulting services use these downstream capabilities in order to capture additional value. Based on our pre-understanding, we will now outline aspects that have been raised by our interviewees but could not be considered directly within the framework. First, it does not differentiate between the modes of value creation but within our data we found indication for the different modes of value co-creation [14, 17]. Second, it has been emphasized that feedback mechanisms with customers as well as market observation is necessary to improve the platform and meet customer requirements. These absorptive capacities [48] may provide an additional mechanism which provide timelier signals to reconsider the strategic intent or business model implementation than monitoring market performance. Third, it appeared that partner management capabilities—not only bound to IT—are found to be highly relevant. These activities include business development and marketing strategies, which have therefore only partly been captured within the dyadic IT customization activities. Fourth, subject to network IT standardization, modularization has been highlighted; nonetheless, different levels of modularization (e.g. inter- or intra-platform) may play a different role in value creation and value appropriation. For example, if in the case of complementary generation or innovation development newly created services can be included in other solutions and thereby extend the platform, it is different from using APIs to utilize added-value-services of the platform provider. This is in line with our finding that novel sales channels are often a source of value creation for these newly created services or complementarities.

## 5 Summary and Outlook

To address the research question how Cloud platforms create and appropriate value and which IT capabilities they require, we built on four case studies. Based on these, four instantiations of dominant strategic intents (improve market responsiveness, develop innovative services, develop market und customer relationships, generate complementarities) were identified. These strategic intents each generated business model requirements in the context of cloud platforms prevalent in our empirical data. Furthermore, these drive the development of unique B2B IT capabilities of such platform providers, which then enable value creation and appropriation mechanisms. In particular, we propose three dyadic IT customization and two network IT standardization capabilities based on our cross case analysis. We found that all three value creation mechanisms (novelty, efficiency, complementarity) were prevalent in almost each case [except Delta (novelty)]. In terms of value appropriation, bundling is the prevalent mechanism combined with other strategies. We suggest two additional mechanisms: downstream capabilities (billable consulting and support) and platform resourcing (increase in scope and reach of the platform by integrating complements). In summary, we propose that capabilities are intended to leverage solutions and services that are then multiplied in order to create value. Value appropriation mechanisms are designed that rents grow with the success of these and to occur repeatedly.

We believe our contribution is twofold. First, we show the validity of the framework of Rai and Tang [12] by the instantiation with our empirical case data. Second, we advance the field of business models of Cloud platform ecosystems by extending (value appropriation) and bridging (BM implementation through IT capabilities) previous work in this domain. We believe that by providing rich empirical examples, we help to advance the understanding of business models, necessary capabilities as well as value creation and appropriation mechanisms of Cloud platforms. Based on our gained insights, we provide indicators for further research in order to strengthen the understanding of value creation mechanics in this context. The instantiated framework helps to understand the underlying logic and mechanisms of Cloud platform business models in terms of strategic intents, derived business model requirements and necessary capabilities to create and appropriate value. Eventually this may help fellow researchers to explore this phenomenon in more detail. In particular, we propose to extend the empirical database in order to overcome the limitations of this study, i.e. finding cases for the missing strategic intent (supply chain efficiency), develop further ideas in terms of similarities and differences for B2B capabilities. Furthermore, we think it is worthwhile to explore the other phenomena that serve as the theoretical boundaries in order to create a more robust framework in the context of Cloud platform ecosystems and other IT-enabled business models.

# References

1. van der Meulen, R. (2015). (Gartner): Gartner CIO survey shows digital business means platform business.
2. Cusumano, M. (2010). Cloud computing and SaaS as new computing platforms. *Communications of the ACM, 53,* 27.
3. Leimeister, S., Riedl, C., Böhm, M., & Krcmar, H. (2010). The business perspective of cloud computing: Actors, roles, and value networks. In *Proceedings of 18th European Conference on Information Systems ECIS 2010.*
4. Carvalho, L. (IDC), Mahowald, R. P., McGrath, B., Fleming, M., & Hilwa, A. (2015). *Worldwide competitive public cloud platform as a service forecast, 2015–2019.*
5. Tiwana, A., Konsynski, B., & Bush, A. A. (2010). Research commentary—Platform evolution: Coevolution of platform architecture, governance, and environmental dynamics. *Information Systems Research, 21,* 675–687.
6. Thomas, L., Autio, E., & Gann, D. (2014). Architectural leverage: Putting platforms in context. *Academy of Management Perspectives, 28,* 198–219.
7. Daugherty, P. (Accenture), Banerjee, P. (Accenture), & Biltz, M. J. (Accenture). (2015). *Digital business era: Stretch your boundaries.*
8. Yoo, Y., Henfridsson, O., & Lyytinen, K. (2010). The new organizing logic of digital innovation: An agenda for information systems research. *Information Systems Research, 21,* 724–735.
9. Adner, R., & Kapoor, R. (2010). Value creation in innovation ecosystems: How the structure of technological interdependence affects firm performance in new technology generations. *Strategic Management Journal, 33,* 306–333.
10. Iansiti, M., & Levien, R. (2004). Strategy as ecology. *Harvard Business Review, 82,* 68–81.
11. Basole, R. C., & Karla, J. (2011). On the evolution of mobile platform ecosystem structure and strategy. *Business & Information Systems Engineering, 3,* 313–322.
12. Rai, A., & Tang, X. (2014). Information technology-enabled business models: A conceptual framework and a coevolution perspective for future research. *Information Systems Research, 25,* 1–14.
13. Veit, D., Clemons, E., Benlian, A., Buxmann, P., Hess, T., Kundisch, D., et al. (2014). Business models. An information systems research agenda. *Business & Information Systems Engineering,* 1–9.
14. Sarker, S., Sarker, S., Sahaym, A., & Bjørn-Andersen, N. (2012). Exploring value cocreation in relationships between an ERP vendor and its partners: A revelatory case study. *MIS Quarterly, 36,* 317–338.
15. Huang, P., Ceccagnoli, M., Forman, C., & Wu, D. J. (2012). Appropriability mechanisms and the platform partnership decision: Evidence from enterprise software. *Management Science, 59,* 102–121.
16. Ceccagnoli, M., Forman, C., Huang, P., & Wu, D. (2012). Cocreation of value in a platform ecosystem: The case of enterprise software. *MIS Quarterly, 36,* 263–290.

17. Huntgeburth, J., Blaschke, M., & Hauff, S. (2015). Exploring value co-creation in cloud ecosystems-a revelatory case study. In *ECIS 2015 Completed Research* (pp. 1–16).
18. Giessmann, A., Stanoevska-Slabeva, K. (2012). Platform as a service—A conjoint study on consumers' preferences. In *ICIS 2012* (pp. 1–20).
19. Giessmann, A., & Stanoevska-Slabeva, K. (2012). Business models of platform as a service (PaaS) providers: Current state and future directions. *Journal of Information Technology Theory and Application, 13*, 31–55.
20. Giessmann, A., & Legner, C. (2013). Designing business models for platform as a service: Towards a design theory. In *ICIS 2013* (pp. 1–10).
21. Giessmann, A., Fritz, A., Caton, S., & Legner, C. (2013). A method for simulating cloud business models: A case study on platform as a service. In *ECIS 2013 Completed Research* (pp. 1–12).
22. Giessmann, A., Kyas, P., Tyrväinen, P., Stanoevska, K. (2014). Towards a better understanding of the dynamics of platform as a service business models. In *47th Hawaii International Conference on System Sciences* (pp. 965–974).
23. Zott, C., & Amit, R. (2008). The fit between product market strategy and business model: Implications for firm performance. *Strategic Management Journal, 26*, 1–26.
24. Zott, C., & Amit, R. (2007). Business model design and the performance of entrepreneurial firms. *Organization Science, 18*, 181–199.
25. Teece, D. J. (2010). Business models, business strategy and innovation. *Long Range Planning, 43*, 172–194.
26. Amit, R., & Zott, C. (2012). Creating value through business model innovation. *MIT Sloan Management Review, 53*, 41–49.
27. Christensen, C. M. (2001). The past and future of competitive advantage. *MIT Sloan Management Review, 42*, 105–109.
28. Amit, R., & Zott, C. (2001). Value creation in E-business. *Strategic Management Journal, 22*, 493–520.
29. Kim, S. M., & Mahoney, J. T. (2006). Mutual commitment to support exchange: Relation-specific IT system as a substitute for managerial hierarchy. *Strategic Management Journal, 27*, 401–423.
30. Broadbent, M., Weill, P., & St. Clair, D. (1999). The implications of information technology infrastructure for business process redesign. *MIS Quarterly, 23*, 159–182.
31. Turnbull, P. D. (1991). Effective investment in information infrastructures. *Information and Software Technology, 33*, 191–199.
32. Malhotra, A., Gosain, S., & El Sawy, O. A. (2007). Leveraging standard electronic business interfaces to enable adaptive supply chain partnerships. *Information Systems Research, 18*, 260–279.
33. Ross, J., & Beath, C. (2006). Sustainable IT outsourcing success: Let enterprise architecture be your guide. *MIS Quarterly Executive, 5*, 181–192.
34. Brandenburger, A. M., & Stuart, H. W. (1996). Value-based business strategy. *Journal of Economics & Management Strategy, 5*, 5–24.
35. Eisenhardt, K. M., & Graebner, M. E. (2014). Theory building from cases: Opportunities and challenges. *Academy of Management Journal, 50*, 25–32.
36. Klein, H., & Myers, M. D. (1999). A set of principles for conducting and evaluating interpretive field studies in information systems. *MIS Quarterly, 23*, 67–94.
37. Walsham, G. (1995). Interpretive case studies in IS research: Nature and method. *European Journal of Information Systems, 4*, 74–81.
38. Seawright, J., & Gerring, J. (2008). Case selection techniques in a menu of qualitative and quantitative options. *Political Research Quarterly*, 294–308.
39. Hahn, C., Röher, D., & Zarnekow, R. (2015). A value proposition oriented typology of electronic marketplaces for B2B SaaS applications. In *AMCIS 2015 Proceedings* (pp. 1–15).
40. Sarker, S., & Sarker, S. (2009). Exploring agility in distributed information systems development teams: An interpretive study in an offshoring context. *Information Systems Research, 20*, 440–461.

41. Patton, M. Q. (2002). *Qualitative evaluation and research methods*. London, UK: Sage Publications Ltd.
42. Gawer, A., & Cusumano, M. (2008). How companies become platform leaders. *MIT Sloan Management Review, 49*, 1–13.
43. Hilkert, D., Benlian, A., Sarstedt, M., & Hess, T. (2011). Perceived software platform openness: The scale and its impact on developer satisfaction. In *ICIS 2011 Proceedings* (Vol. 13, pp. 1–20).
44. Markus, M. L., & Loebbecke, C. (2013). Commoditized digital processes and business community platforms: New opportunities and challenges for digital business strategies. *MIS Quarterly, 37*, 649–653.
45. Muylle, S., & Basu, A. (2008). Online support for business processes by electronic intermediaries. *Decision Support Systems, 45*, 845–857.
46. Wareham, J., Fox, P. B., & Cano Giner, J. L. (2014). Technology ecosystem governance. *Organization Science, 25*, 1195–1215.
47. Baldwin, C., & Woodard, C. (2008). *The architecture of platforms: A unified view.*
48. Venkatraman, N., & Pavlou, P. (2014). *Theorizing digital business innovation: Platforms and capabilities in ecosystems.*
49. Henfridsson, O., & Bygstad, B. (2013). The generative mechanisms of digital infrastructure evolution. *MIS Quarterly, 37*, 907–931.
50. Lavie, D. (2007). Alliance portfolios and firm performance: A study of value creation and appropriation in the U.S. software industry. *Strategic Management Journal, 28*, 1187–1212.
51. Grover, V., & Kohli, R. (2012). Cocreating IT value: New capabilities and metrics for multifirm environments. *MIS Quarterly, 36*, 225–232.

# Information Systems Architecture and Organization in the Era of MicroServices

**Maurizio Cavallari**[ID] **and Francesco Tornieri**

**Abstract** The widespread use of cloud computing and services has modified IS architectures which have been well established and consolidated in the past. We can call this "The Era of (software) MicroServices" which has led towards the adoption of Information Systems models independent from traditional tiered-architecture. MicroServices offer a new conceptualization adopting a distributed system decomposing the architecture legacy in micro-components, each one with an independent life-cycle yet interconnected and correlated. Two new concepts arise: "Continuous Integration", referred as CI, and "Continuous Delivery", referred as CD. Each MicroService is hosted within a single object denominated "container" which has a proper lifecycle and often with a unikernel-operating system with minimal sets of executable libraries. The paper then discusses the new technological tendencies under the lens of an organizational approach to new aspects of development and the emerging security solutions introduced by MicroServices, in particular for existing legacy systems.

**Keywords** Cloud computing · IS architectures · Software · Life-Cycle
Micro-Services · Continuous integration · Continuous delivery
Container · Organization · Development

M. Cavallari (✉) · F. Tornieri
Università Telematica Internazionale UniNettuno,
Corso Vittorio Emanuele II, 39, Rome, Italy
e-mail: maurizio.cavallari@uninettunouniversity.net

F. Tornieri
e-mail: francesco.tornieri@uninettunouniversity.net

© Springer International Publishing AG, part of Springer Nature 2018
R. Lamboglia et al. (eds.), *Network, Smart and Open*, Lecture Notes in Information
Systems and Organisation 24, https://doi.org/10.1007/978-3-319-62636-9_11

# 1    Introduction

"MicroServices" is a software architecture which involves building and delivering systems that are characterized by small, granular, independent and collaborative services: breaking down the entire application into individual modular packages of related functionality is what constitutes MicroServices and of which software applications lay behind the frontend of them.

This enables the development of the application in a distributed way and it also loosely part of the business functionality services [1]. Some authors claim that Cloud Computing is the most relevant case of implementation of MicroServices, of need of better and more consistent implementation of them and, more then everything, the desperate need of integration between Cloud Computing and Legacy systems [1, 2].

As a result, this approach removes many of the service limits making it easier to work collaboratively and/or to rework/rewrite code independently [2].

Any developer using a MicroServices approach when designing applications will have the following benefits:

- Services are focused on a single purpose and are built using the best available technology.
- Developers work in collaboration on different services more quickly, which means running concurrent development to shorten development timeline.
- Applications designed in this manner are based on independence (they are a subset of the entire architecture) so is it possible to change and deploy individual components without affecting the entire system (frequent upgrade).
- MicroServices encourage the de-coupling of services and dependencies as well as the focus of services on individual pieces of business logic.

When we think about software development we can say that decomposing the applications business logic into independent functional components has many advantages [3]:

- It allows a development team to be small and highly focused.
- It can choose whichever technology best suits their specific use.
- The Microservices architecture delivers is composed by a set of small individual services modules.
- The MicroServices architecture is designed to be independent and build around individual business functionalities.
- They can then be made deployable on different servers and infrastructure and this would resolve problems that IT had had since the beginning of IT, with scaling enterprise applications within a datacenter.

## 2 Legacy Approach: Monolithic Environment and New Era

The new development approach based on MicroServices is different from the traditional monolithic approach (a single enterprise application would be built as one single unit, and based on the idea of the "tier" levels -a user interface, a server-side application and a database).

Monolithic application architecture has several limitations mainly because many applications are being deployed in the cloud. One of these limitations are due application developers who build as a single unit with all the logic for handling requests running in a single process: this is then delivered as a single software package and is installed on a single server [2].

Research findings demonstrated that self-adaptive software systems are capable of adjusting their behavior at runtime to achieve certain functional or quality-of-service goals [2, 3]. Often a representation that reflects the internal structure of the managed system is used to reason about its characteristics and make adaptation decisions.

Runtime conditions in internal structure can change radically, although, in ways that were not accounted for during their design. As a result, unanticipated changes at runtime violate the assumptions made about the internal structure of the system could degrade the accuracy of the adaptation decisions [3–5].

## 3 Review of Past Research

An approach for engineering self-adaptive software systems highlighted two innovations [6]:

- a feature-oriented approach for representing engineers' knowledge of adaptation choices that are deemed practical, and
- an online learning-based approach for assessing and reasoning about adaptation decisions that does not require an explicit representation of the internal structure of a managed software system [6, 7]. Embedded knowledge, represented in feature-models, adds structure to learning, which in turn makes online learning of MicroServices feasible [1, 3].

Empirical evidence confirms that using a real-world self-adaptive software system could be of great help in MicroServices ability to accurately learn the changing dynamics of the system while achieving efficient analysis and adaptation.

Scalability is achieved by replicating the application on different servers and through load balancing requests: this architectural structure is beneficial and is used successfully in data centers. The reasoning is that it divides the application into classes and functions under one deployable application [1].

The correlation between service and process mean it can be difficult to manage software changes and in case of scaling it requires replicating the whole application. The MicroServices idea permits developers to host the application on different servers in order for resources to be more effectively attributed to those parts of the application of higher importance [1]. However, the separation between business logic and services will require a communication system that permits communications between these parts with additional integration overhead [3].

These are additional benefits of using MicroServices architecture:

- Due to the small size/scale of each service it is easier to develop and deploy [1].
- Each service can be deployed separately from each other [2].
- Development and deployment becomes more efficient as small teams are required to work on individual services' components and they work independently using their own tools to complete the assignment without external limitations [2, 3].
- Improved maintenance and troubleshooting, this is due to the fact that it becomes easier to find faults and isolate problems in one service without including others [1, 3, 5].
- It will be easier to introduce new and emerging technologies even in a monolithic environment as MicroServices can be built to proxy functionality and work alongside a monolithic application [1–3, 5].

The approach of dissecting a large and monolithic application needs to include the identification of areas that need to be either replaced or upgraded making sure that others services are not affected [5, 6].

It is extremely important to remember to drive modularity through the requirement of change: this is to say that whatever needs to be changed is done so, at the same time and in the same module.

Notably, services that change frequently need to be kept separate from those which are updated frequently in their modules [3, 6].

This also implies that services which change with a frequent recurrence should be kept in the same module. By comparing the use-case examples for functionality, a developer can divide the system using inbuilt functionality, which is beneficial, as the original developers designed them to be modular and independent [1, 3, 5].

When MicroServices cover only one well-defined business logic function, which has well defined inputs and outputs, a designer will invariably find the process of decomposing a large enterprise application a lot easier [7]. When a developer has chosen the best option to proceed with the decomposition of an existing monolithic application or to design an application, he will also face the issue of integration.

There is no way around it, MicroServices make integration tasks far more numerous and for those reasons we point out the recommendations from scholarly research, i.e. the need for a well-defined integration policy for protocols and technologies [1, 3, 5, 7, 8].

## 4    The Microservices, API Gateway and Protocols Schema

MicroServices communicate with each other using HTTP (hyper-text transfer protocol) and messaging services protocols. The first protocol is synchronous and is used for communication which requires immediate action. The latter are asynchronous and are used for subscribe/publish commands or information which can be processed when a receiver comes online [7, 8].

Clients of the application when in a monolithic environment use a load balancer to communicate, which receives and manages a client's connection to a particular instance of the application (the services are often distributed on an array of hardware). Bearing in mind today's mobile device working environments, calling these services directly is not an effective method, therefore the best approach is to install an API (application programming interface) gateway which acts as a mediator between the client and services instead of relying on a mobile client.

The API gateway will handle service calls in an aggregate manner, this will make websites performance a lot better. The API gateway also provides an additional layer of abstraction between the client and services, therefore service names can change: only the API gateway will need to be informed and updated and in the meantime a client does not need to be aware of backend changes.

In the legacy monolithic architecture, services communicate via internal method calls: using a single process made quick and easy.

MicroServices need to use a method of inter process communication between disparate services, in order to effectively communicate.

Synchronous HTTP is a well-known method for inter-process communication and is commonly used in MicroServices architectures, HTTP will use REST (Representational State Transfer) or SOAP (Simple Object Access Protocol) service call mechanisms [7–9].

Both REST and SOAP use a standard request/response style of communication making easy to understand and maintain.

However, certain disadvantages exist when using these types of services: both parties must be available at the same time and this might not always be possible in a congested environment as they could sit on different hardware unable to communicate across a busy network [1, 6, 8]. Distributed systems are also inherently prone to application and network induced issues which could result in partial failures [8–10].

HTTP services are vulnerable to these temporary problems and they will see the service as being down resulting in a failed service call. Additional problems are that clients would be required to address their calls to specific servers using an address, a hostname and a port: when considering scaled or cloud deployments this is a critical condition.

We can find an alternative option to synchronous HTTP by using asynchronous messaging which alleviates some problems by not requiring simultaneous availability. MQTT (Message Queue Telemetry Transport), a message queuing protocol, is a typical example [1, 3, 7].

The advantages of a messaging queuing system are that it decouples the sender from the receiver or, technically speaking, from the subscriber, by using a message broker.

Publishers know only the message broker and are not aware of subscribers or clients of their service. Because of this, there is no need for service discovery as the publisher always talks directly with the message broker. A particularly useful feature of message brokers is that by buffering messages for subscribers they can be used to update data in distributed systems. Instead of using distributed transactions which dictates that all participants need to be available at the same time a message broker based system of message publishing allows subscribers to pick up the messages when they become available [7, 9, 11].

The downside is the requirement of a message broker, which is another critical element in the system which brings complexity and an additional point of potential failure.

## 5   MicroServices, Pros Versus Cons

MicroServices architecture is a good solution in the context of critical scalability [1, 11, 12].

Applications in a monolithic architecture are scaled by taking one instance of the application and replicating as necessary to provide redundancy, performance and capacity, so they need to be hosted on a different server, then connected via load balancer devices, which will proxy the incoming client connections and forward them to a particular instance [12].

Load balancers maintain the state of sessions (typically trough a session cookie) and assure that a client is connected to the correct instance of the application.

Creating an application using MicroServices architecture can be an expensive yet lengthy process. Notably MicroServices architecture only delivers benefit when an application reaches the stage where scalability has become an issue: for only then can all benefits be realized [10, 13].

In contrast, startups tend to use a monolithic architecture for fast and cheaper development to build production ready applications and address the issues of scalability at a later stage especially when funding is more accessible.

Let's analyze the main issues as reported in extant literature [11, 12, 14–17]:

- Costs: whereas a monolithic application could be built in a small server, a micro server approach is going to require more hardware and more load balancing and interfacing equipment such as message brokers.
- Developments: application development teams build and deliver as a single application, monolithic enterprise software that are presented or passed onto an operations team for deployment. This approach leads to troublesome deployments and releases due to knowledge gaps between the two teams [18, 19]. There is rarely a lot of operational knowledge resident within the development

team and vice versa. With MicroServices, the problem is resolved to the point that it is a requirement that there is operation experience and knowledge of operational networks within the development team. These are the development skills required to build and run successful MicroServices architecture. These skills certainly do not come cheap but they are mandatory to a successful deployment [6, 18, 20].

- Distributed system: the development team will have to deal with interfacing distributed systems—this is a necessity with MicroServices. As a result, it is mandatory to have strong knowledge of network layer technologies, protocols and how they are optimized and secured. With MicroServices, the shift is towards RPC (Remote Procedure Call), HTTP REST and MQTT and these must be understood and tested for latency and optimized for performance [1, 12, 19, 21].

- Maintenance: one of the biggest challenges when developing a Microservices architecture is to go from the preproduction proof of concept type models to the preproduction stage. It is at this stage that development teams discover that monitoring and testing for availability does not come inbuilt or naturally to the MicroServices architecture. Unlike in the monolithic environment where one needs to check for server availability and service awareness/response within a MicroServices environment, there is a necessity to check many more distributed servers and services to ensure availability and responsiveness [1, 2, 7, 15, 22].

## 6 Practical Significance and Security Aspects

Our research uncovered new and interesting capabilities of the new MicroServices architecture, which can be also very useful in order to enhance the security of the traditional services, i.e. already present in the software applications and not developed with the MicroServices architecture.

This enhancement is achieved by allowing a greater granularity in implementing the hardening of the service, both maintaining the configuration unchanged, as well as utilizing a limited set of libraries and/or executables.

In the first case, the invariable configuration deploys the unique characteristics of MicroServices, e.g. utilization of "namespace" for the management of different resources. In the second case, on the other hand, the utilization of the limited set of libraries or executables is confined within the MicroServices environment.

The security enhancement method hypothesized and proposed by the authors of the present paper, considers two different aspects, shown below.

- Deploying and utilizing the advantages of the modularity of MicroServices by integrating at an architectural level hardened eServices. The hypothesized eServices could implement new security features at the borders of the applications, without the need of modifying application code or structure, and leaving untouched legacy services and even entire applications. This represents the new concept of "MicroGate".

**Fig. 1** The onion model of
eServices security

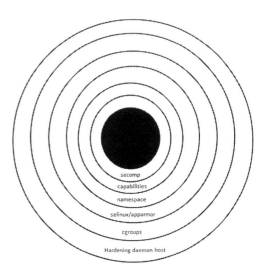

- The particular features of MicroServices could be utilized in order to integrate the MicroServices themselves with the original host so to deploy and take advantage in terms of security of the intrinsic characteristics of the mentioned hosts.

In Fig. 1 we expose the idea of eService security (protection) introducing the, so called, "Onion Model", for the protection of eServices, based on technologies available within MicroServices environments, where the inner part represents the MicroService, along with its respective binaries, while the outer parts represent the different, incremental, host layers utilized to enhance the hardening. The authors considered for this exemplification the model proposed by Newman [1].

Each respective layer of Fig. 1 is discussed in Table 1 that exposes the results of our research, in terms of different checks and verifications that are appropriate and that can be done utilizing the different features of the layers of the proposed model.

## 7 The Issue of Legacy Systems

In the case of need of transformation of legacy services into MicroServices a big issue is left open. The exposure of obsolete services that do not integrate or even do not support necessary security features for today's threats and required security level, e.g. 2FA—two factors authentication, XXS (Cross-Site Scripting)/SQL (Structured Query Language) protections, and the like.

The model and solution proposed in the present paper is the integration of eServices specifically engineered in order to enable the required security features. Those dedicated eServices can be positioned at the borders of the applications before they are exposed on the network (internet, extranet or intranet) so that they

**Table 1** Type/feature/layer and controls that can be implemented for security

| Type/feature/layer | Check |
|---|---|
| SECCOMP | • Verify image binaries of the MicroService<br>• Hardening template creation<br>• Creation of a MicroService functions matrix |
| CAPABILITIES | • Verify what a MicroService image (service) can do at a host level<br>• Creation of a template in order to enroll or to negate enrollment of specific MicroService functions<br>• Creation of variable risk matrix with respect to the basic risk related to the active functions |
| NAME SPACE | • Utilization of "namespace" to differentiate, between host and MicroService, the following:<br>  – pid (process ID)<br>  – username<br>  – network |
| SELINUX/<br>APPARMOR | • Utilization of the typical host security frameworks (e.g. Linux) to confine the MicroService to its limited realm of operations and functions |
| CGROUP | • Limitation of the utilization of the host hardware resources<br>• Template creation |
| HARDENING<br>DAEMON HOST | • Utilization of certificates in order to permit/limit/confine host access to MicroService management<br>• Implementation of TLS to protect information exchange (data streams flow/traffic) from/to MicroServices and host |

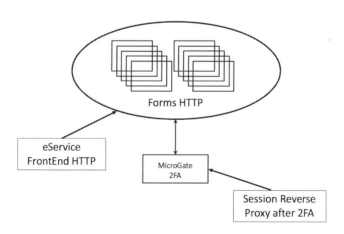

**Fig. 2** Architecture of an access service based on http/https

would represent real MicroGates where all application traffic and interaction should pass through. A sort of fine grain specifically dedicated where there is only one "MicroGate" for a single eService that would filter and discriminate data streams and traffic with respect to the specific security rules and features.

Figure 2 shows an example of an access service based on http/https.

# 8  Conclusions

As discussed in the present paper, MicroServices is the solution for many modern day application and data center scaling issues, it also provides a new idea for developers to use different technologies and tools to resolve specific problems and to leave legacy monolithic applications untouched [1, 2, 21, 23].

However, this solution has inherent drawbacks, such as increased reliance on interfacing, rising costs and reliance on an expensive skill set [24, 25].

Explorations about the specification in a container-based system show that highly customizable monitoring infrastructures can be effectively provided as a service, and that a key step in this process is the definition of an expandable abstract model for them [5, 23, 26]. The steps towards the definition of a standard interface for Monitoring Services allowed the definition of complex, hierarchical monitoring infrastructure by composing multiple instances of two basic components, both for measurement and for data distribution [1, 5, 27, 28]. The conclusion is that functionalities defined through the interface and implemented as MicroServices embedded in containers, along with the internals of each MicroServices, reflect a distinction between core functionalities which are bound to the standard, and custom plugin modules. The deployment of a system of MicroServices that implements the monitoring infrastructure shall pay special attention to maintain the distinction between core and custom functionalities [29, 30].

We can conclude that, to broaden the application spectrum of agent technology in practice and have them more accessible for object-oriented developers, additional communication means for agents are needed. Research findings show that agents can interact using strongly typed service interfaces towards to asynchronous based methods [31].

These allow keeping agents autonomous and further support several recurrent interaction patterns within one method call, that is, avoiding the use of complex message protocols. Improved simplification and higher maintainability would spring from prior research findings and recommendations. Moreover, extensions of binary data streaming via virtual connections resembles established input and output streaming.

This model and approach would allow developers to be able to transfer data between agents and MicroServices in the same way, hence substantially improving a development life cycle along with MicroService efficiency and reliability.

With respect to Security, as discussed above, the advantages of the researched solution can vary in scope, but all have a significant impact on architecture. As for systems and services exposed on Internet, the enablement of up to date security features, would greatly improve efficiency and security update capabilities. For the legacy services that are exposed on Internet, there are no particular modification, and so the implementation of security features with eServices based on MicroServices presents practically a minimal impact on legacy systems and their applications. This would allow rapid deployment of MicroGates and fast security upgrading, while maintaining legacy system untouched (with respect to security).

The creation of standardized and hardened MicroGate templates, would greatly enhance the possibility of re-use and would substantially improve in usability.

At the end, a great flexibility and much easier possibilities of integration are achievable utilizing MicroGates in mixed environments, both exclusively based on MicroService, as well as only partially. Applications and practical impacts may vary from implementing new security features in legacy systems [21, 27], to a new organization of software development process [6, 25], to the technological possibilities of dematerialization and the substitution of the physical business documentation with digital archives [32], to the possibility of enforcing an efficient strategy on Cloud Computing for government and e-Science [33]. Other lines of research could benefit from the present study and research findings, like peer-to-peer (P2P) platforms, and the sharing computation online [34], Cloud Computing reputational impacts [35].

# 9 Limitations

The present research has been pursued both in theory and verified in practical environments, in test laboratories. A substantial empirical analysis is envisaged in order to verify the hypothesis and the conclusions in environment with a great number of connections and a sufficient magnitude of transactions, leaving a huge scope for future investigation and research.

# References

1. Newman, S. (2015). *Building microservices: Designing fine-grained systems*. Sebastopol, CA: O'Reilly Media.
2. Kiess, W., An, X., & Beker, S. (2015). Software-as-a-service for the virtualization of mobile network gateways. In *2015 IEEE Global Communications Conference, GLOBECOM 2015*.
3. Pokahr, A., & Braubach, L. (2016). Elastic component-based applications in PaaS clouds. *Concurrency Computation, 28*(4), 1368–1384.
4. Cavallari, M. (2012). Analysis of evidences about the relationship between organisational flexibility and information systems security. In *Information systems: Crossroads for organization, management, accounting and engineering* (pp. 439–447). ItAIS: The Italian Association for Information Systems.
5. Ciuffoletti, A. (2015). Automated deployment of a microservice-based monitoring infrastructure. *Procedia Computer Science, 68*, 163–172.
6. Malek, S., Edwards, G., Brun, Y., Tajalli, H., Garcia, J., Krka, I., et al. (2010). An architecture-driven software mobility framework. *Journal of Systems and Software, 83*(6), 972–989.
7. Versteden, A., Pauwels, E., & Papantoniou, A. (2015). An ecosystem of user-facing microservices supported by semantic models. In *Proceedings of the CEUR Workshop* (Vol. 1362, pp. 12–21).
8. Ciuffoletti, A. (2015). Open Cloud Computing Interface Monitoring. In *Open Grid Forum*.

9. Viennot, N., Lécuyer, M., Bell, J., Geambasu, R., & Nieh, J. (2015). Synapse: A microservices architecture for heterogeneous-database web applications. In *Proceedings of the 10th European Conference on Computer Systems, EuroSys 2015.*

10. Cavallari, M., Adami, L., & Tornieri, F. (2015). Organisational aspects and anatomy of an attack on NFC/HCE mobile payment systems. In *Proceedings 17th International Conference on Enterprise Information Systems, ICEIS 2015* (Vol. 2, pp. 685–700).

11. Yangui, S., & Tata, S. (2014). An OCCI compliant model for PaaS resources description and provisioning. *The Computer Journal.*

12. Luiz André, B., Clidaras, J., & Hölzle, U. (2013). The datacenter as a computer: An introduction to the design of warehouse-scale machines. *Synthesis Lectures on Computer Architecture, 8*(3), 1–154.

13. Soltesz, S., Pötzl, H., Fiuczynski, M. E., Bavier, A., & Peterson, L. (2007). Container-based operating system virtualization: A scalable, high-performance alternative to hypervisors. In *Operating Systems Review (ACM)* (pp. 275–287).

14. Armbrust, M., Fox, A., Griffith, R., Joseph, A. D., Katz, R., Konwinski, A., et al. (2010). A view of cloud computing. *Communications of the ACM, 53*(4), 50–58.

15. Meyer, D. (2013). The software-defined-networking research group. *IEEE Internet Computing, 17*(6), 84–87.

16. Casalino, N., Cavallari, M., De Marco, M., Gatti, M., & Taranto, G. (2014). Defining a model for effective e-government services and an inter-organizational cooperation in public sector. In *Proceedings of the 16th International Conference on Enterprise Information Systems, ICEIS 2014* (Vol. 2, pp. 400–408).

17. Esfahani, N., Elkhodary, A., & Malek, S. (2013). A learning-based framework for engineering feature-oriented self-adaptive software systems. *IEEE Transactions on Software Engineering, 39*(11), 1467–1493.

18. Andersson, J., De Lemos, R., Malek, S., & Weyns, D. (2009). *Towards a classification of self adaptive software system LNCS* (Vol. 5525).

19. Zhang, J., & Cheng, B. H. C. (2006). Using temporal logic to specify adaptive program semantics. *Journal of Systems and Software, 79*(10), 1361–1369.

20. Kramer, J., & Magee, J. (2007). Self-managed systems: An architectural challenge. In *FoSE 2007: Future of software engineering* (pp. 259–268).

21. Sousa, J. P., Balan, R. K., Poladian, V., Garlan, D., & Satyanarayanan, M. (2008). User guidance of resource-adaptive systems. In *Proceedings of the 3rd International Conference on Software and Data Technologies, ICSOFT 2008* (pp. 36–44).

22. Esfahani, N., & Malek, S. (2012). Utilizing architectural styles to enhance the adaptation support of middleware platforms. *Information and Software Technology, 54*(7), 786–801.

23. Cooray, D., Malek, S., Roshandel, R., & Kilgore, D. (2010). RESISTing reliability degradation through proactive reconfiguration. In *Proceedings of the IEEE/ACM International Conference on Automated Software Engineering, ASE'10* (pp. 83–92).

24. Esfahani, N., Kouroshfar, E., & Malek, S. (2011). Taming uncertainty in self-adaptive software. In *Proceedings of the 19th ACM SIGSOFT Symposium on Foundations of Software Engineering, SIGSOFT/FSE 2011* (pp. 234–244).

25. Malek, S., Medvidović, N., & Mikic-Rakic, M. (2012). An extensible framework for improving a distributed software system's deployment architecture. *IEEE Transactions on Software Engineering, 38*(1), 73–100.

26. Salehie, M., & Tahvildari, L. (2009). Self-adaptive software: Landscape and research challenges. *ACM Transactions on Autonomous and Adaptive Systems, 4*(2).

27. Krintz, C. (2013). The appscale cloud platform: Enabling portable, scalable web application deployment. *IEEE Internet Computing, 17*(2), 72–75.

28. Pokahr, A., & Braubach, L. (2015). Towards elastic component-based cloud applications. In *Intelligent Distributed Computing* (Vol. VIII, pp. 161–171). In D. Camacho, L. Braubach, S. Venticinque & C. Badica (Eds.), *Studies in Computational Intelligence* (p. 570). Cham: Springer.

29. Braubach, L., Jander, K., & Pokahr, A. (2014). A middleware for managing non-functional requirements in cloud PaaS. In *Proceedings of the International Conference on Cloud and Autonomic Computing (CAC-2014)* (pp. 83–92). London: IEEE Computer Society.
30. Bahga, A., & Madisetti, V. K. (2013). Rapid prototyping of multitier cloud-based services and systems. *Computer, 46*(11), 76–83.
31. Kächele, S., & Hauck, F.J. (2013). Component-based scalability for cloud applications. In *Proceedings of the 3rd International Workshop on Cloud Data and Platforms, CloudDP 2013—Co-located with ACM 13th EuroSys* (pp. 19–24).
32. Bellini, F., D'Ascenzo, F., Ghi, A., Spagnoli, F., & Traversi, V. (2013) The impact of e-invoicing on businesses eco-systems: Evidences from Italian supply chains and suggestions for a research agenda. In *Lecture Notes in Information Systems and Organisation* (Vol. 3, pp. 325–336).
33. Bellini, F., D'Ascenzo, F., Ghi, A., Spagnoli, F., & Traversi, V. (2013). Legal issues and requirements for cloud computing in e-science In *Lecture Notes in Information Systems and Organisation* (Vol. 2, pp. 61–70).
34. Meleo, L., Romolini, A., & De Marco, M. (2016). The sharing economy revolution and peer-to-peer online platforms. The case of Airbnb In *Lecture Notes in Business Information Processing* (Vol. 247, pp. 561–570).
35. Patrignani, N., De Marco, M., Fakhoury, R., & Cavallari, M. (2016). Cloud computing: Risks and opportunities for corporate social responsibility In *Lecture Notes in Information Systems and Organisation* (Vol. 15, pp. 23–32).

# Hosting Mission-Critical Applications on Cloud: Technical Issues and Challenges

**Massimo Ficco⊙, Alba Amato⊙ and Salvatore Venticinque⊙**

**Abstract** Deployment in Cloud of applications affected by restrictive security and dependability requirements, and currently considered too critical to be hosted on existing public Clouds, can be a challenge, but at the same time, a necessity for owners of mission-critical applications and services and a new business opportunity for federated Clouds. In particular, new paradigms should be designed to leverage the greater scalability and elasticity offered by federated Cloud infrastructures, as well as tools should be developed to implement a more secure, resilient and performing inter-cloud ecosystem. Such solutions can enable application owners to control in a finer-grained manner the security and dependability of their resources across federated Clouds, in order to satisfy the same critical requirements achieved by hosting the application on its private Cloud. This paper presents the main technical issues and challenges, which must be addressed to migrate mission-critical applications on public Clouds.

**Keywords** Cloud federation · Mission-critical applications · Cloud elasticity Security

## 1 Introduction

Although, virtualization, elasticity and resource sharing enable new levels of flexibility, convenience and economy benefits, they also add new challenges and more areas for potential failures and security vulnerabilities, which represent the major concerns for companies and public organizations that want to shift their business

M. Ficco (✉) · A. Amato · S. Venticinque
Università Degli Studi Della Campania "Luigi Vanvitelli", Aversa, Italy
e-mail: massimo.ficco@unina2.it

A. Amato
e-mail: albaamato@gmail.com

S. Venticinque
e-mail: salvatore.venticinque@gmail.com

© Springer International Publishing AG, part of Springer Nature 2018
R. Lamboglia et al. (eds.), *Network, Smart and Open*, Lecture Notes in Information Systems and Organisation 24, https://doi.org/10.1007/978-3-319-62636-9_12

and mission critical applications and sensitive-data to the Cloud. For example, physical co-residency of a virtual machine (VM), which hosts critical applications with other tenants, makes it more difficult to predict application performance (due to resource stealing), as well as failures may affect multiple co-residency applications; multi-tenancy can represent an increased vulnerability associated to malicious co-resident VMs. Therefore, deployment and migration of critical applications and data should be managed in accordance with more restrictive security, resiliency, performance, and regulatory requirements. Likewise, hosting data-intensive applications is challenging not only due to the size of the data, but also due to its heterogeneous nature and its geographic distribution [1]. Thus, comprehensive and efficient analysis of such data requires distributed and parallel processing, as well as extreme scalability and flexibility essential to respond to non-deterministic resource and performance demands of such applications [2].

In order to cope with the resilience and scalability limits of small Clouds, as well as to surmount the single point of failure associated to the choice of a single proprietary Cloud solution, the concepts of adopting distributed Clouds, federating multiple heterogeneous organizations (governmental Clouds, private and public Clouds) are receiving an increasing attention by the key players in the Cloud services market. The geographic distribution of Cloud data-centers can reduce the access latency to data and services, improve cost efficiency of a single Cloud service provider (CSP), as well as meet customer's legal issues and regulations.

However, contrarily to multi-Cloud paradigm, in which the underlying Clouds are quite visible as separate to the customers, and where customers are directly responsible for managing resource provisioning and scheduling, Cloud federation potentially represents a new business model, in which a multitude of resources and services can be orchestrated in a transparent manner to customers, in order to create large-scale distributed virtual computing clusters, operating as within a single Cloud organization from the customer point of view.

The migration in the federation of applications affected by restrictive security and dependability requirements, currently considered too critical to be hosted on existing Clouds, can be a challenge, but at the same time, a necessity for owners of critical applications and services and a new business opportunity for federated Clouds. The success depends on employing of new models, methods and technologies to manage and impress higher reactivity to the elasticity and scalability capabilities offered by the federated paradigm, as well as to offer greater security and privacy, needed to meet the more stringent requirements of critical applications, data and network traffic, while effectively managing risk and reducing cost and complexity.

In this direction, we believe that new paradigms to implement a more secure, resilient and performing inter-Cloud ecosystem should be designed, as well as new tools should be implemented; on the other hand, to support the federated CSPs to implement new scaling and live-migration Cloud models [3], which are aimed at optimizing the resource allocation and re-allocation in a federated Cloud infrastructure, according to the criticality of the hosted applications and sensitive-data; on the other hand, to support the application owners to perform end-to-end assessment of critical requirements as in a private Cloud.

The rest of the paper is organized as follows: Sect. 2 introduces the opportunity to migrate critical applications in federated environments; Sect. 3 presents the challenges to be addressed to host such applications on existing public Clouds; and Sect. 4 presents the final remarks.

## 2 Critical Applications Migration in Federated Environments

According to the survey by Harvard Business Review Analytic Services (sponsored by Oracle [4]), it is no longer enough to deliver speed and simplicity; the Cloud must also support mission-critical operations. At the state of the art, Cloud providers consider business critical functionalities, at least at theoretical level, just those ones which are essential in disaster planning, maintaining high availability and scalability. However, the same report states, for example, that "*the greatest barrier to Cloud adoption for migrating mission-critical application and services to Cloud is security*".

Cloud federation potentially represents a new business model, in which multiple resources and services from different cloud providers can be orchestrated to create large-scale distributed virtual computing clusters, operating as within a single cloud organization, and able to offer greater guarantees in terms of resilience and scalability required by data- and media-intensive critical applications [5, 6]. Cloud federation can provide abstraction at a much higher level with resulting benefits of elasticity, mobility, and transparency, but it still works at Cloud infrastructure level. Thus, claiming a support for mission-critical applications means: "*shifting from a resource centric Cloud to an application centric Cloud*".

In the case of federated environments, services to support mission-critical applications are still described in terms of functional requirements, but assuring the level of dependability is always in charge of the user. For example, RadiantOne Cloud Federation Service (CFS) offers federated authentication and authorization services, providing an abstraction layer that interfaces with user's identity system: "*delegating to the user critical requirements applications addressing*".

What is expected from service providers is delivering of deeper service-level monitoring, reallocation services and governance capabilities across data-centers. It means: "*a portfolio of tools to provide the control, visibility, security, and scalability that you need to run smoothly*". For example, this is essential to ensure every bit of data moving around in the Cloud ends up exactly where it is supposed to be, at exactly the right time. It is more difficult to be achieved in multi-Cloud scenarios.

As regards current research projects, the SWITCH Horizon 2020 project [7] aims at improving the existing development and execution model of time critical applications, and provides an interactive environment for developing applications and controlling their execution. SUPERCloud Horizon 2020 project [8] proposes a user-centric paradigm, for self-service Clouds-of-Clouds, where customers define their own protection requirements, that reduce administration complexity through security automation. It focuses mainly on security and partially on resilience, in terms of integrity and consistency data requirements [9].

*Therefore, the key players in the Cloud services market should aim at supporting the migration in public Cloud, of critical applications currently already deployed in private data-center and Clouds, providing to the application owner major controllability of the Cloud environments, as well as monitoring in a finer-grained manner the security and dependability of their resources in the Cloud. Moreover, a multi-objective optimization planner for application deployment, and an autonomous application-centric reactive platform for reallocation of resources, on the base of critical requirements and the forecasted behavior of the application, may be the key success factor provided by federated environments for mission-critical applications.*

## 3   Challenges to Be Addressed to Host Mission-Critical Applications on Public Clouds

### 3.1   Resource Provisioning and Planning with Respect to Critical Multi-objectives

Much effort has been spent by the research community to allow for dynamic scheduling, resource allocation, and VM migration to meet Service Level Agreements (SLAs), also in federated Clouds [10]. It is mandatory in Cloud federation to provide information related to Cloud's availability, pricing and SLA rules, and made available to the outside domains. Other mechanisms are needed, such as brokers, which act on behalf of users to identify suitable CPSs for an allocation of resources that meets Quality of Service (QoS) needs of users.

Cloud applications may have different requirements, which must be addressed, such as availability, cost, performance, robustness, and others. On the other hand, mission-critical applications usually have several parts that are critical, because of security and resiliency concerns, workloads, temporary faults, and so on. Moreover, these are usually not independent. For this reason, multi-objective optimization models should allow an effective Cloud resource provisioning and application deployment [11]. Moreover, such different kinds of objectives require to advance the state of art in resource planning and provisioning. For example, maintaining fault tolerance usually means deploying the application on resources fully redundant all the time, forever. That gets costly fast, but when fault tolerance (FT) is not required, the application can be throttled back to a non-FT infrastructure seamlessly with no interruption of service [12]. This saves money, optimizes utilization of computing resources, and provides the availability required when it is most critical [13, 14].

**Challenge**: *It should be provided dynamic re-planning and provisioning of services in a Cloud Federation, to preserve dependability of mission critical applications, only when its critical service levels are expected to be violated and the application is going to fail.*


## 3.2 Cloud Scalability and Elasticity in Federated Environments

Capacity is the maximum workload a service can handle as bound by its SLA. Scalability is the ability of a service to increase its capacity by consuming more resources. Elasticity is the degree of Cloud resources to autonomously adapt its capacity to workload over time. While scalability is mostly a feature of a service itself, elasticity is mostly a feature of the Cloud resources. Precise scalability and elasticity metrics are a key part of the SLA. CloudScale [15] has developed precise metrics for scalability and elasticity, but without considering federated Clouds.

With federated Clouds both scalability and elasticity may improve, but the complexity also increases. Scalability improves because it is possible to get a better match between the workload and the federated Cloud resources, but then more Cloud resources also needs to be taken into consideration in the optimal provisioning and deployment selection. For elasticity, fast reactions to workload changes is key. With a federated Cloud, we get more Cloud resources to choose from, but then the challenge is to keep the reaction time down.

**Challenge**: *It should be defined clear application-centric (instead of infrastructure-centric) metrics for both scalability and elasticity. Then, both design time and runtime adaptations should be developed supporting these novel metrics. It should also find out how to best represent the information in the scalability and elasticity metrics internally, so that, it is possible to use this information for good provisioning and fast (predictive) reallocation decisions.*


## 3.3 SLA Violation Monitoring, Prediction and Reaction

Cloud Federation, Multi-Clouds environments, composition and resource orchestration have increased the complexity of Cloud architecture, but they have opened the Cloud to complex and critical applications. The management of application and resources is crucial, in particular, in critical applications, both users and providers have to monitor performances and other QoSes continuously in order to forecast, prevent or manage hazards and failures.

Existing works on management and forecasting in Cloud Computing usually focus on energy efficiency, SLA awareness, load balancing, costs optimization and on Mobile Cloud Computing [15, 16].

In this critical application context, it is crucial the use of forecasting and profiling models for resource management and for planning reconfiguration actions [17, 18]. Several works focused on workload and resources usage modeling [19]. The main effort in literature was spent in virtual machine and data optimization. In the second case, many forecast models have been provided in order to reduce cost, increase availability and to effectively migrating data in case of problems [20]. In order to increase trustiness towards Cloud systems for critical applications, proper models must be developed in order to rank providers' capabilities. This problem was introduced in recent works [21], but the problem of developing formal trust models for critical applications in the Cloud is still an open issue. The main results in literature about Cloud application profiling and forecasting models focus on workload prediction of single Cloud provider; main models are used to monitor and analyze VMs elements (CPUs, memory etc.) at Infrastructure as a Service (IaaS) level. Some approaches exploit autoregressive [22], reactive [23], proactive [24] or Markovian [25] models of responses of Cloud resources with given workloads. Anyway, most of these models are based on time series to acquire and have a long-time prediction [26]. Despite of the need of profiling and forecasting models for proper resource management, resource management in Hybrid/Federated Clouds mainly addresses scheduling with the goal of optimizing resources over-all costs [27]. The most used optimization methods are based on Pareto Front Approximations [28].

Moreover, rules-based approaches have been used to predict the behavior of the system loads; then, these predictions have been used to decide how to scale Cloud resources. For example, the AzureWatch [29] offers an elasticity service based on information, such as workload, history, date and time or size of the queue of requests, to adjust the number of instances used to run applications on the platform. Dawoud et al. [30] present Elastic VM, an architecture that re-sizes the VM resources dynamically to cope with workload demand and maintain the service level objectives (SLO). To predict the CPU allocations, Elastic VM uses a mechanism based on adaptive control that considers the last allocations and CPU utilization history. Roy et al. [31] describes a look-ahead resource allocation algorithm, based on an autoregressive-moving-average model (ARMA), which predicts future workload based on a limited workload history and adjusts the virtual machines amount allocated to users. The algorithm objective is to minimize the used resources, satisfying the application QoS and keeping operational costs low. PRESS [32] is a predictive elasticity system based in patterns generated with Fast Fourier Transform (FFT). PRESS first employs FFT to identify repeating patterns and, called signature, which are used for its predictions. If no signature is discovered, PRESS employs a statistical state-driven approach to capture short-term patterns in resource demand, and uses a discrete-time Markov chain to predict that demand for the near future. Vasic et al. [33] identifies workload classes and assigning to each one a signature generated by the relationship between the load and the resources used to handle it. When the workload conditions have changed, it loads the resource configuration related to the signature.

**Challenge**: *Monitoring and forecasting should be used to predict behaviors that could lend to some kind of violations of contracted application critical require-ments, as well as to react and avoid application failures. In particular, it should be introduced forecasting models into federated Clouds able to increase trustiness in Cloud system by critical application owners. Forecasting and profile models can overcome the problems outlined in [21], by providing proper models and tech-niques to forecast unexpected behaviors under typical and atypical/malicious workloads. It should not address only optimal scheduling of resources, but define proper formal forecasting models able to prevent or at least early detect errors, QoS-related problems, incorrect or faulty behaviors. These predictions will be used to decide how to scale and/or reallocated Cloud resources, as well as where relocate the workload (e.g., reallocation of users to different VM instances).*

## 3.4  Security Issues and Measures in Federated Environments

Cloud security is still considered one of the inhibitors for migration critical application in the public Cloud. Users with sensitive data are still reluctant to move applications and data to commercial Clouds, mainly due to a lack of trust in CSPs and on the need of respecting still unclear data protection regulations. Moreover, Cloud is perceived as an additional source of risks, which hardly can be addresses.

Lack of trust is often derived from the difficulties of applying common security methodologies in the Cloud: system security assessment usually relies on verifi-cation of checklists of (standard) security controls manually made by an audit. Framework like NIST SP800-53, ISO 27000, CSA Cloud Control Matrix, lists the proposed controls. In a Cloud environment, which relies on the service model, it is difficult to make such audits and verification, due to the delegation to third party of many of the issues: *"Who controls the CSP supports? Does it correctly apply to my specific service?"*.

Recently, international community is adopting Security SLA as a mean to address such problem: Security SLAs are Service Level Agreements that include terms devoted to identify the security granted when providing the service [34]. ENISA documents offer an overview of the state of art of the security and Security SLA adoption in the Cloud.

FP7 and H2020 projects are proposing models and techniques to address and manage security SLAs: FP7 SPECS project [35] proposes a SLA model and a machine readable format able to model Security SLA and a framework to automate their negotiation, automatic enforcement and monitoring. SLAReady [36] and SLALOM [37] project proposes SLA models that include specific legal terms and contractual forms in order to correctly address security in such documents. MUSA

[38] proposes a framework to develop multi-Cloud applications, taking security into account from the very early development stages.

In the context of Cloud federation, several research work state that relying on multi-Cloud solutions can improve security. Others believe that, on the contrary, this will bring new security risks and vulnerabilities. For instance, on one hand, the authors of [39] offers simple surveys of solutions that try to improve the security using multi-Cloud techniques. For example, [40] proposes techniques to distribute a file over multiple providers or untrusted networks, granting higher confidentiality and data integrity. On the other hand, [41] face the security in multi-Cloud application in different perspectives. They analyze different multi-Cloud solutions and try to make a security assessment of the overall application behavior. According to such vision, multi-Cloud is open to new security threats that decrease the global security level. At best of the authors' knowledge, there are no concrete techniques that try to address the issue of granting a security SLA to a critical application running in a Cloud federation.

**Challenge**: *Critical applications often have strict security requirements that restrict their adoption in Cloud environments. Therefore, SLA should include security terms, as well as SLA models should include the formalisms and machine readable formats proposed in the above cited project (particularly SPECS and MUSA projects). Moreover, it should be offered solutions to both implement SLA and react to (possible) SLA violations, using federated resources: such approaches enable to offer to critical application owner, security SLA that can be continuously monitored and can take advantages of the offerings of multiple providers. Cloud federation should protect infrastructure security offering Security SLAs, which grant secure boot, secured crashes, and back-doors disclosure via virtualized test and monitoring. Finally, it should be offered specific services to address security issues, for example, offering Intrusion Detection System as a service and granting secure storage services. Furthermore, it could guarantee better security when user comes to Authentication, Authorization, Accounting (AAA). In particular, it should be provided an Authenticated Time Service to solve two issues: i) AAA regarding the network and virtualization infrastructure (e.g., identifying the tenant or guest service providers) and ii) AAA regarding the network function (e.g., identifying the end-user).*

## 4 Conclusions and Future Remarks

The past 3–4 years have seen significant growth of enterprise that need to migrate their secure workloads in the cloud, as well as predictable performance and support for their mission-critical applications. As reported by 'State of the Market: Enterprise Cloud 2016' [42], 84% of business critical enterprises said that private cloud usage has increased in the past year, and half of enterprises said they would like to migrate in public clouds at least 75% of their critical workloads by 2018. This requires designing cloud services that specifically fit such critical workloads, taking into account geography, networking, security, resilience, scalability, and service management expectations, as well as the ability to quickly deploy the solution to meet rapidly changing business requirements. Moreover, according to [43], there were an estimated 1.2 billion business-to-business IoT connections in 2014 up from less than one billion in 2011. That number is expected to grow to more than 5 billion over the next five years. The key to success is creating a tailored solution that considers each workload security, resiliency, agility, elasticity and scalability requirements.

Taking the most out of the cloud technologies means to rapidly evolve to federated environments, where the scalability and the combination of multiple offerings makes the difference in terms of application resilience and performance (availability, scalability, etc.), reduced cost, or reliable data protection mechanisms. Critical application growth, rise in complexity and need for interoperability create market opportunity for cloud integrators and federated cloud providers, by offering new capabilities in the existing complex cloud landscape [44].

On the other hand, the complexity of meeting critical application requirements in public cloud involves technologies and practices that are still maturing, including recognition of what and where new points of vulnerability and failures cloud could introduce. Solutions to such types of problems stem from the potentialities offered by federated environments, whose resources, if appropriately managed, can guarantee scalability and resiliency features which, coupled with security aspects, could be used to satisfy more restrictive critical requirements of applications.

Therefore, innovative Frameworks to setup federated CSPs and exploit the greater scalability and elasticity offered by federated cloud infrastructures, as well as a Platforms enabled to implement a more secure, resilient and performing inter-cloud ecosystem, should be implemented.

As represented in Fig. 1, the federation consists of a group of CSPs that voluntarily collaborate with each other, in order to share network, computing, storage resources and services from one or several distributed data-centers. From architectural perspective, future solutions should not adopt a centralized resource management model, but, as defined by Buyya [10], it should be implements a Peer-to-Peer (p2p) based inter-cloud platform, in which each federated CSP represents a peer enabled to communicate and negotiate directly with each other without mediator.

The platform should support the negotiation process among a federated CSP, its customers (critical application owners), and the other federated peers. It should implement decision support and planning services, in order to optimize dynamic resource allocation and reallocation needed to satisfy critical requirements and avoid application failures. Automatic provisioning and deployment services integrated in the platform should be implemented to manage network, computing, and storage resources in the federation.

Mechanisms should be offered for real-time monitoring of critical properties of the application, the operating environment, and the hosting infrastructure, and used to implement services to predict the system behavior, and based in these results, to predict when and how to reallocate resources. Open source tools and application

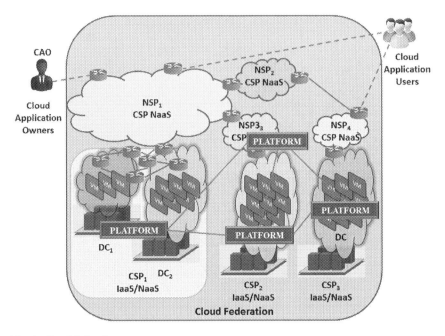

**Fig. 1** Cloud federation ecosystem

programming interfaces should be investigated and extended in order to implement application-centric elasticity capability, including replication (horizontal scaling), and live migration. It can be expressed as a multi-objective optimization problem, covering both more restrictive requirements of critical application, and CSP's benefits (minimize the number of active hosts, energy saving, etc.). Such mechanisms should assign to the federation more predictive scalability and elasticity guarantees indispensable to avoid and mitigate failure, security incidents and performance degradation of the critical application. Moreover, security services should be provided to grant security features according to Security SLA.

Administrator of each federated CSP should runs the platform on local resources. Each Platform should be able to interact with other federated peers, by using specific distributed enabling services, which should be implemented to support the p2p cooperation among the federation (including communication overlay network, authentication service, distributed resource register, etc.).

As Fig. 2 shows, the framework, through a Web dashboard should provide a set of tools, which can be offered to the critical application owners for (i) SLA negotiation, (ii) deploying application components in the federated infrastructure, (iii) SLA monitoring, and (iv) intrusion detection. Such services and tools should enrich cloud services offered by each federated CSP, in order to ensure more restrictive requirements of critical applications and workloads.

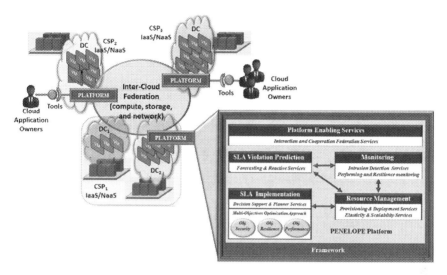

**Fig. 2** Cloud federation P2P framework

**Acknowledgements** This research is partially supported by the projects CoSSMic (Collaborating Smart Solar-powered Micro-grids—FP7-ICT-608806), CRYSTAL (Critical System Engineering Acceleration—no. 332830), and ITINERE (Integrated and Interoperable System for Railway Enhanced Applications—P.O.R. FESR Campania 2007/2013).

# References

1. Esposito, C., Ficco, M., Palmieri, F., & Castiglione, A. (2015). A knowledge-based platform for big data analytics based on publish/subscribe services and stream processing. *Journal of Knowledge-Based Systems, 79,* 3–17.
2. Diaz-Montes, J., Diaz-Granados, M., Zou, M., & Tao, S. (2015). Supporting data-intensive workflows in software-defined federated multi-clouds. In *IEEE Transactions on Cloud Computing* (Vol. 99).
3. Ficco, M., Esposito, C., Chang, H., & Raymond Choo, K. K. (2016). Live migration in emerging cloud paradigms. *IEEE Cloud Computing, 3*(2), 12–19.
4. Cloud Computing Comes of Age, available at https://hbr.org/resources/pdfs/comm/oracle/19128_HBR_Oracle_Report_webview.pdf.
5. Esposito, C., Ficco, M., Palmieri, P., & Castiglione, A. (2013). Interconnecting federated clouds by using publish-subscribe service. *Cluster Computing, 6*(4), 887–903.
6. Ficco, M., Tasquier, L., & Di Martino, B. (2014). Interconnection of federated clouds. *Intelligent Distributed Computing VII, 511,* 243–248.
7. SWITCH project, Software Workbench for Interactive, Time Critical and Highly self-adaptive Cloud applications, available at http://www.switchproject.eu/.
8. SUPERCLOUD project, User-centric management of security and dependability in clouds of clouds, available at https://supercloud-project.eu/.
9. Ficco, M., Palmieri, F., & Castiglione, A. (2015). Modeling security requirements for cloud-based system development. *Concurrency and Computation: Practice and Experience, 27*(8), 2107–2124.

10. Buyya, R., Ranjan, R., & Calheiros, R. N. (2010). InterCloud: Utility-oriented federation of cloud computing environments for scaling of application services. *Algorithms and Architectures for Parallel Processing, LNCS, 6081*, 13–31.

11. Ficco, M., & Rak, M. (2013). SLA-oriented security provisioning for cloud computing. *LNCS, 367*, 230–244.

12. Ficco, M., & Rak, M. (2012). Intrusion tolerance of stealth DoS attacks to web services. *Information Security and Privacy, LNCS, 376*, 579–584.

13. Andersen, J. (2015). Moving mission-critical applications to the cloud. *Network Computing*, available at: http://www.networkcomputing.com/cloud-infrastructure/moving-mission-critical-applications-cloud/2132272314.

14. Ficco, M., & Rak, M. (2015). Stealthy denial of service strategy in cloud computing. *IEEE Transactions on Cloud Computing, 3*(1), 80–94.

15. Brataas, G., Stav, E., Becker, S. (2013). CloudScale: Scalability management for cloud systems. In *Proceedings of the 4th ACM/SPEC International Conference on Performance Engineering* (pp. 335–338).

16. Rak, M., & Ficco, M. (2012). Intrusion tolerance as a service: A SLA-based solution. In *Proceedings of the 2nd International Conference on Cloud Computing and Services Science (CLOSER 2012)* (pp. 375–384). Porto, Portugal.

17. Weingärtner, R., Bräscher, G. B., & Westphall, C. B. (2015). Cloud resource management: A survey on forecasting and profiling models. *Journal of Network and Computer Applications, 47*, 99–106.

18. Ficco, M., Rak, M., & Di Martino, B. (2012). An intrusion detection framework for supporting SLA assessment in cloud computing. In *Proceedings of the 4th International Conference on Computational Aspects of Social Networks (CASoN 2012)* (pp. 244–249). Sao Carlos, Brazil.

19. Geronimo, G., Werner, J., Westphall, C., & Defenti, L. (2013). Provisioning and resource allocation for green clouds. In *Proceedings of the International Conference on Networks* (pp. 81–86).

20. Raja Wasim, A., et al. (2015). A survey on virtual machine migration and server consolidation frameworks for cloud data centers. *Journal of Network and Computer Applications, 52*, 11–25.

21. Macías, M., & Guitart, J. (2016). Analysis of a trust model for SLA negotiation and enforcement in cloud markets. *Future Generation Computer Systems, 55*, 460–472.

22. Calheiros, R. N., et al. (2015). Workload prediction using ARIMA model and its impact on cloud applications' QoS. *IEEE Transactions on Cloud Computing, 3*(4), 449–458.

23. Bonvin, T., Papaioannou, G., & Aberer, K. (2011). Autonomic SLA-driven provisioning for cloud applications. In *Proceedings of the 11th International Symposium on Cluster, Cloud and Grid Computing* (pp. 434–443).

24. Islam, S., Keung, J., Lee, K., & Liu, A. (2012). Empirical prediction models for adaptive resource provisioning in the cloud. *Future Generation Computing System, 28*(1), 155–162.

25. Pacheco-Sanchez, S., et al. (2011). Markovian workload characterization for QoS prediction in the cloud. In *Proceedings of the 4th International Conference on Cloud Computing* (pp. 147–154).

26. Tran, V. G., Debusschere, V., & Bacha, S. (2012). Hourly server workload forecasting up to 168 hours ahead using seasonal ARIMA model. In *Proceedings of the 13th International Conference on Industrial Technology* (pp. 1127–1131).

27. Mustafa, S., et al. (2015). Resource management in cloud computing: Taxonomy, prospects, and challenges. *Computers & Electrical Engineering, 47*, 186–203.

28. Farahabady, M. R. H., Lee, Y. C., & Zomaya, A. Y. (2014). Pareto-optimal cloud bursting. *IEEE Transactions on Parallel Distributed System, 25*(10), 2670–2682.

29. AzureWatch, available at: www.paraleap.com/azurewatch/.

30. Meinel, C., Dawoud, W., & Takouna, I. (2011). *Elastic vm for dynamic virtualized resources provisioning and optimization* (Technical Report), Hasso Plattner Institute, University of Potsdam.

31. Roy, N., Dubey, A., & Gokhale, A. (2011). Efficient autoscaling in the cloud using predictive models for workload forecasting. In *Proceedings of the 4th International Conference on Cloud Computing* (pp. 500–507).
32. Gong, Z., Gu, X., & Wilkes, J. (2010). Press: Predictive elastic resource scaling for cloud systems. In *Proceedings of the 6th International Conference on Network and Service Management* (pp. 9–16).
33. Vasi, N., Novakovi, D., Miu, S., Kosti, D., & Bianchini, R. (2012). Dejavu: Accelerating resource allocation in virtualized environments. In *Proceedings of the 17th International Conference on Architectural Support for Programming Languages and Operating Systems* (pp. 423–436).
34. Ficco, M., Venticinque, S., & Di Martino, B. (2012). mOSAIC-based intrusion detection framework for cloud computing. In *Move to Meaningful Internet Systems: OTM 2012, LNCS* (Vol. 7566, pp. 628–644).
35. SPECS Project. Secure Provisioning of Cloud Services based on SLA management. FP7-ICT-2013.1.5, available at: http://specs-project.eu/.
36. SLAReady—Making Cloud SLAs readily usable in the EU private sector, available at: http://www.sla-ready.eu/.
37. SLALOM—SLALOM—Service Level Agreement—Legal and Open Model, available at: http://slalom-project.eu/.
38. MUSA Project. MUlti-cloud Secure Applications, H2020-ICT-2014-1, available at: www.musa-project.eu.
39. Bennani, N., Ghedira-guegan, C., Vargas-solar, G., & Musicante, M. A. (2015). Towards a secure database integration using SLA in a multi-cloud context. In *Proceedings of the Computer Software and Applications Conference* (pp. 4–9).
40. Bohli, J. M., Gruschka, N., Jensen, M., Iacono, L. L., & Marnau, N. (2013). Security and privacy-enhancing multicloud architectures. *IEEE Transactions on Dependable and Secure Computing, 10,* 212–224.
41. Singhal, M., et al. (2013). Collaboration in multicloud computing environments: Framework and security issues. In *IEEE Computer* (pp. 76–84).
42. 5 questions to consider as you shift more business critical applications to the cloud, available at: http://www.networkworld.com/article/3027682/cloud-computing/5-questions-to-consider-as-you-shift-more-business-critical-applications-to-the-cloud.html (Retrieved January 2015).
43. Trending: Enterprises Move Business-Critical Application to the Cloud, available at: http://news.verizonenterprise.com/2015/06/enterprise-cloud-workloads-applications-adoption/ (Retrieved February 2015).
44. The future of cloud computing, 3rd annual survey 2013. North Bridge in partnership with GigaOM Research. Available at http://www.northbridge.com/2013-cloud-computing-survey (Retrieved February 2015).

# The Impact of XBRL on Financial Statement Structural Comparability

Steve Yang⑩, Fang-Chun Liu⑩ and Xiaodi Zhu⑩

**Abstract** The quality of corporate financial reporting has long been an important interest of financial reporting users, including investors, financial analysts, and regulators. Comparability is a key qualitative characteristic of accounting information that facilitates the comparison of financial statements. However, various reporting formats and accounting taxonomy standards result in inconsistent reporting structures that indirectly affect comparability. To improve information comparability, the U.S. Securities and Exchange Commission (SEC) mandated the adoption of the eXtensible Business Reporting Language (XBRL), a search-facilitating technology, to reduce the costs of information search and improve the efficiency of information processing. Leveraging on the XBRL adoption enforced by the SEC, this study investigates whether the comparability of financial statement structure has improved in the post-mandate XBRL period. The results show a significant, consistent comparability improvement in the post-XBRL adoption period, providing empirical evidence of the positive impact of XBRL on enhancing financial statement structural comparability.

**Keywords** XBRL · Financial reporting quality · Comparability
Financial statement structure

S. Yang (✉) · F.-C. Liu · X. Zhu
Stevens Institute of Technology, Hoboken, NJ, USA
e-mail: syang14@stevens.edu; steve.yang@stevens.edu

F.-C. Liu
e-mail: fangchun.liu@stevens.edu

X. Zhu
e-mail: xzhu@stevens.edu

© Springer International Publishing AG, part of Springer Nature 2018
R. Lamboglia et al. (eds.), *Network, Smart and Open*, Lecture Notes in Information Systems and Organisation 24, https://doi.org/10.1007/978-3-319-62636-9_13

# 1  Introduction

The quality of financial reporting has long been an important interest of financial reporting users, including investors, financial analysts, and regulators. Prior literature has proposed different models that consider quantitative information (e.g. earnings persistence) and/or qualitative information (e.g. choice of accounting methods) to investigate the issue of financial reporting quality [1, 2]. In the Financial Accounting Standards Board (FASB)'s conceptual framework for financial reporting, comparability is recognized as a key enhancing qualitative characteristic of accounting information [3, 4]. More comparable financial statements have the potential to reduce information processing costs for both users and preparers of financial statements and further improve capital market efficiency [5]. Accounting standard setters, such as the FASB, therefore work on converging accounting standards and promoting the use of new technology to improve financial reporting comparability. However, financial statement structure, an important qualitative attribute of comparability, has not yet been examined.

Financial statement structure consists of a series of accounting concepts and their semantic relationships presented in taxonomies. Different reporting formats and taxonomies permitted under the U.S. Generally Accepted Accounting Principles (GAAP) lead to inconsistent reporting structures that affect comparability. The complexity of inherent data structures and the diversity of reporting preferences and accounting choices also hinder comparability. To address the comparability issue, accounting standard setters and regulators prompt and mandate the adoption of the eXtensible Business Reporting Language (XBRL) as well as the standardized U.S. GAAP taxonomy, to provide better information transparency, accessibility, and efficiency [6]. XBRL is a search-facilitating technology which defines text data by tags. XBRL tags are used to uniquely identify each piece of business information and can be processed by a variety of software. Therefore, XBRL is expected to facilitate information creation, exchange, and comparison, which in turn improves financial reporting quality [5, 7]. In 2004, the U.S. Securities and Exchange Commission (SEC) initiated a voluntary filer program to evaluate the extent to which XBRL enhances comparability. The investigation of companies' financial statement structural differences is a challenge in the pre-XBRL adoption period. With the mandatory use of XBRL, we are able to extract the semantic structure information to examine the issue of financial reporting structures that affect comparability.

This study investigates whether the comparability of financial statement structures has improved in the post-XBRL mandate period. We construct a large scale dataset of XBRL filings and utilize the graph similarity approach proposed by [8] to examine the structural differences of financial statements. The sample includes 27,971 corporate filings from ten industries for the period 2010–2014. The results show a consistent reporting structure comparability of XBRL filings. By controlling the effect of firm size and industry characteristics, we further show that the improvement is more significant after the enactment of the SEC mandatory filing rule. To the best of our knowledge, this is the first study to investigate the comparability of financial statement structure by conducting large scale XBRL data analyses to examine financial statement structure changes in the post-XBRL adoption period. The empirical results of the study not only provide important policy implications but also fill the current gap in accounting and XBRL research by addressing the qualitative attribute of financial statement comparability, the reporting structure comparison.

## 2  Literature Review

As the major source for accounting information users to evaluate corporate value, financial statements are expected to provide clear, accurate, and comprehensive information of a firm's business. High quality financial reporting could reduce the information asymmetry issue that indirectly affects the efficiency of the capital market [9]. As one of accounting information characteristics proposed by the FASB to evaluate the quality of financial reporting, comparability helps reduce the costs of information acquisition and processing [10]. As such, data quality and comparability improvement are the primary motivation for the implementation of the new financial statement filing techniques and standardized accounting taxonomy [11].

The document markup language using standardized tags is developed to improve data processing efficiency [12]. XBRL, an eXtensible Markup Language (XML) standard search-facilitating technology, was created to standardize the electronic format of a financial report and help improve the transparency of financial reports [6, 13]. Given the flexible characteristics of XBRL technology, financial reporting preparers, namely firms, can adopt the standardized XBRL format to present their financial information with some alterations for presenting the uniqueness of their business. Financial reporting users, including analysts, investors and regulators, can use a variety of software to access, exchange, and compare information in XBRL format automatically. The advocates of XBRL expect that XBRL improves financial statement comparability by adopting standard tags and interpretable hierarchical relationships [14, 15]. XBRL also helps improve the efficiency of information processing and reduce the cost of financial statement preparation [14, 16]. Given the expected benefits of XBRL technology, the SEC issued mandatory XBRL rules in early 2009 which require companies to provide their financial statements to the SEC and on their corporate websites using XBRL [17].[1]

---

[1]By June 15, 2009, domestic and foreign large accelerated filers that use U.S. GAAP and have a worldwide public float above $5 billion were required to submit XBRL documents using the U.S. GAAP taxonomy in addition to HTML files, while other large filers needed to file XBRL filings by June 15, 2010 and all remaining filers were required to submit their XBRL filings by June 15, 2011.

The FASB codifies the U.S. GAAP into XBRL taxonomies for companies to file their financial reports using XBRL. In the early stages of XBRL adoption, mapping errors were detected in XBRL filings, which were mainly caused by errors in the U. S. GAAP taxonomy, including multiple elements with similar names and missing key elements [18]. By 2011, the FASB has made significant updates on the U.S. GAAP XBRL taxonomy standards by expanding the existing standards, in order to include more accounting items that are commonly reported in company filings, correct existing technical errors, eliminate duplicated tag items, and update the taxonomy structural models [19]. Such continuous update effort done by the FASB is expected to provide the taxonomy with better quality to "minimize any interference that common extensions might have with data comparability issue" so that better financial reporting quality can be provided for information users to make relevant decisions [17].

Many prior studies examine the impact of XBRL on financial reporting quality by investigating the quantitative attribute of comparability, the reported numbers of certain accounting items [5, 20]. For example, [20] measures financial reporting comparability by the extent of the mapping from economic events to corporate accounting numbers. Such a measure is based on the assumption that firms with similar financial performance under similar economic conditions are expected to have comparable accounting systems. They find a decline of comparability in the post-XBRL adoption. The possible reasons of such decline can be attributed to the use of different accounting choices allowed under U.S. GAAP and the common use of custom XBRL tags. The learning curve associated with the adoption of new technology, XBRL, is one main reason causing XBRL errors found in the early adoption stage [21].

Several studies thus focus on examining the data quality of XBRL filings. For example, a line item matching approach proposed by [22] compares the XBRL file using U.S. GAAP taxonomy with companies' financial statements prepared in other presentation formats. XBRL taxonomy in the early adoption stage is found to have low completeness, low relevancy, and low interoperability, due to the prevalent use of companies' customized tags [23]. The metric method developed in [24] measures the completeness and relevancy of XBRL data standards and also shows a large proportion of companies' customized tags in early XBRL adoption period. With more available XBRL data, research has shown that, compared to traditional reporting formats such as PDF or HTML, XBRL technology provides better financial reporting quality in terms of increased information transparency and efficiency [6, 25–27]. Yang et al. [28] applies a structural pattern method to quantify the financial statement structural differences in order to help detect the unconventional reporting structural patterns chosen by firms. However, the question of whether there exists the structure comparability of financial reporting after the XBRL mandate is not yet empirically examined in the literature.

# 3 Methodology and Data

## 3.1 Graph Similarity Measure

To evaluate the impact of XBRL on financial statement structure, it is important to consider the classifications of financial statement items and the inter-relationships among financial statement items. Yang and Cogill [8] proposes that, by using the standard U.S. GAAP taxonomy concepts or the permissible company customized concepts, financial statement items can be uniquely identified. In addition, the semantic relationships of financial statements in XBRL format can be further modeled in an ordered tree structure with a unique label of each node, as shown in Fig. 1. The similarity between financial statement structures transformed into the tree editing distance can be approximated as the string edit distance with dynamic programming [29]. A greater string editing distance suggests the financial statement structures between two examined companies are less similar.

In Fig. 1, the graphs under consideration can be transformed into property strings in a level oriented way (level order tree traversal). Here we denote the root of the $k$-th tree as $r_k^{T_k}$, and it has $h_k$ levels and $\sigma_{h_k}$ number of nodes at level $h_k$. The value of the property string at $i$-th level and $j$-th position for tree $T_k$ is denoted as $v_{i,j}^{T_k}$. Hence we can represent the property strings of tree $T_1$ and $T_2$ as:

$$s_1 := r_1^{T_1} \cdot v_{1,1}^{T_1} \cdot v_{1,2}^{T_1} \cdot \cdots \cdot v_{h_1,\sigma_{h_1}}^{T_1} \tag{1}$$

$$s_2 := r_2^{T_2} \cdot v_{1,1}^{T_2} \cdot v_{1,2}^{T_2} \cdot \cdots \cdot v_{h_2,\sigma_{h_2}}^{T_2} \tag{2}$$

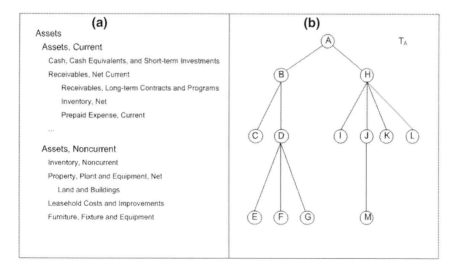

**Fig. 1** **a** Balance sheet; **b** A labeled, directed, rooted tree representation

First, the tree edit distance is defined. Suppose $T_1$ and $T_2$ are two labeled trees, and labels assigned to nodes are chosen from a finite alphabet $\Sigma$. Let $\lambda \notin \Sigma$ denote a special blank symbol and define $\Sigma_\lambda = \Sigma \cup \lambda$. An edit script S between these two trees is a sequence of edit operations turning tree $T_1$ into $T_2$. The cost of an edit script S is the sum of the costs of the operations in S. The tree edit distance is the optimal edit script between $T_1$ and $T_2$ such that the cost of the edit script is minimal. The approximated tree edit distance from $T_1$ and $T_2$ has an upper bound, which can be obtained from the string alignment distance between $T_1'$ and $T_2'$ that can be computed using a dynamic programming algorithm—Levenshtein distance [29].

## 3.2  Local Outlier Factor Algorithm

Local outlier factor (LOF) is an algorithm to find abnormal data points in a dataset by measuring the local deviation of a given data point to its neighbor [30]. It is an extension combining the distance-based outlier detection method and density-based clustering by transferring the global view distance to local density. LOF is the average ratio of reachability density of point $p$ and its neighborhoods. If one point $p$ has lower density and its neighbors have high density, the LOF will become larger. A larger LOF indicates a higher possibility of object $p$ being an outlier. We measure the comparability convergence based on the LOF distribution of the sample. The converged LOF distribution suggests a higher financial reporting structure similarity among observations. Figure 2 shows the plot of LOF density results using our sample data.

To measure the level of convergence in each sample year, we compare the quantiles of LOF score distribution on each data set. We further apply the

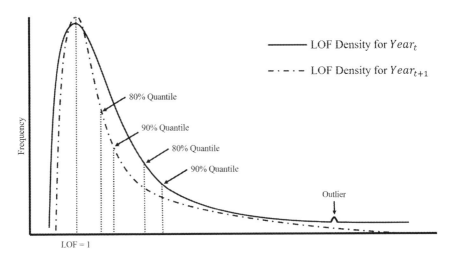

**Fig. 2**  The Local Outlier Factor (LOF) density plot

**Table 1** Sample observations by industry, by year

|      | Mining | Manufacturing | Transportation | Finance | Service | Others |
|------|--------|---------------|----------------|---------|---------|--------|
| 2010 | 81     | 435           | 183            | 212     | 162     | 206    |
| 2011 | 498    | 1919          | 465            | 935     | 1039    | 1247   |
| 2012 | 629    | 2207          | 484            | 1020    | 1191    | 1371   |
| 2013 | 586    | 2196          | 494            | 983     | 1221    | 1519   |
| 2014 | 542    | 2200          | 480            | 987     | 1213    | 1266   |

nonparametric Mann-Whitney U test on LOF between $Year_t$ and $Year_{t+1}$ to statistically examine the trend of convergence across years. Our hypotheses are the following:

$H_0$: $Year_t$ and $Year_{t+1}$ come from the same distribution; that is, $P(Year_t > Year_{t+1}) = P(Year_{t+1} > Year_t)$.

$H_1$: The probability of an observation in $Year_t$ exceeds an observation in $Year_{t+1}$ is greater than the probability of an observation in $Year_{t+1}$ exceeds an observation in $Year_t$; that is, $P(Year_t > Year_{t+1}) > P(Year_{t+1} > Year_t)$.

The unpaired two-year test is to statistically examine the difference between LOF from different years. If $H_0$ is rejected, it suggests the observations from $Year_t$ are significantly larger than observations from $Year_{t+1}$. In other words, LOF in $Year_{t+1}$ is more converged than LOF in $Year_t$ if the p-value is significant.

## 3.3 Data

In this study, we collect the XBRL format of annual reports submitted to the SEC under the "Interactive Data to Improve Financial Reporting Rule".[2] We employ an open source software product, Arelle,[3] to extract the accounting concepts and the financial statement structures from companies' filings. We focus our analyses on three main financial statements, including balance sheets, income statements, and cash flow statements.

The data includes fiscal years 2010 through 2014. After eliminating missing data, the resulting dataset consists of 27,971 valid filings. We then classified the filings into ten groups based on the Standard Industry Classification (SIC) code. The five smallest sectors and observations with missing SIC codes are combined into an "other" sector. The five largest industry sectors in the sample are mining, manufacturing, transportation, finance and services (see Table 1).

---

[2]The rules apply to public companies and foreign private issuers that prepare their financial reports in accordance with U.S. GAAP. For more details of the rules, please refer to the SEC's final rule: http://www.sec.gov/rules/final/2009/33-9002.pdf.

[3]Arelle is an open source software for XBRL, which can be also used on measuring comparability and data mining [31, 32]. Further information can be found at http://arelle.org.

## 4  Empirical Results and Discussion

As we stated earlier, financial statement comparability measures how well the information users can compare across different financial reports for better decision making. Our proposed comparability convergence measure incorporates the two aspects of the comparability of financial reports, including the common financial concepts and the degree of structural similarity. By collecting a large number of corporate XBRL filings, we are able to extract the unique concepts and their corresponding semantic relationships in financial statements.

We first apply the graphic similarity method to calculate distance matrices for each sector across different years. Considering the efficiency of analysis, all distance matrices are reduced to three-dimensional matrices using principal component analysis. Then, the local outlier factor algorithm is applied on the distance matrices to compute LOF scores for each reporting structure. In Fig. 3, we compare the LOF scores at different quantiles to evaluate the pattern of structure convergence over time.

The results show the LOF score at three different quantiles (that is, 70, 80 and 90%, respectively). Lower quantiles will have LOF score closer to 1 which satisfies

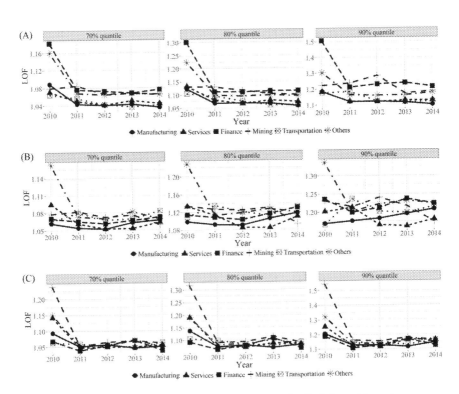

**Fig. 3** LOFs for **a** Balance sheets, **b** Income statements, and **c** Cash flow statements

the definition of LOF method. Figure 3 shows a clear and consistent trend for balance sheets and cash flow statements. On average, all three types of financial statements have relative high LOF in 2010, and decrease to a significantly lower level after 2011. The results indicate the consistent convergence across industries since the mandatory XBRL enactment. Between 2011 and 2014, the results show a relatively flat trend with minor changes. The results of income statements, on the other hand, do not have a clear trend compared to balance sheets and cash flow statements. This is possibly due to the varied choices of accounting methods such as different revenue recognition practices adopted by firms. We believe the relatively weak results of income statements still support the notion of positive standardized XBRL adoption on comparability improvement. At 70% quantile, the trend of income statements is still kept at a relatively low level since 2011. The trends become inconsistent for higher quantile, in particular at 90% quantile. Companies belonging to highest 10% LOF score group are more likely to be outliers, which may cause the inconsistent trend between high quantile and lower quantile. The LOF scores at lower quantiles measure the majority scores, which can represent the convergence better. Our sector analyses of balance sheets show that the finance sector has relatively high LOF score at different quantile points. The result is similar to the interoperability finding examined in prior research [24]. The results of cash flow statements across industries are consistently converged since 2011.

Table 2 shows the statistical results of the Mann-Whitney U test. For all three types of statements, the comparison between 2010 and 2011 using the whole sample shows a significant convergence. The industry sector results also show similar convergence. The results of balance sheets and cash flow statements in the column of 2013 versus 2014 are also significant. This may be due to more updates of the taxonomy done during that time frame. Overall, the statistical test results are consistent with the observed LOF quantile convergence. The statistical results of income statements show a less significant convergence trend. The possible explanation for such insignificant results may due to the more flexible presentation styles of income statements. A firm can choose to present its income statement using either a single statement of comprehensive income or two separate statements for its comprehensive income. In addition, a firm can decide between a multiple-step income statement or a single-step income statement to report its operational results. We believe such flexibility of income statement presentations is the main reason why our finding shows less structural convergence in the income statement analysis.

The users of accounting information rely on high quality financial reporting to evaluate business performance and the effectiveness of strategies implemented by companies. Since the adoption of the XBRL program in 2009, research has started to evaluate the comparability of financial statements using XBRL format, such as the examination of interoperability [33]. Although interoperability measures the taxonomy similarity, its main constraint is to compare only two companies simultaneously. To overcome such a constraint, our proposed method is able to measure the semantic structural convergence within the whole sample by applying the local outlier detection method combined with the distance matrix from the graph

**Table 2** Mann-Whitney U test results

| (A) Balance sheets | 2010 versus 2011 | 2011 versus 2012 | 2012 versus 2013 | 2013 versus 2014 |
|---|---|---|---|---|
| Whole sample | 0.000*** | 0.118 | 0.616 | 0.097* |
| *Sector analysis* | | | | |
| Manufacturing | 0.000*** | 0.345 | 0.630 | 0.002*** |
| Service | 0.002*** | 0.385 | 0.829 | 0.348 |
| Finance | 0.000*** | 0.196 | 0.628 | 0.793 |
| Mining | 0.686 | 0.057* | 0.122 | 0.637 |
| Transportation | 0.332 | 0.115 | 0.430 | 0.642 |
| Others | 0.000*** | 0.740 | 0.463 | 0.586 |
| (B) Income statements | 2010 versus 2011 | 2011 versus 2012 | 2012 versus 2013 | 2013 versus 2014 |
| Whole sample | 0.030** | 0.118 | 0.980 | 0.379 |
| *Sector analysis* | | | | |
| Manufacturing | 0.287 | 0.604 | 0.997 | 0.670 |
| Service | 0.283 | 0.142 | 0.528 | 0.819 |
| Finance | 0.340 | 0.135 | 0.768 | 0.727 |
| Mining | 0.633 | 0.234 | 0.524 | 0.132 |
| Transportation | 0.292 | 0.152 | 0.554 | 0.717 |
| Others | 0.001*** | 0.524 | 0.659 | 0.023** |
| (C) Cash flow statements | 2010 versus 2011 | 2011 versus 2012 | 2012 versus 2013 | 2013 versus 2014 |
| Whole sample | 0.000*** | 0.907 | 0.990 | 0.002*** |
| *Sector analysis* | | | | |
| Manufacturing | 0.000*** | 0.728 | 0.050** | 0.902 |
| Service | 0.000*** | 0.748 | 0.765 | 0.232 |
| Finance | 0.000*** | 0.922 | 1.000 | 0.000*** |
| Mining | 0.000*** | 0.785 | 0.712 | 0.216 |
| Transportation | 0.005*** | 0.301 | 0.228 | 0.996 |
| Others | 0.000*** | 0.524 | 0.996 | 0.000*** |

$***p < 0.01$, $**p < 0.05$, $*p < 0.1$

similarity measure. In addition, our measure is not only able to examine the level of convergence using a large scale dataset, but also incorporates the similarity of both semantic structure and adopted taxonomies. We believe our method can provide a more comprehensive measurement of financial reporting quality, in particular shedding light on the investigation of comparability.

The empirical results overall show a significant converged trend among semantic structures after 2011, when the U.S. GAAP taxonomy had a major update. The revised U.S. GAAP taxonomy helps the convergence of financial reporting structure by reducing the use of firm's self-developed concepts. For example, Monsanto Company, one of the firms in first adoption phase, increased the use of standardized

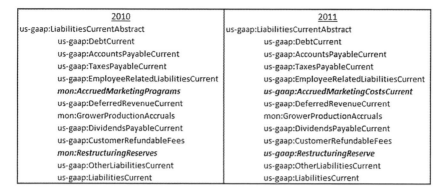

| 2010 | 2011 |
|---|---|
| us-gaap:LiabilitiesCurrentAbstract | us-gaap:LiabilitiesCurrentAbstract |
| us-gaap:DebtCurrent | us-gaap:DebtCurrent |
| us-gaap:AccountsPayableCurrent | us-gaap:AccountsPayableCurrent |
| us-gaap:TaxesPayableCurrent | us-gaap:TaxesPayableCurrent |
| us-gaap:EmployeeRelatedLiabilitiesCurrent | us-gaap:EmployeeRelatedLiabilitiesCurrent |
| *mon:AccruedMarketingPrograms* | *us-gaap:AccruedMarketingCostsCurrent* |
| us-gaap:DeferredRevenueCurrent | us-gaap:DeferredRevenueCurrent |
| mon:GrowerProductionAccruals | mon:GrowerProductionAccruals |
| us-gaap:DividendsPayableCurrent | us-gaap:DividendsPayableCurrent |
| us-gaap:CustomerRefundableFees | us-gaap:CustomerRefundableFees |
| *mon:RestructuringReserves* | *us-gaap:RestructuringReserve* |
| us-gaap:OtherLiabilitiesCurrent | us-gaap:OtherLiabilitiesCurrent |
| us-gaap:LiabilitiesCurrent | us-gaap:LiabilitiesCurrent |

**Fig. 4** Example of migration from customized concept to the U.S. GAAP unified concept

labels in 2011, compared to its 2010 filings. Figure 4 is the excerpt from Monsanto's 2010 and 2011 balance sheets. The custom labels used in 2010 filings, "mon:AccruedMarketingPrograms" and "mon:RestructuringReserves", were replaced by the U.S. GAAP taxonomy, "us-gaap:AccruedMarketingCostsCurrent" and "us-gaap:RestructuringReserve", in 2011, showing the increased taxonomy relevancy and the convergence of semantic reporting structure within a single company. It is expected that the improvement of the standardized U.S. GAAP taxonomy is associated with the increasing use of the standard labels, which in turn contributes to the comparability of different companies' financial statements.

Taken together, our results show the quality of financial statements has improved through the mandatory XBRL GAAP taxonomy, as demonstrated in increased comparability of financial reporting. Furthermore, the empirical results provide evidence to support regulator's assertion that XBRL adoption benefits information users by providing better quality and effectiveness of financial reporting practice, and complements the continuous efforts of regulators in updating the XBRL taxonomy.

## 5   Conclusion

The quality of financial reporting has long been the focus of accounting standards setters. However, the measure of qualitative attributes of financial reporting such as comparability is scarce because of the data availability. With the prevalent use of XBRL technology, the study analyzes the semantic quality of financial statement structures by analyzing a large scale XBRL dataset. We collect annual corporate XBRL filings submitted to the SEC between 2010 and 2014. The dataset consists of 27,971 firm-year observations. We propose a comprehensive method to address the issue of the financial statement comparability by investigating the changes of financial statement structure in the post-XBRL adoption period. The method not only measures the commonly used accounting taxonomies but also evaluates the relative relationships of semantic structures.

We show that the overall accounting semantic quality has improved through the SEC's XBRL project. The results of balance sheets and cash flow statements demonstrate significant and robust convergence of statement structure, suggesting that comparability has improved over time. Our sector analyses also show a consistent trend of convergence. To the best of our knowledge, this is the first study to address the issue of reporting comparability by focusing on financial statement structure. The study contributes to accounting literature, in particular XBRL, by showing the significant improvement of structural comparability with the use of XBRL technology. Our findings provide supportive evidence for the benefits of XBRL. For regulators, the convergence of financial reporting documented in the study provides supportive evidence of the continuous development of XBRL program made by the FASB and the SEC.

Certain confounding factors such as firm-specific characteristics and year-over-year taxonomy updates are associated with the usefulness of XBRL technology. To provide a more comprehensive understanding of the impact of XBRL on financial statement comparability, particularly the reporting structural comparison, we plan to conduct the following analyses in our future work to: (1) address the impact of year-over-year XBRL taxonomy updates, (2) examine the learning effects of XBRL adoption for firms classified in different adoption phases, and (3) propose a more comprehensive comparability measure that not only considers the semantic structure measure but also includes the quantitative measure that evaluates the extent of the mapping from economic events to reported accounting numbers.

# References

1. Archer, S., Delvaille, P., & McLeay, S. (1995). The measurement of harmonisation and the comparability of financial statement items: Within-country and between-country effects. *Accounting and Business Research, 25,* 67–80. https://doi.org/10.1080/00014788.1995. 9729930.
2. Krisement, V. M. (1997). An approach for measuring the degree of comparability of financial accounting information. *European Accounting Review, 6,* 465–485. https://doi.org/10.1080/ 713764728.
3. FASB. (2010). Conceptual framework for financial reporting. http://www.fasb.org/jsp/FASB/ Document_C/DocumentPage?cid=1176157498129&acceptedDisclaimer=true.
4. Miller-Nobles, T. L., Mattison, B. L., & Matsumura, E. M. (2015). *Horngren's Accounting* (11th ed.). Prentice Hall.
5. De Franco, G., Kothari, S. P., & Verdi, R. S. (2011). The benefits of financial statement comparability. *Journal of Accounting Research, 49,* 895–931.
6. Hodge, F. D., Kennedy, J. J., & Maines, L. A. (2004). Does search-facilitating technology improve the transparency of financial reporting? *The Accounting Review, 79,* 687–703. https:// doi.org/10.2308/accr.2004.79.3.687.

7. Engel, P., Hamscher, W., Shuetrim, G., vun Kanno, D., & Wallis, H. (2004). Extensible Business Reporting Language (XBRL). http://www.xbrl.org/Specification/XBRL-RECOMMENDATION-2003-12-31+Corrected-Errata-2004-04-29.pdf.

8. Yang, S., & Cogill, R. (2013). Balance sheet outlier detection using a graph similarity algorithm. In *IEEE* (pp 135–142).

9. Turner, L. E. (2000). Speech by SEC staff: Charting a course for high quality financial reporting. https://www.sec.gov/news/speech/spch356.htm.

10. Ball, R. (2006). International Financial Reporting Standards (IFRS): Pros and cons for investors. *Accounting and Business Research, 36,* 5–27. https://doi.org/10.1007/s00113-013-2415-0.

11. FASB. (1980). Statement of financial accounting concepts No. 2: Qualitative characteristics of accounting information. http://www.fasb.org/cs/BlobServer?blobcol=urldata&blobtable=MungoBlobs&blobkey=id&blobwhere=1175820900526&blobheader=application%2Fpdf.

12. SEC. (2003). XBRL Voluntary financial reporting program on the EDGAR system. https://www.sec.gov/rules/proposed/33-8496.htm#P125_13776.

13. Hannon, N. (2002). XBRL enters a new phase. *Strategic Finance, 83,* 61–62.

14. Baldwin, A. A., & Trinkle, B. S. (2011). The impact of XBRL: A Delphi investigation. *The International Journal of Digital Accounting Research, 11,* 1–24. https://doi.org/10.4192/1577-8517-v11.

15. Vasarhelyi, M. A., Chan, D. Y., & Krahel, J. P. (2012). Consequences of XBRL standardization on financial statement data. *Journal of Information Systems, 26,* 155–167.

16. Cox, C. (2008). Opening statement-open meeting on the use of technology to improve financial reporting. Washington, D.C.

17. SEC. (2009). Interactive data to improve financial reporting. https://www.sec.gov/rules/final/2009/33-9002.pdf.

18. Bartley, J., Al-Chen, Y. S., & Taylor, E. (2010). Avoiding common errors of XBRL implementation. *Journal of Accountancy, 209,* 46–51.

19. FASB. (2011). FASB US GAAP financial reporting taxonomy release notes. http://www.fasb.org/cs/ContentServer?site=FASB&c=Document_C&pagename=FASB/Document_C/DocumentPage&cid=1176157270751.

20. Dhole, S., Lobo, G. J., Mishra, S., & Pal, A. M. (2015). Effects of the SEC's XBRL mandate on financial reporting comparability. *International Journal of Accounting Information Systems, 19,* 29–44. https://doi.org/10.1016/j.accinf.2015.11.002.

21. Du, H., Vasarhelyi, M. A., & Zheng, X. (2013). XBRL mandate: Thousands of filing errors and so what? *Journal of Information Systems, 27,* 61–78.

22. Bovee, M., Ettredge, M. L., & Srivastava, R. P. (2002). Does the year 2000 XBRL taxonomy accommodate current business financial-reporting practice? *Journal of Information Systems, 16,* 165–182.

23. Zhu, H., & Fu, L. (2009). Towards quality of data standards: Empirical findings from XBRL. In *30th International Conference on Information Systems* (p. 66).

24. Zhu, H., & Wu, H. (2011). Quality of data standards: Framework and illustration using XBRL taxonomy and instances. *Electronic Markets, 21,* 129–139. https://doi.org/10.1007/s12525-011-0060-4.

25. Kim, J. W., Lim, J.-H., & No, W. G. (2012). The effect of first wave mandatory XBRL reporting across the financial information environment. *Journal of Information Systems, 26,* 127–153.

26. Perdana, A., Robb, A., & Rohde, F. (2014). An integrative review and synthesis of XBRL research in academic journals. *Journal of Information Systems, 29,* 115–153.

27. Wang, Z., & Gao, S. S. (2012). Are XBRL-based financial reports better than non-XBRL reports? A quality assessment. *International Journal of Social, Behavioral, Educational, Economic, Business and Industrial Engineering, 6,* 511–516.

28. Yang, S. Y., Liu, F., & Zhu, X. (2015). An exploratory study of financial reporting structures: A graph similarity approach using XBRL.

29. Levenshtein, V. I. (1966). Binary codes capable of correcting deletions, insertions, and reversals. *Soviet Physics Doklady, 10,* 707–710.
30. Breunig, M. M., Kriegel, H.-P., Ng, R. T., & Sander, J. (2000). LOF: Identifying density-based local outliers. *ACM SIGMOD Record, 29,* 93–104. https://doi.org/10.1145/335191.335388.
31. Fischer, H., & Mueller, D. (2011). Open source & XBRL: The Arelle® project. In *2011 Kansas University XBRL Conference* (pp. 29–30).
32. Fischer, H., & Mueller, D. (2011). Enabling comparability and data mining with the Arelle® open source unified model. In *First Conference on Financial Reporting in the 21st Century: Standards, Technology, and Tools.*
33. Zhu, H., & Wu, H. (2014). Assessing the quality of large-scale data standards: A case of XBRL GAAP taxonomy. *Decision Support Systems, 59,* 351–360. https://doi.org/10.1016/j.dss.2014.01.006.

# Digital Governmental Financial Reporting: First Evidence from Italy

**Andrea Fradeani⊙, Michela Soverchia⊙ and Eldi Metushi⊙**

**Abstract** The aim of this paper is to analyze the role that XBRL, the open standard for digital business reporting (which is being widely adopted around the world in the private sector), could play within governmental financial reporting. Literature on this issue is poor, and this research topic seems to be particularly relevant: considering the strong need for governments' information transparency strengthened by the recent financial crisis, XBRL could be a useful digital standard to push and improve governments' accountability, and thereby preventing or avoiding potential future crisis. This issue needs specific research because the role of XBRL within governmental financial reporting is slightly different to its role in the private sector. The theoretical analysis provided in the paper is accompanied by a case study concerning Italy, where two recent projects realized by the Court of Auditors and the State General Accounting Department introduced the use of XBRL as a tool to collect financial information from Italian Regions and Local Governments.

**Keywords** Government financial reporting · XBRL · Accountability
Transparency

## 1 Introduction

Last decades have been characterized by frequently reforming processes involving public administration. The organizational, managerial and financial dimensions of governments have been changed in order to not only recover efficiency and

A. Fradeani (✉) · M. Soverchia
University of Macerata, Macerata, Italy
e-mail: andrea.fradeani@unimc.it; a.fradeani@unimc.it

M. Soverchia
e-mail: michela.soverchia@unimc.it

E. Metushi
Canadian Institute of Technology, Tirana, Albania
e-mail: eldi.metushi@cit.edu.al

© Springer International Publishing AG, part of Springer Nature 2018     207
R. Lamboglia et al. (eds.), *Network, Smart and Open*, Lecture Notes in Information
Systems and Organisation 24, https://doi.org/10.1007/978-3-319-62636-9_14

effectiveness, but also to improve their transparency and accountability [1, 2]. Within these processes, technology plays a significant role. In the early 2000s e-Government phenomenon exploded: it concerns the use of new technologies, in particular ICT, in governments' working and public services' delivering [3].

Nevertheless, it is well known that in 2008 one of the deepest recessions since the early 1930s began. One of its main effects is the national sovereign debt crisis, which has highlighted governments' lack of transparency and accountability as well as poor public finance management and government financial reporting. As governments raise funds through debt markets, and considering that banks and private investors hold governments' debt, there is a strong demand for financial transparency and accountability from governments as it is required already for business entities. Therefore, governments are called to reinforce their own credibility and restore trust between themselves and citizens, taxpayers, markets, and investors [4]. Within this context, it is evident that government financial disclosure plays a crucial role.

The aim of the paper is to explore and deepen the role that eXtensible Business Reporting Language (XBRL)—the electronic language for business financial reporting increasingly widespread in Europe [5] and in the rest of the world[1]—can play within public sector, in particular concerning governmental financial reporting.

At the moment in several countries (for example Australia, Belgium, Brazil, Canada, Chile, China, Colombia, Denmark, France, Germany, India, Indonesia, Israel, Italy, Japan, Korea, Luxembourg, Singapore, Spain, Sweden, UK, United Arab Emirates and USA) XBRL is either mandatory or voluntary used in regulatory filing programs in all business sectors (i.e. banking, insurance, securities market sectors, business registers and tax), as a mean to improve the transparency and effectiveness of publicly lodged financial reports and to achieve efficiency, as shown also in recent theoretical and empirical studies [6–13].

However, this is not the same for governments and their financial reporting, and the literature focused on this issue is quite poor [14–22]. This research topic seems to be particularly relevant: considering the strong need for governments' information transparency strengthened by the financial crisis, XBRL could be a useful digital standard to boost governments' accountability and information transparency and comparability.

The remainder of the paper is structured as follows: we proceed in the next paragraph by giving few sketches on what XBRL is; then research questions and methodology will follow; the fourth paragraph regards the literature review concerning innovation and ICT within governments, as well as government financial reporting supply chain; in the fifth paragraph the Italian case study is illustrated; finally, some concluding remarks are provided.

---

[1]For further information on the international adoption of XBRL refer to the content on XBRL International website at http://www.xbrl.org, last accessed 2017/04/11.

## 2 What Is XBRL?

XBRL is a freely available mark-up language, based on XML and managed by XBRL International (a global not for profit consortium), designed to code business data in a way that computers can directly manage it (use, store, transfer, and so on). Business data are not treated as a block of text, as in the case of a PDF file or of a printed document, because XBRL is based on a different philosophy: business reports are decomposed—following specific vocabularies ("taxonomies")—into their basic items, each marked by a specific tag which identifies their features so business data can be read, understood and used by any software which can recognize the tags (like barcodes) regardless of the computer platform used.

Financial reports thus become digital systems of alphanumeric values that can be automatically and electronically processed, and so dynamic and adaptable to their users' needs [23, 24]. In short, thanks to XBRL-enabled software, business data can be used interactively and in real time, with no longer need to re-type or do any complex manual tasks, thus streamlining the process for collecting and reporting financial information, saving costs in terms of time, resources and lowering the risk of errors. This open standard also lets to mitigate significantly the trade-off "richness versus reach", allowing to produce information that is characterized by richness and quality that can be spread interactively among a very high number of recipients [25].

As a real language, XBRL is based on the interaction between a grammar (i.e. the specifications) and a vocabulary (i.e. the taxonomy): the former, globally the same, is defined by XBRL International and reflects the IT aspects of the digital language (the current version is still the version 2.1 of 31 December 2016, however integrated with additional modules for encoding more complex data such as, for example, multidimensional data); the latter, which varies according to the type of accounting data to be disclosed, reflects all the elements used to encode the financial reports and their features, and thus represents the key component of the companies' digital language. That is why at a national level local jurisdictions are born, in order to develop the taxonomies in accordance with the guidelines issued by the international consortium: for every set of accounting principles there will be a specific taxonomy.

To benefit from XBRL potential, the existence of a complete and shared vocabulary appears to be a prerequisite. This has to be reconciled with the difficulties arising from such incomparability of information contained in financial statements, especially if prepared in accordance with accounting standards that do not contemplate rigid financial documents, such as IFRS. Therefore, the development of a taxonomy is a complex and delicate task, as it affects the effective disclosure of financial documents and the quality and reliability of the information provided [26–30].

# 3 Research Questions and Methodology

The aim of this paper is to explore and deepen the role that XBRL can play within public sector, in particular reference to governmental financial reporting. Our work is based on the following research questions:

– can XBRL be used also in public sector organizations, as well as in private companies, for mandatory financial reporting?
– may it be considered an additional bureaucratic tool or rather a useful tool for boosting public sector transparency and control?

To answer these questions, both a theoretical analysis on the research topic, and an empirical one—case study—have been conducted. In particular, the Italian case has been analyzed, where the Court of Auditors and the State General Accounting Department have recently implemented two projects concerning the use of XBRL with reference to Regions and Local Governments' budgets and financial reporting. It is well known, in fact, that the case study methodology is particularly important when analyzing a complex subject, allowing investigating it in depth and detail [31]. To study this case, we conducted a document analysis—based on the institutional website and on the informational materials provided by the Court—and interviews with key-actors involved in the project.

# 4 Theoretical Background and Framework

## 4.1 The Use of ICT Within Government

There are numerous studies showing that innovation is a key element determining Nations and Regions' competitiveness [32], especially in times of financial crisis. Positive effects resulting from the innovations implementation have been proved both within companies that improve their performances, and within governments that boost quality and quantity of services provided and, therefore, public value produced [33, 34]. The e-government phenomenon, exploded since the early 2000s, concerns the ICT use by government in carrying out its functions and in managing the communications with citizens, in order to simplify procedures and improve the usability of information and services, making delivery activities more rapid and efficient. Therefore, e-government refers not very much to government computerization in the strict sense—that is also a strategic issue as a precondition for carrying out e-government programs—but mainly to the implementation of ICT in achieving better government working, producing and delivering products and services for several government stakeholders: individuals, families, business, and other public organizations.

ICT not only affects the organizational structure of a single public organization, but also impacts the whole public sector, strengthening the interrelationships and interdependencies between the various actors: accompanied by normative and regulatory changes, it encourages the creation of a governance model based on inter-institutional collaboration and on public/private/non-profit cooperation through the development of network systems between several organizations [35–38].

The e-government phenomenon can be better described focusing the analysis on networks that it allows to create or improve, resulting from different relationships qualified by three main key-elements:

- the objects, referring to the relation contents of the interaction, tangible or intangible, strictly related to the needs supporting the creation of the relation: the object can be information, money, services, etc.;
- the subjects, which are the actors between whom relations are built; interactions may be of different kinds: government to government (different levels such as local, regional, national, supranational and international government), government to business (private organizations, for profit or not for profit), government to citizens (individually or organized, end-users of public services) [39, 40];
- the tools, which are the means and technologies used to support these interactions.[2]

As mentioned above, innovation implementation within an organization is not neutral: usually, to release its utility, technologies require standardized processes, so that some scholars question whether is ICT to influence administrative processes or otherwise. Many scholars identify the changes of this kind of relations as a transition from "government" to "governance", providing for the abandonment of relationships based purely on hierarchical patterns, considered inadequate to solve the problems that characterize the current socio-economic scenarios, for new forms of collaboration/cooperation between public and private actors.

Thus, this development finds an indispensable support on ICT, including promoting the attainment of the objectives with the processes of modernization given above, such as operational efficiency, simplification, transparency, accountability. Furthermore, these innovative forms of governance need new information and monitoring tools, which cannot disregard the use of new ICT: appropriate reporting models should be defined, to enable the consolidation of public expenditures, and the results and outcomes achieved for the benefit of the overall community.

## 4.2   Governments Financial Reporting and XBRL

Theoretical and empirical research shows that there is an increasing participation of stakeholders in government actions and policies. There is an increasing cooperation

---

[2]ICT, however, should not be relegated to a mere instrumental role, as it changes the access way to information and services, impacting on the relations referred above and, ultimately, on the internal and external decision making processes.

between governments and other actors in policy networks and public-private partnerships: information arrangements should reflect and follow these patterns of relations between government and different other actors, public and private ones, and financial information too. Furthermore, the information produced by public and private organizations (governments, companies and non-profit organizations) is designed to support decision-making processes of several stakeholders; the ability to store, process and disseminate vast amounts of information characterizing modern technologies is one of the main drivers that contributed to the emergence of knowledge economy [41].

However, the question is who is actually interested in government financial information? This is a very important issue, in order to identify who could benefit from the XBRL implementation within government. All subjects having direct and indirect relationships with the government could benefit from XBRL.

A public entity transforms inputs in outputs, delivers services and creates public value, therefore, there are actors with which it establishes direct economic and financial transactions (subjects providing money and other kind of inputs—such as tax payers, banks, business, other public entities—and subjects getting outputs, consuming public services: citizens, business, other public entities). Furthermore, there are also some actors with which the public entity has no direct transactions, but nevertheless, are still interested in its financial information to support their decision-making processes: for example, other public entities, for controlling and benchmarking purposes; and the overall community leaving and working in that region, because of the outcomes deriving from public activities improving the social and economic conditions of the population.

This issue needs specific research because the role of XBRL within governmental financial reporting is particularly different to the role of XBRL in corporate disclosure, first of all because different levels of government have different reporting obligations not only within the nation but also outside it. Local Governments, for example, have to report about their financial situation to central governments in different ways; and the same central governments have accountability obligations toward the supranational or international organizations to which they belong: this is the case of EU and its member states, regarding the need of consolidating public expenditures.

In which cases XBRL could be particularly useful? It allows reusing data, manipulating and displaying financial information in different ways, for different purposes, according to the various user needs: these XBRL features make it a highly appropriate digital standard in contexts where different entities need to share the same information and when an entity has to provide the same information to several other subjects [14, 16]. This seems to be the case of many public sector entities. This kind of situations are very common for government entities, as different reporting relationships link the various administrative levels of government: often a certain public entity must provide the same information to several other public entities (such as ministries), but in time and especially different ways (sizes, means of transmission). Just as often some information, provided to a particular office, then will be shared with others. Public entities have reporting obligations with different subjects (other entities), with redundant data-entry processes, because the objects (information) are sometimes the same, but should be provided in different times, ways and formats. In these cases, XBRL could help public entities to better meet their reporting requirements [20].

In summary, each public entity has numerous reporting obligations, often marked by insertion and process redundancy of the same data, involving the use of substantial resources (human, financial, time) to meet its needs, but not strictly related to the aim of its institutional goals. This requires retyping and reconfiguration of the integrated management system, generating costs and consuming-time activities. Furthermore, each step of the retyping process can invite errors that distort information.

The reporting, which is typically a supporting activity, may represent a possible area of improved efficiency by saving resources that could be devoted to improving quality and quantity of public services provided. Furthermore, people involved in the government financial reporting supply chain will be able to carry out interpretations and comparisons easily, because of flexibility [20]. Despite the undoubted importance of reporting, it is evident that the underlying processes have no value in itself, but only because they lead to an outcome, represented by the quality-quantity size of produced and disseminated information.

The introduction of XBRL can help to streamline and simplify the government reporting processes by reusing information, both with reference to the subject to whom it is addressed, and with regard to how that subject needs it, according to its specific purposes and user needs. As an interoperable language, in fact, XBRL allows the customization of the display and the possibility of information processing, safeguarding their integrity and in short time.

XBRL refers to the production of external reports, thus the external actors engaged in forms of control required by law may be interested primarily. It could be used as a digital standard with which to encode and transmit the financial reports that the legislation in force plans to disclose to outside parties, usually other public entities: consider, for example, financial controls carried out by the European Court of Auditors, which sometimes require the whole budget accounts and financial statements, in other cases only some sets of financial data, referred to specific categories of expenditures. These individuals could get data in their databases without the need to re-type the figures they are interested, being able to use in real time data, for example calculating specific ratios, for public entities, part of the public sector, and so on.

XBRL implementation could also help getting government financial information —financial statements, budget accounts, and eventual voluntary reporting, such as social, environment reporting—in a rapid and economic way, and thus strongly improving government financial transparency and comparability for all the people interested in: both for other public institutions (for example the EU or other public body who have to assess government performances), and for citizens, business, media, workers, analysts and so on. Last but not least, XBRL offers the possibility to submit the encoded information in an interactive way, easily integrated with the

Web and, therefore, independent from the characteristics of the hardware and software in possess of the recipients. This could improve government level of transparency and accountability, key elements of public trust [42, 43].

## 5 The Experience of the Italian Court of Auditors and the State General Accounting Department

The use of XBRL in the public sector, in specific for coding government financial statements, has not received a success comparable to that received in the private sector. In fact, several projects have been initiated over the last fifteen years, however with mixed results and often limited in scope. We refer, to the case of New Zealand where it was attempted—and later abandoned—to use XBRL as part of a wider and more general e-government project named e-GIF [44]. Particularly important are also the projects developed in Netherlands, especially those related to the trimester reporting practices of the municipalities and the Dutch Water Boards [45].

In addition, interesting to point out are also the US experiments conducted in the state of Nevada [46] and Oregon [19], while still waiting the possible XBRL developments as a consequence of the introduction of Digital Accountability and Transparency Act (DATA Act) [47]. Still, the most successful experiences are those achieved in Spain [48] and Brazil [49], where XBRL is used by the central authorities to collect the economic and financial reporting of the Local Governments.

Among these cases, also Italy recently moved within this field, implementing a couple of interesting projects.

### 5.1 The SMART Project of the Italian Court of Auditors

The Italian Court of Auditors plays a very important role in controlling public finances and expenditures: it is a constitutional institution that controls and reports to the parliament on the financial situations of all Italian public sector entities, in order to assure an effective and strong control of the public financial resources use, also to avoid corruption.

In recent years, starting from 2009, a large and important public-sector accounting and financial reporting reform has been implemented. It involves different kind of public entities, such as the State, Local Governments, universities and healthcare institutions, in order to harmonize public financial management and improve transparency and accountability; furthermore, the new budgeting and accounting framework is supposed to be consistent with the European System of

National and Regional Accounts (ESA), used by the European Commission to consolidate financial information coming from the EU member states.

Among the most important changes introduced by the reform, is the implementation of the accrual accounting system based on double-entry bookkeeping, along the traditional modified cash accounting system, based on the single-entry bookkeeping. Additionally, a mandatory integrated common chart of accounts has been introduced, in order to identify precisely the nature of the transactions entered, together with the common financial statements (also consolidated ones).

Within this context, the Italian Court of Auditors launched an ambitious project that concerns the use of XBRL to collect financial statements and relative detailed accounting data produced by more than 8000 Italian Local Governments (20 Regions, 110 Provinces and about 8000 Municipalities).[3] This project, called SMART (Sistema Monitoraggio ARmonizzazione Territoriale—Local Government Harmonized Monitoring Control System), benefits from a previous experience of the Italian Court of Auditors in the use of XBRL with SICE (Information System for Control of Central Public Bodies), even though it was not on such a large scale.

It is important to point out that this is not a new requirement for the Italian local authorities: they already had to submit to the Court of Auditors their budgets and financial statements. However, the novelty is the use of the XBRL protocol, and therefore its potential to improve the transparency and make easier the disclosure and exchange of financial information.

The project's objectives included the acquisition of financial statements of Local Government entities in digital editable format, in order to dematerialize the information flows by replacing paper-based submission obligation of accounting data with the telematics one. The implementation of SMART helps the procedures for receiving data without burdening the activities of Local Governments and, through its cognitive component, allows the strengthening of analysis instruments, investigation and control, including also the business intelligence tools, allowing a quicker comparison of homogeneous accounting items of different entities belonging to the same sector. Altogether, the associated benefit is the growth of the overall knowledge system on public finance for supporting the Court of Auditors' activities.

The implementation of the SMART project followed a step-by-step approach. Initially, on December 2015 the Italian Court of Auditors released two taxonomies (Decree of the President of the Court of Auditors No. 112/2015, published in the Italian Official Journal n. 5 of 8/01/2016): one for financial statements and one for detailed accounting data [50]. In fact, two groups of data have been managed, transmitted by each Local Government that uploads XBRL instance files via internet. Thus, two XBRL taxonomies based on XBRL specification 2.1.

---

[3]With particular reference to Local Governments (municipalities and provinces), the budgeting, accounting and financial reporting reform drawn by the Legislative Decree n. 118/2011 started with a 3-year pilot phase (2012–2013–2014) and involved about 400 Local Government entities. This reform is fully operational from 2016.

The first one includes all the accounting concepts related to the financial statements that each Local Government has to approve: it takes into account all the possible rows-column combinations contained in the 27 different financial statements defined by the new accounting system (because of the different types of Local Governments—Municipalities, Provinces, Regions and their bodies), so more than 26,700 items have been defined. In particular, all the "concepts" present in more than one financial statement have been identified, in order to allow the reporting entity to avoid data redundancy; furthermore, all the relationships between different financial statements have been identified, to trace the arithmetical relationships and check the data reliability.

The second taxonomy contains all the detailed data transactions underlying the financial statement values (revenues, costs, payments, receipts, liabilities, etc.): this taxonomy is built by taking into consideration the standard codes required by the new accounting rules. In particular, different data structures have been identified, related to cash modified expenditure and receipt data, accrual income statement data (revenues and costs) and accrual balance sheet data (debts, credits, assets, etc.), according to the integrated chart of accounts. In fact, the chart of accounts items are the main taxonomy items, organized according to their own hierarchical structure: each leaf node (that is the items used for the accounting entries) is linked with the tuple, which structure is defined according to a proprietary layout (XSD complex type). In this way, more than 12,700 items and more than 7800 tuples have been defined [50].

The SMART project has been merged with a broader project stemming from the collaboration between the Italian Court of Auditors and the Italian Ministry of Economy and Finance, in particular by its State General Accounting Department.

## 5.2    The Intervention of the Italian State General Accounting Department

In 2016 the Italian State General Accounting Department launched the new system "Banca Dati Amministrazioni Pubbliche (BDAP)—Bilanci Armonizzati" (Public Administration Database—Harmonized Budgets and Accounts).[4]

Following the request of Regions and Local Governments concerning the need of integrating and centralizing their financial data collection, in order to reduce their reporting obligations (following the idea of a "one-stop shop"), on May 12, 2016, the Ministry of Economy and Finance, in concert with the Italian Court of Auditors, issued the Decree to define the procedure for filing budgets, financial statements and consolidated financial statements of Italian Regions, Local Governments and their operating entities to BDAP, via XBRL. This submission is requested within 30 days from the official approval of the documents; if this does not happen,

---

[4]The database BDAP is available online at http://www.bdap.tesoro.it, last accessed 2017/04/10.

penalties for non-compliance will be imposed, such as the impossibility to hire new staff.

It is important to highlight that the use of XBRL for transmission to BDAP of the "harmonized" public sector accounts is the first large-scale application of XBRL to the public sector in Italy—following the mandatory adoption of XBRL for business entities [51, 52]—and one of the first of this size at the international level. This has been made possible thanks to the XBRL experience gained by the Court of Auditors, which shared with the Ministry of Economy and Finance documents, technologies and know-how generated with the previous SICE and SMART projects.

With the above-mentioned Decree, XBRL has become mandatory for more than 8000 public entities throughout the Italian territory. The new system, set to acquire also analytical accounting data at the level of the integrated chart of accounts, operates with the XBRL taxonomies that will be gradually released by the State General Accounting Department. At the time, it was decided to limit the use of the basic XBRL specification 2.1 without extensions (using the same limit for the customizations as that applied to business entities), and provide a gradual adoption of the technical possibilities offered by the standard language.

The financial statements submission will be made, with reference to local entities reporting on the traditional modified cash accounting system, through the three available taxonomies[5]: the first related to the budget, the second to the management report, and the third to the consolidated financial statements. As for the financial reports of entities adopting financial accounting, they will use the XBRL taxonomy that already exists for filing the financial statements of private companies (Italian GAAP taxonomy) to the Italian Business Register, without further implementations or changes. Furthermore, the accounting documents sent to BDAP by public entities will undergo a series of checks (blocking and non-blocking controls) to verify the quality and consistency of the reported data.

## 6    Discussion and Conclusions

XBRL is an increasingly popular language, and this is also confirmed by the growing literature contributions on this topic [13]. However, little research, both theoretical and empirical, has been conducted on the use of XBRL by public sector organizations. The aim of this paper is to contribute to fill this gap, examining the role that XBRL could play within governmental financial reporting, both from a theoretical point of view and from a specific case-study analysis.

The globalization of socio-economic scenarios has involved a growing need for in-formation necessary for making choices. XBRL seems to intercept some of the most pressing needs of the global market: timeliness, accuracy and interoperability

---

[5]The taxonomies is available online at http://www.bdap.tesoro.it, last accessed 2017/04/10.

of information concerning financial business communication, and costs savings. Reducing administrative burdens is one of the main reasons that led to the choice of XBRL for financial statements of firms [53]. Such savings, in fact, can be achieved along different paths: by eliminating or simplifying the rules, by using new technologies, or a combination of the two options.

Concerning the first research question (can XBRL be used also in public sector organizations, as well as in private companies, for mandatory financial reporting?), the answer is yes. Even though this was only briefly mentioned at the beginning of the fifth paragraph, some projects in this regard have already been realized in different countries, European and not. And the case-study here analyzed confirms this possibility. In fact, even though the paper is focused on governmental use of XBRL, we think that the real challenge ahead concerns the realization of a full use of XBRL without distinction between the public or private nature of the user organization. Furthermore, nowadays is being more difficult to make this distinction clear and unambiguous and in fact is progressively being less significant, partly because of the widespread forms of collaboration and partnership between public and private organizations that have been mentioned. In summary, the success of XBRL seems will be determined by the scale of its adoption [40, 54].

Concerning the second research question (may XBRL be considered an additional bureaucratic tool for public sector organizations or useful to boost their transparency and control?), the case-study analyzed in this paper shows that XBRL can be used to replace reporting relationships that already exist: the Italian Regions and Local Governments, according to the two projects, have not experienced an increase in their administrative compliance, they are simply using a different tool that allows improved reliability, timeliness and, above all, the possibility for the Court of Auditors and the State General Accounting Department to elaborate the significant amount of information (referring to more than 8000 Local Governments) without having to reinsert it into a software or other tool, and thus achieving significant benefits for both parties involved. This project may be considered a "first step": in fact, XBRL may help simplify and streamline the relationships between different public entities; the resulting benefits from its use probably would be much higher than are the organizations linked by reporting relationships that adopt it, with a resulting improvement in controls. The use of XBRL, along with web technologies, may also simplify and make more interactive the data usage by citizens, and thus increase their awareness (and control) on public finance issues.

With particular reference to the Italian context, it is clear that the incomplete accounting harmonization of Italian public administration still does not allow using XBRL uniformly, thus increasing the necessity of several taxonomies. Nevertheless, as a digital and open standard for the use of which it is necessary to standardize the syntactic and semantic information that will be filed into the reports, it can assist and encourage the process of governmental accounting and financial reporting harmonization and simplification, at both national and international level. With particular reference to the European context, the need of monitoring and consolidating member states' public expenditures is particularly acute. Recently EUROSTAT, on behalf of the European Commission, has conducted a public consultation to assess the suitability of the International Public Sector Accounting Standards for the Member States [55]: the public sector budgeting and accounting systems harmonization is considered a very urgent need and the development of accrual-based European Public Sector Accounting Standards (EPSAS) is currently being discussed, in order to improve financial management of European public entities and try to prevent future crises [56]. XBRL, considering its features, could help realizing this, as in the private sector it has been associated with the IFRS diffusion [57]. This is even more relevant in light of the proposal of the European Securities and Markets Authority (ESMA) to adopt XBRL (in its new version Inline XBRL), from the 1st January 2020, as a mandatory format for submitting the consolidated financial statements of the European[6] listed companies.

As for the limits of this article, it is exclusively based on a documental analysis and the Italian application of XBRL for public entities is very recent, some years will be necessary to understand the related benefits. The research issue addressed in this paper needs to be strengthened by further empirical studies concerning projects that are taking place abroad, to compare and verify the actual and effective contribution that XBRL may give to public administration.

With respect to the research implications, we suggest greater attention of the regulators to the use of XBRL in governmental financial reporting.

# References

1. Pollitt, C., & Bouckaert, G. (Eds.). (2004). *Public management reform. A comparative analysis* (2nd ed.). Oxford: Oxford University Press.
2. Kettl, D. F. (2005). *The global public management revolution* (2nd ed.). Washington: Brookings.
3. Aikins, S. K. (2012). *Managing e-government projects. Concepts issues and best practices.* Hershey: IGI Global.
4. Sapienza, P., & Zingales, L. (2012). A trust crisis. *International Review of Finance, 12*(2), 123–131.
5. Enachia, M., & Andoneb, I. I. (2015). The progress of XBRL in Europe—Projects, users and prospects. *Procedia Economics and Finance, 20,* 185–192.
6. Bonsón, E., Cortijo, V., & Escobar, T. (2009). Towards the global adoption of XBRL using international financial reporting standards (IFRS). *International Journal of Accounting Information Systems, 10*(1), 46–60.
7. Roohani, S., Furusho, Y., & Koizumi, M. (2009). XBRL: Improving transparency and monitoring functions of corporate governance. *International Journal of Disclosure and Governance, 6*(4), 355–369.
8. Debreceny, R., Farewell, S., Piechocki, M., Felden, C., & Gräning, A. (2010). Does it add up? Early evidence on the data quality of XBRL filings to the SEC. *Journal of Accounting and Public Policy, 29*(3), 296–306.

---

[6]For further details refer to the Feedback Statement on the Consultation Paper on the Regulatory Technical Standards on the Single European Electronic Format (ESEF) available at http://www.esma.europa.eu, last accessed 2017/04/10.

9. Yoon, H., Zo, H., & Ciganek, A. (2011). Does XBRL adoption reduce information asymmetry? *Journal of Business Research, 64*(2), 157–163.
10. Chen, Y. (2012). A comparative study of e-government XBRL implementations: The potential of improving information transparency and efficiency. *Government Information Quarterly, 29*(4), 553–563.
11. Kim, J. W., Lim, J. H., & No, W. G. (2012). The effect of first wave mandatory XBRL reporting across the financial information environment. *Journal of Information Systems, 26* (1), 127–153.
12. Efendi, J., Park, J. D., & Smith, L. M. (2014). Do XBRL filings enhance informational efficiency? Early evidence from post-earnings announcement drift. *Journal of Business Research, 67*(6), 1099–1105.
13. Perdana, A., Robb, A., & Rohde, F. (2015). An integrative review and synthesis of XBRL research in academic journals. *Journal of Information Systems, 29*(1), 115–153.
14. Abdolmohammadi, M., Harris, J., & Smith, K. (2002). Government financial reporting on the Internet: The potential revolutionary effects of XBRL. *Journal of Government Financial Management, 51*(2), 24–31.
15. Rezaee, Z., & Turner, J. L. (2002). XBRL-based financial reporting: Challenges and opportunities for government accountants. *Journal of Government Financial Management, 51* (2), 16–22.
16. American Council for Technology, Industry Advisory Council. (2007). Transforming financial information. Use of XBRL in federal financial management. White paper available at http://www.actiac.org. Last accessed April 4, 2017.
17. Ball, C. (2007). Better information better management. *Journal of Government Financial Management, 56*(2), 16–19.
18. Kull, J., & Abraham, C. (2008). XBRL and public sector financial reporting. *Journal of Government Financial Management, 57*(2), 28–37.
19. Kull, J., & Abraham, C. (2008). XBRL and public sector financial reporting. Standardized business reporting: The Oregon CAFR project. AGA CPAG Research Series, Report No. 16 available at http://www.agacgfm.org. Last accessed April 4, 2017.
20. Mauss, C. V., Bleil, C., Balloni, A. J., & Vanti, A. A. (2008). XBRL in public administration as a way to evince and scale the use of information. In K. Elleithy (Ed.), *Innovations and advanced techniques in systems, computing sciences and software engineering*. Dordrecht: Springer.
21. Soverchia, M. (2015). How can technology improve government financial transparency? The answer of the eXtensible Business Reporting Language (XBRL). *International Journal of Public Administration in the Digital Age, 2*(1), 24–38.
22. Snow, N. M., & Reck, J. L. (2016). Developing a government reporting taxonomy. *Journal of Information Systems, 30*(2), 49–81.
23. Bergeron, B. (2003). *Essentials of XBRL: Financial reporting in the 21st century*. Hoboken: Wiley.
24. Debreceny, R., Felden, C., Ochocki, B., & Piechocki, M. (2009). *XBRL for interactive data. Engineering the information value chain*. Berlin: Springer.
25. Evans, P., & Wurster, T. (2000). *Blown to bits. How the new economics of information transforms strategy*. Boston: Harvard Business School Press.
26. Boritz, J. E., & No, W. G. (2008). The SEC's XBRL voluntary filing program on EDGAR: A case for quality assurance. *Current Issues in Auditing, 2*(2), A36–A50.
27. Plumlee, R. D., & Plumlee, M. A. (2008). Assurance on XBRL for financial reporting. *Accounting Horizons, 22*(3), 353–368.
28. Bartley, J., Al-Chen, Y. S., & Taylor, E. (2010). Avoiding common errors of XBRL implementation. *Journal of Accountancy, 209*(2), 46–51.
29. Debreceny, R. S., Farewell, S. M., Piechocki, M., Felden, C., Gräning, A., & D'Eri, A. (2011). Flex or break? Extensions in XBRL disclosures to the SEC. *Accounting Horizons, 25* (4), 631–657.

30. Fradeani, A., Regoliosi, C., D'Eri, A., & Campanari, F. (2017). Implementation of mandatory IFRS financial disclosures in a voluntary format: Evidence from the Italian XBRL project. In K. Corsi, N. G. Castellano, R. Lamboglia, & D. Mancini (Eds.), *Reshaping accounting and management control systems. New opportunities from business information systems.* Cham: Springer.

31. Yin, R. K. (2014). *Case study research: Design and methods* (5th ed.). Thousand Oaks: SAGE.

32. Porter, M. E. (1990). *The competitive advantage of nations.* New York: The Free Press.

33. Moore, M. H. (1995). *Creating public value. Strategic management in government.* Cambridge: Harvard University Press.

34. Contini, F., & Lanzara, G. F. (2009). *ICT and innovation in the public sector.* New York: Palgrave Macmillan.

35. Klijn, E. H., Koppenjan, J., & Termeer, K. (1995). Managing networks in the public sector: A theoretical study of management strategies in policy networks. *Public Administration, 73*(3), 437–454.

36. Milward, H. B., & Provan, K. G. (2001). Do networks really work? A framework for evaluating public-sector organizational networks. *Public Administration Review, 61*(4), 414–423.

37. Goldsmith, S., & Eggers, W. D. (2004). *Governing by network: The new shape of the public sector.* Washington: Brookings.

38. Considine, M., Lewis, J., & Alexander, D. (2009). *Networks, innovation and public policy.* New York: Palgrave Macmillan.

39. European Commission. (2004). *European interoperability framework for pan-European e-government services.* Luxembourg: Office for Official Publications of the European Communities.

40. de Winne, N., Janssen, M., Bharosa, N., van Wijk, R., & Hulstijn, J. (2011). Transforming public-private networks: An XBRL-based infrastructure for transforming business-to-government information exchange. *International Journal of Electronic Government Research, 7*(4), 35–45.

41. Dodgson, M. (2000). *The management of technological innovation.* Oxford: Oxford University Press.

42. Dawes, S. S., Cresswell, A. M., & Pardo, T. A. (2009). From "need to know" to "need to share": Tangled problems, information boundaries, and the building of public sector knowledge networks. *Public Administration Review, 69*(3), 392–402.

43. Di Piazza, S. A., & Eccles, R. G. (2002). *Building public trust. The future of corporate reporting.* New York: Wiley.

44. David, J. (2016). The non-adoption of XBRL by professional and government organisations in New Zealand and its implications for stakeholders. Ph.D. thesis, available at http://researcharchive.vuw.ac.nz. Last accessed April 9, 2017.

45. Bakhshi, N., Versendaal, J., van den Berg, J., & van den Ende, D. (2007). Impact of the extensible business reporting language on the administrative burden of organizations: A case study at the Dutch water boards. In *Proceedings of the 4th International Conference on Enterprise Systems, Accounting and Logistics.* Corfou: ICESAL.

46. Bills, H. W., & Hansen, J. (2008). *Enabling grants with XBRL reporting: A case study.* Paper presented at the 18th XBRL International Conference, Washington.

47. Bloch, R., Issa, H., & Peterson, A. (2015). The DATA Act. *The CPA Journal, 85*(6), 36–42.

48. Cano, C. (2011). XBRL projects in Spain. *iBR, 1*(3), 19–20.

49. Garbellotto, G., De Sousa Simões, B., & Silveira Do Nascimento, L. (2015). Driving efficiency and transparency in government reporting with XBRL global ledger. The experience of the National Treasury in Brazil. Case study available at http://www.xbrl.org. Last accessed April 9, 2017.

50. Minerva, M., & Virguti, E. (2016). *The Italian Court of Auditors SMART project—A pioneering initiative in the public sector based on XBRL standard protocol.* Paper presented at the 16th XBRL Europe Day available at http://www.xbrleurope.org. Last accessed April 10, 2017.
51. Avallone, F., Ramassa, P., & Roncagliolo, E. (2016). XBRL extension to the financial statement notes: Field-based evidence on unlisted companies. *The International Journal of Digital Accounting Research, 16,* 61–84.
52. Fradeani, A., Panizzolo, D., & Metushi, E. (2016). Financial reporting in XBRL: First evidence on financial statement notes of Italian unlisted companies. *The International Journal of Digital Accounting Research, 16,* 85–115.
53. OECD. (2008). *Programs to reduce the administrative burden of tax regulation in selected countries.* Paris: OECD Publishing.
54. Doolin, B., & Troshani, I. (2007). Organizational adoption of XBRL. *Electronic Markets, 17* (3), 199–209.
55. European Commission. (2013). Towards implementing harmonized public sector accounting standards in Member States. The suitability of IPSAS for the Member States. Brussels, COM (2013) 114 final.
56. Mussari, R. (2014). EPSAS and the unification of public sector accounting across Europe. *Accounting, Economics and Law: A Convivium, 4*(3), 299–312.
57. Markelevich, A., Riley, T., & Shaw, L. (2015). Towards harmonizing reporting standards and communication of international financial information: The status and the role of IFRS and XBRL. *Journal of Knowledge Globalization, 8*(2), 23–38.

# The Propensity of Being "Openness" of Italian LGAs. A Study of Possible Relationships with Financial Performance

**Lepore Luigi** and **Paolone Francesco**

**Abstract** Tools of Web 2.0 and Open Data source have witnessed a massive improvement and become the most used platforms to divulgate information and to shrink the gap between Local Government Authorities (LGAs) and their stakeholders. The aim of this work is to test the effect of financial performance on the Openness of the Italian LGAs, in order to assess transparency and participation for improving accountability. Our results show no significant relationship between "*Openness*" and traditional performance focused on financial autonomy but, on the other hand, we find a strong association between "*Openness*" variables and a score deriving from the ten financial performance indexes (*"Financially Distress" Score*). Notice that the use of only one traditional financial indicator is not able to explain the relationship while a more complex indicators derived from a set of 10 financial ratios (as we call *"Financially Distress" Score*) is considered more appropriate.

**Keywords** LGAs · Openness · Financial distress · Transparency

## 1 Introduction

Over the past decades, many countries in Europe have carried out reforms in public sectors to improve the propensity of being openness that, together with financial performance, represent crucial elements at both central and local levels. Research about the relationship between openness and performance are often based on agency theory framework able to explain the information asymmetry between Local Government Authorities (LGAs) and their stakeholders. This could explains the potential free riding of politicians and manager that could choose a way to use public money that expropriate citizens, that are tax payers and so the lenders of

L. Luigi (✉) · P. Francesco
Parthenope University of Naples, Naples, Italy
e-mail: luigi.lepore@uniparthenope.it

P. Francesco
e-mail: francesco.paolone@uniparthenope.it

© Springer International Publishing AG, part of Springer Nature 2018                    223
R. Lamboglia et al. (eds.), *Network, Smart and Open*, Lecture Notes in Information
Systems and Organisation 24, https://doi.org/10.1007/978-3-319-62636-9_15

public administrations. This study aims at examining the relationship between Openness and performance of Italian LGAs after the reform issued in 2009, that requires Italian LGAs to disclose performance data on their website, in order to enhance transparency. We also seek to understand how factors such as the presence of Open Data source, Social Media and YouTube channels define the Openness for LGAs and how they do matching with financial performance. We also investigate the role of web 2.0 that enhances to spreading information about public value and facilitates citizens in making judgments about the ways public administrations communicate and deliver public services.

## 2 Background and Hypothesis Development

Reforms in public management realized in the last two decades posit the attention on the accountability in order to improve effectiveness and efficiency within LGAs. The concept of accountability may be defined as the state of being answerable, responsible and/or accountable for results in the own area of responsibility. Accountability goes beyond rendering an account of the resources used, but also includes the efficient use of those resources and the ability of policy decisions and managerial activities to satisfy public needs [1]. The state of being responsible can be referred both to the organizational level—in this case, for example, we consider the accountability of LGAs—and at the individual level—i.e. the accountability of manager or politicians [2]. These reform processes derived from the need of enhancing public performances are necessary to ensure transparency on data. This allows citizens to make judgments about the ways public administrations spend public money to deliver public services (social control). Citizens, that is the electorate, have the right to be informed about the actions and expenditures of the executive and legislative arms of government [3, 4]. Transparency, through the use of Social Media, has the intent of improving engagement, involvement and participation in political and public issue by a large part of stakeholders group. According to Farneti [5], this concept is relevant for keeping politicians and managers accountable.

Contributions on the relationship between accountability and performance are often based on the Agency Theory framework [6]. However, there have also been other theoretical approaches used to deeply analyse the implementation of mandatory performance measurement system in government organizations, including the Institutional Theory. According to Cavalluzzo and Ittner [7], the Institutional Theory is useful to explain implementation success of performance measurement system in public management. Principals are the voters, citizens and other stakeholders, while the Agents are the politicians and managers. It is hard to define the relationship between principal and agent in public sector for the reason that many different accountability relationships exist: those between elected officials and managers, those between elected officials and citizens and those between citizens and managers [8]. This is consistent with what happened in other European countries, whose most emblematic case is represented by the United Kingdom, the reform of Italian LGAs issued in 2009 by the Law 15/2009 and implemented by the Legislative Decree 150/2009 requires LGAs to disclose their objectives, performance indicators and data about resources spent to deliver public services, as well as information about organization, on their website (hereafter Openness) in order to improve performances.

Furthermore, the Legislative Decrees 118/2011 and 126/2014 require the transition to an accounting system which integrates the traditional system based on financial perspective with an accrual-based accounting system oriented to economic results, in order to overcome the limits of cash-accounting system. This reform requires that the financial and economic accounting systems formed a unique accounting system that facilitate financial reporting to external individuals and, therefore, the social control.

Despite considerable interest of scholars all around the world, relatively few investigations were conducted on the impact of such reforms on the performance of LGAs. We may think that the above reforms will lead to better performance has not yet been found, particularly in Italian public sector and in countries characterized by a public administration style affected by structures, principles, logics and instruments inherited from a bureaucratic, hierarchical public administration based on administrative law [8, 9].

In the light of the reform issued in 2009, we investigate the relationship between accountability "in terms of Openness" and performance of Italian LGAs in the more recent year 2014, considering the accountability relationships between citizens and elected officials and those between citizens and managers. In particular, we seek to provide a starting point in which better financial performance at organizational level may have a positive impact on the propensity of being openness, enhancing the accountability and visibility on social media.

We mainly address our study to the agency theory, because it better explains the information asymmetry between LGAs and stakeholders that inhibits the supervision of government activities by citizens and consequently the performance improvement. Agency theory suggests that information asymmetry between citizens and politicians and managers pushes agents to free ride. For this reason, in order to reduce the opportunity of free riding, a more social control is needed. The progresses of Internet in the use of Web 2.0 tools have made easier the diffusion of information and the interaction between LGAs and stakeholders. Internet became the most important "highway" to disclose information, to reduce the gap between LGAs and its stakeholders as well as to maintain politicians, managers and public administrations visible, accountable and opened.

Many authors have emphasized the fundamental contribution of the Open data source in order to promote new forms of accountability, enhancing interactivity, transparency and, thus, the openness of LGAs [10–13]. These are all considered as positive values to improve social control and, thus, to strengthen citizens trust in governments [11, 14]. However, the presence of the information on Internet

(Open Data source) does not assure that citizens receive and use that information to exercise the social control. So, it becomes important that Web 2.0 tools in the forms of Social media and YouTube channels disclose further information. The relevant role of social media and YouTube platform in stimulating public opinion and social control is clear. In the light of the above considerations, we decide to address the following hypothesis:

$H_1$ There is a significant association between LGAs financial performance and the Openness through Open Data source, Social Media and YouTube platform;

$H_2$ Only one financial indicator is not able to explain the relationship between LGAs financial performance and the "Openness". On the other hand, a more complex financial indicator originated from a set of 10 performance indicators (so called "Financially Distress" Score) is more able to explain the above relationship.

## 3   Research Methodology

### 3.1   Data and Sample Analysis

This part of the work aims to empirically investigate what is the impact of financial indicators of Italian LGAs on their propensity of being "Openness". This goal is pursued through the implementation of OLS regressions, considering that a set of different financial indicators may affect the level of openness. The final objective is thus to underline whether and how the indicators positively or negatively interacts with Openness.

The sample is composed of 5703 Italian Local Government Authorities in the period of 2014 belonging to the following 72 provinces: Alessandria, Ancona, Andria, Aosta, Arezzo, Asti, Bari, Barletta, Benevento, Bergamo, Bologna, Bolzano, Brescia, Brindisi, Cagliari, Campobasso, Caserta, Catania, Catanzaro, Como, Cosenza, Ferrara, Firenze, Foggia, Forlì, Genova, La Spezia, L'Aquila, Latina, Lecce, Livorno, Lucca, Matera, Messina, Milano, Modena, Monza, Napoli, Novara, Olbia, Padova, Palermo, Parma, Perugia, Pesaro, Pescara, Piacenza, Pistoia, Pordenone, Potenza, Prato, Ragusa, Ravenna, Reggio Calabria, Reggio Emilia, Rimini, Roma, Salerno, Sassari, Savona, Siracusa, Taranto, Terni, Torino, Trento, Treviso, Trieste, Udine, Varese, Venezia, Verona, Vicenza, Viterbo. The remaining provinces have been excluded because of missing data. Table 1 indicates the number of LGAs in each province and the related percentages.

We gathered financial data from the AIDA PA database (Italian Database of Public Administrations), which is the Italian provider of the Bureau Van Dijk European Database; it is the most complete and reliable economic and financial information source about entities of public administration in Italy. Financial data are

**Table 1** Sample

| Provinces | N. of LGAs | % | Provinces | N. of LGAs | % |
|---|---|---|---|---|---|
| Alessandria | 190 | 3.3 | Novara | 88 | 1.5 |
| Ancona | 50 | 0.9 | Olbia-Tempio | 26 | 0.5 |
| Aosta | 74 | 1.3 | Padova | 104 | 1.8 |
| Arezzo | 41 | 0.7 | Palermo | 82 | 1.4 |
| Asti | 118 | 2.1 | Parma | 49 | 0.9 |
| Bari | 41 | 0.7 | Perugia | 59 | 1.0 |
| Barletta-Andria-Trani | 10 | 0.2 | Pesaro Urbino | 61 | 1.1 |
| Benevento | 78 | 1.4 | Pescara | 46 | 0.8 |
| Bergamo | 246 | 4.3 | Piacenza | 48 | 0.8 |
| Bologna | 62 | 1.1 | Pistoia | 22 | 0.4 |
| Bolzano | 116 | 2.0 | Pordenone | 52 | 0.9 |
| Brescia | 206 | 3.6 | Potenza | 100 | 1.8 |
| Brindisi | 20 | 0.4 | Prato | 7 | 0.1 |
| Cagliari | 71 | 1.2 | Ragusa | 12 | 0.2 |
| Campobasso | 84 | 1.5 | Ravenna | 18 | 0.3 |
| Caserta | 104 | 1.8 | Reggio di Calabria | 97 | 1.7 |
| Catania | 58 | 1.0 | Reggio nell'Emilia | 46 | 0.8 |
| Catanzaro | 80 | 1.4 | Rimini | 29 | 0.5 |
| Como | 166 | 2.9 | Roma | 121 | 2.1 |
| Cosenza | 155 | 2.7 | Salerno | 158 | 2.8 |
| Ferrara | 27 | 0.5 | Sassari | 66 | 1.2 |
| Firenze | 46 | 0.8 | Savona | 69 | 1.2 |
| Foggia | 61 | 1.1 | Siracusa | 21 | 0.4 |
| Forlì-Cesena | 30 | 0.5 | Taranto | 29 | 0.5 |
| Genova | 67 | 1.2 | Terni | 33 | 0.6 |
| L'Aquila | 108 | 1.9 | Torino | 315 | 5.5 |
| La Spezia | 32 | 0.6 | Trento | 245 | 4.3 |
| Latina | 33 | 0.6 | Treviso | 95 | 1.7 |
| Lecce | 97 | 1.7 | Trieste | 6 | 0.1 |
| Livorno | 20 | 0.4 | Udine | 139 | 2.4 |
| Lucca | 37 | 0.6 | Varese | 142 | 2.5 |
| Matera | 31 | 0.5 | Venezia | 44 | 0.8 |
| Messina | 108 | 1.9 | Verona | 98 | 1.7 |
| Milano | 134 | 2.3 | Vicenza | 121 | 2.1 |
| Modena | 47 | 0.8 | Viterbo | 60 | 1.1 |
| Monza della Brianza | 55 | 1.0 | | | |
| Napoli | 92 | 1.6 | Total | 5703 | 100.0 |

those we need to compute "Financially Distress" score.[1] Once we obtain the ten indexes we build a final score by assigning a value from 0 to 10 according to level of each index.[2]

## 3.2   Variable Description and Statistics

Since the aim of this work is to test the effect of financial performance on the Openness of the Italian LGAs, the three variables are reported as follows.

**Dependent Variables**. The dependent variable aims at capturing the propensity of being Openness. We compute our dependent variable using three different measures of "*Openness*". More specifically, we use an overall score considering the presence or absence of Open Data, Social Media and YouTube channel for each province analysed. We assign 1 point each when a LGA has an Open Data source, a social media and a YouTube channel, 0 otherwise, so that the maximum score would be 3.

**Independent Variables**. With regard to the independent variables, we use two different measure: the *Financial Autonomy*[3] computed as "freedom to impose local taxation, generate revenue within its assigned sources, allocate its financial and material resources, determine and authorize its annual budget without external interference" and, secondly, an overall score of the ten "*Financially distress*" indexes.[4] In the second case, we assign 1 point when a LGA does not overcome the limit of the index, 0 otherwise, so that the maximum score would be equal to 10.

**Control Variables**. We also include control variables that have been shown to have significant impact on the dependent variable: the population of residents and the number of households in the LGA.

Before implementing the OLS regressions an analysis of the descriptive statistics of the variables are provided (Table 2).

---

[1]In accordance with Legislative Decree of 18 February 2013 published in Official Gazette at n. 55 of 6 March 2013 and communicated mentioned in Official Gazette n. 102 of May 3, 2013, these parameters of "Financially Distress" Indexes were established with the aim at highlighting difficulties for financial collapse.

[2]i.e. if a local government authority shows 3 out of 10 indexes up to the limit, it means that score will be 7: 10–3.

[3]We calculated Financial Autonomy as the ratio between revenues obtained from local taxes and tariffs to total current revenues. If this ratio is high, it means that LGA is little dependent on other public administrations for sources of financing. We collected data on our dependent variable from the ANCI website.

[4]These 10 indicators have the goal of monitoring:

 - the institution's capability to collect the claims and payback its debts within a reasonable time;
 - the ability to generate positive operating results;
 - the rigidity of the cost structure;
 - the amount of debt financing;
 - the existence of future costs alleged related to litigations.

**Table 2** Descriptive statistics

| Variables | Number | Min. | Max. | Mean | Std.d. |
|---|---|---|---|---|---|
| Openness Score | 5703 | 0.00 | 3.00 | 1.5862 | 1.05291 |
| Financially Distress Score | 5703 | 0.00 | 10.00 | 8.6609 | 2.24468 |
| Financial Autonomy | 5496 | 0.06 | 1.00 | 0.8430 | 0.16696 |
| Population of residents | 5617 | 37.00 | 2,872,021 | 9048 | 50,724 |
| Households | 5618 | 28.00 | 1,362,599 | 3846 | 24,001 |
| Valid (listwise) | 5485 | | | | |

**Empirical model**. As we above mention, we propose an OLS regression based on a single cross-section in order to assess the relationship between openness and financial status of LGAs, by exploring 5703 observations for the last-available year 2014. The response variable is a linear function of the following regressors:

$$Openness\ Score = b_0 + b_1\ Financial\ Performance + b_2\ Control + \varepsilon \quad (1)$$

where

*Openness Score* = from 0 to 3, attributed to the presence or absence of Open Data (1 if present), Social Media (1 if present) and YouTube Channel (1 if present).
*Financial Performance* = "Financial Autonomy" in the first OLS; "Financially Distress" Score (from 0 to 10) in the second OLS.
*Control* = Control Variables (Populations of residents and Households).

For each of two independent variables ("Financial Autonomy" and "Financially Distress" Score) it will be implemented both the two regression models by using the IBM statistics software, SPSS.

# 4 Empirical Results

As the Table 3 shows, the variables selected as proxies appear to have different impact on the dependent variable.

The results indicate that the two regression models bring to different findings. Regression (1), based on Financial Autonomy as independent variable, shows that, with the except for control variables, Financial Autonomy is negatively related to Openness Score (−0.007) but not significant.[5] We may point out that this variable is not able to capture any relationships with Openness variables.

---

[5]The P-Value of FA not reported in the Table is even equal to 62.5%.

**Table 3** Results from OLS regression

| OLS results with Openness Score | | |
|---|---|---|
| Variables | Regression (1) | Regression (2) |
| Constant | *** | *** |
|  | (21.884) | (22.488) |
| Financial Autonomy | −0.007 | |
|  | (−0.489) | |
| Financially Distress_Score | | 0.028** |
|  | | (2.076) |
| Population | 0.523*** | 0.533*** |
|  | (3.544) | (3.647) |
| Households | −0.466*** | −0.476*** |
|  | (−3.157) | (−3.258) |
| Observations | 5496 | 5703 |
| R-squared | 0.11 | 0.115 |
| F-stat | 9.762 | 11.092 |
| Sig. | 0.000 | 0.000 |

T-statistics are provided in parentheses under the estimated coefficient in the first line. In the second line, two tailed P-Value (Sig.). ***Sig. at 1% level, **Sig. at 5%, *Sig. at 10%. Predictor variables in the multiple regression models are not highly correlated, meaning that there is no multicollinearity between variables

On the other hand, Regression (2), based on "Financially Distress" Score, shows remarkable results, in fact the "Financially Distress" Score is positively related to dependent variable (+0.028) as well as significance at 5% level. Furthermore, both control variables are found to be significant at 1% level and with different impact on Openness: population of residents has a strong positive impact (+0.523) while the number of households is negative related (−0.476).

## 5  Conclusions and Further Developments

We may state that, while Financial Autonomy is not significant, the "Financially Distress" score is highly significant, meaning that the higher number of "Financially Distress" Score (tend to 10), the higher becomes the propensity of being more Openness in terms of three aspects: the presence of Open Data, Social media and Youtube channel. This is in line with our hypothesis addressed that there is a significant relationship between LGAs financial performance and the presence of

Open Data source, Social Media and YouTube platform ("Openness"). But, on one hand, only one financial indicator (Financial Autonomy) is not able to explain to relationship between LGAs financial performance and the "Openness". On the other hand, a score deriving from set of 10 financial indicators (so called "Financially Distress" Score") is more able to explain the above relationship.

In addition, we confirm that positive performance allows to be more open and to achieve better communication skills, to collaborate and interact with citizens and, in doing so, to improve the social control. The above positive relationship is strengthen thanks to the use of Web 2.0 and other tools such as Social Media and YouTube platform. The high interactivity between the users (in our case citizens) and the Local Governmental Institution accelerate the communication process and facilitate a better social control in Italy.

There is considerable scope for further empirical research along the lines of the article discussed above. We think it would be helpful a panel analysis instead a simple cross-section considering a time-period of three years. Furthermore, a limitation of this study is that the analysis considered only financial indicators neglecting the economic measure; this limitation will overcome next year because all the LGAs have to show economic indicators in addition to financial ones. Finally, it would be interesting making a cross-national analysis in order to see any possible differences between European LGAs.

## Appendix—The Proxies of "Openness"

*Open Data.* The open data are commonly defined as data that can be accessed and used freely by anyone, without copyright restrictions, patents or other forms of control that limits playback, typically with only obligation to mention the source and share them with the same type of license under which they were originally released. The open data constitute can be downloaded from the Internet free of charge and are designed to implement interoperability of systems and organizations and constitute an essential prerequisite to the implementation of open government, especially through the use of new information and communications technology. It is important to cite the evolution of the concept of corporate transparency, following the enactment of D.Lgs no. 150/2009, is defined as "total accessibility [...] of information on every organization's aspect", a much broader notion than that contained in the Law no. 241/1990, which governs the right of access to administrative documents.

*Web 2.0 Tools.* Internet is emerging more and more as the preferred tool of communication and has been deeply renewed compared to the first decade. In fact, the corporate website is no longer the only point of access to information. With the development and spread of social networks, the Web has become in fact in a virtual place of interaction, relationship and dialogue in which information is spread with great speed and second viral mode that use the paths designed by the same social networks. Citizens are more and more informed through their networks of relationships, in which nodes can communicate almost instantaneously, in particular through social media, using the multimedia language, allowing them to exchange large amounts of information in the form of text, still images and audio-visual. The *social media* and *The YouTube Channel* represent the two most innovative source of information through the web 2.0 which enhance the accountability of the institution.

# References

1. Osborne, D., & Gaebler, T. (1993). *Reinventing government: How the entrepreneurial spirit is transforming the public sector*. New York: Penguin Book.
2. Royle, M. T., Hall, A. T., Hochwarter, W. A., Perrewé, P. L., & Ferris, G. R. (2005). The interactive effects of accountability and job self-efficacy on organizational citizenship behavior and political behavior. *Organizational Analysis, 13*(1), 53–71.
3. Fountain, J. (1991). Service efforts and accomplishment reporting. *Public Productivity and Management Review, 15*(2), 191–198.
4. Lepore, L., & Pisano, S. (2013). Determinants of Internet-based performance reporting released by Italian local government authorities. In D. Mancini, E. Vaassen, & R. P. Dameri (Eds.), *Accounting information systems for decision making. Lecture Notes in Information Systems and Organisation* (Vol. 3). Berlin: Springer.
5. Farneti, G. (2011). *Ragioneria pubblica. Il "nuovo" sistema informativo delle aziende pubbliche*. Milano: Franco Angeli.
6. Schaltegger, C. A., & Torgler, B. (2007). Government accountability and fiscal discipline: A panel analysis using Swiss data. *Journal of Public Economics, 91*(1), 117–140.
7. Cavalluzzo, K. S., & Ittner, C. D. (2004). Implementing performance measurement innovations: Evidence from government. *Accounting, Organizations and Society, 29*, 243–267.
8. Dunleavy, P., & Hood, C. (1994). From old public-administration to new public management. *Public Money & Management, 14*(3), 9–16.
9. Pollitt, C., & Bouckaert, G. (2000). *Public management reform: A comparative analysis*. Oxford: Oxford University Press.
10. Cyberspace Public Research Group. (2001). Web attribute evaluation system (WAES). Available at http://www.cyprg.arizona.edu.
11. Demchak, C. C., Friis, C., & La Porte, T. M. (2000). Webbing governance: National differences in constructing the public face. In G. D. Garson (Ed.), *Handbook of public information systems* (pp. 179–196). New York: Marcel Dekker.
12. Ke, H. (2007). Can e-government make public governance more accountable? In A. Shah (Ed.), *Performance accountability and combating corruption* (pp. 59–87). Washington, DC: The World Bank.

13. La Porte, T. M., Demchak, C. C., & De Jong, M. (2002). Democracy and bureaucracy in the age of the web. Empirical findings and theoretical speculations. *Administration & Society, 34* (4), 411–446.
14. Kim, P. S., Halligan, J., Cho, N., Oh, C. H., & Eikenberry, A. M. (2005). Toward participatory and transparent governance: Report on the sixth global forum on reinventing government. *Public Administration Review, 65*(6), 646–654.

# Exploring the Effects of Sustainability on Accounting Information Systems: The Role of SBSC

**Katia Corsi** and **Brunella Arru**

**Abstract** In the last twenty years the companies and governments (see the recent directive—2014/95/EU) paid increasing attention to sustainability issues: they gained strategic relevance for the business and deserved interest of stakeholders. According to these sustainability information needs, academics and practitioners examined the development of new accounting information systems (AISs), aimed to collect, elaborate and integrate environmental and social data. In this paper, we consider the Sustainability Balanced Scorecard (SBSC), considering it as an urge to develop and integrate the AISs. The aim of this paper, through a case study, is to investigate the role of SBSC and try to highlight a relationship between the different designs of SBSC proposed by literature and different levels of integration of AISs. This work provides a theoretical contribution to the debate on accounting information system for sustainability and offers useful reflections for the practitioners about the potentialities and critical aspects of SBSC.

**Keywords** Sustainability · Accounting information system · Sustainability balanced scorecard · Information integration

## 1 Introduction

In the last two decades, the companies paid increasing attention to environmental and social issues and now they have gained strategic relevance for the business [1–3]. They represent risks and opportunities that can affect the financial results, it need only consider their positive or negative effects on corporate reputation [4, 5].

K. Corsi (✉) · B. Arru
University of Sassari, Sassari, Italy
e-mail: Kcorsi@uniss.it

B. Arru
e-mail: brarru@uniss.it

© Springer International Publishing AG, part of Springer Nature 2018
R. Lamboglia et al. (eds.), *Network, Smart and Open*, Lecture Notes in Information Systems and Organisation 24, https://doi.org/10.1007/978-3-319-62636-9_16

This attention to environmental and social issues leads companies to pursue a sustainable development defined as "development that meets the needs of the present without compromising the ability of future generations to meet their own needs" [6, p. 54]. Today, many companies are oriented towards sustainability, which "became a multidimensional concept that extends beyond environmental protection to economic development and social equity" [4]. The approach of sustainability is called also the "triple bottom line model" (TBL or 3P: people, planet and performance), suggesting that the organizations cannot realize only economic performance, but they need to engage in activities that positively affect the environment and society [7, 8]. The sustainability strategies are simultaneously focused on environmental, economic and social/ethical goals in order to create value for all stakeholders. Because of this, the increasing attention to corporate sustainability regards also external subjects, with the consequence of increasing and improving the sustainability disclosure. It is confirmed also by recent regulations from UE (Directive 2014/95), which includes the information about the sustainability in the corporate disclosure, showing the need of communicating to market the engagement on environmental and social issues.

According to the corroborated literature on the relationship between strategy and management control systems [9, 10], the sustainability strategies affect control systems and particularly AISs, in order to satisfy new, internal and external, information needs [11–13]. The AISs, supporting the decision-making process of stakeholders, are versatile and flexible, and they adapt to the new strategic orientation [13, 14]. In line with the sustainability, the AISs change by using new tools, techniques and methods to supplement and complement economic goals with environmental and social ones. In sustainable development context, the AISs must provide the information to test the potential growth, the financial viability and the capability to create value: the sustainability, if is not connected to value creation, is untenable and in long terms it generates more costs than benefits. The AISs that support the sustainability decision-making process (such as accounting social responsibility-ASR; environmental management accounting-EMA; social management accounting-SMA, just to name a few) [15, 16], regardless of their name, must be integrated into multidimensional information systems.

A significant stimulus to this integration also comes from the need to use specific tools of management control to support the sustainability strategies. The traditional model of BSC of Kaplan and Norton [17], with its four perspectives, is one of the most used tools for strategic control. It doesn't represent a kind of "straitjacket", but can be reviewed and changed, according to the company context and strategy. Because of its natural multidimensional and flexibility [18, 19], several scholars [20, 21] argue that the balanced scorecard represents the best tools to realize the sustainable development, proposing the Sustainability Balanced Scorecard. It can be considered an upgrade of traditional method of BSC, through the application of the TBL approach and the integration of social and environmental goals. The SBSC allows to pursue a sustainable development, addressing the three sustainable dimensions "in a single integrate management system instead of requiring parallel system" [22, p. 196]. According to literature, there are different SBSC configurations, which present various ways of integrating environmental and social aspects.

The aim of our work is to investigate, through a case study, the role of the SBSC as a tool to formulate, control and communicate the sustainability strategy, and the relationship between the design of SBSC and different levels of integration of AISs designated to measure the environmental and social aspects.

Afterwards, on the basis of the case study findings, this work provides a theoretical contribution to the debate on AISs for sustainability and offers useful considerations for the practitioners about the potentialities and critical aspects of SBSC and the AISs associated to it.

The paper is structured as follows: in the second section we reviewed the literature concerning the AISs to support the sustainable development and about the SBSC; in the third section research framework and methodological notes are presented; in the fourth section is provided a detailed narrative of the SBSC and AISs adopted by the company analysed; in the final section we discussed the main findings and concluded with some consideration, highlighting the limits of the research and suggesting further direction for future research.

## 2 Literature Review

### 2.1 The Accounting Information System for Sustainability

Most companies are struggling to engage sustainability initiatives in their corporate strategy [23]. In order to allow to achieve the sustainable business goals, enterprises can be helped by a new approach to accounting considering the three dimensions of sustainability (TBL): the sustainability accounting [16, 24]. It plays a pivotal role in improving the corporate sustainability [25], as allows to manage and report the social and environmental issues [26, 27]. It is "an updated form of traditional financial accounting with consideration of both economic and environmental issues at multiple levels" [28, p. 2].

In the sustainable companies, the decision-making process is oriented to balance financial and non-financial requirements [29] and it requires to capture the full costs of products, namely economic in stricto sensu, and environmental and social costs [30]. In order to create a framework for sustainability AISs, it is possible to identify at least three types of accounting information sub-systems, according to the three bottom line approach [31–34]:

- Traditional Management Accounting (TMA), that measures economic impacts (with quantitative and financial measures) to support the traditional management accounting and financial accounting. It, generally, provides information on the economic exchange transaction and is not able to collect and process data on sustainability issues and to cover all aspects of the value chain [11].

- Environmental Management Accounting (EMA), aimed to reduce negative impacts on the environment and to improve material efficiency [36]. It identifies, collects and elaborate information on physical unit such as materials, energy, water and wastes and monetary unity, particularly regarding environmental costs [34, 36].
- Social Management Accounting (SMA), aimed to measure social costs in order to reduce negative impacts on society, on employees and all stakeholders as a whole [37–40]. These AISs not only use social and environmental information to support decision-making processes, but also can improve the external disclosure, strengthen the links between management, control and reporting of sustainability [41].

The sustainability accounting is not only a tool for the collection and disclosure social and environmental data but a managerial logic which sometimes can be misinterpreted, losing its substantial meaning. Indeed sometimes the sustainability disclosure could be interpreted as a greenwashing [42] or an half-way "sustainability" approach "based on a win-win situation to demonstrate (and justify) their conduct and development is sustainable only if it can generate economic returns" [43, p. 296]. In order to fully realize a corporate sustainability it needs to increase social accountability, making the organization more aware regarding environmental and social issues [44] and adding value to ensure the sustainability goals [32–34].

The achievement of these purposes also depends on how EMA and SMA are used and integrated between them and with the traditional management accounting system (TMA): this integration is defined as "the basis for sustainable controlling" [40, p. 309].

According to the literature [45], they can be conducted in the companies as shown in Fig. 1:

(1) Autonomous subsystems: EMA and SMA record non financial effects of the environmental and social impacts of corporate strategies. It generally is due to lack of market prices that should facilitate the measurement of these impacts and to frequent use the equivalence ratios determined by an interdisciplinary team of experts.

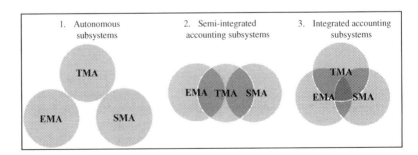

**Fig. 1** Models of integration of AISs for sustainability (our elaboration from Petchard and Mula [46])

(2) Semi-integrated accounting systems: EMA and SMA are more consistent with the traditional accounting system. They regard the measurement, evaluation and recording the resources involved in environmental protection and social engagement, with particular attention paid to financial impacts.

(3) Integrated accounting subsystems: EMA and SMA use different measures (financial, non-financial, qualitative and quantitative) to evaluate the environmental and social issues and create useful information to ensure the companies' sustainability [32–34].

From literature, in this last case, it emerges a new approach, the Sustainability Management Accounting System (SMAS) [16], that allows to add value in three sustainability dimensions. Measurement of social and environmental costs gives more accurate information if their scope is to provide cost information to support financial reports and disclosure of sustainability performance [47, 48], as well as contribute to a sustainable value chain as a whole.

In this integrated use of different AISs, it could use a broader ERP such as Sustainable Enterprise Resource Planning (S-ERP), defined as "holistic, integrative and complete solutions for sustainability business issues" [23, p. 142]. It assists companies to collect, integrate, automate and monitor the information coming from the three dimensions of sustainability [23, 49], and it allows companies to balance the benefits and costs linked to achievement the sustainable goals and satisfy different stakeholders.

## 2.2   The Sustainability Balanced Scorecard

There is a broad range of frameworks to design, measure and communicate the corporate sustainability performance proposed by international governmental, non-governmental and intergovernmental organizations such as ISO 14031, the Global Reporting Initiative (GRI), and the Global Compact [49]. Basing also on them, scholars [51–53] have proposed several strategic management tools, including the SBSC, as an upgrade aimed to sustainability of BSC.

The original framework developed by Kaplan and Norton [17], is a performance measurement system, which represents a close relation between strategies, corporate objectives and performance, using a multidimensional set of financial and non-financial performance metrics, which equally regard four traditional perspectives: financial, customer, internal business process, learning and growth [59]. This tool helps managers to: improve accountability; clarify the strategy (allowing to articulate and communicate the business objectives and priorities); monitor its progress (including the cause-effect linkages and distinguishing leading and lagging measures of performance); define action plan consistent with the strategic objectives in different organizational levels; balance, according to its "philosophy", short, medium and long term indicators, qualitative and quantitative indicators regarding external and internal, tangible and intangible aspects [55–58].

In order to better determine performance measures, managers must understand the cause-effect chains between strategic objectives, that are illustrated by strategy map [60], which represents the BSC's architecture [22, 61, 62].

Among the strengths of BSC [17, 64, 65] there is its flexibility, which allows to combine and adapt the instrument to manage and control the aspects of sustainability, thus creating a new tool, called Sustainability Balanced Scorecard [22] or Sustainability Scorecard [66]. It, compared to traditional BSC, recognizes explicitly objectives and performance measures related to sustainability [55, 67], and shows the relationship between long-term resources and capabilities and short-term financial outcomes, within the cause-effect chains that involves social, environmental and economic, direct and indirect outcomes. The SBSC, in this way, encourages the alignment and management of all corporate activities according to the company's sustainable strategy.

The process of formulating an SBSC elaborated by Figgie et al. [68] includes the following steps:

(1) Choose strategic business unit.
(2) Identify environmental and social exposure.
(3) Determine strategic relevance of environmental and social aspects in the four traditional perspective of the BSC.
(4) Determine whether strategically relevant environmental or social aspects influence significantly the company success via other mechanisms than market system.

Particularly the third step allows to determine the environmental and social aspects' relevance for strategy implementation and execution. To translate the strategy into indicators, causally linked, the company must recognize three levels of strategic relevance of sustainability objectives and indicators [67, 69]:

(a) Sustainability aspects that are strategic core issues for which lagging indicators (that are typically "output" oriented, confirm long-term trends and measure the outcomes achieved through the management of leading indicators) can be developed.
(b) Sustainability aspects that are considered business drivers for which leading indicators (typically input oriented that tend to communicate changes in the environment, and therefore are considered business drivers) can be defined.
(c) Hygienic factors that are necessary but not sufficient to realize a strategic advantage [70], and for this not included in the scorecard.

The fourth step regards the check of the aspects which are non-measurable via market mechanism but equally influencing the company's strategy and then must be included in the SBSC and connected, through the cause-effect links, to strategic objectives.

According to the literature [67, 71], the above-mentioned aspects can be integrated in a BSC tool, following three approaches, progressively extensive:

(1) The first type of integration leads to the inclusion of the environmental and social aspects in the traditional model of BSC. These aspects become an integral part of conventional perspectives like all other potentially relevant strategic aspects: goals and indicators are integrated in the model in their cause-effect links and oriented towards the financial perspective. We call this approach Integration into Traditional BSC (ITB).

(2) The second type of integration adds one or more non-market perspectives regarding the environmental and social aspects [55]. This requires a broader strategic map and the formulation of non-market perspectives in a similar way to conventional scorecard: individuation of the strategic core aspects, leading indicators and linkages with the financial perspective through hierarchical cause-and-effect chains. We call this approach Addition of Non-Market Perspective (ANMP).

(3) Deduction of a derived environmental and social scorecard, which is an extension of one of previous variants and not an independent alternative for integration. This scorecard cannot be developed parallel to the traditional BSC, but it must be carried out only after one of the two previous approaches. The aim of this third approach is to coordinate, organize and further differentiate the environmental and social aspects, once their strategic relevance and position in cause-effect chains between market and not market perspectives have been identified by the previous approaches. We call this approach Deduction of a Derived Scorecard (DDS).

The choice between one of three ways to integrate environmental and social aspects cannot be taken in advance, but during the process of formulating an SBSC [21, 22, 72].

Considering the widespread disagreement on how sustainability can be measured [73, 74] and the companies' need of validated indicators that drive the company's financial long-term success [71], many companies adopt the GRI's reporting methodology, which provides various standard indicators regarding the sustainability performance.

In this way, the companies could design the SBSC using GRI indicators and highlight the links between long-term environmental and social goals and short-term financial benefits of firms [21, 29, 75–77]. The usefulness of GRI indicators is emphasised because of the frequent difficulty of the companies to autonomously identify appropriate sustainability indicators [78], and by the possibility to use "a single language as a bridge of communication between the entity and the stakeholders" [79: 4992].

Compared to traditional BSC, this involves a transformation of the financial perspective in economic perspective, gathering information about the wider economic growth (including financial, social and environmental aspects) [21] and a change of the customer perspective in external stakeholder perspective [66].

# 3 Research Framework and Methodology

The aim of this paper is firstly to investigate the role of SBSC and secondly to try of showing the relationship between the SBSC and the level of integration of AISs designated to measure the environmental and social aspects.

The second aim is based on the literature analysis, carried out in the previous paragraph. It shows three types of SBSC configurations and three different uses of sustainability accounting information systems (EMA and SMA) (as shown in Fig. 2).

According to literature [9, 10], the strategy management affects the management control system and the AISs in it incorporated [81]. In this case, the strategic relevance of the aspects non-measurable via market mechanism should affect the SBSC configuration and the sustainability AISs and their integration. Increasing strategic relevance of the social and environmental aspects should increase: (a) the need to control them and therefore the use of a more complex configuration of SBSC in order to highlight how these aspects contribute to value create; (b) the need of AISs to capture these aspects that are not measurable through financial measures, and integrate all aspects of the triple bottom line, in order to collect, elaborate, control and report data and information which allow to realize the sustainability strategy.

These impacts of strategic relevance of sustainability aspects on SBSC configuration and the integration of AISs could be explained by using the Simons' levers of control (LOC) framework [81, 82]. In this framework there are two possible uses of management control and information system:

- Interactive use, focused on actors' attention on key goals and aimed to support changes aligned with strategic objectives.
- Diagnostic use, aimed to correct actors' actions.

In the conventional BSC, the traditional management accounting has an interactive use because the information "(1) must be simple to understand (…); (2) must provide information about strategic uncertainties (…); (3) must be used by

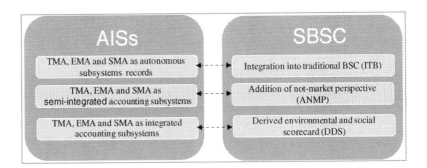

**Fig. 2** Relationship between AISs and SBSC (our elaboration)

managers at multiple levels of the organization (…) and (4) must generate new action plans" [81, p. 220].

In SBSC, the use of sustainability accounting information system (and specifically the EMA and SMA) in an interactive or diagnostic way, depends on the integration between sustainability and strategy [83], reflected also in specific configuration of SBSC.

- In the first configuration of SBSC (ITB) the aspects non measurable via market mechanism do not represent resources with strategical value and therefore do not need a detection and integration with other resources. For this reason, the sustainable issues should be managed diagnostically with EMA and SMA (represented by simple tools of collect data, such as excel), not integrated with TMA, and developed to respond to external pressure to comply with standard [83], such as GRI. This type of companies have a "compliant-driven sustainability strategy" [83].
- In the second configuration of SBSC (ANMP), in which the sustainability aspects have a medium strategic relevance, they frequently represent external constraints "rather than business opportunities" [82, p. 214], which affect strategic choices and the financial results. In this SBSC configuration the aspects non measurable via market mechanism are showed in a new specific perspective in order to highlight the attention paid to these aspects and to improve the control of objectives linked to issues of legality and autonomy of action, such as the ethic objective of no child labour [68]. This configuration of SBSC requires a minimum of integration of AISs to catch the impacts of non-market aspect on financial results. The EMA and SMA are used only in diagnostic way to increase reputation and legitimacy to operate.
- Finally, in the third configuration of SBSC (DDS), in which the sustainability aspects have a high strategic relevance, the firm's commitment to recognizing, measure and disclosure the strategic aspects is stronger. The EMA and SMA should be more integrated in order to allow the deployment and renewal of sustainability strategy and to catch all the cause-effect chains among the TBL's aspects. All AISs must have an interactive use in order to generate organizational learning and new action plans [83].

In order to examine the process of implementation and the use of SBSC and to show the relationship with AISs, we use a qualitative case study methodology [84, 85].

The case examined, from a methodological viewpoint, represents an exploratory case study, according to the Yin's taxonomy [85]. In this work the qualitative case study methodology [84, 85] is justified because it is a preliminary study, aimed to fill the literature gap about the relationship between the AISs and SBSC, and because in accounting study "we can use case studies to provide descriptions of accounting practice, to explore the application of new procedures, to explain the determinants of existing practice" [86, p. 143]. The case study concerns the description of an SBSC adopted by Hera Group, one of the more relevant Italian multi-utility company.

The choice of this case study is due to the attention paid by Hera to aspects of sustainability, as shown by exhaustive sustainability report and by unusual disclosure of SBSC.[1] The information sources used to perform the case study come from the exhaustive website of the company and from the phone calls (about 20 min) with two managers of the Management Control Department, to which we have turned a semi-structured interview and subsequent email, regarding the SBSC use, the existing AISs which support SBSC, their assessment of these tools and future developments.

## 4   Case Study Description

The Hera Group S.p.A. operates in 358 Italian municipalities, including many major cities of Central and Northern Italy. It provides energy (gas, electricity), water (aqueducts, sewerage and purification) and environmental (waste collection and disposal) to more than 4 million citizens, realizing annual revenues (in the 2015) of 4817.8 million Euro, with 8571 employees.

The group has three strengths: the balance between the services in the free market (such as sale of gas and disposal of special wastes) and regulated services (such as gas distribution, integrated water services, collection and disposal of municipal waste); territoriality and strong attention paid to aspects of sustainability; the presence of a free float of about 24,000 shareholders.

Hera, since its establishment in 2002, attributed a central role to sustainability, integrating it into planning and control systems, and then in the activities related to business management. This justifies the implementation of a sustainability balanced scorecard, which allows to formulate the strategy into operational projects that are part of the incentive system of management and the reporting.

The principles underlying the sustainable management are enshrined in the Group's Code of Ethics, in which there are all values that are the basis of the group's strategy and consequently of strategic business plan and of disclosure to stakeholder, including a sustainability annual report.

The process of formulating the SBSC in Hera can be ideally divided into two steps.

The first refers to the formalizing business goals and includes:

- Mission: to be the best multiutility in Italy.
- Vision: to develop an original business model oriented to innovation, to acquire trust of stakeholders and to strengthen the links with the geographical areas in which it operates by respecting the local environment.

---

[1]We selected this case from AIDA, the Bureau van Dijk database. Among 25 listed Italian energy, water and environmental enterprises selected, only 10 draw up a sustainability report and only five of these adopted, or was starting to adopt, the SBSC (Hera, Terna, A2A, ERG, Iren).

- Business goals: a multi-business growth strategy focused on three business areas (energy and gas, environment, water services), keeping a business portfolio that is balanced between regulated activities with low risk and deregulated services offering growth perspectives.
- Priorities: excellence, growth, efficiency, innovation, but also improve the environment, ensure quality and safety, be transparent, engage and motivate workers, have partner suppliers for sustainable growth.

The second step, starting from strategic priorities, relates more closely to the design of the SBSC defining specific objectives and indicators (KPI).

The economic and financial highlights in the business plan to 2019 are: (a) EBITDA of 1030 million Euro; (b) earning per share of 5% per year; (c) total investment of 2.2 billion Euro (d) Net Financial Position/EBITDA of 2,9. The industrial highlights are: (a) keep the ratio "regulated activities-to-liberalized activities" substantially unchanged (55–45% in 2019, vs. 53–47% in 2014); (b) coexistence of internal Growth and External Growth Strategies; (c) exceed 2.3 million "energy clients" in 2019; (d) maintain high levels of sustainability targets. This second step involves the identification of all potential environmental and social exposure of the company, that allows to draw up a list of all environmental and social aspects that may be strategically relevant.

According to the framework elaborated by Figgie [68], Hera recognizes its environmental exposure about the emissions (increasing renewable energy), wastes (further reduction in the use of landfills for municipal wastes) and energy (electricity, gas and water grid modelling).

The social exposure analysis initially involves the identification of all relevant stakeholder groups, which are divided into direct and indirect stakeholders, and subsequently, their social claims and issues are identified. The direct stakeholders of Hera are: internal (employees with regard to the job security, the work conditions, the professional development and enhancement) and along the value chain (customers with regard to the rate tariff, electronic meters, response timing, and on-line services). The indirect stakeholders of Hera are: along the value chain (suppliers' employees with regard to the job security and the legality, social cooperatives); the community (non-profit organization of the territory and educational initiatives) and the society in a broad sense (consumer groups, trade associations, certification institutes, government with regard to the employment, regional development and legislation compliance).

The Hera's relevant commitment to involving stakeholders is manifested in numerous dialogue and consultation initiatives with stakeholders, as well as customers and employees satisfaction surveys, of which results are used to plan improvement actions.

In order to define the perspectives of the SBSC, Hera has adopted the approach proposed by Crawford and Scaletta [77], referring to sustainability report standard (GRI-G4) and using the four traditional perspectives of BSC.

On the basis of the indicators used for sustainability reports, compliant with GRI-G4, Hera group has mapped the relations of cause-effect between the 29 strategic objectives to increase the company's value in the long-term. Furthermore, the financial perspective is renamed as the economy-financial viewpoint, the customer perspective as the customer and region viewpoint, and the learning and growth perspective as the training and development viewpoint (as shown by strategic map in Fig. 3).

- In the economic-financial perspective, the lagging indicators are those identified in the strategic formulation step and represented by three financial highlights and four industrial highlights, previously exposed.
- The customer and region perspective shows three strategically important issues, namely aimed to increase their market share, to grow in new territories, and to increase customer loyalty. The relationship with customers has three performance drivers, such as: (a) characteristics of the product linked to reliability and renewable sources; (b) customer relationship focused on the tariff plan, the timing and on-line services; (c) the image and reputation. These performance drivers are accounted for both consumers and trade associations.
- The third perspective, focused on internal processes, reveals the presence of three environmental aspects, regarding the increasing alternative energy sources, reducing waste in landfills, and standards compliance, as well as the social aspects concerning prevention and health of workers, the reduction of the response timing to the customers and the increase in online services.
- The employee satisfaction is a strategic core business of fourth perspective and its performance drivers identified concern the employees (prevention, safety, involvement, and professional development), the promotion of QSE policy, the alignment with the principles of the code of ethics, the effectiveness of information systems, and the focus on the result-based strategy and culture.

According to Figgie [67, 68] the choice of SBSC configuration is linked to relevance of social and environmental aspect, measurable with non-market mechanism, such as legitimacy and legality. In the Hera's SBSC there are many environmental and social indicators closely linked to economic one and integrated in market system, but there are also non-market aspects such as dialogue with stakeholders and region and reputation that influence the business via non-market mechanisms. Hera recognizes the relevance of the latter, but it does not attribute them a strategic identity in contributing to the success of the company. For example, Hera identifies the dialogue with stakeholders and the region as relevant non-market aspect, defining three main objectives: (a) the further development of initiatives of involvement and dialogue with stakeholders; (b) the consolidation and promotion of the CSR to improve the long-term competitiveness and create shared value in the region; (c) the further contribution to the economic, social and environmental development for the relevant territory and for all stakeholders. Hera, although recognizes that this non-market aspect is relevant, does not believe that his contribution is so significant to justify a separate representation. For this reason, it decided to include this aspect in the four perspectives (in particular in the third perspective), without creating another perspective (as shown in the Fig. 3).

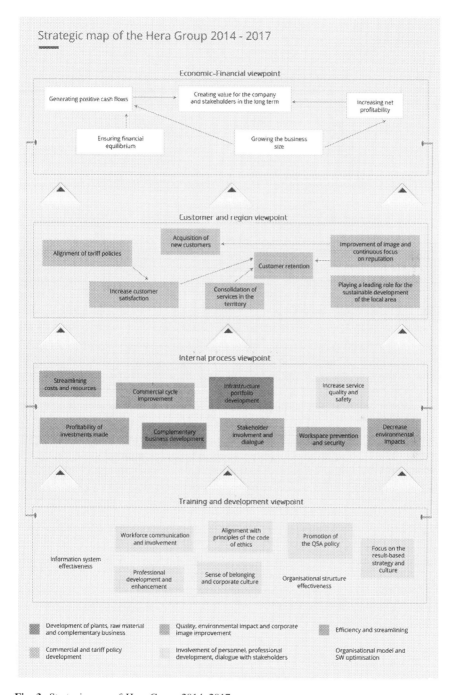

**Fig. 3** Strategic map of Hera Group 2014–2017

In this way, Hera does not use the SBSC to its full potential. In Hera, the SBSC is closely linked to incentives' system: it articulates the strategy into operative projects that are linked to bonus system of management and to reporting. All projects include: (a) the assignment to a manager and their inclusion in the incentives' system for managers; (b) the process and result indicators; (c) the key action plan for achievement of the project objectives in terms of time and cost; (d) a monitoring, on a quarterly basis, at central and local (budget units) level.

The main link of the SBSC with AISs regards the collection of indicators, which are related to management of individual projects target, included in the SBSC system. This is often a general problem in traditional BSC, but it is amplified in SBSC due to the heterogeneous data, generally non-financial and coming from different sources according to the typology of KPI.

In order to manage the SBSC projects, Hera recently implemented a simple software, which allows the project managers to develop their projects and to carry out quarterly an upgrade of the project. Particularly this system allows to enter the following information: project plan (such as GanttProject); a description of the project; working group; results and activity indicators. The implementation of the new information system required a specific training initiative addressed to all managers and executives. This initiative aimed to provide operating instructions on systems use, to present the techniques of project management and to ensure greater capacity for planning and managing the project in a sustainable perspective.

There is not an automatic interface between the information system and the SBSC that allows the recovery of the indicators loaded by project managers or in other planning and control system: the integration of social, environmental and financial aspects is made as a function of sustainable reporting. Despite this, there is always a consistency control between the financial, environmental and social objective loaded by the project managers and the indicators included in the SBSC.

The use of the information system at project managers level, even if not integrated with other accounting systems ensures a great efficient and effective management of the balanced scorecard process through:

- The simplified updating and monitoring of projects.
- Better control of the correct monitoring of project sheets (inability to change the assigned objectives), through the maintenance of initial planning (no change objectives assigned).
- Increasing the visibility of the projects by the members of the working group.
- Automatic generation of displays and summary reports.
- The definition of procedures to facilitate the retrieval and management of data.

## 5  Discussion

The role of sustainability issues is becoming more prominent on company agendas. The most of listed companies are actively integrating sustainability principles into their businesses, and are managing the three dimensions of sustainability to improve processes, pursue growth, and create value for the company and stakeholders and finally are providing the exhaustive disclosure also on environmental and social issues. In order to support the sustainability, enterprises should seek an integrative and complete view spanning all sustainable value chain elements of the organization, requiring an information system able to allow the achievement, jointly, of economic, social and environmental goals.

The SBSC allows a diversified integration of financial objectives with social and environmental aspects on the basis of the strategic importance attributed to them. According to literature [87] the SBSC could have the following strengths: improvement in understanding of corporate environmental and social responsibilities; improvement in planning of environmental and social targets; improvement in employees' attitude toward their environmental and social responsibilities; improvement in environmental and social performance; improvement in resource allocation; potential facilitation of the introduction of other AISs; improvements in data collection and data quality; connection between environmental, social and financial targets; alignment of different business units in common environmental and social targets.

Among the three configurations of SBSC derived by literature, Hera adopts the first configuration, integrating the environmental and social aspects in the four traditional perspectives of balanced scorecard. Hera believes that the non-market aspects (such as stakeholder dialogue) are important to be "a good citizen" but are not enough strategically relevant to generate a new perspective. Hera uses the SBSC especially to take over the sustainability issues in multi-utilities sector and to link the incentive mechanisms also to sustainability goals. The AISs support the process of collection and manage the information to implement and use this tool. There are different AISs to achieve this task in relation to not only economic dimension, but also the social and environmental aspects (manifested through market and non-market mechanisms), such as EMA and SMA.

The AISs of Hera are the autonomous subsystems: several information systems separately detect, collect and process social, environmental and economic information. The integration of information arising from the social, environmental and economic dimensions, takes place through the product manager control, recording environmental and social data in an autonomous way. Recently, Hera implemented a simple software to allow the project managers to manage the project plan, working group, result and activities' indicators, and to carry out quarterly an upgrade of the projects.

According to literature, the strategic relevance of the social and environmental aspects non measured via market mechanism affects the SBSC configuration, the sustainability AISs and their integration.

The greater strategic importance of social and environmental non-market aspects, generates (1) a progressive evolution of the SBSC configuration, that drives towards (2) the use of SAISs, increasingly integrated.

If the company's strategy is strongly focused on social and environmental issues, the company needs of AISs more integrated in order to collect and elaborate data and information to monitor and evaluate all aspects of sustainability, in a way more timely and with less efforts. The case examined allows us to, only partly, explore this problem and the findings from it are indicative rather than conclusive.

Hera adopts the first configuration of SBSC (ITB), which not fully takes strategic advantages of this tool, supported by a "diagnostic" use of AISs. Hera considers that the AISs will allow to facilitate investigation and monitoring of projects, and to increase the commitment of the working group to realize the sustainable project objectives. However, the EMA and SMA in Hera are autonomous systems which provide useful data to create indicators needed in multiutilities sector and compliant with GRI, but they do not allow to recover all non-market aspects which can contribute to achieving the company's long-term success.

## 6   Conclusion

The main purpose of this study was to advance understanding of the role of sustainability in the evolution of control and accounting information systems.

To achieve this, the authors examined literature regarding sustainability and accounting information systems, focusing on the contributes regarding: (1) the role of SBSC as a tool for formulating, controlling and communicate the sustainability strategy; (2) the role of the new accounting information systems to support the sustainable commitment of business; (3) the possible relationship between AISs (especially in terms of their integration) and SBSC (which reflects the strategic relevance of sustainability aspects).

The accounting and control systems evolve consistently with the strategy and complexity of decision-making process. Academics and practitioners proposed many accounting and control instruments: one of the most important instruments, which link sustainability and strategy, is the SBSC, an integrated system of indicators, aimed to evaluate the corporate sustainability performance.

The SBSC requires specific AISs to collect, process and report information relating to the three dimensions of sustainability and that can interact in different ways and be variously integrated. According to literature, there are several AISs, which recognize the social and environmental dimensions in addition to the economic dimension, such as EMA and SMA, which use market and non-market mechanisms.

If the company's strategy is strongly focused on social and environmental issues, the company should use the more evolved configurations of SBSC (such as ANMP or DDS as shown in Fig. 2). This requires AISs more integrated in order to collect and elaborate data and information to monitor and evaluate all aspects of sustainability, in a way more timely manner and with less efforts. In this way, the company could avoid the risk of not being able to manage a significant part of the strategy or the risk of inefficiencies associated with recovery and processing times of information and with duplication, unreliability, incompleteness of data.

The case examined allows us to, only partly, explore the relationship between the environmental and social aspects considered strategically relevant and AISs to detect them, because of the exploratory nature of this work.

The case study illustrated can be collocated in the first relationship (as shown in Fig. 2), showing a basic SBSC configuration (ITB) in which the sustainability aspects are included in the four traditional perspectives and the EMA and SMA are autonomous and not integrated with traditional information system, providing only environmental and social data. This does not allow us to explore the full relationship supposed between AISs and SBSC, but it represents the first step to fill the gap in literature about the integration issue of information, which seems to be the pivotal aspect to make effective the sustainability management and each strategic control tools. Consequently, the main outcome of this work is to show how a leading company in the multiutilities sector oriented towards sustainability uses the SBSC and the AISs to manage all aspects of corporate sustainability, but we intend to expand it in a larger research. We believe that a greater number of case studies, also in no Italian context, is needed, in order to better validate our considerations and test all possible relationships between AISs and SBSC. There are many possible directions for future research, in particular, it would be interesting to improve the investigation of the different AISs to sustainability, which can be used to draw-up the SBSC but also to satisfy the disclosure need, as recently required by the new EU Directive.

# References

1. Hall, J. K., Daneke, G. A., & Lenox, M. J. (2010). Sustainable development and entrepreneurship: Past contributions and future directions. *Sustainable Development and Entrepreneurship, 25*(5), 439–448.
2. Hartmann, B., & Farkas, C. (2016). Energy efficient data centre infrastructure—Development of a power loss model. *Energy and Buildings*.
3. Morioka, S. N., & de Carvalho, M. M. (2016). A systematic literature review towards a conceptual framework for integrating sustainability performance into business. *Journal of Cleaner Production*, 1–13.
4. Choi, D. Y., & Gray, E. R. (2008). The venture development processes of «sustainable» entrepreneurs. *Management Research News, 31*(8), 558–569.
5. Hansen, A. (2014). *Media and the environment*. London: Routledge.
6. WCED. (1987). *Our common future*. Oxford: Oxford University Press.
7. Elkington, J. (2004). Enter the triple bottom line. In A. Henriques & J. Richardson (Eds.), *The triple bottom line: Does it all add up* (1–16). Earthscan.
8. Porter, M. E., & Kramer, M. R. (2006). Strategy and society: The link between competitive advantage and corporate social responsibility. *Harvard Business Review*.
9. Langfield-Smith, K. (2007). *A review of quantitative research in management control systems and strategy. Handbook of management accounting research* (pp. 753–784). Oxford, UK: Elsevier.
10. Otley, D. (2016). The contingency theory of management accounting and control: 1980–2014. *Management Accounting Research, 31*, 45–62.

11. Brown, D., Dillard, J., & Marshall, S. (2005). Incorporating natural systems as part of accounting's public interest responsibility. *Journal of information system, 19*(2), 79–104.
12. Busco, C., & Quattrone, P. (2015). Exploring how the balanced scorecard engages and unfolds: Articulating the visual power of accounting inscriptions. *Contemporary Accounting Research, 32*(3), 1236–1262.
13. Rinaldi, L., Binacchi M. (2007). Managing and measuring sustainability: The business case of public utility industry. *Economia Aziendale 2000 Web, 1,* 147–174
14. Dillard, J. (2008). Responding to expanding accountability regimes by re-presenting organizational context. *International Journal of Accounting Information Systems, 9*(1), 21–42.
15. Brown, J. (2009). Democracy, sustainability and dialogic accounting technologies: Taking pluralism seriously. *Critical Perspectives on Accounting, 20*(3), 313–342.
16. Petcharat, N., & Mula, J. M. (2009). Identifying system characteristics for development of a sustainability management accounting information system: Towards a conceptual design for the manufacturing industry. *IEEE,* 56–64.
17. Kaplan, R. S., & Norton, D. (1992). The balanced scorecard: Measures that drive performance. *Harvard Business Review, 70*(1), 71–79.
18. Broccardo, L. (2010). An empirical study of the balanced scorecard as a flexible strategic management and reporting tool. *Economia Aziendale Online, 1*(2), 81–91.
19. Kaplan, R. S., & Norton, D. P. (1996). The balanced scorecard: Translating strategy into action. *Harvard Business Press.*
20. Fülöp, G., & Hernádi, B. H. (2013). *Sustainability accounting: A success factor in corporate sustainability strategy* (pp. 229–241). Riga: Present at New Challenges of Economic and Business Development–2013.
21. Caraiani, C., Lungu, C. L., & Cornelia, D. (2015). *Green accounting initiatives and strategies for sustainable development.* IGI Global.
22. Hansen, E. G., & Schaltegger, S. (2016). The sustainability balanced scorecard: A systematic review of architectures. *Journal of Business Ethics, 133*(2), 193–221.
23. Chofreh, A. G., Goni, F. A., Shaharoun, A. M., Ismail, S., & Klemeš, J. J. (2014). Sustainable enterprise resource planning: Imperatives and research directions. *PSE Asia for Cleaner Production, 71,* 139–147.
24. Lodhia, S., & Hess, N. (2014). Sustainability accounting and reporting in the mining industry: Current literature and directions for future research. *Journal of Cleaner Production, 84,* 43–50.
25. Schaltegger, S., & Burritt, R. (2010). Sustainability accounting for companies: Catchphrase or decision support for business leaders? *Journal of World Business, 45,* 375–384.
26. Bebbington, J., Unerman, J., & O'Dwyer, B. (2014). *Sustainability accounting and accountability.* London: Routledge.
27. Burritt, R. L., & Schaltegger, S. (2010). Sustainability accounting and reporting: fad or trend? *Accounting, Auditing & Accountability Journal, 23*(7), 829–846.
28. Zhang, B., & Chen, B. (2016). Sustainability accounting of a household biogas project based on emergy. *Applied Energy.*
29. Möller, A., & Schaltegger, S. (2005). The sustainability balanced scorecard as a framework for eco-efficiency analysis. *Journal of Industrial Ecology, 9*(4), 73–83.
30. Gray, R., Javad, M., Power, D. M., & Sinclair, C. D. (2001). Social and environmental disclosure and corporate characteristics: A research note and extension. *Journal of Business Finance Accounting, 28*(3–4), 327–356.
31. Burritt, R. L., Hahn, T., & Schaltegger, S. (2002). Towards a comprehensive framework for environmental management accounting: Links between business actors and environmental management accounting tools. *Australian Accounting Review, 12*(2), 39–50.
32. Berkel, R. V. (2003). Managing for sustainable development: Using environmental management accounting and sustainable development reporting. *CPA Congress, 21,* 1–18.

33. Gadenne, D., & Zaman, M. (2002). Strategic environmental management accounting: An exploratory study of current corporate practice and strategic intent. *Journal of Environmental Assessment Policy and Management, 4*(2), 123–150.
34. Hubbard, G. (2009). Measuring organizational performance: Beyond the triple bottom line. *Business Strategy and the Environment, 17,* 171–191.
35. Qian, W., & Burritt, R. (2007). Environmental accounting for waste management: A study of local governments in Australia. *The Environmentalist, 27*(1), 143–154.
36. Gale, R. (2006). Environmental management accounting as a reflexive modernization strategy in cleaner production. *Journal of Cleaner Production, 14*(14), 1228–1236.
37. Nachtmann, H., & Al-Rifai, M. H. (2004). An application of activity based costing in the air conditioner manufacturing industry. *The Engineering Economist, 49*(3), 221–236.
38. Bengo, I., Marika, A., Giovanni, A., & Calderini, M. (2016). Indicators and metrics for social business: A review of current approaches. *Journal of Social Entrepreneurship, 7,* 1–24.
39. Gray, R., O'Dochartaigh, A., & Rannou, C. (2016). Organisational effectiveness and social and environmental accounting: Through the past darkly. In J. Haslam & P. Sikka (Eds.), *Pioneers of critical accounting: A celebration of the life of Tony Lowe* (pp. 53–71). London: Palgrave Macmillan UK.
40. Heupel, T. (2015). Social management accounting: Development of an integrative framework for environmental and social costing. In L. O'Riordan, P. Zmuda, & S. Heinemann (Eds.), *New perspectives on corporate social responsibility: Locating the missing link* (pp. 301–319). Wiesbaden: Springer Fachmedien Wiesbaden.
41. Maas, K., Schaltegger, S., & Crutzen, N. (2016). Integrating corporate sustainability assessment, management accounting, control, and reporting. *Journal of Cleaner Production,* 1–12
42. Parguel, B., Benoît-Moreau, F., & Larceneux, F. (2011). How sustainability ratings might deter "Greenwashing": A closer look at ethical corporate communication. *Journal of Business Ethics, 102,* 15.
43. Passetti, E., Cinquin, L., Marelli, A., & Tenucci, A. (2014). Sustainability accounting in action: Lights and shadows in the Italian context. *The British Accounting Review, 46,* 295–308.
44. Lamberton, G. (2005). Sustainability accounting—A brief history and conceptual framework. *Accounting Forum, 7,* 13–14.
45. Ferens, A. (2015). Best information system in achieving social responsibility strategy of the company. *Economy & Business Journal, 9*(1), 799–809.
46. Petcharat, N., & Mula J. M. (2009). Identifying system characteristics for development of a sustainability management accounting information system: Towards a conceptual design for the manufacturing industry. *IEEE,* 56–64.
47. IFAC. (2005). Environmental management accounting: International guidance.
48. The Sigma Project. (2003). *Sustainability accounting guide.* London: The UK, & Department of Trade And Industry (DTI).
49. Brooks, S., Seidel, S., & Recker, J. (2012). Unpacking green IS: A review of the existing literature and directions for the future. In J. vom Brocke (Ed.), Green business process management (pp. 15–37). Berlin: Springer.
50. Atkinson, G. (2000). Measuring corporate sustainability. *Journal of Environmental Planning and Management, 43*(2), 235–252.
51. Rabbani, A., Zamani, M., Yazdani-Chamzini, A., & Zavadskas, E. K. (2014). Proposing a New Integrated Model Based on Sustainability Balanced Scorecard (SBSC) and MCDM approaches by using linguistic variables for the performance evaluation of oil producing companies. *Expert Systems with Applications, 41*(16), 7316–7327.
52. Chen, F.-H., Hsu, T.-S., & Tzeng, G.-H. (2011). A balanced scorecard approach to establish a performance evaluation and relationship model for hot spring hotels based on a hybrid MCDM model combining DEMATEL and ANP. *International Journal of Hospitality Management, 30*(4), 908–932.

53. Chai, N. (2009). Sustainability performance evaluation system in government: A balanced scorecard approach towards sustainable development. Springer Science & Business Media.
54. Johanson, H., Skoog, M., Backlund, A., & Almqvist, R. (2006). Balancing dilemmas of the balanced scorecard. *Accounting, Auditing & Accountability Journal, 19*(6), 842–857.
55. Schaltegger, S., & Dyllick, T. (2002). Nachhaltig managen mit der Balanced Scorecard. Konzept und Fallstudien Sustainability Management with the Balanced Scorecard – Concept and Cases. Wiesbaden: Gabler.
56. Birch, C. (2000). *Future success*. Melbourne: Prentice Hall.
57. Lipe, M. G., & Salterio, S. E. (2000). The balanced scorecard; Judgmental effects of common and unique performance measures. *The Accounting Review, 3,* 289–298.
58. Martinsons, M., Davison, R., & Tse, D. (1999). The balanced scorecard: A foundation for the strategic management of information systems. *Decision Support Systems, 25*(1), 71–88.
59. Johanson, H., Skoog, M., Backlund, A., & Almqvist, R. (2006). Balancing dilemmas of the balanced scorecard. *Accounting, Auditing & Accountability Journal, 19*(6), 842–857.
60. Kaplan, R. S., & Norton, D. P. (2004). *Strategy maps: Converting Intangible assets into tangible outcomes (1st ed., Fourth Impression)*. Boston: Harvard Business Review Press.
61. Kaplan, R. S., & Norton, D. P. (2001). Transforming the balanced scorecard from performance measurement to strategic management: Part I.
62. Kaplan, R. S., & Norton, D. P. (2001). *The strategy-focused organization: How balanced scorecard companies Thrive in the new business environment*. Brighton: Harvard Business Press.
63. Kaplan, R. S. (2008). conceptual foundations of the balanced scorecard. *Handbooks of Management Accounting Research, 3,* 1253–1269.
64. Simons, R. (1994). How New top managers use control systems as levers of strategic renewal. *Strategic Management Journal, 15,* 169–189.
65. Epstein, M. J., & Manzoni, J. F. (1997). The balanced scorecard and Tableau de Bord: Translating strategy into action. *Management Accounting (US), 79*(2), 28–36.
66. The Sigma Project (2003, september) The Sigma Guidelines toolkit—Sustainability scorecard.
67. Figgie, F., Hahn, T., Schaltegger, S., & Wagner, M. (2002). The sustainability balanced scorecard—Linking sustainability management to business strategy. *Business Strategy and the Environment, 11*(5), 269–284.
68. Figgie, F., Hahn, T., Schaltegger, S., & Wagner, M. (2002). The sustainability balanced scorecard—Theory and application of a tool for value-based sustainability management. Presented at Greening of Industry Network Conference, Göteborg, Sweden.
69. Schaltegger, S. (2004). Sustainability balanced scorecard. *Controlling, 16*(8–9), 511–516.
70. Herzberg, F., Mausner, B., & Snyderman, B. B. (1993). The motivation to work. Piscataway: Transaction Publishers.
71. Butler, C. J., Henderson, S. C., & Raiborn, C. (2011). Sustainability and the balanced scorecard. Management Accounting Quarterly. *Management Accounting Quarterly, 12*(2), 1–10.
72. Elijido-Ten, E. (2010). Sustainability and balanced scorecard reporting: What determines public disclosure decision? *Presented at Proceedings of the 6th Asia Pacific Interdisciplinary Research in Accounting Conference (APIRA 2010)*. Sydney, Australia.
73. Govindan, K., Khodaverdi, R., & Jafarian, A. (2013). A fuzzy multi criteria approach for measuring sustainability performance of a supplier based on triple bottom line approach. *Journal of Cleaner Production, 47,* 345–354.
74. Rosano, M., & Schianetz, K. (2014). Measuring sustainability performance in industrial parks: A case study of the Kwinana industrial area. *International Journal of Sustainable Development, 17*(3), 261.
75. Länsiluoto, A., & Järvenpää, M. (2008). Environmental and performance management forces: Integrating «greenness» into balanced scorecard. *Qualitative Research in Accounting & Management, 5*(3), 184–206.

76. Nikolaou, I. E., & Tsalis, T. A. (2013). Development of a sustainable balanced scorecard framework. *Ecological Indicators, 34,* 76–86.
77. Crawford, D., & Scaletta, R. (2006). The balanced scorecard and corporate social responsibility: Aligning values for profit. *FMI Journal, 17*(3), 39–45.
78. Savalia, J. D. (2016). Social and environmental performance indicators: Dimensions of integrated reporting and benefits for responsible management and sustainability. *International Journal of Trend in Research and Development, 3*(2), 257–259.
79. Caraiani, C. (2012). Social and environmental performance indicators: Dimensions of integrated reporting and benefits for responsible management and sustainability. *African Journal of Business Management, 6*(14), 4990–4997.
80. Malmi, T., & Brown, D. A. (2008). Management control systems as a package—Opportunities, challenges and research directions. *Management Accounting Research, 19,* 287–300.
81. Simons, R. (2000). *Performance measurement and control systems for implementing strategies.* Upper Saddle River: Prentice Hall.
82. Gond, J.-P., Grubnic, S., Herzig, C., & Moon, J. (2012). Configuring management control systems: Theorizing the integration of strategy and sustainability. *Management Accounting Research, 23,* 205–223.
83. Gond, J. P., & Herrbach, O. (2006). Social reporting as an organizational learning tool? A theoretical framework. *Journal of Business Ethics, 65,* 359–371.
84. Eisenhardt, K. M. (1989). Building theories from case study research. *The Academy of Management Review, 14*(4), 532–550.
85. Yin, R. K. (2013). *Case study research: Design and methods.* Thousand Oaks, CA: Sage.
86. Ryan, B., Scapens, R. W., Theobald, M. (2002) *Research method and methodology in finance and accounting.* London: Thomson.
87. Tsalis, T. A., Nikolaou, I. E., Grigoroudis, E., & Tsagarakis, K. P. (2013). A framework development to evaluate the needs of SMEs in order to adopt a sustainability-balanced scorecard. *Journal of Integrative Environmental Sciences, 10*(3–4), 179–197.

# The Moderating Effect of Proprietary Costs in the Relation Between Ownership Structure and Human Capital Disclosure in Sustainability Report

**Sabrina Pisano**, **Luigi Lepore**, **Assunta Di Vaio** and **Loris Landriani**

**Abstract** This paper investigates the relationship between ownership concentration and human capital disclosure in sustainability report, using both the agency theory and the proprietary costs theory. The findings show a negative relationship between ownership concentration and the level of human capital disclosure. The results also reveal that the association between ownership concentration and human capital disclosure is stronger for companies characterized by higher proprietary costs. This study contributes to the literature on human capital disclosure in different ways. First, we develop a wider human capital disclosure index, that could be utilized in future studies, and use this index to investigate the information released in the sustainability report. Moreover, this is the first study, to the best of our knowledge, examining the role of proprietary costs as a potential explanatory determinant, in conjunction with ownership structure, of human capital disclosure released in sustainability report.

**Keywords** Human capital disclosure · Sustainability report · Ownership structure
Agency theory · Proprietary costs theory

S. Pisano (✉) · L. Lepore · A. Di Vaio · L. Landriani
Parthenope University of Naples, Naples, Italy
e-mail: sabrina.pisano@uniparthenope.it

L. Lepore
e-mail: luigi.lepore@uniparthenope.it

A. Di Vaio
e-mail: susy.divaio@uniparthenope.it

L. Landriani
e-mail: loris.landriani@uniparthenope.it

© Springer International Publishing AG, part of Springer Nature 2018
R. Lamboglia et al. (eds.), *Network, Smart and Open*, Lecture Notes in Information
Systems and Organisation 24, https://doi.org/10.1007/978-3-319-62636-9_17

# 1   Introduction

Over the last decades the relevance of human capital (HC) disclosure has been widely recognized by scholars for different reasons. Releasing HC information permits to increase the transparency to capital markets [1], informing stakeholders on the company's ability to create economic value, to establish trustworthiness with stakeholders [2], to appear legitimate in the eyes of society [3, 4] and so on.

HC disclosure is considered the most valuable asset within the three intellectual capital (IC) categories [5]. According to previous studies [6–8], in fact, knowledge is considered a key factor in the value creation process of companies.

Researchers conducted several studies aiming at analyze the amount of HC disclosure and, more generally, of IC disclosure voluntarily released by firms operating in different Countries and its determinants.

This paper aims at analyzing the association between HC disclosure released in the sustainability report and two possible explanatory determinants: ownership structure and proprietary costs. More specifically, we consider proprietary costs as a moderating variable, that affects the relation between ownership structure and HC disclosure explained using the type II of agency conflicts.

We conducted the analysis on a sample of Italian non-financial listed companies. We decided to focus on the Italian context because the ownership of these companies is traditionally concentrated in the hands of few large shareholders; as a consequence, these firms suffer from type II of agency conflicts. We analyzed the information released in the sustainability report. This is a document voluntarily drawn up by companies and published on their website. We decided to focus on this report because it is considered a suitable document to report IC disclosure [9]. According to Oliveira et al. [10], IC report guidelines and sustainability report guideline present some similarities in terms of purpose, content and users of the document. In particular, the GBS (Working group on issuing of social report preparation principles) guidelines (2013) offer a wide range of HC contents that sustainability reports should show. In the first part of the GBS guidelines, the measurement of the value added per employee is explained, while in the second part the following items are presented: (a) Remuneration and incentives systems (levels of salaries, benefits provided); (b) Health and safety (safety policies, number of accidents at work, number of work-related accidents, training expenses), (c) Job organization (number of hours per employee), (d) Socio-demographic and work profile (gender, age, origin, working class, education); (e) Career development (internal promotions); (f) Union activity (Trade union activities, hours of strikes, number of signed agreements); (g) Internal relationships (intranet, mailing list); (h) Social activity (type and number of social events, percentage of participation, associations); (i) Welfare and motivation (employee turnover, job rotation opportunities, new hirings classified for work class/gender, employee satisfaction, servicescape); (j) Warnings (numbers, appeals/petitions); (k) Charity work (number of hours); (m) fundraising (charity events). However, previous studies on IC disclosure mainly focused on the annual report and only few researchers [11] analysed the IC information released in the sustainability report.

The results showed a negative relationship between ownership concentration and the level of HC disclosure released in sustainability report. Moreover, we found that the association between ownership concentration and HC disclosure is stronger for companies characterized by higher proprietary costs.

The paper is organized as follows: Sect. 2 shows a literature review on the determinants of HC disclosure; Sect. 3 describes the sample and the research model; Sect. 4 highlights the results obtained by the study and the discussion about them. Finally, Sect. 5 draws some final considerations and the main limits of this study.

## 2 Literature Review and Hypotheses Development

The HC is a category of most IC models developed by academics and practitioners, together with external capital and internal capital [12–17] (see [18] for a review of the main guidelines and frameworks developed with a focus in reporting IC). More precisely, HC is considered the most valuable asset within the three IC categories [5], so that Roslender and Fincham [19] defined HC as primary IC and the other two categories as secondary IC, promoting an HC-centred perspective on IC.

Companies release HC information for several reasons: to create an image of its hidden value [20], to communicate the link between HC and performance to stakeholders [21], to mimic the "best practice" firms [5], to achieve an effective management of the critical resources [3], to reduce tension between firms and their constituents in the interest of further capital accumulation [22].

Several studies have analyzed the amount of HC disclosure and, more generally, of IC disclosure voluntarily released by firms operating in different Countries and its determinants. Most of the previous research investigated the information released in the annual report and found that size [23], industry [24], leverage [25], profitability [26], board composition [27] and ownership concentration [28, 29] are possible determinants of HC disclosure.

In this study, we focus on the relationship between HC disclosure released in sustainability report and two possible explanatory determinants: ownership structure and proprietary costs. We use both the agency theory (type II of agency conflicts) and the proprietary costs theory.

In the last years, several research focused on the relation between ownership structure and IC disclosure in order to understand its effects in mitigating the agency problem between competing parties in the firms [24, 27–30]. In fact, ownership structure influences both the level of monitoring function that minority shareholders can exercise on largest shareholder/s and also the level of voluntary disclosure released [31].

Empirical research usually suggested and tested a negative relationship between ownership concentration and voluntary disclosure [32, 33], considering that firms with greater concentration of capital were less likely to voluntarily disclose information, because the largest shareholders have means and power to obtain the information they need. Also with specific regard to IC disclosure, previous studies [27–29] tested and found a negative relationship between ownership concentration and IC disclosure released by companies.

Agency theory, in fact, argues that firms characterized by greater ownership diffusion among shareholders normally experience more pressure from shareholders for greater disclosure to reduce agency costs and information asymmetry [34, 35]. Instead, firms characterized by concentrated ownership have less information asymmetry between minority shareholders and management/dominant shareholders who typically have access to the information they need and can provide an active governance system that is difficult for smaller and less-informed investors [36].

Hence, we hypothesize that:

*H₁ There is a negative relationship between ownership concentration and the level of HC disclosure released in sustainability report.*

There are also some disincentives for companies to make full HC voluntary disclosure in their sustainability report. A possible explanation is given by the proprietary costs theory [37, 38], which states that companies limit voluntary disclosure when proprietary costs arise from it. These proprietary costs include the costs of preparing, disseminating and auditing information, as well as the costs deriving from disclosing information which may be used by competitors, undermining the firm's competitive advantage. So, according to the proprietary costs theory companies tend to not provide too much proprietary information in order to avoid of eroding their competitive position.

Most previous studies that have analyzed how competition affects managers' disclosure referred to the segment reporting [39–45]. The results found support for the hypothesis that firms operating in less competitive industries have less incentive to provide proprietary information to competitors. On the other hand, firms operating in higher competitive industries may have greater incentive to disclose, because there is less risk to harm their competitive position.

With respect to HC disclosure, Singh and Van der Zahr [46] found a negative influence of proprietary costs on the association between ownership retention and the IC disclosure released in the prospectuses of IPO. Beattie and Smith [3] found that the most important disincentive to the disclosure of HC information externally is avoiding giving away information which may harm the company's competitive position.

In this study we consider proprietary costs as a moderating variable, given the highly proprietary nature of IC disclosure [46], and in particular HC disclosure. In other words, we hypothesize that the influence of ownership concentration on HC disclosure is moderated by the existence of proprietary costs:

*H₂ The negative association between ownership concentration and the level of HC disclosure released in sustainability report is stronger for companies with higher levels of proprietary costs.*

# 3 Method

## 3.1 Sample Selection and Data Source

The sample is composed by 45 Italian non-financial companies listed at 31st December 2015. We selected all Italian non-financial companies listed at the MTA market that voluntarily drawn up and published on their website the sustainability report.

We gathered accounting and financial data and information on ownership structure from the Orbis database, created by Bureau Van Dijk, and the HC information from the sustainability report of each company drawn up for the fiscal year 2014. We collected data in May, 2016.

## 3.2 Measurement

**Dependent Variable**. To collect data on our dependent variable, the HC disclosure released in sustainability report (*HCD*), we used content analysis [47], that is the research method most used in IC disclosure studies [48] (see also Dumay and Cai [49], which examine and criticize how scholars applied content analysis methodology in the IC disclosure research, in order to understand why this stream of research presents conflicting results).

The coding procedure was organized as follows. Firstly, we identified the items of HC disclosure using the IC literature. We decided to not define too many items in order to avoid the possibility of coding errors deriving from a great number of content categories [4]. As a consequence, we identified 9 HC disclosure items and grouped these items in two categories: (1) the stock of knowledge and capabilities of employees and (2) the human resource management practices (see Table 1), as suggested by Abhayawansa and Abeysekera [50].

We investigated both these categories of information because, although HC has been widely recognized as the most important asset of the firm [51], the findings of most prior studies on IC disclosure do not confirm this assumption, showing that the most reported category is external capital. Authors justified these results with different arguments: the lack of an established and generally accepted framework for IC reporting [52], the risk of such information being used by competitors [23], the lack of perception by firms that employees may be relevant as value drivers or the risk of losing HC [53].

According to Abhayawansa and Abeysekera [50], the low level of HC disclosure, compared to the information released on both external and internal capital, is the consequence of the framework used to construct the disclosure indices, that mainly refers to the Sveiby's [12] IC tripartite and considers the stock of knowledge and capabilities of employees, but does not take into account the human resource management practices implemented within the company to motivate and leverage

**Table 1** HC disclosure items

| HC disclosure item | Definition and examples of information |
|---|---|
| *Stock of knowledge and capabilities* | |
| Employee related measurements | Number of employees, median age distribution of employees, racial distribution of employees, gender distribution of employees, number of disabled employees, employee breakdown by job function, value added per employee, revenue per employee |
| Education | Education of directors as well as other employees |
| Know-how and experience | Knowledge, know-how, expertise or skills of directors and other employees, employee work-related competences and knowledge |
| *Human resource management practices* | |
| Recruitment | Recruitment policies, description of job requirements |
| Training | Training policies, description of training programs, training expenses, number of training programs, number of training days per employee, share of employees participating in training programs |
| Career development | Employee development policies and programmes, internal promotion |
| Welfare and motivation | Remuneration and incentives systems, pension, insurance policies, employee share option scheme, employee benefits, employee satisfaction, employee motivation, job rotation opportunities, employee turnover, flexibility, absence |
| Health and safety | Safety policies, number of accidents at work |
| Union activity | Trade union activities |

these knowledge resources. However, as noted by Bontis and Fitz-enz [54], both training and employee satisfaction have positive effects on HC, and Roslender et al. [55] suggested that employee wellness should be a component of primary IC. As a consequence, Abhayawansa and Abeysekera [50] recommended developing new HC disclosure indices that consider both the stock of knowledge and the human resource management practices involved within the firm. To our knowledge, so far few studies have developed such wider indices [21, 22, 24, 27, 29, 51, 56].

In this paper, we responded to the call for research of Abhayawansa and Abeysekera [50], developing a HC disclosure index that includes items concerning both the stock of knowledge and capabilities of employees and the human resource management practices.

Once the HC disclosure items were identified, the sustainability report published on the website of each sampled company was analyzed and data were collected for each item of information.

The analysis was conducted by two associate professors. The text units have been chosen as the recording units, in order to avoid the limits deriving from the use of sentences. The use of sentence, in fact, requires to determine which item dominates if different items are mentioned in the same sentence [4]. With the text unit, instead, we broke down the sentences according to how many pieces of information they contain and, then, we coded each text unit to a HC disclosure item.

Each text unit was coded with a score of 0 if the company did not provide information and with a score of 1 if the information was released. If the same information was repeated, we did not consider the repetitions [23]. We also coded the tables and considered each disclosure as different theme [57].

The amount of HC disclosure was measured by counting the frequency of occurrence for each item. An overall score was assigned to each firm in relation to the total amount of HC disclosure released in both the categories identified, by the following formula:

$$HCD_j = \sum_{i=1}^{2} TextUnit_{ij} \tag{1}$$

The score (*HCD*) awarded to firm j is equal to the sum of text units disclosed across the two categories i identified.

To verify inter-coders reliability, the two coders firstly defined a set of coding rules. Then, each researcher independently coded three sustainability reports, in order to identify the differences between coders. Finally, these differences were discussed and, on the basis of this discussion, the final set of coding rules was defined. To quantify the level of inter-coders reliability, the Krippendorff Alpha was calculated, obtaining an acceptable result (76%).

**Independent and Moderating Variables**. Previous studies investigating the relationship between ownership structure and IC disclosure mainly used the percentage of shares held by the first or the largest shareholders as a proxy for ownership concentration [28–31].

In this paper, we measured our independent variable, i.e. the ownership concentration (*OwnConc*), using the accumulated ownership of the first, second and third largest shareholders. The higher the value of this variable, the higher is the concentration of power in the hands of the largest shareholders.

To measure our moderating variable, that is the proprietary costs (*PropCost*), we investigated the level of competitiveness in a given industry as proxy. More specifically, we used the Herfindahl index, that is widely used to measure the level of industry concentration (see, for example, [39, 41, 44]) and is computed as follows:

$$Herfindahl\,Index = \sum_{i=1}^{n} \left(\frac{s_i}{S}\right)^2 \tag{2}$$

where:

$s_i$ = firm'i sales
$S$ = the sum of sales for all firms in the industry
$n$ = the number of firms in the industry

The greater the Herfindahl index, the higher the level of industry concentration and, consequently, the lower the level of industry competition. Because we were interested in the level of competition, the predicted sign of the Herfindahl index was negative.

**Control Variables**. We also included some control variables that have been shown to have significant impact on the dependent variable. We inserted some firm-specific characteristics that represent factors influencing HC disclosure according to prior literature (see, for example, [23–26]).

We included firm size (*Size*), measured as the natural logarithm of total assets, and predicted to find a positive association with *HCD* because larger firms are expected to provide more information in order to satisfy the investors' demand for information, considering that they support lower average costs of collecting and disseminating information, compared to smaller firms [30]. We inserted leverage (*Lev*), calculated as the total long term debt over equity and predicted to find a positive association with HC disclosure because, according to Jensen and Meckling [58], firms with higher leverage have more incentive to disclose information voluntarily, hoping to reduce agency costs with long-term and short-term creditors. Finally, we included profitability (*Profit*), calculated as return on assets, and predicted to find a positive relation with our dependent variable because companies characterized by high profitability could have incentives to make more corporate disclosures [35], in order to underscore their good performance to investors.

**Descriptive Statistics**. Table 2 shows the descriptive statistics for the variables of our research model. It shows the mean, standard deviation, minimum, median and maximum value for each model variable.

The level of HC disclosure released in sustainability report is on average 28.11 text units. The minimum value is 5 and the maximum is 71. This result is partially different from the findings of previous studies showing low levels of HC disclosure for companies operating both in Italy [23] and in other Countries. Our different result, compared to those of previous studies, could be the consequence of the framework used to construct our index. Unlike previous researches, our HC disclosure index does not exclusively consider the stock of knowledge and capabilities of employees but, according to the suggestion of Abhayawansa and Abeysekera [50], we also took into account the human resource management practices implemented within the company to motivate and leverage the knowledge resources. In fact, when we compare our finding with those of other studies whose HC disclosure indices also include the human resource management practices [21, 22, 51], we find similar results.

**Table 2** Descriptive statistics

| Variables | Mean | Std.d. | Min. | Median | Max. |
|---|---|---|---|---|---|
| HCD | 28.119 | 18.351 | 5.000 | 20.000 | 71.000 |
| OwnConc | 55.730 | 20.707 | 11.380 | 57.550 | 100.000 |
| PropCost | 0.081 | 0.143 | 0.005 | 0.025 | 0.873 |
| Size | 14.566 | 2.139 | 10.508 | 14.340 | 18.931 |
| Lev | 0.820 | 2.158 | −8.911 | 0.729 | 9.662 |
| Profit | 1.847 | 4.793 | −9.899 | 2.247 | 14.764 |

The standard deviation is 18.35, revealing that the disclosure behaviours adopted by the sampled companies have not been homogeneous.

Companies gave more importance to the items concerning the human resource management practices (61%), rather than those concerning the stock of knowledge and capabilities of employees (39%). This result confirms the importance to develop a wider HC disclosure index, that does not exclusively consider the stock of knowledge and capabilities of employees but, according to the suggestion of Abhayawansa and Abeysekera [50], takes into account the human resource management practices implemented within the company to motivate and leverage the knowledge resources. The use of a wider HC disclosure index, in fact, permits a better understanding of the disclosure behaviour adopted by companies with respect to the HC information released.

The item with the highest percentage of text units is the *Employee related measurements*. It follows the *Welfare and motivation* item. In the *Employee related measurements*, the sampled companies mainly reported the number of employees; this result is not unexpected, considering that art. 2427 of the Italian civil code requires companies to release information on the number of employees in the note of the financial statement. So, the sampled firms repeated the information contained in the note in their sustainability report. Almost all companies reported data on the distribution of employees per age, gender or job function. Few companies gave information on the value added per employee.

Passing to the independent variable, the results show that the ownership of the sampled companies is concentrated in the hands of the first three shareholders: the average value of *OwnConc* is 55.73%, with a minimum value of 11.38% and a maximum of 100%.

The average level of industry concentration, instead, is low (8.2%). This means that the level of industry competition is high.

Finally, the sampled companies present a discrete level of size (14.56), as well as an high level of leverage (82%) and a low level of profitability (1.84).

## 4  Regression Analysis

### 4.1  Statistical Model

In order to test the hypotheses developed, we used the following model:

$$HCD = \alpha + \beta_1 \, OwnConc + \beta_2 \, PropCost + \beta_3 \, OwnConc * PropCost + \beta_4 \, Size$$
$$+ \beta_5 \, Lev + \beta_6 \, Profit + \varepsilon$$

$$(3)$$

The additional term (*OwnConc * PropCost*) affects the direction and the strength of the relationship between prediction variables and our dependent variable. More specifically, in this research we state that the simple slope of the independent variable (*OwnConc*) on the dependent variable (*HCD*) changes depending on the level of the moderator (*PropCost*).

## 4.2 Results

Table 3 reports the results of the regression analysis for our model.

The explanatory power of previous regression is 22.7%; our findings are comparable with other studies on the determinants of IC disclosure that considered the same control variables of this paper.

The results provide support for both the hypotheses developed.

With respect to $H_1$, we found a negative relationship between *OwnConc* and *HCD* ($\beta = -0.440$, $p < 0.05$). This result is in line with the results of previous studies. Firer and Williams [28], Li et al. [27] and Oliveira et al. [29] found a negative relationship between ownership concentration and IC disclosure released by companies. Similar results are those of Patelli and Prencipe [33], that found a positive relationship between diffusion of the capital and voluntary disclosure, and those of Brammer and Pavelin [32], that found a negative relationship between ownership concentration and practice of environmental reporting.

The coefficient of our moderating variable (*PropCost*) is negative and statistically significant ($\beta = -106.013$, $p < 0.01$), showing that companies operating in higher concentrated (less competitive) industries have less incentive to provide proprietary information to competitors. On the other hand, firms operating in lower concentrated (higher competitive) industries may have greater incentive to disclose, because there is less risk to harm their competitive position.

**Table 3** Results from OLS regression

| Dependent variable: HC disclosure | | | | |
|---|---|---|---|---|
| Variables | Predicted sign | Estimated coefficient | t-Statistic | |
| OwnConc | − | −0.440 | −2.320 | ** |
| PropCost | − | −106.013 | −2.914 | *** |
| OwnConc * PropCost | + | 1.056 | 2.816 | *** |
| Size | + | 3.652 | 2.502 | ** |
| Lev | + | −1.578 | −1.336 | |
| Profit | + | 0.369 | 0.678 | |
| Observations | 45 | | | |
| $R^2$ | 0.349 | | | |
| Adjusted $R^2$ | 0.227 | | | |
| F-statistic | 2.868 | ** | | |

** $= p < 0.05$; *** $= p < 0.001$

With respect to $H_2$, the result of importance is the coefficient of the interaction term *OwnConc * PropCost*, which is positive and statistically significant ($\beta = 1.056$, $p < 0.01$). This means that, according to our expectation, the influence of ownership concentration on HC disclosure increases when the proprietary costs rise. In other words, the relationship between ownership concentration and the level of HC disclosure released in sustainability report is stronger for companies with higher levels of proprietary costs.

The control variable *Size* also contributes to the explanatory power of the regression model ($\beta = 3.652$, $p < 0.05$). Contrary to our expectations and findings from some prior studies, the coefficients related to leverage and profitability are not statistically significant.

## 5   Conclusions

This paper contributes to existing literature on HC reporting by examining the role of proprietary costs as a potential explanatory determinant, in conjunction with ownership structure, of HC disclosure released in sustainability report.

To investigate the HC information released by companies in the sustainability report voluntarily drawn up and published on their website, we developed a disclosure index that includes items concerning both the stock of knowledge and capabilities of employees and the human resource management practices.

We found that companies gave more importance to the items concerning the human resource management practices, rather than those concerning the stock of knowledge and capabilities of employees. This result demonstrates that the use of a wider index, compared to those mainly referred to the Sveiby's model, permits a better understanding of the companies' disclosure behaviour. As a consequence, this study contributes to the literature on HC disclosure developing a wider HC disclosure index, that could be utilized in future studies.

With respect to the determinants of HC disclosure, we found a negative relationship between ownership concentration and the level of HC disclosure released in sustainability report, in line with the results of previous studies [27–29]. Moreover, our findings showed that the association between ownership concentration and HC disclosure is stronger for companies characterized by higher proprietary costs. To the best of our knowledge, this is the first study examining the role of proprietary costs as a potential explanatory determinant, in conjunction with ownership structure, of HC disclosure released in sustainability report.

The results obtained in this study could support management in reconsidering the voluntary disclosure released in sustainability report. Indeed, the HC disclosure in companies characterized by an high ownership concentration is often considered as "the transfer" of own competencies to competitors, but not as a factor that can be used to improve the company's image or, more generally, to add value. However, the HC information might be used as a key factor in obtaining a competitive advantage.

The study presents some limitations. So, further work needs to be done in several ways. First, the sample includes only 45 listed companies, hence the results may not be generalized to all Italian firms. In addition, it could be interesting both to examine the HC disclosure provided over a longitudinal period in order to better understand its development, and to compare the characteristics of HC disclosure in sustainability report to HC disclosure released via traditional media, such as the annual report, in order to shed some lights on possible differences or similarities and understand the reasons for that. Finally, it could be interesting to analyze further attributes of disclosure, such as the time orientation (forward-looking or present or past), the nature (quantitative or qualitative) and the type (financial or non-financial) of the HC information disclosed.

**Acknowledgements** The research has been published thanks to the financial support received by the Parthenope University, Naples, entitled "Bando di sostegno alla ricerca individuale per il triennio 2015–2017. Annualità 2016".

# References

1. Cormier, D., Aerts, W., Ledoux, M. J., & Magnan, M. (2009). Attributes of social and human capital disclosure and information asymmetry between managers and investors. *Canadian Journal of Administrative Sciences, 26*(1), 71–88.
2. Van der Meer-Koistra, J., & Zijlstra, S. M. (2001). Reporting on intellectual capital. *Accounting, Auditing & Accountability Journal, 14*(4), 456–476.
3. Beattie, V., & Smith, S. J. (2010). Human capital, value creation and disclosure. *Journal of Human Resource Costing & Accounting., 14*(4), 262–285.
4. Beattie, V., & Thomson, S. J. (2007). Lifting the lid on the use of content analysis to investigate intellectual capital disclosures. *Accounting Forum., 31*(2), 129–163.
5. Petty, R., & Guthrie, J. (2000). Intellectual capital literature review. Measurement, reporting and management. *Journal of Intellectual Capital., 1*(2), 155–176.
6. Chen, H. M., & Lin, K. (2003). The measurement of human capital and its effects on the analysis of financial statements. *International Journal of Management., 20*(4), 470–478.
7. Claver-Cortés, E., Zaragoza-Sáez, P. C., Molina-Manchón, H., & Úbeda-García, M. (2015). Intellectual capital in family firms: Human capital identification and measurement. *Journal of Intellectual Capital., 16*(1), 199–223.
8. Massingham, P., Nguyen, T. N. Q., & Massingham, R. (2011). Using 360 degree peer review to validate self-reporting in human capital measurement. *Journal of Intellectual Capital., 12* (1), 43–74.
9. Cordazzo, M. (2005). IC statement vs environmental and social reports. An empirical analysis of their convergences in the Italian context. *Journal of Intellectual Capital., 6*(3), 441–464.
10. Oliveira, L., Rodrigues, L. L., & Craig, R. (2010). Intellectual capital reporting in sustainability reports. *Journal of Intellectual Capital., 11*(4), 575–594.
11. Cinquini, L., Passetti, E., Tenucci, A., & Frey, M. (2012). Analyzing intellectual capital information in sustainability reports: Some empirical evidence. *Journal of Intellectual Capital., 13*(4), 531–561.
12. Sveiby, K. (1997). *The new organizational wealth. Managing and measuring knowledge-based assets.*. San Francisco: Berret-Koehler Publishers Inc.
13. Brooking, A. (1996). *Intellectual capital. Core asset for the third millennium enterprice.* London: International Thomson Business Press.

14. Edvinsson, L., & Malone, M. S. (1997). *Intellectual capital*. New York: Harper.
15. Kaplan, R. S., Norton, D. P. (1992, January–February) The balanced scorecard. Measures that drive performance. *Harvard Business Review, 70*(1), 71–79.
16. Kaplan, R. S., Norton, D. P. (1996, January–February). Using the balanced scorecard as a strategic management system. *Harvard Business Review, 74*, 75–85.
17. Kaplan, R. S., & Norton, D. P. (2000, September–October). Having trouble with your strategy? Then map it. *Harvard Business Review, 78*(5), 167–176.
18. Asanga Abhayawansa, S. (2014). A review of guidelines and frameworks on external reporting of intellectual capital. *Journal of Intellectual Capital., 15*(1), 100–141.
19. Roslender, R., & Fincham, R. (2004). Intellectual capital: Who counts, controls? *Accounting and the Public Interest, 4*(1), 1–23.
20. De Pablos, P. O. (2002). Evidence of intellectual capital measurement from Asia, Europe, and the Middle East. *Journal of Intellectual Capital., 3*(3), 146–193.
21. Abeysekera, I., & Guthrie, J. (2004). Human capital reporting in a developing nation. *British Accounting Review, 36*(3), 251–268.
22. Abeysekera, I. (2008). Motivations behind human capital disclosure in annual reports. *Accounting Forum., 32*(1), 1–13.
23. Bozzolan, S., Favotto, F., & Ricceri, F. (2003). Italian annual intellectual capital disclosure. An empirical analysis. *Journal of Intellectual Capital., 4*(4), 543–558.
24. Bukh, P. N., Nielsen, C., Gormsen, P., & Mouritsen, J. (2005). Disclosure of information on intellectual capital in Danish IPO prospectuses. *Accounting, Auditing & Accountability Journal, 18*(6), 713–732.
25. Williams, S. M. (2001). Is intellectual capital performance and disclosure practices related? *Journal of Intellectual Capital., 2*(3), 192–203.
26. Garcia-Meca, E., & Martinez, I. (2005). Assessing the quality of disclosure on intangibles in the Spanish capital market. *European Business Review., 17*(4), 305–313.
27. Li, J., Pike, R., & Haniffa, R. (2008). Intellectual capital disclosure and corporate governance structure in UK firms. *Accounting and Business Research., 38*(2), 137–159.
28. Firer, S., & Williams, S. M. (2005). Firm ownership structure and intellectual capital disclosures. *Journal of Accounting Research., 19*(1), 1–18.
29. Oliveira, L., Rodrigues, L. L., & Craig, R. (2006). Firm-specific determinants of intangibles reporting: Evidence from the Portuguese stock market. *Journal of Human Resource Costing & Accounting., 10*(1), 11–33.
30. Cerbioni, F., & Parbonetti, A. (2007). Exploring the effects of corporate governance on intellectual capital disclosure: An analysis of European biotechnology companies. *European Accounting Review., 16*(4), 791–826.
31. Eng, L. L., & Mak, Y. T. (2003). Corporate governance and voluntary disclosure. *Journal of Accounting and Public Policy, 22*(4), 325–345.
32. Brammer, S., & Pavelin, S. (2006). Voluntary environmental disclosures by large UK companies. *Journal of Business Finance & Accounting, 33*(7–8), 1168–1188.
33. Patelli, L., & Prencipe, A. (2007). The relationship between voluntary disclosure and independent directors in the presence of a dominant shareholder. *European Accounting Review., 16*(1), 5–33.
34. Li, H., Wang, Z., & Deng, X.-I. (2008). Ownership, independent directors, agency costs and financial distress: Evidence from Chinese listed companies. *Corporate Governance: The International Journal of Business in Society, 8*(5), 622–636.
35. Raffournier, B. (1995). The determinants of voluntary financial disclosure by Swiss listed companies. *European Accounting Review, 4*(2), 261–280.
36. Cormier, D., Magnan, M., & Van Velthoven, B. (2005). Environmental disclosure quality in large German companies: Economic incentives, public pressures or institutional conditions? *European Accounting Review, 14*(1), 3–39.
37. Dye, R. A. (1986). Proprietary and nonproprietary disclosures. *Journal of Business, 59*(2), 331–366.

38. Verrecchia, R. E. (1983). Discretionary disclosure. *Journal of Accounting and Economics, 5* (3), 179–194.
39. Birt, J. L., Bilson, C. M., Smith, T., & Whaley, R. E. (2006). Ownership, competition, and financial disclosure. *Australian Journal of Management., 31*(2), 235–263.
40. Botosan, C. A., & Stanford, M. (2005). Managers' motives to withhold segment disclosures and the effect of SFAS No. 131 on analysts' information environment. *The Accounting Review, 80*(3), 751–771.
41. Harris, M. S. (1998). The association between competition and managers' business segment reporting decisions. *Journal of Accounting Research, 36*(1), 111–128.
42. Hayes, R. M., & Lundholm, R. (1996). Segment reporting to the capital market in the presence of a competitor. *Journal of Accounting Research, 34*(2), 261–279.
43. Nichols, N. B., & Street, D. L. (2007). The relationship between competition and business segment reporting decisions under the management approach of IAS 14 Revised. *Journal of International Accounting, Auditing and Taxation., 16*(1), 51–68.
44. Pisano, S., & Landriani, L. (2012). The determinants of segment disclosure: An empirical analysis on Italian listed companies. *Financial Reporting., 1,* 113–132.
45. Prencipe, A. (2004). Proprietary costs and determinants of voluntary segment disclosure: Evidence from Italian listed companies. *European Accounting Review, 13*(2), 319–340.
46. Singh, I., & Van der Zahn, J. L. W. M. (2008). Determinants of intellectual capital disclosure in prospectuses of initial public offerings. *Accounting and Business Research., 38*(5), 409–431.
47. Krippendorf, K. (1980). *Content analysis: An introduction to its methodology.* Beverly Hills: Sage Publications.
48. Guthrie, J., Petty, R., Yongvanich, K., & Ricceri, F. (2004). Using content analysis as a research method to inquire into intellectual capital reporting. *Journal of Intellectual Capital., 5*(2), 282–293.
49. Dumay, J., & Cai, L. (2015). Using content analysis as a research methodology for investigating intellectual capital disclosure. *Journal of Intellectual Capital., 16*(1), 121–155.
50. Abhayawansa, S., & Abeysekera, I. (2008). An explanation of human capital disclosure from the resource based perspective. *Journal of Human Resource Costing & Accounting., 12*(1), 51–64.
51. Abeysekera, I., & Guthrie, J. (2005). An empirical investigation of annual reporting trends of intellectual capital in Sri Lanka. *Critical Perspective on Accounting, 16*(3), 151–163.
52. Guthrie, J., & Petty, R. (2000). Intellectual capital: Australian annual reporting practices. *Journal of Intellectual Capital., 1*(3), 241–251.
53. Garcìa-Meca, E. (2005). Bridging the gap between disclosure and use of intellectual capital information. *Journal of Intellectual Capital., 6*(3), 427–440.
54. Bontis, N., & Fitz-enz, J. (2002). Intellectual capital ROI: A causal map of human capital antecedents and consequents. *Journal of Intellectual Capital, 3*(3), 223–247.
55. Roslender, R., Stevenson, J., & Kahn, H. (2006). Employee wellness as intellectual capital: An accounting perspective. *Journal of Human Resource Costing & Accounting., 10*(1), 48–64.
56. Pisano, S., Lepore, L., Alvino, F. (2017). Italian web-based disclosure: A new index to measure the information released on human capital. In: Mancini, D., Castellano, N., Corsi, K., Lamboglia, R. (Eds.), *Reshaping accounting and management control system through digital innovation.* Berlin: Springer.
57. Husin, N. M., Hooper, K., & Olesen, K. (2012). Analysis of intellectual capital disclosure— An illustrative example. *Journal of Intellectual Capital, 13*(2), 196–220.
58. Jensen, M. C., & Meckling, W. H. (1976). Theory of the firm: Managerial behavior, agency costs and ownership structure. *Journal of Financial Economics, 3*(4), 305–360.

# Mapping Financial Performances in Italian ICT-Related Firms via Self-organizing Maps

**Marina Resta⊙, Roberto Garelli⊙ and Renata Paola Dameri⊙**

**Abstract** In this work, we explore the application of machine learning models (MLM) to the analysis of firms' performance. To such aim, we consider a bunch of financial indicators on firms operating in the Information and Communication Technology (ICT) sector, with attention to enterprises providing ICT related-services. The rationale is to highlight the potential of MLM to exploit the complexity of financial data, and to offer a handy way to visualize the related information. In fact, instead of performing classical analysis, we discuss how to apply to those indicators Self-Organizing Maps-SOMs—that are well suited to manage high dimensional and complex datasets to extract their relevant features. It emerges that SOMs are useful in clustering companies depending on multi-dimensional criteria and in analysing hidden relations in companies' performances.

**Keywords** ICT-related firms · Financial performances · Self-organizing maps

## 1 Introduction

Over the past twenty years there has been a flourishing of accountancy papers with focus on the use of machine learning methods [1] to analyze firms' financial data. In particular, the attention of the researchers was directed to test the efficacy of neural classifiers [2] in clustering firms' determinants and exploiting relevant features which might be able to explain the complexity of financial data. Towards this direction, a preeminent role has been played by Kohonen's Self-Organizing

M. Resta (✉) · R. Garelli · R. P. Dameri
University of Genova, Genoa, Italy
e-mail: resta@economia.unige.it

R. Garelli
e-mail: rgarelli@economia.unige.it

R. P. Dameri
e-mail: dameri@economia.unige.it

© Springer International Publishing AG, part of Springer Nature 2018
R. Lamboglia et al. (eds.), *Network, Smart and Open*, Lecture Notes in Information Systems and Organisation 24, https://doi.org/10.1007/978-3-319-62636-9_18

Maps-SOMs [3, 4]. This is a data analysis and visualization technique, of widespread use to mine interesting relations and dependencies among the observed variables, as it creates an ordered representation of high-dimensional data by mapping them into an intuitive two-dimensional (checkerboard-like) space.

Although originally conceived as a technique for patterns recognition in image processing [5], SOM has been widely employed in the accountancy literature, starting from the seminal paper of Serrano-Cinca and Martin del Brio (1993) who employed this methodology for the analysis and representation of financial data and for aid in financial decision-making [2].

From that time on, the efforts of researchers mainly focused on two trails: (a) the use of SOM in search of pathologic patterns to explain either the route of firms towards solvency/bankruptcy or to detect fraudulent financial behaviour; (b) the analysis of SOMs capabilities to manage big financial datasets.

Within the first stream, notable works include the contributions of Kiviluoto [6] who employs a SOM to generate trajectories of firms by way of financial indicators derived from companies' annual financial statements over several years. More recently, SOMs confirmed superior capabilities in bankruptcy prediction for Korean firms [7]; in addition, they have been applied to both financial data and ratios to reduce the dimensionality curse in the financial distress prediction problem [8]. In this light, SOMs exhibited great capabilities to accurately predict business failures [9]. For what is concerning the detection of fraudulent financial behaviours, Kirkos et al. [10], as well as Thiprungsri and Vasarhelyi [11] compared various data mining techniques, and highlighted that SOM is a very effective method to identify counterfeits [10, 11]. Furthermore, Koyuncugil and Ozgulbas [12] applied SOMs to automate fraud filtering during an audit and to develop a financial early warning system for risk prevention [12]. More generally, SOMs can be applied to uncover patterns neglected by common techniques, and to assess the reliability of financial statements [13].

Moving to the second research trail, many papers have been developed, highlighting the suitability of SOM to investigate financial variables [14, 15], and underlying the capability of SOMs to handle the complexity embedded in those data without reducing data multidimensionality [16–19]; moreover, SOMs revealed very effective in grouping firms based on their similarities [20, 21]. Towards this direction, an interesting application of SOM uncovers the differences in financial structures between keiretsu and non-keiretsu firms [22]. Finally, more recently some contributions have dealt with the application of SOM to manage data at micro territorial level, to address policy interventions [23].

Despite this huge apparatus of journal papers and monographs, a limited attention has been devoted to the features mapping for firms that work in emerging sectors, like that of ICT, as defined by OECD: "a combination of manufacturing and services industries that capture, transmit and display data and information electronically" [24]. This is clearly an important issue: as highlighted in [25] ICT has traditionally played a catalyst role in expanding and letting economic opportunities to emerge. To fill in this gap, we selected firms operating on ICT-related areas, with a major focus on those providing services, and we run SOM on a bunch of financial indicators to map these firms depending on their performance profile.

In accordance to what stated on previous rows, the paper is organized as follows. Section 2 describes the data and the methodology in use; Sect. 3 provides results discussion, while Sect. 4 concludes.

## 2 Description of the Sample

The dataset in use has been extracted from the AIDA database[1] and considers firms of the ICT area, providing intangible services. ICT related-service firms are detectable by the coding suggested in the "Osservatorio ICT Piemonte", as stated in [26]. This coding arises by the instances from many sources, with particular attention to:

1. The Italian ATECO codes which in turn follow the indications provided by the OECD.[2]
2. The ASIA (Italian Statistical Business Register) codes.

The ICT related-service companies in Italy are 42,523, spread along 14 ATECO codes (see attachment 1). To the aim of our analysis, we extracted from this huge database a sample of 1809 firms sharing the following requirements:

- The financial statement filed on 31/12/2014.
- A number of employees equal or greater than ten.
- An amount of revenues greater than 1,999,999 Euro.

Although this number is sensitively smaller than the overall number of ICT related-service firms, as outlined in previous rows, they cover approximately 75% of the revenues of the whole sector, and provide employment for 65% of the workers in the sector (see attachment 1). We derived a set of financial indicators featuring firms' performance, whose complete listing and description is provided in Table 1.

For each indicator, Column 1 contains the formula, Column 2 the description, and Column 3 the featuring dimension, that can assume the following meaning. R abbreviates the Italian accounting term "Rigidità" that stresses the weight of various kinds of assets on total assets; CL&SE is the acronym for "Composition of Liabilities and Shareholders' Equity"; P indicates the firms' profitability; finally, Pd identifies productivity-related indexes. As a result, the input for our data mining procedure was a 1809 × 13 matrix, where each row represents a company and each column represents an indicator as listed in Table 1.

---

[1]Analisi Informatizzata delle Aziende Italiane, Bureau Van Dijk, http://www.bvdinfo.com/it-it/home.

[2]http://www.oecd.org/sti/ieconomy/2766494.xls.

**Table 1** Listings and description of the indicators

| Name | Description | Feat. Dim. |
|---|---|---|
| F/K | Fixed assets/total assets | R |
| Fm/K | Tangible fixed assets/total assets | R |
| Fi/K | Intangible fixed assets/total assets | R |
| N/K | Shareholders' equity/total assets (total liabilities and shareholders' equity) | CL&SE |
| Sh/N | Share capital/shareholders' equity | CL&SE |
| N/F | Shareholders' equity/fixed assets | CL&SE |
| C/p | Receivables short term/payables short term | CL&SE |
| ROE | Profit (loss) for the accounting period/shareholders' equity | P |
| ROA | Operating profit (loss)/total assets | P |
| ROS | Operating profit (loss)/revenues | P |
| Rev/K | Revenues/total assets | P |
| VA/Emp | Value added/employees | Pd |
| W/Emp | Wages/employees | Pd |

## 3 The Case Study

### 3.1 Methodological Aspects

We applied the SOM algorithm on the matrix of data described in the previous Sect. 2. SOM is an unsupervised learning algorithm in the family of neural networks, with which high-dimensional input data can be projected into a 2-dimensional space.

The basic ratio is that of ordering a set of neurons, often arranged in a 2-D rectangular or hexagonal grid, to form a discrete topological mapping of the input space that can be therefore interpreted and perceived more easily. Let us indicate by $\mathbf{w_i} \in R^n$ ($i = 1, ..., M$) the weight vector associated to neuron $i$; at the start of the learning, all the weights $\{\mathbf{w_1}, \mathbf{w_2}, ..., \mathbf{w_M}\}$ are initialized to small random numbers. Each input vector $\mathbf{x(t)} \in \mathbf{X}$ is associated to neurons in the map through a synaptic weight connection which from arbitrary values is led to learn or update during the learning process as described in Table 2.

**Table 2** The SOM algorithm at work

Repeat
1 At each step $t$, present an input $\mathbf{x(t)} \in \mathbf{X}$ and select the winner:
$$v(t) = \mathrm{argmin}_i \|\mathbf{x(t)} - \mathbf{w_i(t)}\|$$
2 Update the weights of the winner and its neighbours:
$$\Delta\mathbf{w_i(t)} = \alpha(\mathbf{t})\eta(v, \mathbf{i}, \mathbf{t})(\mathbf{x(t)} - \mathbf{w}_v)$$
**until** the map converges

Here the notation $\|.\|$ indicates the Euclidean distance operator, while $\eta(v, i, t) = \exp\left(\frac{\|-r_v - r_i^2\|}{2\sigma^2}\right)$ is the neighbourhood function, with $\sigma$ representing the effective range of the neighbourhood; finally $\alpha(t)$ is the so called *learning rate*, that is a scalar-valued function, decreasing monotonically, and satisfying: (i) $0 < \alpha(t) < 1$; (ii) $\lim_{t \to +\infty} \alpha(t) = 0$.

## 3.2 Results and Discussion

Running SOM on our data, from the initial 13-dimensional input space we obtained a 2-dimensional mapping which is shown in Fig. 1a together with the corresponding induced clustering provided in Fig. 1b.

The left-hand side plot is the so-called U-Matrix (Unified distance matrix): moving from dark blue to yellow, different color shades identifies closer and more distant nodes according to the Euclidean distance among them. The right-hand side plot shows the induced clustering, obtained by positioning each ICT firm in the map according to the similarity with the SOM nodes.

The mapping identifies five clusters, with lower values concentrated in the first group (CL01) up to increasingly higher values, moving from CL02 to CL05. The groups shown on the map are based on the commonalities among the firms in the sample that can been used as starting point for further analysis.

A straightforward question at this point, for instance, concerns the significance of the employed variables. In other terms: we are arguing whether or not it is possible to state that all the 13 variables contribute to both the final trim of the map and to the clustering. In giving an affirmative answer, we provide the evidence from the ANalysis Of VAriance (ANOVA) test made on both the final map (Table 3) and on the clusters for each variable as factor (Table 4).

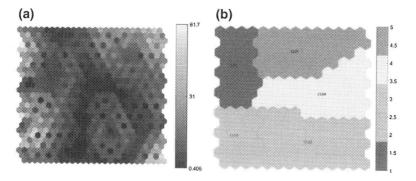

**Fig. 1** From left to right: overall mapping of the ICT-related service firms and induced clusters

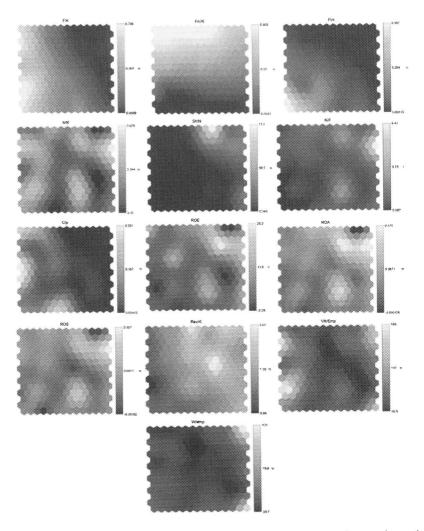

**Fig. 2** Components maps: from top to bottom and from left to right each map shows the organization of the nodes values for each determinant

Here, for what it concerns the final map (U-Matrix) all the variables except than Sh/N, have significantly different means, i.e. only Sh/N cannot be considered relevant for the map definition. A preliminary conclusion is therefore that Sh/N might be as not significant as originally imagined to characterize ICT firms (or at least those in the examined sample). Nevertheless, looking at Table 4, also Sh/N recovers a role in forming the firms' clusters in the map.

Moving to the clusters' composition, provided in Table 5, we can observe that CL01 and CL03 are lower populated than clusters CL02, CL04 and CL05.

**Table 3** ANOVA test on the input variables as determinants of the map

|  | F | $p$-value | Significativity |
|---|---|---|---|
| F/K | 24.679 | 0 | *** |
| Fm/K | 4.771 | 0 | *** |
| Fi/k | 9.472 | 0 | *** |
| N/K | 16.855 | 0 | *** |
| Sh/N | 0.475 | 1 | |
| N/F | 5.924 | 0 | *** |
| C/p | 7.487 | 0 | *** |
| ROE | 2.382 | 0 | *** |
| ROA | 9.265 | 0 | *** |
| ROS | 7.468 | 0 | *** |
| Rev/K | 6.438 | 0 | *** |
| VA/Emp | 31.761 | 0 | *** |
| W/emp | 8.168 | 0 | *** |

*** markes the variables with significantly different means

**Table 4** ANOVA test on the input variables as determinants of the induced clustering

|  | F | $p$-value | Significativity |
|---|---|---|---|
| F/K | 489.181 | 0.00E+00 | *** |
| Fm/K | 46.6 | 0.00E+00 | *** |
| Fi/k | 255.313 | 0.00E+00 | *** |
| N/K | 276.033 | 0.00E+00 | *** |
| Sh/N | 7.571 | 4.78E−06 | *** |
| N/F | 136.811 | 0.00E+00 | *** |
| C/p | 211.437 | 0.00E+00 | *** |
| ROE | 54.673 | 0.00E+00 | *** |
| ROA | 199.078 | 0.00E+00 | *** |
| ROS | 156.598 | 0.00E+00 | *** |
| Rev/K | 85.474 | 0.00E+00 | *** |
| VA/Emp | 99.674 | 0.00E+00 | *** |
| W/emp | 110.885 | 0.00E+00 | *** |

*** markes the variables that consistently participate in the induced clustering process

**Table 5** Clusters' composition

|  | Nr | Perc. (%) |
|---|---|---|
| CL01 | 190 | 10.50 |
| CL02 | 432 | 23.88 |
| CL03 | 238 | 13.16 |
| CL04 | 532 | 29.41 |
| CL05 | 417 | 23.05 |

In order to investigate that difference and, eventually, its financial significance, we turned our attention to the components maps generated by the SOM procedure. An appealing feature of SOM, in fact, is that in addition to the summary map (as the one in Fig. 1a), it makes possible to spread the contribution of each variable by way of component maps which, likewise to the U-Matrix, represent the similarity of nodes (and hence firms) with respect to each determinant, i.e. the indicators listed in Table 1 (Fig. 2).

Being the distribution of colors the same as explained for Fig. 1, here we can capture the (eventual) correlation or anti-correlation of each variable in determining the final clustering. Looking at the maps, for instance, it is possible to capture that Fi/K (Intangible fixed assets/Total assets), Sh/N (Share capital/Shareholders' equity), N/K (Shareholders' equity/Total assets), and, in minor part, ROA (Operating profit (loss)/Total assets), ROS (Operating profit (loss)/Revenues) and W/Emp (Wages/Employees) seem being correlated in creating CL01, as all those variables exhibit lowest value in the left-hand corner of the correspondent map. Similar considerations hold for F/K (Fixed assets/Total assets), Fi/K, N/K, C/p (Receivables short term/Payables short term) and W/Emp in defining CL02; for Fm/K (Tangible fixed assets/Total assets), N/K, ROE (Profit (loss) for the accounting period/Shareholders' equity), ROA and ROS in forming CL03; Fm/K and Rev/K (Revenues/Total assets) for CL04, and finally for Fm/K, N/K, ROE, ROA and ROS to identify CL05.

Moving to the financial analysis of the results, the evidence outlined in the previous rows seems being confirmed. To make an example, the indicators representing the firms' profitability are at the highest level in CL02, and at the lowest in CL03, where we have also the lowest level in N/K. Furthermore, CL02 is characterized by lower significance of indicators belonging to the R dimension (especially for what is concerning intangible assets). On the other hand, CL01 includes firms with both higher values for F/K, N/K and C/p. Notably in this case we also encounter both the higher values on VA/Emp (Value added/Employees) and the lowest on W/Emp, i.e. the indicators in the Pd layer. Finally, CL05 is quite similar on average to CL02 but in this case we observe that the values of ROE and ROA (P featuring dimension) enhanced by the higher levels of Rev/K. Finally, CL04 gathers firms in a quite residual fashion.

SOMs therefore return a clustering of ICT-related service firms thanks to a multi-dimensional analysis simultaneously taking into consideration all the 13 indicators. On the contrary, traditional financial analysis considers each indicator separately. Moreover, components maps permit to individuate which indicators mostly affect the clustering and therefore contribute to profile companies included in each cluster.

## 4 Conclusion

In this paper, we examined a sample of firms working in ICT-related service area by way of Self-Organizing Maps (SOMs). The rationale was to highlight the potential of machine-learning methods to exploit the complexity of financial data, and to offer a handy way to visualize the related information. To this aim we extracted a dataset of 1809 firms with balance sheet filed at 31 December 2014, and complaining with two basic requirements, i.e. having ten or more employees and annual revenues greater than 1,999,999 Euro. We then evaluated thirteen indexes well representing the financial performance of these firms, running SOM on the resulting input matrix. Furthermore, we analysed the clusters emerging from the procedure, trying to interpret the outcomes within a financial light. The SOM discovered five clusters, and we observed that the contribution provided by each determinant in forming them was quite different, with some indexes moving towards the same direction (i.e. exhibiting positive correlation), and other showing anti-correlation.

From the financial viewpoint, the analysis of the induced clusters confirmed this evidence, and highlighted groups having different dominant financial dimensions.

Future works will include the extension of the analysis with SOM to the whole Italian ICT sector and the comparison with those therein discussed.

# Appendix

See Fig. 3.

| ISTAT | Description | Italian Enterprises | | | | Italian M-L enterprises | | | | E/A | F/B | G/C | H/D |
|---|---|---|---|---|---|---|---|---|---|---|---|---|---|
| | | A | B | C | D | E | F | G | H | | | | |
| 5821 | Publishing of computer games | 26 | 6.396 | 8.083 | 48 | 0 | 0 | 0 | 0 | 0,00% | 0,00% | 0,00% | 0,00% |
| 6110 | Wired telecommunications activities | 109 | 1.001.618 | 5.075.159 | 2.025 | 15 | 854.374 | 1.720.570 | 1.906 | 13,76% | 85,30% | 33,90% | 94,12% |
| 6120 | Wireless telecommunications activities | 37 | 2.735.973 | 8.347.144 | 3.301 | 6 | 2.640.651 | 8.253.321 | 3.245 | 16,22% | 96,52% | 98,88% | 98,30% |
| 6130 | Satellite telecommunications activities | 28 | 347.939 | 767.585 | 1.398 | 7 | 339.326 | 754.792 | 1.310 | 25,00% | 97,52% | 98,33% | 93,71% |
| 6190 | Other telecommunications activities | 1.726 | 2.053.819 | 1.476.746 | 6.464 | 69 | 940.339 | 774.571 | 3.829 | 4,00% | 45,78% | 52,45% | 59,24% |
| 6201 | Computer programming activities | 12.994 | 22.075.650 | 24.186.535 | 145.993 | 928 | 18.088.960 | 19.174.767 | 111.890 | 7,14% | 81,94% | 79,28% | 76,64% |
| 6202 | Computer consultancy activities | 4.073 | 2.848.973 | 2.882.596 | 22.043 | 180 | 1.636.773 | 1.562.849 | 13.350 | 4,42% | 57,45% | 54,22% | 60,56% |
| 6203 | Computer facilities management activities | 111 | 116.260 | 129.545 | 538 | 6 | 27.334 | 40.251 | 301 | 5,41% | 23,51% | 31,07% | 55,95% |
| 6209 | Other information techn. and computer service act. | 3.790 | 6.107.016 | 5.829.744 | 31.718 | 190 | 5.093.546 | 4.487.463 | 22.920 | 5,01% | 83,40% | 76,98% | 72,26% |
| 6311 | Data processing, hosting and related activities | 17.082 | 6.862.874 | 11.123.748 | 66.347 | 307 | 3.780.266 | 4.626.487 | 24.711 | 1,80% | 55,08% | 41,59% | 37,25% |
| 6312 | Web portals | 949 | 390.377 | 546.133 | 1.465 | 11 | 302.871 | 373.470 | 742 | 1,16% | 77,58% | 68,38% | 50,65% |
| 9511 | Repair of computers and peripheral equipment | 1.204 | 916.302 | 787.230 | 6.006 | 64 | 529.083 | 437.691 | 3.169 | 5,32% | 57,74% | 55,60% | 52,76% |
| 9512 | Repair of communication equipment | 278 | 259.541 | 246.401 | 2.149 | 20 | 188.827 | 143.158 | 1.462 | 7,19% | 72,75% | 58,10% | 68,03% |
| 9521 | Repair of consumer electronics | 116 | 71.833 | 59.612 | 457 | 6 | 30.398 | 18.321 | 153 | 5,17% | 42,32% | 30,73% | 33,48% |
| | Total | 42.523 | 45.794.570 | 61.466.262 | 289.952 | 1.809 | 34.452.746 | 42.367.711 | 188.988 | 4,25% | 75,23% | 68,93% | 65,18% |

A = Number of enterprises providing ICT related services    E = Number of enterprises providing ICT related services (with defined characteristics)

B = Total revenues                                    F = Total revenues

C = Totale asset                                       G = Totale asset

D = Number of employees                         H = Number of employees

**Fig. 3** Situation of ICT related-services Italian firms, from an authors' proprietary elaboration

# References

1. Mitchell, T. (1997). *Machine learning*. NY: McGraw Hill.
2. Martín-del-Brío, B., & Serrano-Cinca, C. (1993). Self-organizing neural networks for the analysis and representation of data: Some financial cases. *Neural Computing and Applications, 1*(3), 193–206.
3. Kohonen, T. (1982). Self-organized formation of topologically correct feature maps. *Biological Cybernetics, 43,* 59–69.
4. Kohonen, T. (1997). *Self-organizing maps* (2nd ed.). Berlin: Springer.
5. Amerijckx, C., Verleysen, M., Thissen, P., & Legat, J. D. (1998). Image Compression by self-organized Kohonen Map. *IEEE Transactions on Neural Networks, 9*(3), 503–507.
6. Kiviluoto, K. (1998). Two-level self-organizing maps for analysis of financial statements. In *Neural Networks Proceedings, 1998. IEEE World Congress on Computational Intelligence* (Vol. 1).
7. Lee, K., Booth, D., & Alam, P. (2005). A comparison of supervised and unsupervised neural networks in predicting bankruptcy of Korean firms. *Expert Systems with Applications, 29*(1), 1–16.
8. Alfaro-Cid, E., Mora, A. M., Merelo, J. J., Esparcia-Alcázar, A. I., & Sharman, K. (2009). Finding relevant variables in a financial distress prediction problem using genetic programming and self-organizing maps. In *Natural computing in computational finance* (pp. 31–49). Berlin: Springer.
9. Tsai, C. F. (2014). Combining cluster analysis with classifier ensembles to predict financial distress. *Information Fusion, 16,* 46–58.
10. Kirkos, E., Spathis, C., & Manolopoulos, Y. (2007). Data mining techniques for the detection of fraudulent financial statements. *Expert Systems with Applications, 32*(4), 995–1003.
11. Thiprungsri, S., & Vasarhelyi, M. A. (2011). Cluster analysis for anomaly detection in accounting data: An audit approach. *The International Journal of Digital Accounting Research, 11*(17), 69–84.
12. Koyuncugil, A. S., & Ozgulbas, N. (2012). Financial early warning system model and data mining application for risk detection. *Expert Systems with Applications, 39*(6), 6238–6253.
13. Huang, S. Y., Tsaih, R. H., & Lin, W. Y. (2012). Unsupervised neural networks approach for understanding fraudulent financial reporting. *Industrial Management & Data Systems, 112*(2), 224–244.
14. Schreck, T., Tekušová, T., Kohlhammer, J., & Fellner, D. (2007). Trajectory-based visual analysis of large financial time series data. *ACM SIGKDD Explorations Newsletter, 9*(2), 30–37.
15. Budayan, C., Dikmen, I., & Birgonul, M. T. (2009). Comparing the performance of traditional cluster analysis, self-organizing maps and fuzzy C-means method for strategic grouping. *Expert Systems with Applications, 36*(9), 11772–11781.
16. Back, B., Sere, K., & Vanharanta, H. (1998). Managing complexity in large data bases using self-organizing maps. *Accounting, Management and Information Technologies, 8*(4), 191–210.
17. Back, B., Toivonen, J., Vanharanta, H., & Visa, A. (2001). Comparing numerical data and text information from annual reports using self-organizing maps. *International Journal of Accounting Information Systems, 2*(4), 249–269.
18. Back, B., Irjala, M., Sere, K., & Vanharanta, H. (1998). Competitive financial benchmarking using self-organizing Maps. In M. A. Vasarhelyi & A. Kogan (Eds.), *Artificial intelligence in accounting and auditing: Towards new paradigms. Rutgers series in acccounting information systems* (pp. 69–81).
19. Eklund, T., Back, B., Vanharanta, H., & Visa, A. (2003). *Financial benchmarking using self-organizing maps studying the international pulp and paper industry. Data mining: Opportunities and challenges.* Hershey: IGI Global.

20. Di Tollo, G., Tanev, S., & Ma, Z. (2012). Neural networks to model the innovativeness perception of co-creative firms. *Expert Systems with Applications, 39*(16), 12719–12726.
21. Haga, J., Siekkinen, J., & Sundvik, D. (2015). Initial stage clustering when estimating accounting quality measures with self-organizing maps. *Expert Systems with Applications, 42* (21), 8327–8336.
22. Cheh, J. C., Lapshin, E. A., & Kim, I.-W. (2006). An application of self-organizing maps to financial structure analysis of Keiretsu versus non-Keiretsu firms in Japan. *Review of Pacific Basin Financial Markets and Policies, 09,* 405.
23. Resta, M. (2016). *Computational intelligence paradigms in economic and financial decision making.* Berlin: Springer International Publishing.
24. OECD. (2002). *Measuring the information economy.* Paris: OECD Publishing.
25. Kramer, W. J., Jenkins, B., & Katz, R. S. (2007). *The role of information and communications technology sector in expanding economic opportunity. Harvard economic opportunity series* (Vol. 22).
26. Osservatorio ICT Piemonte. (2007). Proposta di aggiornamento della definizione del settore ICT secondo la nomenclatura Ateco.

# The Impact of Business Intelligence Systems on Management Accounting Systems: The Consultant's Perspective

Andrea Nespeca and Maria Serena Chiucchi

**Abstract** The use of Business Intelligence (BI) and Business Analytics for supporting decision-making is widespread in the world of praxis and their relevance for Management Accounting (MA) has been outlined in non-academic literature. Nonetheless, current research on Business Intelligence systems' implications for the Management Accounting System is still limited. The purpose of this study is to contribute to understanding how BI system implementation and use affect MA techniques and Management Accountants' role. An explorative field study, which involved BI consultants from Italian consulting companies, was carried out. We used the qualitative field study method since it permits dealing with complex "how" questions and, at the same time, taking into consideration multiple sites thus offering a comprehensive picture of the phenomenon. We found that BI implementation can affect Management Accountants' expertise and can bring about not only incremental changes in existing Management Accounting techniques but also more relevant ones, by supporting the introduction of new and advanced MA techniques. By identifying changes in the Management Accounting System as well as factors which can prevent or favor a virtuous relationship between BI and Management Accounting Systems this research can be useful both for consultants and for client-companies in effectively managing BI projects.

**Keywords** Business intelligence · Management accounting · Field study
Management accountants · Consultants

A. Nespeca (✉) · M. S. Chiucchi
Università Politecnica delle Marche, Ancona, Italy
e-mail: a.nespeca@pm.univpm.it

M. S. Chiucchi
e-mail: m.s.chiucchi@univpm.it

# 1   Introduction

"Management Accounting (MA) is the process of identification, measurement, accumulation, analysis, preparation, interpretation, and communication of information that assists executives in fulfilling organizational objectives" [17]. In order to perform these activities the Management Accounting System (MAS) requires the contribution of the Information System which consists of "an integrated set of computer-based components" [13] involved in collecting, processing, storing, and disseminating information for decision making and control purposes [19].

Over the years, scholars have studied the relationship between the MAS and different kinds of Information Systems. Early studies aimed to unveil changes in the MAS due to legacy systems and ERP systems [4, 14, 26, 30] while, more recently, the academic interest has been directed toward analysis-oriented information systems, such as Business Intelligence (BI) systems and Big Data analytics, which are becoming more relevant due to companies' growing need for analysis of both structured and unstructured data. In order to contribute to the knowledge on the impact of BI systems on the Management Accounting System this research adopts a field study approach to explore possible changes in Management Accounting techniques and in the role of Management Accountants which can be fostered by BI implementation and use.

From a theoretical perspective, this study identifies those techniques which are influenced by the implementation of BI systems, unveils the nature of this influence, and sheds light on changes in Management Accountants' expertise due to the implementation of BI systems. Additionally, this study improves the knowledge about the process through which Information Systems affect the MAS by highlighting factors which can play a role in this process, either as reinforcements or obstacles to the impact of BI systems on the MAS.

Moreover, from a practical point of view, this study provides useful findings both for consultants and for client-companies involved in BI implementation projects by disclosing factors that should be exploited (levers) or prevented (barriers) in order to allow BI systems to produce changes in the MAS. Furthermore, this study can support management accountants who are looking for an improvement in the MAS of their companies by showing the contribution that a BI system can offer to different MA techniques.

# 2   Literature Review

Management Accounting Systems support managerial decisions by gathering raw data, processing, analyzing, and transforming it into information and then delivering the information to managers. In data gathering, storing, and analysis and in information communication MA is supported by the Integrated Information System (IIS).

The IIS can be defined as a "system of systems" [27] since it includes both ERP systems and analysis-oriented information systems, like the BI system. Despite ERP systems providing "a platform for accounting and control information to flow" [12], they are more concerned with transaction processing [3]. Moreover, according to Booth et al. [1], their role in supporting MA analysis for decision making is limited. Differently, Business Intelligence systems are specifically designed to provide "complex and competitive information to planners and decision makers" [22] and are perceived as an innovation in Management Accounting Systems [11].

Researchers have studied the relationship between the MASs and ERPs mainly exploring how ERPs impact on MA techniques and Management Accountants' role [4, 7, 14, 26, 30]. More in detail, researchers have identified changes in Management Accounting tools which existed before implementing ERPs and that can be considered "incremental" [7], and they have highlighted how ERPs help Management Accountants to develop new competences [4, 14].

Similarly, the research on the impact of analysis-oriented information systems on the MAS has focused mainly on changes in MA techniques fostered by BI systems [27, 31, 34]. BI systems are analysis-oriented information systems resulting from the combination of three elements [33]:

- The process for collecting, analyzing, and disseminating information from internal and external sources [21].
- The set of tools, technologies, and software products used in the abovementioned process [23].
- The knowledge, which represents the product of the process of data collection and analysis, and is embedded in the information disseminated inside the companies [33].

Regarding BI systems, they seem to be the "primary enablers of change in reporting and analysis, budgeting, non-financial, external and ad hoc management accounting and allocation of costs" [27] even if the nature of these changes has not been highlighted. Moreover Candiotto and Gandini [5] have suggested that the application of BI systems to existing Balanced Scorecards can improve the strategic management process and many authors have observed that BI systems can support the design, the calculation process, the analysis, and the visualization of the indicators of a Performance Measurement System [3, 6].

Researchers have also reflected on the potentialities of an advanced approach to Business Intelligence [9, 10], i.e. Business Analytics, in unveiling and verifying causal relationships in Performance Measurement Systems (PMSs) [31, 34]. Specifically, Business Analytics are considered a possible solution to the limited implementation and controversial effectiveness of PMSs. By identifying and proving causal relations among context factors, inputs, processes, outputs, and outcomes of PMSs [31, 34], Business Analytics could improve their effectiveness and consequently ensure a widespread adoption of PMSs in the world of praxis. However, no empirical evidence of such a positive effect for PMSs has been provided up to now.

Additionally, aspects related to MA techniques and Management Accountants' roles have been identified in non-academic studies on BI systems. In highlighting Business Intelligence "capabilities", Gartner analysts have considered reporting, predictive modelling and performance measurement as essential "capabilities" for BI solutions [29]. In this perspective, Management Accounting techniques such as reports, scorecards, and predictive analytics have been considered BI tools [32]. Concerning the relationship between BI and Management Accountants, it has been suggested that BI systems can change the traditional role of Management Accountants into a business partner role and release Management Accountants from preparing budgets, consolidations, forecasts, and reports [8].

To conclude, our current understanding of the impact of BI systems on Management Accounting is still limited [15]. The literature review carried out has shown that although it has been acknowledged that BI systems do influence MA techniques [27], "how" MA techniques change as a consequence of BI implementation and use is still an area open to research. Furthermore, while Business Analytics are believed to transform the Management Accountant's role [2] and to shift it towards a business partner role [16], no empirical evidence of such a change has been provided.

In order to fill these gaps and to contribute to the literature on BI system implications for Management Accounting, we asked: "How do Business Intelligence systems affect Management Accounting techniques and the Management Accountant's role?".

## 3   Design of the Study

In order to answer this research question, we conducted an explorative field study [14, 20, 28] involving consulting companies which had developed BI implementation projects in Italian companies.

Drawing from Lillis and Mundy [20], by field study method we mean a qualitative research method that involves "limited-depth studies conducted at a non-random selection of field sites, thus lying somewhere between in-depth cases and broad-based surveys" [20]. The field study method is suitable to deal with complex "how" questions and to offer a "wide and comprehensive picture of the phenomenon" [14]. More specifically, by including multiple research sites as a means for identifying patterns in the observations [20], it allows researchers to gather insights on a phenomenon of interest and on its present extension [28]. Moreover, this method is less structured in data collection than surveys and involves shorter, less intensive data collection on site than in-depth case studies [20].

Considering that our aim was to provide a wide and comprehensive picture of changes in MA due to BI systems and not an in-depth analysis of such changes, the field study allowed us to investigate a larger number of units of study than multiple case studies [20]. We chose not to conduct intensive case research focused on one or on a limited number of companies on the grounds that "it may not capture the range of such perceptions and insights" [28].

We also considered the survey method to provide a general understanding of the impact of BI systems on Management Accounting Systems; nonetheless, we decided not to adopt this method: the scarcity of prior research did not allow us to develop a questionnaire in specific terms to guide empirical enquiry [14].

This study is based on the evidence collected from twelve Italian consulting companies specialized in BI implementation projects. We chose to focus on consultants rather than on client companies because of their experience in several BI implementation projects. Since consulting companies implement BI systems in several companies, they could have witnessed different reactions and impacts of BI systems on Management Accounting Systems.

Consulting companies were selected using purposeful sampling [24]. Starting from "Gartner BI magic quadrant 2015"[1] we focused on BI vendors which were positioned in the "leaders" section: Sap, Sas, Oracle, IBM, Microstrategy, Microsoft BI, Qlik, Tableau, and Information Builders. We considered leading vendors because they were top performers in the Business Intelligence market. Therefore, we assumed that their solutions were the most widespread and that the BI consultants who implemented leading solutions probably managed a high number of implementation projects.

It is worth highlighting that in our study, BI vendors' solutions did not represent the units of analysis. Specifically, we focused our attention on leading vendors in order to select specific consulting companies to be contacted for participation in our research. In this regard our study is different from those that consider leading vendors as a starting point for comparing BI analytics tools (from different vendors). For instance, Sherman [32] adopted this starting point to suggest which BI analytics tools suit specific companies' "use cases".

From a methodological point of view, through leading vendors' websites we identified BI consulting partners in order to build a sample of consulting companies officially recognized as BI implementation experts. It is worth underling that for one of these leading vendors, Tableau, it was not possible to identify any consulting partners since Tableau's website did not disclose information on them.

Considering the overlapping cases, 109 companies were identified and were contacted via mail. Out of the 109 identified organizations, ten participated in the research; eleven declined to participate, while eight companies declared that they were involved in mergers and acquisitions, so they could not contribute to the study, or the companies either no longer existed or could not be found on the Web. The remaining 79 companies did not answer. Out of the ten companies that accepted to take part in the research, two were Oracle partners, two were Sap partners, four were Sas partners, one was a Qlik partner, and one was a

---

[1]Gartner Magic Quadrant for BI and Analytics Platform provides an overview of the relative positions of BI vendors. BI vendors' position in the table depends on their capability to execute their stated visions and to perform against Gartner's market view. According to Gartner, four types of technology providers are identified: leaders, visionaries, niche players, and challengers.

Microsoft BI partner. Therefore, the consulting partners of some of the leading BI vendors were missing. In order to consider at least one consulting company for each BI leading vendor, the results of the desk research were integrated with four additional consulting companies suggested by some informed Italian scholars and consultants operating in the fields of Management Accounting and Business Intelligence. We considered these additional consulting companies because, although they were not recognized as official consulting partners by leading BI vendors, they actually implement BI solutions developed by leading vendors.

These additional four consulting companies were asked to take part in the research and two of them accepted. Nonetheless, it was not possible to identify consulting partners for IBM, Microstrategy, or Information Builders. In the end, a total of twelve consulting companies participated in the field study.

We used the semi-structured interview to gather data [18, 25] because it allows the interviewer to ask for clarification and to carry out in-depth exploration of emergent issues [35]. In this study, consultants that managed BI implementation projects were interviewed via Skype, by telephone, and also face-to-face. Interviews were conducted in the early months of 2016 and lasted approximately 60 min each. They were tape-recorded and then transcribed for analysis. Respondents were interviewed on the organization of BI implementation projects, on the reasons why companies implement BI solutions, on the changes in MA techniques and Management Accountants' roles which occurred as a consequence of BI implementation, on the factors that may have favored or hindered the abovementioned changes, and on the effects produced on the MAS by BI systems.

Post-communications with the respondents helped the authors to ensure the accuracy of the collected data.

# 4 Findings

The interviewees were asked to give information about some preliminary issues concerning the number of BI implementation projects they had managed in their experiences as consultants, the size of their client companies, the sector they belong to, and aspects concerning the organization of BI projects in client companies.

In Table 1 the number of BI implementation projects managed by each consulting company is shown: most of the companies managed from 20 to 100 projects while some of them (B, E, and F) worked on fewer than 20 projects. This happened when the interviewed consulting company was a start-up or had only recently developed a business unit for carrying out BI projects.

Every interviewee claimed to have managed from a minimum of 10 to a maximum of 100 BI projects and all together, the consultants had an overall experience of more than 300 projects.

Moreover, 75% of the consultants provided information about the size and the sector of client companies. The interviewees stated that companies that had

| Consulting company | Number of BI projects |
|---|---|
| A | 40 |
| B | 7 |
| C | 30 |
| D | 20 |
| E | 10 |
| F | 15 |
| G | 21 |
| H | Several dozens |
| I | 20 |
| L | N.a. |
| M | More than 100 |
| N | 40 |

**Table 1** Number of BI projects managed

undertaken a BI project were medium-large organizations which operated predominantly in the energy, telecommunication, banking, and insurance sectors.

As far as the organization of BI implementation projects is concerned, the consultants were asked to provide information about people in client companies who played the roles of the promoter and the sponsor and about the composition of the team in charge of the BI project. Moreover, they were asked to explain what role that management accountants had in the above-mentioned projects.

We defined the promoter as the person who decides to implement BI systems in order to support his/her decision-making process and/or activity. In this regard, line managers were identified as promoters by 75% of the consultants even if this role was also played by top managers and by people from the IT area or from the areas which are directly supported by the BI system. Line managers promoting BI projects mainly belonged to the sales and marketing area, the management accounting area, or the IT area.

As for the sponsor, he/she supports and legitimizes the BI project in the client companies. According to the majority of the consultants, this role was played by people holding managerial positions of which most were top managers. Only consultants from companies B and D provided further details on this point: both of them took part in projects in which the sponsor was the client company's CEO or CFO.

In order to manage BI implementation projects, client companies tended to create dedicated teams, as observed by 75% of the interviewed consultants. These teams were mainly composed of the promoters and professionals from the IT area.

Finally, in the preliminary phase of the interviews, the consultants were asked to describe the role that management accountants had in BI implementation projects. According to 75% of the consultants, management accountants took part in BI implementation projects and in many cases they played a role as promoters. One of the reasons why management accountants promoted the introduction of BI systems was due to the limitations of existing management accounting techniques, as underlined by the consultant from company E: "*they need specific information which cannot be provided by existing management accounting tools*". In contrast, the remaining consultants explicitly declared that management accountants did not take part in the projects and some of the interviewees did not provide any answer to this question.

The structure of the remainder of this section is as follows: Sect. 4.1 presents the reasons why companies implement BI systems, focusing on those which are related to Management Accounting. Section 4.2 describes changes in Management Accounting Systems due to the implementation and use of BI systems. Section 4.3 illustrates the levers and barriers which can respectively favor or hinder the changes in the MAS due to the BI. Finally, Sect. 4.4 discusses the effects that the implementation and use of the BI produce on the MAS.

## *4.1   Reasons to Implement BI Systems*

Several reasons drove companies to implement a BI system. Here we comment only on those that seem to be related to Management Accounting. According to the interviewees, client companies had implemented BI systems in order to achieve an improvement in information timeliness and information reliability. Concerning information timeliness, BI systems were implemented by companies "*to have information when it is necessary and not after a long time*", as suggested by the consultant from company E, or so that decision makers could "*take decisions at the right moment*" (consultant from company C). Regarding the need to improve reliability, it can be due to the fact that, without BI systems, data could be manipulated by data owners, as one consultant highlighted: "*I mean, the old way of preparing reports involved individuals who actually produce reports have the possibility to rig reporting contents*".

Other reasons related to MA, referred to information gathering and analysis, were outlined by consultants from companies E and G, who suggested that BI systems were implemented in companies to perform analysis on new dimensions or to enrich the stock of information provided by the existing information system: "*the Management Accounting people needed certain information and the tools they got were not able to produce this information or to provide a satisfactory level of detail*".

Additionally, three consultants reported that BI systems were implemented to support cost accounting practices on new cost objects. As argued by the consultant from company G, "*these [BI] tools were used to accurately account for costs and revenues with the possibility of allocating them to cost objects such as the bus line, which is a cost object in public transport, in order to understand which lines result in a profit and which ones result in a loss*".

## 4.2  Changes in Management Accounting Systems

In this section changes in Management Accounting techniques and the Management Accountant's role are analyzed.

It is worth highlighting that not all consultants observed changes in MA. A few of them (17%) declared that their experience with BI projects to support the controlling function was limited and consequently, they could not properly answer this part of the interview.

Concerning MA techniques, the consultants observed how the implementation and use of BI systems had an impact on existing MA techniques and how it fostered innovation in the companies' MAS by introducing advanced MA techniques. Specifically, changes in existing MA techniques were observed in reporting and budgeting practices while, if we consider advanced MA techniques, the Performance Measurement System was the most common technique introduced thanks to the implementation of the BI system.

Regarding managerial reporting, BI systems had an impact on the reporting content by introducing new dimensions of analysis and enriching information. As suggested by the consultant from company G, the reporting content became flexible since it could be customized according to specific decision makers' needs: "*before, the report was very static, I mean, it could be prepared in just one way. Now we play with some dimensions and we realize the great benefit of playing with these dimensions*".

Budgeting was also influenced by the implementation and use of BI systems. Most of the consultants who noticed changes in budgeting practices stated that BI systems could provide IT support for each phase of the budgeting process. As one consultant explained: "*when we talk about Business Analytics we mean not only to provide [IT] tools, but also to provide applications for preparing, managing, and monitoring budgets*". Worthy of note is the fact that BI systems required the implementation of a workflow to support the budgeting process. In this way, the latter became structured, rationally organized, and consequently faster than before. As reported by the consultant from company E, BI systems allowed client companies "*to prepare a raw version of budgets by loading actual data, adopting a rough formula to modify them by adding 20%, for example, and finally, distributing all these data sheets to agents. Then, the data sheets are gathered and consolidated. And all this process is managed via web. Before, we sent excel files via mail, excel files came back [...] Moreover, concerning the process of budget revision, once it was quite approximate but now it can be managed in a structured way. Therefore, all the process of budget creation was surely made faster and more rational*". Nonetheless, the illustrated change did not necessarily occur and the logic underlying the budgeting process may have not been modified, as reported by the consultant from company H: "*this tool [BI] is useful to centralize information and to provide a front end to access data but the logics at the base of the [budgeting] process are not modified*".

The consultants highlighted also the relationship between BI systems and PMSs. More specifically, the BI implementation seemed to precede the introduction of the Balanced Scorecard (BSC), which was considered a sort of evolution of the BI system itself. In this regard, the consultant from company B noticed that: "*generally, when we [consultants and clients] decide to implement the BSC, the BI system already exists. Therefore we seek an evolution; we want to raise the bar*". BI systems enabled companies to take real time data from the information system to measure indicators "*in an automatic or semi-automatic way*". More in detail, the automatic calculation of indicators made it possible to get a dynamic BSC which was frequently updated with fresh data, as reported by one consultant: "*consulting companies promoted this kind of projects [BSC implementation] but they had great trouble making them work because several of them are not manageable without the software. The Balanced Scorecard cannot work without data. Moreover, it cannot be a photograph, it should be prepared everyday [...] real time data should be gathered and used to do frequent analysis and to do tests*".

According to the consultants, the Management Accountants' roles also changed as a consequence of the BI system implementations. In particular, the interviewees observed that the implementation of BI systems allowed Management Accountants to reduce the time spent in routine activities, such as data gathering or preparing reports, and consequently, this allowed them to devote more time to performing analysis. As one consultant reported, "*...what changes is the allocation of time among activities. More time is allocated to data analysis than to data control because most of the data control is performed by the system*".

Moreover, the consultants explained how the implementation of BI systems pushed Management Accountants to improve their knowledge on the company business. Nonetheless, it is worth highlighting that one consultant observed that the enhancement of those Management Accountants' competences which were referred to company business occurred (only) when the management accountant was the promoter of the project.

## 4.3   Levers and Barriers to Changes in Management Accounting Systems

The consultants were also asked to identify the factors that favor or hinder the changes in the MAS. In this regard, it is worth underlining that over a third of the consultants did not answer the questions about levers and barriers to changes in the MAS nor did they report the factors which were related to the implementation of the BI in the company rather than to the changes in the MAS.

According to the consultants, a strong top management sponsorship of BI implementation projects and the need to manage a high volume of data were relevant factors in favoring changes in the MAS. Specifically, top manager sponsorship was indicated as a lever to changes in the MAS by most of the consultants.

Concerning the barriers to changes in the MAS, the fact that individuals who gathered data were "jealous" of their data was considered by most of consultants to be a factor that hindered the changes in the MAS. More specifically, individuals considered themselves "data owners" and therefore, they were reluctant to share data, as noted by the consultant from company E: "*sometimes there is the problem of jealousy, I mean, the feeling that the data is mine and I want to control it before it is delivered to others*". Other barriers identified were the fact that the users of BI systems did not easily understand what the benefits produced by the BI were and that people from the IT department could show resistance to the implementation of BI systems.

## 4.4 Effects on Management Accounting Systems

In order to unveil any other possible effects of BI on MA systems, besides asking specific questions on changes in the MA techniques and in the Management Accountant's role, the consultants were asked whether they had noticed any positive and/or negative effects on the MAS and if so, what kind of effects they had observed.

A large number of consultants (75%) reported that the MAS took advantage of BI systems. Specifically, BI positively affected the quality and timeliness of information by improving the level of detail in data analysis, reducing errors, and improving timeliness in the processes of data gathering, data processing and information reporting. Moreover, the interviewees also highlighted another positive effect produced by BI systems on the MAS, i.e., the fact that, thanks to BI systems, the data was no longer ambiguous and was no longer owned by individuals from different areas. In this regard, one consultant observed that "*data has become a company asset. It is no longer necessary to ask for data from different areas since the data gathering process is automatic*".

Lastly, while half of the interviewed consultants declared that they had not observed any negative effects on the MAS, the rest either remained silent on this aspect or identified factors which were negative for the company as a whole, so they were not related to the MAS. However, it is important to observe that consultants are official suppliers of this kind of IT solution and therefore, their point of view in this regard may have been influenced by their role, as suggested by one of them: "*I actually cannot identify any negative effects, but maybe I am not impartial because I produce BI systems and I sell them*".

## 5    Discussion and Conclusions

In this paper we have explored how Business Intelligence systems affect Management Accounting techniques and the Management Accountant's role. To address this research question, we conducted a field research involving Italian BI consulting companies.

Our research contributes to the literature on the impact of BI systems on Management Accounting [15] in several ways. More in detail, this study improves the understanding of the influence of BI systems on MA techniques and contributes to filling the gap concerning the impact that BI systems have on the Management Accountant's role. Finally, this study provides insights on the process through which BI systems affect the MAS by highlighting factors that can favor or hinder changes in MA techniques due to BI system implementation.

Concerning the influence of BI systems on existing MA techniques, first, our study confirms the role that BI systems play in fostering changes in budgeting and reporting practices [27]; second, our research contributes to explaining how these techniques change. More specifically, as far as the budgeting process is concerned, while its underlying logics do not seem to change, the introduction of workflows (driven by the BI) makes the process more structured, more rational, and faster. With reference to changes in the reporting practices, our evidence shows how the BI can affect the reporting content. By implementing BI systems, reports can be customized according to decision makers' needs and can be enriched with new dimensions of analysis. The observed changes can be considered "incremental" since they represent an improvement in existing MA techniques but not a shift in the underlying logics of the MAS.

Additionally, our findings make a contribution by providing empirical evidence on the role that BI systems have in improving the strategic management process [5]. More specifically, BI systems foster the implementation of an advanced MA tool, i.e., the Balanced Scorecard. Even if we cannot conclude that this radical change is brought about exclusively by the BI implementation, we can argue that, by favoring the introduction of this kind of MA technique, BI can contribute to changing companies' MA logics, which become more strategically oriented.

Furthermore this study sheds light also on how BI systems contribute to the calculation process of PMS indicators. First, by getting real time data, BI systems affect the quality of data used in the calculation process; second, by allowing companies to calculate indicators in an automatic way and updating data contained in the Balanced Scorecard, BI systems affect the way the calculation process is carried out.

As far as Management Accountants are concerned, in the literature it has been highlighted that BI systems can affect the Management Accountant's role [2, 8, 16]. In this regard, our study provides empirical evidence on how this transformation can occur. More in depth, by developing business-oriented competences and devoting more time to business analysis, Management Accountants can carry out more "value-added" activities and their role shifts towards that of a "business partner".

Our evidence suggests that these changes cannot occur without a strong top management sponsorship of BI implementation projects and that, conversely, the reluctance of individuals to share "their" data is a factor that prevents modifications in the MAS. While top management sponsorship and the reluctance of people to share their knowledge/information have been amply studied in managerial literature, here we show how these factors are, respectively, the most relevant lever and barrier in the process through which BI deploys its potentialities for MA development.

Additionally, our results suggest that the overall effect of BI systems on the MAS is positive. More specifically, improvements in information quality and timeliness were pointed out by the interviewed consultants as positive effects on the MAS while, on the contrary, no negative effects were identified. However, it is important to underline that the interviewed consultants were official suppliers of BI solutions and that, therefore, their point of view and their silence in this regard may be influenced by their role.

In conclusion, it is necessary to highlight the major limitations of this paper. Our research was focused only on the consultants' perspective and the analysis was limited to the Italian context. In order to overcome these limitations in the future it could be interesting to explore client companies' perspectives. Moreover, a similar analysis can be carried out in different countries in order to identify possible cross-country patterns.

# References

1. Booth, P., Matolcsy, Z., & Weider, B. (2000). The impacts of enterprise resource planning systems on accounting practice—The Australian experience. *Australian Accounting Review, 10,* 4–18. https://doi.org/10.1111/j.1835-2561.2000.tb00066.x.
2. Brands, K., & Holtzblatt, M. (2015). Business analytics: Transforming the role of management accountants. *Management Accounting Quarterly, 16,* 1–12.
3. Brignall, S., & Ballantine, J. (2004). Strategic enterprise management systems: New directions for research. *Management Accounting Research, 15,* 225–240. https://doi.org/10.1016/j.mar.2003.10.003.
4. Caglio, A. (2003). Enterprise resource planning systems and accountants: Towards hybridization? *European Accounting Review, 12,* 123–153. https://doi.org/10.1080/0963818031000087853.
5. Candiotto, R., Gandini, S. (2013). Strategic enterprise management in the taps and fittings sector: Application of the balanced scorecard methodology to business intelligence systems. In D. Mancini, E. D. J. Vaassen, & R. P. Dameri (Eds.), *Accounting information systems for decision making. LNISO* (Vol. 3, pp. 175–183). Berlin: Springer. https://doi.org/10.1007/978-3-642-35761-9_1.
6. Chen, H., Ciang, R. H. L., & Storey, V. C. (2012). Business intelligence and analytics from big data to big impact. *MIS Quarterly, 36,* 1165–1188.
7. Chiucchi, M. S., Gatti, M., Marasca, S. (2012). The relationship between management accounting systems and ERP systems in a medium-sized firm: A bidirectional perspective. *Management Control, 3,* 39–60 (2012). https://doi.org/10.3280/MACO2013-SU3003.

8. CIMA. (2008). Improving decision making in organizations: Unlocking business intelligence, executive report.
9. Davenport, T. H., & Harris, J. G. (2007). *Competing on analytics: The new science of winning*. Boston: Harvard Business School Press.
10. Davenport, T. H. (2014). *Big data @ work: Dispelling the myths, uncovering the opportunities*. Boston: Harvard Business Review Press.
11. Elbashir, M. Z., Collier, P. A., & Sutton, S. G. (2011). The role of organizational absorptive capacity in strategic use of business intelligence to support integrated management control systems. *The Accounting Review, 86*, 155–184. https://doi.org/10.2308/accr.00000010.
12. Ferreira, A., & Otley, D. (2009). The design and use of performance management systems. An extended framework for analysis. *Management Accounting Research, 20*, 263–282. https://doi.org/10.1016/j.mar.2009.07.003.
13. Gelinas, U. J., Jr., & Oram, A. E. (1996). *Accounting information systems*. Cincinnati: South-Western College Publishing.
14. Granlund, M., & Malmi, T. (2002). Moderate impacts of ERP on management accounting: A lag or permanent outcome? *Management Accounting Research, 13*, 299–321. https://doi.org/10.1006/mare.2002.0189.
15. Granlund, M. (2011). Extending AIS research to management accounting and control issues: A research note. *International Journal of Accounting Information Systems, 12*, 3–19. https://doi.org/10.1016/j.accinf.2010.11.001.
16. Hagel, J. (2013). Why accountants should own big data, 20.
17. Horngren, C. T., & Sundem, G. L. (1990). *Introduction to management accounting*. Englewood Cliffs: Prentice-Hall Inc.
18. Kreiner, K., Mouritsen, J. (2005). The analytical interview: Relevance beyond reflexivity. In S. Tengblad, R. Solli, B. Czarniawska (Eds.), *The art of science* (pp. 153–176). Kristianstad: Liber & Copenhagen Business School Press.
19. Laudon, K. C., & Laudon, J. P. (1988). *Management information systems. A contemporary perspective*. New York: Macmillan Publishing Company.
20. Lillis, A. M., & Mundy, J. (2005). Cross-sectional field studies in management accounting research—Closing the gaps between surveys and case studies. *Journal of Management Accounting Research, 17*, 119–141. https://doi.org/10.2308/jmar.2005.17.1.119.
21. Lönnqvist, A., & Pirttimaki, V. (2006). The measurement of business intelligence. *Information Systems Management, 23*, 32–40. https://doi.org/10.1201/1078.10580530/45769.23.1.20061201/91770.4.
22. Negash, S. (2004). Business Intelligence. *Communications of the association for information systems, 13*, 177–195.
23. Olszak, C. M., & Ziemba, E. (2007). Approach to building and implementing business intelligence systems. *Interdisciplinary Journal of Information, Knowledge, and Management, 2*, 135–148.
24. Patton, M. Q. (1990). *Qualitative evaluation and research methods (2/e)*. Thousand Oaks: Sage.
25. Qu, S. Q., & Dumay, J. (2011). The qualitative research interview. *Qualitative Research in Accounting & Management, 8*, 238–264. https://doi.org/10.1108/11766091111162070.
26. Quattrone, P., & Hopper, T. (2005). A "time-space odyssey": Management control systems in two multinational organizations. *Accounting, Organizations and Society, 30*, 735–764. https://doi.org/10.1016/j.aos.2003.10.006.
27. Rom, A., & Rohde, C. (2006). Enterprise resource planning systems, strategic enterprise management systems and management accounting. *Journal of Enterprise Information Management, 19*, 50–66. https://doi.org/10.1108/17410390610636878.
28. Roslender, R., & Hart, S. J. (2003). In search of strategic management accounting: Theoretical and field study perspectives. *Management Accounting Research, 14*, 255–279. https://doi.org/10.1016/S1044-5005(03)00048-9.
29. Sallam, R. L., Richardson, J., Hagerty, J., & Hostmann, B. (2011). *Magic quadrant for business intelligence platforms*. Stamford, CT: Gartner Group.

30. Scapens, R. W., & Jazayeri, M. (2003). ERP systems and management accounting change: Opportunities or impacts? A research note. *European Accounting Review, 12,* 201–233. https://doi.org/10.1080/0963818031000087907.
31. Schläfke, M., Silvi, R., & Möeller, S. K. (2013). A framework from business analytics in performance management. *International Journal of Productivity and Performance Management, 62,* 110–122. https://doi.org/10.1108/17410401311285327.
32. Sherman, R. A buyer's guide to choosing the right BI analytics tool. http://searchbusines sanalytics.techtarget.com/buyersguide/A-buyers-guide-to-choosing-the-right-BI-analytics-tool.
33. Shollo, A., & Kautz, K. (2010). Towards an understanding of business intelligence. In *21st Australian conference on information systems, paper 86, ACIS proceedings.*
34. Silvi, R., Bartolini, M., Raffoni, A., & Visani, F. (2012) Business performance analytics: Level of adoption and support provided to performance measurement systems. *Management Control, 3,* 118–142. https://doi.org/10.3280/MACO2013-SU3006.
35. Wengraf, T. (2001). *Qualitative research interviewing: Biographic narrative and semi-structured methods.* Beverley: Sage.

Printed in the United States
By Bookmasters